£14.95

AHMED RASHID

The Resurgence of
Central Asia

Islam or Nationalism?

D1080589

OXFORD UNIVERSITY PRESS

Karachi

ZED BOOKS

London & New Jersey

The Resurgence of Central Asia: Islam or Nationalism?
was first published in:

South Asia
Oxford University Press, 5-Bangalore Town
Sharae Faisal, PO Box 13033, Karachi-75350

Rest of the World
Zed Books, 7 Cynthia Street, London NI 9JF, UK and
165 First Avenue, Atlantic Highlands, New Jersey 07716, USA

Copyright © Ahmed Rashid, 1994

Set in Monotype Bembo by Ewan Smith
48 Shacklewell Lane, London E8 2EY
Cover design by Andrew Corbett
Map by Jenny Ridley
Printed by Biddles Ltd, Guildford and King's Lynn

A catalogue record for this book is available from the
British Library

US CIP data is available from the Library of Congress

ISBN I 85649 131 5 hb
ISBN I 85649 132 3 pb
South Asia ISBN 0 19577548 I

Contents

Tables

Acknowledgements

This book could not have been written without the help of my editors and fellow journalists, who realized the importance of Central Asia and gave me the opportunity, the space in their newspapers and the resources to travel there frequently.

The *Far Eastern Economic Review* has been the most consistent backer of coverage from Central Asia. For that I have to thank three regional editors, Susumu Awanohara, Charles Smith and the great Hamish McDonald, who despite his own interest in Central Asia never stopped me from going there. But my frequent trips would not have been possible without the backing of deputy regional editor V.G. Kulkarni, who ensured that my requests always got a good hearing at the *Review*.

At the *Independent* in London I have to thank its very first foreign editor, Stephen Glover, and his successor the late Nicholas Ashford, who both realized that I was onto something when I first suggested that the story in Central Asia could be as interesting as the one developing in Moscow. East Europe editor Steve Crawshaw was a great support. However, without the savage humour and the unrelenting encouragement given by Michael Fathers, the first and best Asia editor the paper ever had, my stories might not have seen the light of day.

At the BBC World Service there are too many people to thank. The presenters on first '24 Hours' and then 'Newshour' put up with erratic long-distance calls, bad telephone lines, and showed much patience in hearing me out. At the BBC Eastern Topical Unit, good friends such as Nicholas Nugent, George Arney, Lyse Ducett and Larry Jagan have always been extremely helpful.

In Pakistan I have to thank Arif Nizami, editor of the *Nation*, who ensured that my stories ran and ran in his paper, which was the first to bring on the spot coverage of Central Asia to a Pakistani audience. Sherry Rehman and Talat Aslam, editor and deputy editor of the monthly magazine *Herald*, never flinched when I bombarded them with thousands of words on Central Asia. Sherry's desire to be the first magazine editor to run a regular slot on Central Asia was a great help. I owe my thanks to all the others who work in the madhouse at the *Herald*.

Friends at the Pakistan Foreign Office also gave me unstinting help. I have to thank Ashraf Jahangir Qazi, Pakistan's ambassador in Moscow, for ensuring that I always got my visas, whilst his encyclopaedic knowledge of Central Asia was a major source for ideas. To his wife Abida I owe a great deal. Pakistan's ambassador in Alma Ata, Riaz Mohammed Khan, and Pakistan's ambassador in Tashkent, Shafqat Sheikh, have been enormously helpful, for they always treated me as a friend. Sardar Asif Ali, the former Minister of Economic Affairs, who opened Central Asia for Pakistan, was also a great help.

In Central Asia there are too many people to mention, from taxi drivers to government officials: many have become good friends. Some of the best days of my life have been spent in the company of Safarbai Kuchkarov, from Djizak in Uzbekistan. He is a Sufi, a medicine man, entrepreneur, philosopher and master of many tongues. The hospitality of his wife Gulbahar and their children was extraordinary. I also could not have done without the repeated hospitality of Valery and Elena Novikov in Alma Ata, of Nozigul Zamanova and Maujuda and Akmal Alimova in Dushanbe, and of Marina Belskaya, the best translator in Kazakhstan.

Robert Molteno of Zed Books has pressed me for years to write a book for him and it was at his suggestion that I at last did. I owe a great deal to the time and effort he has put into the manuscript.

My sisters Sultana and Kokee were always supportive, and my mother kept pushing me back to my desk. However I could have written no book without the love, patience and devotion of my wife Angeles, who has put up with a great deal as a result of my repeated absences. My children Raphael and Saara finally got used to the idea that I had to be at my desk, so long as I took time off to give them their swimming lessons.

A Note on Spellings

Since 1989 the names and the spellings of cities and towns in the former Soviet Union, and in Central Asia in particular, have been in a state of continual flux. The desire to revert to the past has spared not even the names of states and their capital cities. Kirgizia shed its Russian-language name and became Kyrgyzstan. Its capital Frunze, named after the conquering Soviet General, reverted to its original Turkic name Beshkek. Throughout the text I have used the name that is most common in Central Asia now and used by newspapers and news agencies.

Many names have numerous spellings. Thus, there are several ways to spell the two famous rivers of Central Asia, the Amudarya and the Syrdarya. In such cases I have used the spelling that is most common in Central Asia itself and is also recognizable in the West.

Abbreviations

CIS	Commonwealth of Independent States
CPK	Communist Party of Kyrgyzstan
CPKZ	Communist Party of Kazakhstan
CPSU	Communist Party of the Soviet Union
CPT	Communist Party of Turkmenistan
CPTJ	Communist Party of Tajikistan
CPU	Communist Party of Uzbekistan
DMK	Democratic Movement of Kyrgyzstan
DPT	Democratic Party of Turkmenistan
DPTJ	Democratic Party of Tajikistan
IRP	Islamic Renaissance Party
NDP	National Democratic Party of Uzbekistan

About the Author

Ahmed Rashid was educated at Malvern College and the University of Cambridge. Following a prolonged period of political involvement on behalf of the rights of national minorities in Pakistan – which resulted eventually in his enforced exile – he later returned to his country. He is now a respected journalist. In addition to writing for the Pakistan press, for six years he was the Pakistan correspondent for the *Independent* (London). He is now the Pakistan, Afghanistan and Central Asia Bureau Chief for the *Far Eastern Economic Review* and the *Daily Telegraph* (London). He has also reported for the BBC World Service and various other international TV and radio services.

This book is dedicated to my beloved mother and late father, who were the first to urge me to write it.

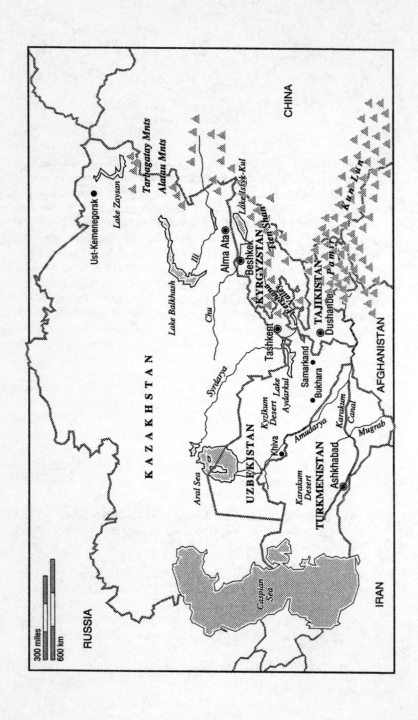

1

Conquerors, Khans and Communists

As it had been so many times before, the fate of Central Asia was to be decided. The khans, or chiefs, of the great tribes – the Kazakh ordas, the Mongol hordes, the Uzbek Shaybanis and the Tajik clans – were gathering to discuss their fate on a cold winter's evening. They arrived wrapped up in great fur coats and fur hats with earflaps that stretched across their faces hiding them from view. Flurries of snow swept across the earth as the chiefs, with their advisers and bodyguards in tow, greeted each other with the customary Muslim warmth.

An honour guard, its members shivering in the cold, went through an elaborate military drill to welcome each delegation. Their hands were close to freezing as they grasped their weapons and brought them level to present arms to the guests. In one corner of the arrival ground a band of musicians played the national anthems of the tribes and traditional tunes. In between the arrival of the delegations, the musicians clapped their hands to keep warm and rubbed their lips to prevent them chapping. In another corner young girls, dressed in elaborate and colourful costumes, waited to present frozen flowers to the guests.

Tonight the khans would feast together, sitting cross-legged on the floor surrounded by carpets and silk pillows, and discuss the critical situation informally, gauging what the others felt and what positions they were likely to take in public. Tomorrow there would be a grand tribal assembly, the *ulus* or *majlis* or *jirga* – there are many names for it – where they would all present their views. The leaders that gathered that night were the heirs of the conquerors of the world, men such as Genghis Khan, Babar and Tamerlane. Their ancestors were also some of the greatest scientists, poets, philosophers and mystics that the steppe has ever produced. The majority of these leaders had never seen the sea: they lived in a landlocked region among the highest mountain ranges in the world, the harshest deserts and the most lush oases ever tilled by man. Yet that night there was a strange tension in the air, a disquiet and nervousness that old-timers had never seen before. Some of the leaders looked fearful, which was hardly normal for the warriors of the Central Asian steppe.

The setting for the meeting was Ashkhabad, the capital of the Soviet Republic of Turkmenistan. The chiefs were the old communist party bosses and now presidents of the republics of Kazakhstan, Uzbekistan, Kyrgyzstan, Turkmenistan and Tajikistan. The date was 12 December 1991. The reason for the meeting was the collapse of the Soviet Union.

These heirs of Genghis Khan's warrior nomads and Stalin's communist party machine had suddenly been orphaned; everything they had known for the past seventy-four years was disappearing before their eyes. Four days earlier at a dacha near Brest, 3,000 kilometres away, presidents Boris Yeltsin of Russia, Leonid Kravchuk of Ukraine and Stanislav Shuskevich of Belarus (formerly Byelorussia) had signed a treaty formally disbanding the Soviet Union and creating a new Commonwealth of Independent States (CIS). In getting rid of the 1917 Revolution and the legacy of Lenin, these Slavic leaders had not bothered to inform or consult with their fellow republican presidents in Central Asia.

Whereas once the Muslims of Central Asia had decided the fate of Russia, now the Slavs were taking their own decisions and seemed prepared to dump Central Asia in the process. That day, shivering on the airport tarmac in Ashkhabad as I watched each delegation arrive, the band strike up and the honour guard salute, I witnessed people's palpable fury at the Slavs and, in particular, the anti-Russian feeling. There was talk of racial discrimination, of ethnic overlordship, and anger that those who had most stood by the idea of a united Soviet Union in the aftermath of the August coup attempt against President Gorbachev had been ditched in order to elevate the leadership of Yeltsin and Russia. It was as if the centuries-long battles that raged across Russia between the Mongols and the Principality of Moscow, between the Tartars and Ivan the Terrible, between the Crescent and the Cross, were again coming to life. Once again history was repeating itself.

The next day at Ashkhabad the five presidents of the Central Asian republics sat down together at a press conference and declared, more or less, that they had eaten humble pie. On a long, elevated platform, presidents Nursultan Nazarbayev of Kazakhstan, Rakhmon Nabiev of Tajikistan, Askar Akaev of Kyrgyzstan, Islam Karimov of Uzbekistan and Saparmurad Niyazov of Turkmenistan said that they were willing to join the CIS, but on the basis of equality. They demanded that they too be made founder members of the CIS. There was not a word of anger against Russia or Yeltsin - in public the leaders swallowed their resentment. Russia was still too powerful to annoy. A week later, on 21 December in Alma Ata, the capital of Kazakhstan, the new CIS was formed with eleven out of the fifteen former Soviet republics becoming members. The three Baltic republics were gone for good and Georgia stood aloof. The Soviet state had ceased to exist.[1]

The life blood of the Soviet state had been ebbing away ever since the August coup attempt in Moscow. That had been carried out by Communist hardliners to prevent President Gorbachev signing a new Union treaty that would have still retained some of the close links between the republics. The irony was that the failed coup ensured that public opinion in Russia and Ukraine, the two most powerful of the fifteen Soviet republics, demanded that they leave the Soviet Union altogether. It was as though a mother was preparing to see her children drown. 'Why should we bail out these strife-torn regions of Central Asia, who share nothing with us – least of all our religion. We would be much better off on our own, for then Russia could become a great power again,' said an aide to Russian Deputy Prime Minister Yegor Gaidar, one of the principal economic advisers to President Yeltsin.[2] If this was the mood in Moscow in the offices of the highest in the land, the mood in the streets was even more militantly in favour of Russian independence.

Decades of indoctrination, about the principals of the Soviet State and its internationalist duties had been thrown out of the window. Central Asia in particular was no longer considered part of the great and glorious Soviet motherland, but instead was seen as culturally, racially and in religious terms totally separate from Russia. The socialist premiss of equality, and specifically that the poorer regions of the Soviet state should be developed to become equal to Russia, was now nothing but a naïve and expensive policy that was draining the Russian exchequer. The new Soviet man whom communism was supposed to create was now suddenly reduced to defending ethnic frontiers.

The leaders meeting in Ashkhabad knew well the present mood amongst the Slavs, which was being pandered to by leaders such as Yeltsin and Kravchuk, and they were furious. Since the August coup attempt, the Central Asian leaders had backed Gorbachev in his demand for a strong centre. President Nursultan Nazarbayev of Kazakhstan was in the forefront of those arguing for a strong centre in order to keep the military, the nuclear arsenal, the currency and the economy under a single control. He was firmly backed by other Central Asian leaders – except for the president of Kyrgyzstan, Askar Akaev, who six months earlier had supported the idea of a loose commonwealth structure instead of the Soviet state.

Delegation members spoke in private about how Yeltsin had abused and humiliated them by secretly going ahead with the Minsk treaty. The leaders spoke bravely of how they would form a new Central Asian common market. 'All the Central Asian states must get together to form a new confederation or our economic development will be stalled,' said President Islam Karimov of Uzbekistan. 'A Central Asian community is the need of the hour,' echoed the Kyrgyz president, Askar Akaev.[3] Yet everyone knew that for the time being these were merely words. Their faces showed their real fears. Since 1917 Central Asia, the land of the greatest trading routes in history, had become little more than an economic colony for Moscow, producing cotton, metals and other raw materials for the Soviet economic powerhouse. When that powerhouse was seen to be built on sand, Central Asia had nowhere else to turn. By thousands of threads, from electricity grids to oil pipelines to telephone lines, the Central Asian republics were tied into Russia. Moscow was an economic and financial spider's web from which no leader on that day could ever see himself disentangled.

That night in Ashkhabad there were no celebrations. 'We are not celebrating, we are mourning,' said a Turkoman Foreign Ministry official. 'The future is extremely bleak. The West will help Russia and other Slav republics to survive, but who will help us?' asked a member of the Uzbek delegation. Here was the final and tragic irony. The break-up of the Soviet Union had given Central Asia that very independence that their forefathers had struggled for, but they were hesitating to eat from it. Economically dependent on Moscow and politically desirous of a strong centre that would guarantee a peacekeeping role for the CIS army, the five states were now faced with rebuilding their economies, forging independent foreign policies and ensuring some degree of foreign aid. The communist bureaucracies that these leaders had risen from had only known subservience and dependency on Moscow for the party line. Now there was no line and no party. All lines had been cut.

Moreover they were all faced in varying degrees with radical Islam, assertive ethnic nationalism and inter-ethnic rivalries, and now had to create their own security forces to maintain law and order. Kazakhstan had suddenly become an independent nuclear power – for the only reason that intercontinental ballistic missiles (ICBMs) were based on its soil. When Islamic fundamentalists in Iran and Pakistan hailed Kazakhstan as the first independent Muslim state to have nuclear weapons, that only added to Nazarbayev's nervousness. Anti-Russian feeling amongst the local populations had to be contained so that it would not create a new bloody battleground and a further excuse for Moscow to abandon Central Asia. There was a large and powerful

Russian minority in every republic, the largest being in Kazakhstan where it formed nearly half the population. These Russians faced their own crisis: whether to brave the coming ethnic storms in Central Asia or to migrate back to Russia, a move that could trigger off large-scale economic disruption in the republics because it was the Russians who were the technical brains and manpower behind the economy. All these problems, for which the former communist bureaucracies were ill prepared, came as shops emptied fast and food shortages grew.

If the end of tsarist Russia was a turning point for Central Asia in the first part of the twentieth century, because it introduced the region to the modern era and a new ideological and economic system, then the end of the Soviet Union has been an equally traumatic turning point, for it created five new independent states in the heart of Muslim Asia. Whereas the transformation of Central Asia after October 1917 was carried out with an unprecedented degree of bloodletting, which decimated the population, the transformation in December 1991 took place without a single dead body in the streets. It was a remarkable way to achieve independence, even though just a few months later Tajikistan was to be in the grip of a brutal civil war.

Today Central Asia comprises five independent republics, Kazakhstan, Kyrgyzstan, Uzbekistan, Turkmenistan and Tajikistan. From its beginning in 1917, the Soviet state never included Kazakhstan in Muslim Central Asia, preferring to give it a non-Asian identity by linking it closely to Russia and Siberia. Today, however, the Kazakhs themselves and the world at large believe they are very much part of the region. Central Asia covers an area of 3,994,300 square kilometres which includes some of the most sparsely populated regions in the world. Its population of only 51 million people includes more than 100 different ethnic groups, from Germans and Austrians to Tibetans and Koreans. The largest ethnic group is the Uzbeks. Uzbekistan has a population of 20.5 million, and Uzbeks form substantial minorities in all other four republics. There were some 10.6 million Russians living in Central Asia in 1992, but there has been a large-scale exodus of Russians from Tajikistan and Uzbekistan because of fears of ethnic violence and Islamic fundamentalism.

Tashkent and Ashkhabad, the capitals of Uzbekistan and Turkmenistan, have long urban histories but the other three capital cities, Dushanbe in Tajikistan, Alma Ata in Kazakhstan and Beshkek in Kyrgyzstan, were created by the Bolsheviks to give a sense of ethnic identity to those nationalities. Uzbekistan contains all the most famous historical cities of Central Asia: Samarkand, Bukhara, Khiva and Kokand. They were the seats of nomadic empires and settled kingdoms in the past, as well as being centres in the development of Islam throughout the region. For centuries the hundreds of madrasahs, or Islamic colleges in Bukhara and Samarkand attracted students from as far away as Morocco and Indonesia. Bukhara is seen by many Muslims as a place of pilgrimage and the most important city in Islam after Mecca, Medina and Jerusalem. Central Asia was also the birthplace of Sufism, the mystical trend in Islam which spread rapidly to Africa and Asia.

Central Asia lies at the heart of the Eurasian continent. Completely landlocked, it borders Iran and Afghanistan to the south, China to the east and Russia to the north and west. The main Central Asian steppe is bounded by the Caspian Sea in the west, the Hindu Kush and Pamir mountain ranges in the south and the Tien Shan mountains in the east. There are no fixed boundaries in the north: where the Kazakh steppe merges into the Siberian steppe in a flat landscape that is punctured with numerous lakes. Although thousands of rivers start in the mountains, only two rivers travel for any length and finally reach the landlocked Aral Sea. The Amudarya, the Oxus river of ancient mythology, originates in the Hindu Kush range, runs along the southern-border of Central Asia skirting Afghanistan and Iran, and reaches the Aral Sea after a journey of 2,500 kilometres. The Syrdarya or Jaxartes river originates in the Tien Shan (where it is first called the Naryn river), passes through the Ferghana valley and journeys north of the Kyzlkum desert to reach the Aral Sea after travelling 2,200 kilometres. Thousands of smaller rivers flow down from the mountains but their waters disappear into the sands of the great deserts.

The lands between these two rivers, which today comprises Uzbekistan and Tajikistan, have produced the main developments of Central Asian history and culture. Both these broad rivers formed formidable frontiers for the ancient world. The Amudarya divided the Persian empire and its culture from the Turkic nomadic empires of the Central Asian steppe. The same river later formed the frontier for the Tsar and the communists, separating Central Asia from first the British empire in India and then the Muslim world to the south. Meanwhile the Syrdarya formed the only northern barrier for the Persian, Greek, Arab and then Turkic kingdoms in Central Asia, protecting them from nomadic invasions from Mongolia and the Gobi desert.

All the mountain ranges of Central Asia and Afghanistan converge at the Pamirs, known as the Roof of the World, mountains which until only recently were considered to form one of the most inaccessible ranges because of its height, its snows and its freezing temperatures. In the eighteenth century the Pamirs were called the Third Pole, after the North and South poles, because they were so unknown. The Tien Shan and Kun Lun ranges run north and east from the Pamirs. It was only in the 1850s that Russian explorers first set foot on the Tien Shan, locally called the Mountains of the Spirits because of the voices that seemed to emanate from their glaciers. Marco Polo was the first Western traveller to traverse the Tien Shan range. 'Even by daylight men hear the voices of the Spirits and often you fancy you are listening to the strains of many instruments. Travellers make a point of staying close together,' he wrote. The Kun Lun were known in ancient Chinese mythology as the Celestial Peaks.

In the centre of the region lie two of the largest deserts in the world. In the south, covering much of present-day Turkmenistan, is the Karakum or 'desert of black sands', which covers 350,000 square kilometres of some of the most arid terrain on earth, where rain is so rare that rainstorms are events recounted decades later by the local nomads. To its north in present-day Uzbekistan is the Kyzlkum or 'red sands' desert, which covers another 300,000 square kilometres and is one and a half times the size of Britain. Despite the scarcity of water, both these deserts have distinctive fauna and flora, as well as being home for some of the toughest nomadic tribes in the world, in particular the Turkomen.

As fearsome as the mountains and deserts are, so the valleys are lush, fertile and capable of producing an abundance and huge variety of crops. In 1900 the total irrigated land in Central Asia was an estimated 46,000 square kilometres of which 12,500 square kilometres lay in the oases of Bukhara, 9,000 square kilometres in the Ferghana valley and 300 square kilometres in and around Khiva. Ancient irrigation was carried out by digging wells and using the wheel system to raise water, as well as the kareez method, and by taking water from the rivers.[5] Agriculture in Central Asia has always been carried out around oasis settlements where water was readily available. Each oasis was a self-contained economic unit and autonomous except for the barter trade with surrounding nomads and the caravans that passed through them. Oases were frequently devastated or ransacked by the nomadic armies sweeping through, but it took them only one or two agricultural cycles to revive. It was only in the eighteenth century that the pauperized local rulers of Central Asia began to squeeze farmers for taxes and tributes.

At the heart of Central Asia is the Ferghana valley, once a cohesive economic unit but divided in the 1930s by Stalin between Uzbekistan, Tajikistan and Kyrgyzstan. The valley is 300 kilometres long and 170 kilometres wide and its history, the power of its princes and mullahs and its ability to mount sustained resistance against all outsiders, has made it the political and Islamic nerve centre of Central Asia (see Chapter 4). With a population of 7 million people, the narrow valley

is the most densely populated region in Central Asia. The Soviet regime changed this natural geography of oasis settlements by irrigating
vast areas of the steppe for cotton and grain cultivation. The project
was initially highly successful, but the lack of planning and foresight
later created massive problems which the Soviet regime refused to
acknowledge and which are only coming to the surface today. Acute
water shortages, pollution, the drying-up of lakes and seas, desertification
and environmental catastrophes brought on by nuclear waste are only
some of the problems that these newly independent republics now
face. This tragedy is compounded by the fact that the nomads have
always lived at one with their environment. The nomad's respect for
the environment is unmatched anywhere in the world. Thus the cal-
lousness with which the Soviet system treated the land has been particularly galling to the nomadic population.

Much of the world's ancient history originated in Central Asia for
it was the birthplace of the great warrior tribes that conquered Russia,
Europe, India and China. Later chapters of this book look in greater
detail at the history of the individual races of Central Asia, even
though it is difficult to split the ancient history of a region that, until
Stalin, considered itself as one geographical and even historical entity.
For example, in the history of which modern day republic does one
include the story of Alexander the Great or of Genghis Khan, two
conquerors who affected the whole region, or the story of the Saminid
kings who laid the foundations for the lasting influence of the Persian
language and culture in Central Asia? Later chapters attempt to discuss these figures according to the regions where they had the most
influence. However, a brief outline of Central Asian history is necessary if one is to understand the cut and thrust of its present-day
politics.

To the classical world of the Greeks and the Romans, Central Asia
was known as Transoxiana, or the region beyond the Oxus river. The
Oxus was only one of many ancient names given to the Amudarya
river. To the Arabs Central Asia was known as 'the land between two
rivers' – the Syrdarya and the Amudarya. To the English Elizabethans
it was known as Tartary. It was the fourteenth-century Moroccan
traveller and writer Ibn Battuta, who coined the word *Turkestan,* meaning
'the land inhabited by Turks'[6]. The nineteenth-century British writer
Rudyard Kipling called Central Asia the 'Back of Beyond'. The Chinese built the Great Wall of China precisely to keep out the tribes from
Mongolia and Central Asia. European writers wrote about Central
Asia without having the slightest idea what it was really like and often
even where it was. The Elizabethan playwright Christopher Marlowe
in his verse drama *Tamburlaine the Great* describes Central Asia and the

exploits of Tamerlane in some detail, much of it wrong. Nevertheless, Marlowe's poetry helped to build the image of awesome power and megalomania that Central Asian leaders came to represent. As Tamburlaine says in a more modest moment:

> I hold the Fates bound fast in iron chains,
> And with my hand turn Fortune's wheel about;
> And sooner shall the sun fall from his sphere
> Than Tamburlaine be slain or overcome.[7]

Poets such as John Milton and the Romantics John Keats and Percy Bysshe Shelley helped build up the mystique of Central Asia in European eyes. Writers such as G.A. Henty and Kipling described it in their adventure novels as a barbaric, unpredictable region – even though neither had ever been there. For the European outsider, Central Asia was a land where the imagination could run riot and take whatever liberty it liked, so few Westerners ever travelled there.

In one way or another Central Asia has always gripped the imagination of outsiders, whether they be Muslim or Christian, European or Asian. For the West it has epitomized the mystery of the Orient and the wide open spaces of the steppe punctuated by bazaars, ruthless tyrants and nomadic armies. In the nineteenth century Central Asia was permanently etched in the minds of British schoolboys because the Great Game played between the Russian and the British empires led to numerous adventure stories about the region. For Muslims Central Asia has epitomized the distant and inaccessible, but still the second holiest region after Saudi Arabia – steeped in Islam and mysticism, and the originator of so many Muslim races.[8] For the Russians it has been a reminder of one of the most painful parts of their history, as they lived for centuries under Mongol rulers and their successors, the Tartars. Russian mothers still use the threat 'the Tartars are coming' to frighten little children into bed or into doing their homework. Russian prejudices remain deeply ingrained. Ethnic riots in Central Asian cities are still described by Russian commentators as 'riots between rampaging mobs' or 'crazed Islamic fundamentalists'. In 1990, after ethnic riots between Uzbeks and Kyrgyz, no less a person than the Soviet interior minister Vadim Bakatin described them as 'a reflection of primitive and medieval nationalism'. The same kind of nationalism being espoused in the Baltic republics or Ukraine at the time was never described in such a way.[9]

Central Asia has always been different. At the heart of the history of Central Asia is not the story of princes and their courts, but the story of the nomad and his horse. In recent years Soviet archaeological research has pushed back the date when man first began herding animals in Asia to around 4000 BC. It is now thought that the horse was first domesticated in the Ukraine and that the cult of the horse spread rapidly eastward. During the Neolithic Age, between 4,000 and 2,000 BC, Central Asia saw the development of mixed farming in which tribes hunted, herded and grew some crops. Based around the Caspian Sea these tribes developed pottery and stone tools as they steadily moved eastward into Central Asia. Recent excavations at Altyn Tepe, near present-day Ashkhabad, revealed Neolithic settlements whose peoples traded with Persia and Mesopotamia in the Middle East. Later, pure pastoralism developed as tribes wandered further afield from their oasis settlements looking for pasture for their ever-larger herds of animals.[10]

From around 1700 BC a distinct nomadic culture emerged. The evidence of unearthed burial mounds points to the importance given to horses and camels, which were killed and buried alongside their owners. Later, between 1700 and 1000 BC, mounted nomadism became common, with the training of horses for war and their harnessing to chariots once the spoked wheel had been invented. When the Hittites conquered Anatolia in 1286 BC, mounted warriors and chariots were used for the first time as part of the established battle order.[11]

The Saka tribes settled around the Caspian Sea and the Aral Sea were the first mounted nomads to found a dynasty in the region. At its height around 800 BC, this dynasty ruled an area including that of modern-day Iran, western Turkey and Central Asia. Squeezed by growing Persian power, the Sakas later retreated into the Pamirs and the Tien Shan mountains, in the region today known as Kyrgyzstan. They remained here until 200 BC, when they were finally conquered by the Persians.[12] From 700 to 300 BC the Scythian tribes, who were settled north of the Syrdarya, swept southward conquering Central Asia and then India and Syria. The Scythians became the main antagonists of the Persian kings and later Alexander the Great, but today there is little evidence of what became of them; they must have been assimilated into the great ethnic melting pot of Central and South Asia.[13]

The early Persian kings were the first to demarcate Central Asia, now inhabited by the offshoots of the Saka tribes. They divided the region between the Amudarya and Syrdarya rivers (darya means 'river' in Persian) and stretching from the Caspian Sea to the Pamir mountains into three distinct regions. From west to east these were Chorasmia, Bactria and Sogdiana. The latter included modern-day Tajikistan, eastern Uzbekistan and northern Afghanistan, while Bactria included much of present-day Uzbekistan. The Persian empire founded by Cyrus the Great in 550 BC was to rule Central Asia for the next two hundred years, until the arrival of the Greeks. It was in Bactria that Zoroaster, who was born in modern Azerbaijan, first appeared with a new religion of fire worship. Zoroastrianism spread rapidly through Bactria and Sogdiana and was later adopted by the Persians.[14]

The single aberration in this history of invasions from the east and south was the arrival from Europe of the Greeks under Alexander the Great. After defeating the Persians, Alexander conquered Bactria and Sogdiana between 329 and 327 BC. Alexander left an indelible mark on Central Asia, founding cities, promoting Hellenic culture and creating far greater uniformity within the region than it had ever known before. One of his successors, General Selucucos, founded the Selucid dynasty which ruled Bactria and large parts of Sogdiana. In 239 BC another Greco-Bactrian kingdom was established which ruled from the Afghan city of Balkh. The Bactrians were to be finally overthrown by nomadic invaders from the east in around 140 BC.

Meanwhile the western region of Central Asia in present-day Turkmenistan continued to be ruled by the Parthian dynasty which was based on the Saka tribes. In 224 BC they were defeated by the Persian Sassanids. With the southern belt of Central Asia firmly under the control of the Persians, the north of Central Asia was invaded in the last century BC by successive waves of more Sakas, who continued south to Afghanistan and India. After these invasions, Buddhism also arrived and much closer contact was established between Central Asia and China to the east and India to the south.[15]

In the eastern region of Central Asia in what is now Kyrgyzstan, the Sarmatian nomads with their Siberian animal culture moved south from Siberia and dominated the region from around 500 BC onwards. The first raids into Central Asia by Chinese princes took place around 100 BC and for a time they captured the Ferghana valley and imposed an annual tribute of 1,000 stallions on their victims. The Chinese were convinced that the famous horses of the Ferghana sweated blood. These horses were not only highly prized in the Chinese army, but also served as models for all horse sculpture across China.[16]

In time both the Sarmatians and the Chinese were pressed from the east by the Huns, the forefathers of the Mongols, who came out of the Gobi desert to occupy Kasghar in Xinjiang around 200 BC, crossed Central Asia and reached the Volga river in Russia by AD 400. Their empire – the first nomadic Mongol empire – stretched from Korea to the Ural mountains in Russia. The descriptions of the Huns fit the modern Kazakhs, who retain the same stocky physique and still have the largest mean head size of any people in the world. The Hepthalities, or White Huns, went on to conquer eastern Europe and parts of India, and in the fifth century Huns settled on the Danube rallied around their chief Attila and marched on Rome.

As the Huns moved westward, the vacuum in the east was filled by the Turkic tribes, who began what was to be a series of invasions westward spread over several centuries. The Turkic tribes originally inhabited the Alatau mountains in eastern Central Asia, from around 1000 BC onwards. The word *Tur* or *Turkic* was given by the Chinese to signify all those nomadic tribes who occupied the region from Mongolia to the Black Sea and who posed a threat to the Chinese empire. Raids by the early Turkic tribes forced the Chinese to build the Great Wall of China.[17] Around AD 200 these tribes turned around from attacking the Chinese in the east to attacking the oasis towns in Central Asia to the west. Some Turkic tribes settled in the Ferghana valley. By AD 500 these Turkic nomads were to defeat both the Persian Sassanids and the remainder of the Huns in the western part of Central Asia. Meanwhile eastern Central Asia was in the hands of the Uighur Turkic tribes, who set up a nomadic empire that straddled the border between present-day former Soviet Central Asia and Xinjiang.

Soon after the death of the Prophet Mohammed, Central Asia was invaded by the Arabs of the Umayyad dynasty based in Damascus. Crossing Persia, the Arabs first defeated Zubil, the Turkic king of Kabul, and then, crossing the Oxus for the first time, defeated the Sassanids at Merv in AD 651. The Arabs began the process of converting Central Asia to Islam, and some 50,000 Arab families arrived to settle in Merv. The second wave of Arab conquests began in 705 when Bukhara and Samarkand were conquered. By 713 the Arabs ruled over the Ferghana valley and had ventured as far east as Kasghar. The Zoroastrian fire temples in Samarkand and Bukhara were destroyed as the conquered people converted to Islam.[18] The Arabs ruled Central Asia from the kingdom of Khorasan, which covered what is today western Afghanistan, northern Iran and Turkmenistan. The Arab capital was at Merv, near the present-day Turkoman city of Mary. Merv, called the Queen of the World, developed as a major centre of Islamic learning under the Arabs and later the Seljuk Turks, until it was destroyed by the Mongols.

The Arab conquests saw a flowering of Islamic thought, philosophy and mysticism which was to turn Bukhara into a city second only to Mecca for its religiosity and learning. Al Bokhari (809–69), the philosopher and commentator on the Koran, wrote the Hadith, the sayings of the Prophet, which is still revered as one of the most important works in Islam. As the Arabs drove northwards, the Chinese were expanding into eastern Central Asia, and in 751, at Talas, the Muslim Arabs and the Chinese at last met in battle. The decisive victory of the Arabs ensured that the Chinese would encroach no further into Central Asia than Xinjiang.[19]

By AD 900 several independent Muslim kingdoms had sprung up in Central Asia. The most important of these dynasties were the Persian Samanids who ruled from 874 to 999 and made their capital at Bukhara, from where they acted as patrons to one of the greatest periods of Islamic art, culture and science that Central Asia was ever to see. The Samanids were descended from Saman, a Zoroastrian from Balkh in Afghanistan, whose son Ismail captured Khorasan and later the whole of Persia. With a well-organized army and bureaucracy, the Samanids built up extensive trading links with Europe and China, thus regulating the Silk Route. During Samanid rule Central Asia became a recognized entity, considered to be not at the edges of the world but at the very centre of the known world, and which armies, merchants and peoples travelling from west to east had to traverse. With physicians such as Ibn Sina, mathematicians such as Al Biruni and poets such as Firdausi, the Samanid court left an indelible mark on the development of the Persian language and culture that was not to be eroded in Central Asia until the advent of communism.

The defeat of the Samanids by Alptgin, a Turkic officer of slave origins who formerly belonged to the Samanid army, saw the end of Persian political domination in Central Asia and the advent of Turkic domination. At Ghazni in Afghanistan the Turkic tribes created the Ghaznavid dynasty, which was to rule over a region that included parts of Central Asia and India. Its strongest ruler, Mahmood of Ghazni, undertook seventeen campaigns into India between 1001 and 1024 and conquered much of Central Asia.[20] A series of invasions from the north by fresh Turkic tribes brought the Seljuk Turks to centre stage. The Seljuks first settled near Bukhara before they moved south. They captured Merv and then defeated the Ghaznavids in 1041, establishing an empire that spread as far as Turkey. By 1055 the Seljuk chief, Tughril Beg, stood outside the gates of Baghdad. For over 200 years the Seljuks ruled from the Pamirs to Iraq, thus uniting for the first time under Turkic hegemony Central Asia with Persia and the Arab world. At the height of Seljuk rule, King Malikshah (1072–92) ruled from Kasghar to Jerusalem and protected the booming trade along the Silk Route between Syria, Central Asia and China. The Seljuks were challenged and finally defeated by the Mongols under Genghis Khan. The Seljuk execution of Genghis Khan's envoy in 1218 and the murder of 450 Muslim merchants who had traded with the Mongols led Genghis Khan to attack their domains in Central Asia. Seljuk high-handedness is thus often blamed for the Mongol onslaught over Asia and Europe that was to follow.[21]

When the Seljuks and other Turkic tribes had moved westward they left behind in the Gobi desert their kinsmen, the Mongols, who gradually came to inhabit the region south of Lake Baikal. Genghis Khan, born in 1155, succeeded in uniting the local tribes and in 1206 he was elected the Great Khan at a tribal meeting which adopted the name Mongol for a new tribal confederacy. Later called the Golden Horde, this confederacy included all the tribes that today make up the major ethnic groups in Central Asia. The exception are the Tajiks who derive their ancestry directly from the ancient Sogdians. The ancient Kazakhs, Kyrgyz and Turkomen were the warriors, whilst the Uighurs formed the bulk of Genghis Khan's bureaucracy because under Chinese influence they had developed a written script and a code of laws, which Genghis Khan was to adapt to Mongol needs.

Nobody in Central Asia or Europe could imagine what was about to appear over the horizon. The Mongols captured Bukhara in 1220, killing 30,000 people and burning the city to the ground in the process. In Bukhara, Genghis Khan declared, 'You ask who I am, who speaks this to you. Know, then, that I am the scourge of God, if you had not sinned God would not have sent me hither to punish you.' In the next twelve months the whole of Central Asia fell to the Mongols. In 1223 an army of Tartar tribes led by Mongol generals defeated far superior Russian forces at the battle of Kalka and then pushed on through Russia in the dead of winter, finally reaching Hungary. The conquest of Russia was not to be avenged by the Russian princes for another three hundred years, until Ivan the Terrible captured the Tartar capital of Kazan in 1552. The Tartars were the heirs of the Mongols.

It is ironic that, despite untold massacres carried out by the Mongols and the destruction of entire cities, Genghis Khan was a strong protector of trade and the Silk Route between Europe and China across Central Asia. During his lifetime, under a 'pax mongolica' merchants could travel from Korea to the Crimea in absolute security, not least because entire populations had been decimated along the way. The cost of this peace is now estimated to be about 5 million people who were killed by the Mongols. After the death of Genghis Khan, Central Asia was ruled by his son Chagatai, whose descendants divided Central Asia into two – the khanate of Transoxiana in the west and Turkestan in the east.

The last great explosion out of Central Asia was to be perhaps the most important and lasting cultural influence in the region. Taimur, or Tamerlane as he is known in the West, was born in 1336 and did not begin his conquests until he was forty years old. Born south of Samarkand amongst the Barlas Turks, Tamerlane captured most of Turkestan by 1380 and then moved south to Persia and India, west to Russia, and eastward to China. In 1393 he captured Baghdad. Two years later he took Moscow. As he conquered he moved the cream of the vanquished regions' intelligentsia and craftsmen to Samarkand, where he began to build the grandest capital city of ancient Asia. Tamerlane established the Timurid dynasty, and his grandson Ulugh Beg continued his artistic and intellectual traditions, turning Samarkand and Bukhara into the seat of all learning in the decorative arts, architecture, poetry, philosophy, painting and astronomy.[22]

After two thousand years the military machine perfected by the nomads of Central Asia appeared to be finally running its course. Except for slight variations, their weapons had not changed for centuries. The short and powerful bow with which a rider could shoot off dozens of arrows accurately from the saddle, the dagger and small shield remained the same. From around AD 600 the short sword for close-quarters fighting was replaced by a steel sabre. Only in the seventeenth century did the introduction of firearms change the weaponry and tactics of nomadic warfare. The nomads' standard dress of pantaloons, wide at the waist and fitted into knee-high leather boots with a high heel, together with a long shirt, barely changed except for differences of style amongst the various ethnic groups. A similar dress was adopted by Muslims in India during the Mogul empire. Elaborate saddles and harnesses for the horses made of leather, fur and a felt underlay had become standard by the thirteenth century. With the Huns ruling in central and western Europe, the Goths in Spain and Italy, and the Avars in Hungary, it appeared for a time that the whole world was in the grip of Central Asian nomads. They influenced European military tactics and weapons, and European attitudes to the use of cavalry.[23] Amir Khusrun, a Muslim writer living in India in 1289, gave historians a vivid description of the Mongol army on the move, which was similar to many of the nomadic warrior armies of Central Asia:

> There were more than a thousand Tartar infidels and warriors of other tribes, riding on camels, great commanders in battle, all with steel-like bodies clothed in cotton; with faces like fire, with caps of sheep-skin, with their heads shorn. Their eyes were so narrow and piercing that they might have bored a hole in a brazen vessel. Their stink was more horrible than their colour. Their faces were set on their bodies as if they had no necks. Their cheeks resembled soft leather bottles, full of wrinkles and knots. Their noses extended from cheek to cheek, their mouths from cheek bone to cheek bone. Their moustaches were of extravagant length. They had scanty beards around their chins. The King marvelled at their beastly countenances and said that God had created them out of hell-fire.[24]

The Timurid dynasty was to be replaced by a new tribal grouping, the Shaybani Uzbeks. The Uzbeks were of mixed Turkish and Mongol blood and part of the Golden Horde of Genghis Khan, but they had remained nomads, untouched by the civilizing influences of urban life. Under their dynamic chief Mohammed Shaybani, who was born in 1451, the Uzbeks united other tribes and then defeated the Timurid heir Babar at the decisive battle of Serpul, near Samarkand. This battle was to change the course of Indian history, for Babar went on to conquer Afghanistan and India and to found the Mogul dynasty in Delhi. In a brief decade, from 1500 to 1510, the Uzbeks defeated the Turkomen and the Persians, thus extending their empire to much of Central Asia and northern Persia.[25]

But Persian power was again on the rise with the coming to power of the Safavids, who ruled from 1501 to 1722 and who changed the state religion from Sunni to Shia Islam – a step that considerably reduced Persia's influence in Central Asia. Persia's main challenge was to contain Ottoman power in Turkey and Uzbek power in the north – the Uzbek chief Mohammed Shaybani was killed in 1510 in battle against the Safavids. In any case the Uzbeks soon broke up into smaller principalities, and the frequent wars of succession amongst them led to the evolution of three khanates, based on the cities of Khiva in the west, Bukhara in the centre and Kokand in the east. With the discovery of the sea route to India, the importance of the Silk Route had declined and, semi-forgotten, Central Asia slipped into a limbo.

Russia had made its opening move eastward as early as 1552 when Ivan the Terrible captured Kazan from the Tartars and massacred the entire population. Ivan built Saint Basil's Cathedral in Moscow's Red Square to commemorate the victory and topped its domes with onion shapes to symbolize the severed heads of the turbaned Tartars. The battle and its grim memento was to be etched into Russia's collective memory for ever. As one writer has noted, the only time after 1552 that Russian forces ever retreated in the face of Muslim power was four centuries later in Afghanistan.[26] Ivan the Terrible swept on in 1556, taking Astrakhan, the strategically important city where the Volga empties into the Caspian Sea. Military expeditions were then mounted beyond the Ural mountains and into Siberia. Within a century, by 1650, the Russians had reached the Pacific, subduing the Siberian khanate along the way. Over the next two centuries the Muslim tribes in Central Asia were rolled back by a Slav crusade. Peter the Great seized Dagestan, along the Caspian Sea, in 1723, which began a long and bloody war by Russia to conquer the Caucasus, which was to last until 1859 because of the spirited resistance put up by Caucasian guerrilla leaders such as Mullah Shamyl (1797–1871).

By the time Russia could claim that it had complete control of the Caucasus, it had also moved steadily southeastward into present-day Kazakhstan, building forts and roads and making treaties with local chiefs.[27] By 1750 the Russians had built forts over some 2,500 kilometres from Gurev, on the northern tip of the Caspian Sea, north to Orenburg and then east as far as the Alatau mountains and the town of Ust-Kamenogorsk (see map). Meanwhile the Russians had also expanded southward from the Siberian steppe as far as Lake Balkash. The Kazakhs were the first to be subdued, through a series of treaties with their chiefs between 1731 and 1740, but the three main Kazakh *ordas* or hordes still provided formidable resistance to Russian settlers (see chapter 5).

As with Siberia, the pressure to conquer Central Asia was a mixture of imperial policy, ambition to rule the entire continent east of Moscow, and unrelenting economic pressure from merchants, bankers and industrialists. The expansion into Siberia was fuelled by the hunger for land, furs or 'soft gold' and the sudden requirement by the Tsar for penal colonies.[28] In Central Asia, Russian expansion was fuelled by the military-bureaucratic apparatus which suddenly found itself, at the end of the war in the Caucasus, without an enemy to fight. Senior officers of the 200,000-strong Army of the Caucasus lobbied at the Tsar's court for permission to advance eastward. At the same time, under Tsar Alexander the Second (1855–81), a similar aim was given to foreign policy by Foreign Minister Prince A. Gorchakov. In his first memorandum to the Tsar he wrote that Russia should turn away from Europe and expand its national interest in Asia, even at the price of confronting the British empire.[29]

Merchants had been trading with Central Asia since the time of Peter the Great, and they had already discovered the merits of Central Asian cotton when the American Civil War (1861–65) suddenly cut off American cotton supplies. Merchants demanded that Moscow advance into Central Asia to secure cotton supplies. They increased the yield by importing Russian farmers and more scientific methods of cultivation. The abolition of serfdom in Russia had created a huge potential free peasant class, who wanted land, while Russian industrialists were anxious to sell their goods to Central Asia. Once the economic and military imperatives had been determined, the court and the intellectual elite produced the necessary moral justification so common to other empire-building states in the colonial era. Mikhail Pogodin (1800–75), a history professor at Moscow University, became popular for preaching the superiority of the Russian race and its civilizing mission in Asia. Other historians and writers joined him, helping to build an intellectual consensus for an aggressive, expansionist policy on Russia's borders.

The Russian Geographical Society, founded in 1845 in St Petersburg and largely manned by retired military officers, used its expeditions to

Central Asia to advocate seizing the region. Pyotr Semyonov (1827–1914), vice president of the society and himself an explorer of the Tien Shan range, argued for an expansionist policy on the basis of Russia's need for military security. He was later given the title 'Tyan-Shansky' by the Tsar in recognition of his work in opening up Central Asia. The Russian Orthodox Church demanded that Russia end the slave trade in Khiva and bring Christianity to a barbaric people. For a time in Moscow everyone believed that it was Russia's manifest destiny to move into Asia and expand the empire.[30] None other than the great Russian novelist and humanist Feodor Dostoevsky was to write in 1881:

> ...the Russian is not only a European, but also an Asiatic. Not only that; in our coming destiny, perhaps it is precisely Asia that represents our main way out. In Europe we were hangers-on, whereas to Asia we shall go as masters. In Europe we were Asiatics, whereas in Asia we, too, are Europeans. Our civilizing mission in Asia will bribe our spirit and drive us thither.[31]

The first expedition to the east had been a disastrous attempt by Peter the Great to conquer Khiva, in 1717, in which an entire Russian army was decimated. Another military expedition, sent out in 1839, also failed, but from then on the Russians followed a more cautious policy. They advanced east along the Syrdarya river building forts and subduing local tribes, and also moved west from the Tien Shan mountains which they had reached from Siberia. The two prongs of this move converged on Chimkent, which was captured in 1864; Kyzl Orda, the main seat of Kazakh resistance, had fallen in 1853 and Vierny, now Alma Ata, was founded a year later. The Land between the Two Rivers was now encircled from three sides and the Russians moved in to conquer the rich agricultural heartland of Central Asia that comprises modern Uzbekistan. Military campaigns were mounted to capture Tashkent in 1865 and Samarkand in 1868: Bukhara became a Russian protectorate. Meanwhile campaigns against the Turkomen in the south resulted in the capture of Khiva in 1873. Finally Kokand, in the east, fell in 1876.[32]

Russia's advance into Central Asia had been watched with great trepidation by another great colonial power, Britain, which scrambled to try to capture Afghanistan in a bid to hold back what it feared would be a Russian advance on British India. Thus began the Great Game between Russia and England which was played out over the vast landscapes of Afghanistan, Persia, Xinjiang and Central Asia. Sensing the coming tensions, Russia quickly legitimized its presence in Central Asia. The conqueror of Central Asia and its governor-general from 1867 to 1881, General K. Von Kaufman, signed a peace treaty with the khan of Khiva abolishing slavery and making Khiva a vassal state. A similar treaty was signed with the emir of Bukhara. Britain tried to trump it in neighbouring Xinjiang by signing a friendship treaty with the emir of Kashgar to ensure that the Russians did not try and move further east into Chinese Turkestan.

Russia also legitimized the borders of Central Asia with its new neighbours. In 1860 a Sino-Russian treaty established the border with Xinjiang. This was to divide permanently the ethnic groups that spanned that border: the Kazakhs, Kyrgyz, Uighurs and others. Russia neutralized the Persians by signing a peace treaty with Teheran in 1881, after the Russian army had defeated the Turkomen. In 1887 Russia began a long series of demarcations of the Afghan border with the British, to ensure that Afghanistan remained a buffer zone between the two imperial powers. The rivalry between the two had intensified after Moscow began laying tracks for the first railway lines in Central Asia, which in twenty years were to traverse the whole region.

The strategic 1,400-kilometre railway line from the Caspian Sea to Samarkand was completed in 1888 after its creators had overcome the enormous problems of building a track in waterless deserts. When the railway line reached Merv and then Kushk on the Afghan border, Russia was only 112 kilometres from Herat in western Afghanistan, which created near-panic in London and Delhi. Russian hawks insisted that a track be laid to Herat while British hawks managed to persuade their government to take the British railway line up the Khyber and Bolan passes in the North West Frontier Province and Baluchistan to the border with Afghanistan. British military historian Major-General Henry Rawlinson saw Russia advancing towards India 'like an army investing a fortress', and when news leaked that the Russian general M. D. Skobelegv had put forward a plan to the Tsar to invade India through Afghanistan with just 15,000 men, there was consternation in the British Parliament and in the press.[33]

The pressure from the British in India ensured that Moscow quickly integrated Central Asia into the Russian empire. Within a few years Central Asia had become a cotton-growing colony for the textile mill owners in Moscow and a virgin market for manufacturers of Russian consumer goods. It was a vast dumping ground for unwanted Russian farm labour, former serfs and political dissidents as well as a playground for adventure-seeking soldiers, priests, explorers and mountain climbers. Unlike the British or French colonists, the Russian empire-builders had no seas to cross and no natural barriers to block their absorption of Central Asia. There was no organized state power in the region to hinder their advance and no foreign competition to interfere with their economic exploitation of the region. Russia had the vast steppes of Central Asia all to itself. By merely controlling the great navigable rivers and key mountain passes and by building railways, Russian access and political control were assured. Geography had given Russia a vast new hinterland that had incalculable natural resources and unparalleled strategic military depth.

Many Russians and a significant school of thought in England led by Sir Halford Mackinder, the founding father of geopolitics, viewed Central Asia in much the same way as the Mongol hordes did: that Central Asia was the centre of the world. 'It is the greatest natural fortress in the world defended by polar ice caps, deserts, arid tableland and mountain ranges.'[34] It was the largest landmass in the world and whoever controlled it exercised enormous power because they were not dependent on sea power. It was the centre of political gravity because it enclosed more frontiers than any other region in the world − those of India, China, Europe and the Middle East. Although overstated, these were appealing notions for Russian and English strategists, who pushed for their respective expansionist policies in Central Asia. This debate about the 'heartland' was only vindicated during World War Two, when Central Asia gave enormous depth and space to Russia's defence and allowed the country to recover industrially from the fury of the German blitzkrieg.

However, like all usurping powers Russia faced unrelenting resistance from the people. The Kazakh and Kyrgyz nomads periodically rose in revolt against the new Russian farm owners who were seizing their grazing grounds. Revolts were crushed by the army and thousands of nomads were killed; many fled to China to escape persecution. The Turkomen continued a hit-and-run guerrilla war in the desert that continued unabated until the 1930s. The Tajiks and the Uzbeks under various political guises − first Pan-Turkism and then Pan-Islamism − resisted the Tsar's policies just as fiercely. The history of this resistance, which is described in much greater detail in the chapters to follow, was studiously ignored by first tsarist and then Bolshevik historians. The collective memory of this resistance is now playing a major role in shaping the future of the newly independent republics. The brutal repression and exploitation by Russia, which in arable areas led to the cultivation of cotton replacing all major food crops, plunged Central Asia into a grave economic crisis. When on 25 June 1916 the Tsar ordered the mass mobilization of Central Asian manpower between the ages of nineteen and forty-three to carry out labour duties in the rear of the Russian army that was locked in battle with Germany, this simple edict was all that was need for a generalized revolt.

Within a few months Kazakh and Kyrgyz nomads were waging an

all-out guerrilla war against the Russian army. But without coherent leadership and common goals, and with vast distances to be covered to maintain communications, the revolts were suppressed – with great bloodshed, the slaughter of entire villages and the hanging and forced deportation of thousands of rebels north to Siberia. Nevertheless the political divide between Russia and Central Asia had grown enormously in the process and a new local leadership of intellectuals, tribal chiefs and merchants formed new parties and military organizations across the region. Prevalent amongst them was the desire for independence, not just from tsarism but from Russia itself.

Russian colonialism had led to an intellectual revival amongst Muslims, especially in the cities of present-day Uzbekistan. Fierce debates erupted between those who believed in a purely Islamic revival in Central Asia and those who believed in an independent united Turkestan under a Pan-Turkic nationalist leadership. Others, particularly Tartar intellectuals, were sympathetic to a socialist revolution, which they hoped would not only do away with Russian oppression but also rid their own societies of feudal and tribal elites. At the heart of these debates was the reformist Jadid movement, begun in 1883 by the Crimean Tartar Ismail Gasprinsky and later led by Uzbek and Tartar intellectuals. The Jadids believed that only by modernizing Islam, spreading education and allowing greater freedom to women could Central Asian Muslims combat growing Russian influence and shape their own future. These trends are all discussed in greater detail in Chapter 4, on Uzbekistan.[35]

When the Bolshevik Revolution took place in 1917 there was considerable hope in Central Asia that Lenin's promises of self-determination meant that Russia would now grant either full independence to Central Asia or at least much greater autonomy. In Lenin's first appeal to the 'Muslims of Russia and the East' on 5 December 1917, he linked the Bolshevik programme, particularly the right of self-determination, to the revolt in Central Asia against tsarism. But the Bolsheviks' real attention was directed to Europe, where they believed the incipient insurrection in Berlin would quickly engulf Europe in revolution. Only in late 1918 did Stalin write the first articles in *Pravda* focusing attention on the revolutionary potential of Central Asia, which could help consolidate the Bolsheviks. A Commissariat of Nationality Affairs, or 'Narkomnats', headed by Stalin had been created in November 1917, but it had failed to address Muslim nationalist feeling in Central Asia. Only after the hopes of revolution in Europe had diminished did Moscow create the All-Russian Congress of Muslim Communist Organizations in the winter of 1918–19 to direct the developing civil war in Turkestan.[36]

Tashkent, a city with a population of 200,000 Muslims and some 50,000 Russian settlers, was the centre of Turkestan's political life.[37] Russian workers and soldiers overthrew the Provisional Government on 31 October 1917 (Julian calendar) and established the first soviet in Central Asia, but local Muslims were not invited to join it. They held a separate Muslim Congress which demanded autonomy for Central Asia but was ignored by the Tashkent Soviet. Muslim leaders then held an important congress in Kokand in December 1917 and announced the formation of the Provisional Autonomous Government of Turkestan, which would seek independence from Russia. Thus within a few months two centres of power had emerged, the wholly Russian and communist centre in Tashkent, and the Muslim and clearly nationalist Turkic centre at Kokand. Ethnic and religious differences had already divided Central Asia.[38] In February 1918 Kokand was attacked by troops of the Tashkent Soviet, who slaughtered the city's inhabitants. The direct result of this brutal assault on the aspirations of Central Asian Muslims was the creation of the Basmachi Muslim rebel movement.

The Basmachis were local guerrilla groups led by mullahs, tribal chiefs and landlords who resisted Soviet rule across the whole of Central Asia and sustained their unequal struggle until the 1930s. By 1919 there were some forty Basmachi groups with some 20,000 fighters strung across the steppe from Ashkhabad to Ferghana and Dushanbe. Lenin's appeals to local Russian communists to be more sensitive to Muslim demands, such as his June 1920 appeal 'On Our Tasks in Turkestan', were ignored. As well as joining the Basmachis, Turkic nomads also joined the White armies in great numbers. By ignoring Muslim demands, the Bolsheviks gave the White armies, now fighting the Reds across much of Central Asia, a major recruiting base.

But the White generals, helped for a time by a dozen foreign countries who wanted to see Bolshevism destroyed, failed to capitalize on this support because their slogan, 'Russia one and indivisible,' alienated the Central Asian Muslims and their dream of independence.[39] By 1920 the Civil War was largely won – because tens of thousands of Muslim soldiers crossed lines and joined the Red Army after being appalled by White Russian attitudes and atrocities. These Muslim troops believed that the new communist era promised greater freedom and development for Central Asia. It was a hope that was to be dashed within months of Lenin's death and Stalin's rise to power.

Notes

1. The three Baltic States had refused to become members of the CIS.

2. Interview by the author in Moscow, 24 November 1991, at the office of Yegor Gaidar.

3. Interviews by the author. See Ahmed Rashid, 'Picking Up the Pieces', Far Eastern Economic Review, 9 January 1992.

4. I. Cameron (1984) Mountains of the Gods, Facts on File, USA.

5. The kareez system, which is still practiced in parts of Central Asia, Pakistan and Afghanistan, depends on the digging of inclined underground canals that channel well water to the fields.

6. Ibn Battuta (1984) Travels in Asia and Africa, 1325–1354, Routledge and Kegan Paul, London.

7. From The First Part of Tamburlaine the Great, in Christopher Marlowe (1969) The Complete Plays, Penguin, London.

8. R. Magowan (1989) Fabled Cities of Central Asia: Samarkand, Bukhara, Khiva, Abbeville Press, New York.

9. Ahmed Rashid, 'Islam Rises, Moscow Trembles', Independent, 13 June 1990.

10. T. Rice (1965) The Ancient Arts of Central Asia, Praeger, New York.

11. E. Phillips (1965) The Royal Hordes: nomad peoples of the steppes, Thames and Hudson, London.

12. Rice.

13. I. Spector (1959) The Soviet Union and the Muslim World, 1917–1958, University of Washington Press, Washington DC.

14. A. Vambrey (1873) History of Bukhara, reprinted by Indus Books, Pakistan.

15. J. Kalter (1984) The Arts and Crafts of Turkestan, Thames and Hudson, London.

16. Rice.

17. P. Bowles (1977) The People of Asia, Charles Scribners, New York.

18. P. Hitti (1946) History of the Arabs, Macmillan, London.

19. Ibid.

20. Ibid.

21. Kalter.

22. B. F. Manz (1989) The Rise and Rule of Tamerlane, Cambridge University Press, England.

23. Kalter.

24. Quoted in Kalter.

25. E. Allworth (1990) The Modern Uzbeks from the Fourteenth Century to the Present: a cultural history, Hoover Institution Press, USA.

26. A. Taheri (1989) Crescent in a Red Sky: the future of Islam in the Soviet Union, Hutchinson, London.

27. Spector.

28. R. Clem (1992), 'The Frontier and Colonialism in Russian and Soviet Central Asia', in R. Lewis (ed.) Geographic Perspectives of Soviet Central Asia, Routledge, London.

29. M. Hauner (1990) What Is Asia to Us? Russia's Asian heartland yesterday and today, Unwin Hyman, London.

30. Ibid.

31. Ibid., quoting an article by Dostoevsky on the Russian victory at Goek-Tepe, where thousands of Turkomen were massacred by a Russian force.

32. Hauner.

33. *Ibid.*

24. *Ibid.*

34. *Ibid.*

35. A. Bennigsen, 'Pan-Turkism and Pan-Islamism in History Today', *Central Asian Survey,* Vol. 3, No. 3.

36. H. Carrere d' Enchausse (1979) *Decline of an Empire: The Soviet Socialist Republics in Revolt,* Newsweek Books, USA.

37. F.M. Bailey (1992) *Mission to Tashkent,* Oxford University Press, England.

38. *Ibid.*

39. A. Bennigsen and E. Wimbush (1979) *Muslim National Communism in the Soviet Union: a revolutionary strategy for the colonial world,* University of Chicago Press, USA.

2

The Two Revolutions –
1917 and 1991

When the 1917 Revolution took place, Central Asia was at least a century behind Russia and in the grip of an economic crisis. A handful of industrialists, the merchants and a small proletariat concentrated in the railways lived largely in Tashkent. They were drawn almost entirely from Russian settlers. Tashkent was only in the very first stages of industrialization. The plantation-style cotton economy that Russia had imposed allowed the tribal and landed elite to continue exercising power in the countryside. Whereas Russia was looking towards socialism as the ideology of the future, Central Asia was still emerging from a tribal and nomadic society that was trying to get to grips with the first rumblings of nationalism and capitalism.

During the Civil War both the Red and White armies exploited Central Asia's backwardness, but they ignored the reality that it was in the throes of an internal revolution in which Islam, tribalism, nationalism and socialism were fiercely competing for ideological dominance amongst the local elite and the masses. Ironically, it was a situation not dissimilar to what the conservative regimes of Central Asia faced in December 1991 as the Soviet Union broke up. Then too a severe economic crisis, ideological competition and a reawakening of the people were under way as the new states came into being. Both revolutions were initiated in a distant Moscow, but whereas the first led to years of civil war and massive casualties, the second was to be accomplished without a single dead body on the streets. If in the first revolution the Central Asian people were eager for independence and were denied it, in the second, independence was gifted to a people many of whom were by now highly reluctant to receive it. Such were the changes that had come about in the intervening seventy-four years of communism.

The impact of Russian colonialism in Central Asia was to arouse a dormant elite to political ferment. The Jadid reformers and intellectuals in Bukhara and Samarkand were the first to raise the issue of how to adapt Islam to modernism so that Muslims could compete with Russians. A similar reawakening was going on in India, Iran and Afghanistan in which Muslim modernizers urged their co-religionists to educate themselves in order better to combat the colonial yoke. The Jadids also, however, faced the traditional Islam of the mullahs, who saw the crisis as an opportunity to rid themselves of Russian domination and impose the sharia, or Islamic law. Today such aims would be termed fundamentalist. There appeared to be no meeting ground between these two Islamic trends, and in the Basmachi uprising this split became wider, with the mullahs joining the Basmachis but the Jadid modernizers largely siding with the Bolsheviks. If the Jadids had joined the Basmachis with all their intellectual and organizing abilities, the story of Central Asia would have been quite different.[1]

The power of Islam to unite different tribal and ethnic groups or as an ideology to mobilize the people was weakened, and that allowed the Bolsheviks easily to crush Islam after they had attained absolute power in Central Asia. A parallel evolved in Tajikistan in 1992, when an incipient Islamic movement that seized power in Dushanbe failed to mobilize the people and was driven out by pro-communist forces. Islamic fundamentalists have, so far at least, failed to gain support from the nationalist camp in present-day Central Asia, even though nationalist parties like Birlik in Uzbekistan promote an Islamic revival as part of their political programme. Thus in 1917 and 1992 the Islamic camp remained divided: Muslim modernists and nationalists have not joined with Islamic fundamentalists to resist a common enemy.

In 1917 the peoples of Central Asia were also discovering nationalism. This took first an intellectual and later a more populist form of expression in Pan-Turkism – the desire to unite the Turkic-speaking peoples of Central Asia (which of course also included the Persian-speaking Tajiks) in an independent state free of Russian control. It was a natural progression from the highly separate tribal identity that most Central Asian peoples had until the arrival of Russian colonialism. There was no sense yet of dividing people into separate national groups – which the Bolsheviks were to do later. Thus Uzbeks or Kazakhs identified themselves first by their respective tribes, then as being Muslims, and finally as being part of a wider Turkic-speaking world. Pan-Turkism was killed off by Stalin, but it saw a major revival during Gorbachev's *perestroika*, and after the break-up of the Soviet Union it was seen by many as the only panacea for the economically short-changed Central Asian states.[2]

Another trend, particularly strong amongst the still-nomadic peoples, was tribal nationalism. Tribal nationalism can be described as the nationalism espoused by a nomadic tribal grouping who have no form of political organization other than the tribe to express themselves through. Thus the Kazakhs reconstituted their ordas, or clans, turned them into a political party called Alash Orda and set up an independent state which lasted from 1917 to 1920. The Kazakhs were determined to free themselves not only from the Russians but also from fellow Muslims such as the Tartars and Uzbeks. So strong has the traditional tribal structure remained amongst the nomads that later, under communism, the tribe achieved almost perfect symbiosis with the party system. Kazakh and Kyrgyz communist party leaders surrounded themselves with their kinsmen. Thus Dinmukhamed Kunayev, one of the longest-serving secretary generals of the Kazakh Communist Party, who belonged to the Great Orda, surrounded himself with kinsmen from the same horde. In Kyrgyzstan members of the powerful Bugu clan dominated the party, while in Turkmenistan the Tekkes, the largest and most powerful tribe, dominated the central committee.[3]

During the political ferment in 1917, the native elite was extremely small in number and deeply divided. Landowners, rich merchants, the scions of princely families, mullahs, the leaders of Sufi orders and a few urban intellectuals and teachers remained the sum total of the traditional leadership.[4] The failure of any of the independent political movements in Central Asia to succeed was partly a result of this elite's inability to produce a coherent leadership from within its ranks or to broaden its support base amongst the masses. Once the communists won the Civil War, much of the traditional elite was co-opted into the communist system and thus made the political transition from tsarism to nationalism and then to socialism within a single generation. Those who refused to go through this process invariably were killed by Stalin.

Stalin's repression in Central Asia was only a continuation of the early refusal of the Bolsheviks to acknowledge any of the local political trends or popular aspirations. The Bolsheviks were prepared to impose communism on a society that was least prepared for it. The theoretical problem they identified in Central Asia was not related to the actual contradictions on the ground or the need to carry society with them as they made the revolution, but was how to tackle the 'national question' in Asia within the framework of the Marxist model. The national question was the least understood and certainly one of the worst-formulated doctrines within the core of Marxism. Moreover it was a debate between European Marxists, who had no idea of the conditions the revolution was to face in a nomadic, Muslim society.

The crux of the problem was what degree of self-determination could be given to smaller nationalities, without destroying the larger nation state. A writer in Tashkent in 1918 described the prevalent mood amongst the people:

> The Central government had announced that the Bolshevik programme included self-determination and the native Mohammedan population considered that this referred to them with their 95% majority. They soon discovered that self-determination in the Bolshevik view did not refer to Turkestan, but only referred to India and countries in the British, French and other bourgeois dominion.[5]

Marx himself wrote little on what was to be later termed the national and colonial question, and his articles on Ireland provided the main vehicle for his views. 'The people which oppresses another is forging its own chains,' Marx wrote, a warning that Lenin refused to heed.[6] Marx supported anti-colonial movements because he thought they would hasten the end of European colonialism and so weaken the European bourgeoisie, but he never asked the question of how a Marxist party would cope with nationalism once it had seized power. Lenin handed over this important interpretive task to Stalin while they were both in exile in Europe in 1913. Stalin's narrow definition of the five factors that constitute a nation have given many Marxists nightmares ever since. 'A nation is a historically constituted, stable community of people formed on the basis of a common language, territory, economic life and psychological make-up manifested in a common culture,' he wrote. Stalin refused to consider any other factors and pushed the Bolshevik interpretation of nationalism into a straitjacket that was to create major problems in the future.[7]

At the same time the Austrio-Marxist school devised a theory of cultural autonomy within the multi-national state to fit the Hapsburg empire. Its leading writers, Karl Renner, Otto Bauer and Karl Kautsky, depoliticized the national question by promoting cultural and psychological factors. Bauer's definition of the nation as 'an aggregate of people bound into community of character by a community of fate' was vague and strongly attacked by Lenin.[8] Rosa Luxemburg, the Polish Marxist, went to the other extreme saying that the proletariat 'should not get bogged down in sterile national struggles' – a view that was also hotly contested by Lenin. She demanded the right of self-determination only for the proletariat, while Lenin demanded unequivocal self-determination for all oppressed nationalities. Trotsky also thought that the struggle for self-determination would undermine the revolution and that at all times self-determination must remain subordinate to the proletariat and the revolution.[9]

The basis of Marxist theory on the national question lies indisputably with Lenin. The failure of the 1905 Revolution in Russia had convinced Lenin that only the right of self-determination as a major plank of the revolutionary programme could win over the mass of non-Russians in the tsarist empire. In Asia the anti-colonial movement and the issue of self-determination were hammering at the door of French and British colonialism. The revolution in Persia in 1906, the Young Turks' movement of 1908, the Chinese Revolution in 1912 and the first stirring of Indian nationalism were providing a new political impetus to Asian revolutionaries. Realizing these changes, Lenin went further theoretically than any Marxist of his day, insisting that only by giving smaller nationalities the freedom to secede could the larger nation make possible a free and voluntary union. 'We want a voluntary union of nations – a union which precludes any coercion ... so that the distrust of centuries has a chance to wear off.'[10] But once Lenin came to power he never allowed any nation in Russia to secede or even express a will to do so. Stalin refused to accept self-determination as a legitimate right because it did not reflect working-class interests.

Before his death Lenin appeared, however, to realize his mistake and tried to rectify it by appealing to communists in Central Asia, observing that sensitivity was needed to handle a largely nomadic society. For the Europeanized and intellectual Bolsheviks, Central Asia in 1917 was like a lunar landscape. as Lenin pointed out:

> You are confronted with a task which has not previously confronted the communists of the world: relying upon the general theory and practice of communism you must adapt yourself to specific conditions such as do not exist in the European countries; you must be able to apply that theory and practice to conditions in which the bulk of the population are peasants and in which the task is to wage a struggle against medieval survivals and not against capitalism.[11]

Lenin's pleas were ignored by the Russian-dominated soviet in Tashkent, which looked on the local people as reactionary natives. Russian communists practised such blatant Russian chauvinism in Central Asia that in his last testament Lenin said their attitude was undermining the Communist Party of the Soviet Union (CPSU).[12]

In 1920 the Bolsheviks called the representatives of all Muslim revolutionary organizations and other Asian communists, including Turks, Indians, Persians and Indonesians, to a major congress at Baku. Narbutabekov, a revolutionary from Turkestan, voiced many delegates' aspirations when he said, 'East is not West, Muslims are not Russians. If we want millions of Muslims to accept the communist regime, we must adapt it to their conditions.'[13] Communists from Central Asia demanded the right to set up their own 'Muslim Communist Party'. The Bolsheviks refused to agree and pushed through a resolution that was to shape the future of all Bolshevik–Muslim relations. The resolution insisted upon 'a single indivisible proletarian collective, a single party for the proletarians of all nations of the given state'. The Bolsheviks viewed a separate Muslim communist party, or Muslim national communism as it was then called, as anathema. However, they soft-pedalled on the issue as they could not afford to antagonize Central Asia while the Civil War continued: more than 250,000 Muslims had enlisted in the Red Army.[14]

The foremost advocate of a separate Muslim communist party was Mir Said Sultan Galiev (1880–1939). Son of a Tartar schoolmaster, Galiev worked as a journalist and took part in Muslim nationalist politics before the Revolution. In 1917 he became a leading member of the Muslim Socialist Committee for Kazan and joined the Bolsheviks, rapidly becoming the highest-ranking Muslim in the communist hierarchy. He became a member of the Central Muslim Commissariat, chairman of the Muslim Military Collegium and a member of the Commissariat of Nationality Affairs. Galiev believed that the nationalist struggle must supersede the social and class struggle because 'all Muslim colonized peoples are proletarian peoples, and as almost all classes in Muslim society have been oppressed by the colonialists, all classes have the right to be called proletarians'.[15] For Galiev, the Muslims' only guarantee against Greater Russian chauvinism was the creation of a separate Muslim communist party, which would be more sensitive to local conditions.

Galiev also demanded the creation of an independent Muslim Red Army. He argued that where the party was weak and its propaganda ineffective, the role of a locally recruited army that paid attention to local traditions and customs could be of critical importance in spreading the revolution. It would be a nationalist and populist army rather than a communist one, but the Bolsheviks refused to contemplate such a suggestion. Bennigsen and Wimbush have pointed out that Galiev's views were later to be adopted by communist revolutionaries who led nationalist revolutions, such as Mao Zedong in China and Ho Chi Minh in Vietnam.[16]

Islam also divided the Bolsheviks from these Muslim Marxists. Galiev believed that Marxism and Islam could coexist, even though he himself was an atheist. Galiev advocated gradualism, education and the raising of political consciousness amongst the masses, while insisting that Islam should not be directly attacked. Stalin was later to treat such sensible suggestions as treason and went to the extent of trying to eradicate Islam – a step that was not even contemplated by the Tsar. Stalin was also to cut off Central Asia from any contact with the rest of the Islamic world.

Central Asia threw up dozens of intellectuals and leaders who eventually sided with the revolution. Although many came from the tribal elite, they were to remain the most popular and forceful personalities on the steppe for more than a decade – until Stalin purged them from the CPSU for 'nationalist deviation' and had them executed. There was no attempt by the CPSU to understand the local phenomena of Red Muslims, Islam or nationalism. There was no attempt to understand tribalism, even though it was in part the tribal masses of Central Asia who won the Civil War and secured the revolution against the Whites. Sixty years later the CPSU was to make the same mistakes when it invaded another tribal society in Afghanistan, where it applied the same tactics as it had in Central Asia and met with the same disastrous results. The foundations of these prejudices and the subsequent Afghan defeat were laid by ideologues such as Bukharin and Preobrazhensky in the early 1920s. As authors of the *ABC of Communism*, the primer for party cadres, they described tribalism as carrying 'the origins of enmity and mistrust between nations', and advised cadres to communize tribal peoples by force.[17]

The Bolsheviks tolerated Galiev so long as the Civil War continued, but once it was over, in 1923, he was arrested with his followers and charged with nationalist deviation. He disappeared during the purges of the 1930s. Stalin pronounced an early verdict on Muslim national communism.'Nationalism is the chief ideological obstacle to the training of Marxist cadres and of a Marxist vanguard in the border regions and Republics,' he said.[18] If implemented, Galiev's demands for greater decentralization and democracy within the CPSU and greater sensitivity to Islam and tradition might well have changed the face of Central Asia, for they could have generated greater unity between Russia and Central Asia. Today Galiev's ideas are more relevant than ever as the pro-communist nomenklatura face an Islamic revival, strident ethnic nationalism, the re-emergence of tribalism and the changeover from socialism to capitalism. If Galiev's ghost is still wandering across the steppe, it would have every reason to be smiling.

Central Asia was reorganized into separate republics. In 1921 the Turkestan Soviet Socialist Republic (SSR) was created, and a commission was set up the following year to draft a new constitution for the federation, on which Stalin was responsible for the nationalities policy. On 30 December 1922 the Third Congress of the Soviets adopted the Treaty of Union which formed the Union of Soviet Socialist Republics (USSR) and under which the republics would enjoy autonomous, but not sovereign status.[19] A constitution for the Union was adopted in 1933 and was not changed until 1978, during the Brezhnev era. In 1990 President Gorbachev negotiated a new Union treaty in which the republics were to be given their sovereignty and much more, but its signing was forestalled by the August 1991 coup attempt in Moscow.

In January 1924 the Turkestan SSR was broken up and over a short period five separate republics came into existence – the Uzbek, Turkoman, Kazakh, Kyrgyz and Tajik Soviet Socialist Republics. After a long illness Lenin died in January 1924, warning Stalin that he was exceeding his authority against the smaller nationalities. Lenin wrote in his Last Testament:

> A distinction must be made between the nationalism of an oppressor nation and that of an oppressed nation, the nationalism of a big nation and that of a small nation. In respect of the second kind of nationalism, we, nationals of a big nation, have nearly always been guilty, in historic practice, of an infinite number of cases of violence.

His warning went unheeded by Stalin.[20]

The new borders divided the people into separate ethnic groups which they themselves were reluctant to recognize as such. How were the Kazakh and Kyrgyz nomads, who had lived together for centuries, to be differentiated now? There was confusion in cities like Tashkent where people had to choose, for the benefit of their identity cards, whether they were Tajik or Uzbek, when they themselves were frequently a mixture of both. The integral cultural and social unity of Central Asia and hopes of Pan-Islamic or Pan-Turkic movements were shattered, which is exactly what Stalin wanted. The loss of Turkestan deprived the people of a common homeland, a common language and a common destiny. Stalin's policies were to pit one republic and one ethnic group against another.

The use of the Arabic script, which was the only means of common communication in Central Asia before 1917, was forcibly ended in favour of a Latin script in 1922, and then Cyrillic after 1935 to increase the pace of integration with Russia. These provisions ensured that future generations would grow up knowing little of their past history, literature and poetry because only those works were translated into Cyrillic that the communists thought appropriate. Islam was forcibly uprooted, beginning with the wholesale destruction of mosques and madrasahs, the end of Arabic as a link language and the cutting off of all ties to the Muslim world. In 1917 there were some 26,000 mosques in Central Asia. By 1940 only 1,312 were left and in 1985 there were only 400 active mosques.[21] Anti-Islam propaganda increased dramatically as the communist leadership took measures to create a new 'Soviet man', which in Central Asia was only an excuse for greater Russification.

Russia's communist educational system was transplanted to Central Asia without any concessions to local needs. So was the legal system, despite Central Asia's own traditions of meetings of tribal elders to adjudicate between belligerents. The Red Army was used to absorb Central Asian males, to mould the new 'Soviet man' in its ranks and ensure that everyone spoke Russian. All separate Muslim units in the army were dismantled in 1923 and it became difficult for muslims to gain promotion as officers. Among the generals appointed between 1940 and 1970, 91 per cent were Slavs; none were from Central Asia.[22] Yet despite Russian prejudices many Jadids and nationalists believed that communism offered progress and modernism for their people, and they joined the CPSU in large numbers. Nationalists such as the Uzbek leader Fayzullah Khojaev, who later became the general-secretary of the Communist Party of Uzbekistan, justified Stalin's dictum to divide the nationalities on the grounds that it would promote progress. He was executed by Stalin for treason in 1938.[23]

The staggering losses suffered by the people of Central Asia during the 1916 revolt against the Tsar, the Civil War of 1918–20, the 1923 famine and the Basmachi uprisings were to be followed in 1928 by the forced collectivization of the nomads and peasants. The resistance they put up was brave, but costly and ultimately futile. Robert Conquest estimates that during the collectivization programme, a total of 6.5 million Soviet people lost their lives, one third of them in Central Asia. An estimated 7 million people died in the 1932–33 famine, of whom 2 million died in Central Asia.[24] Later chapters in this book detail the enormous human losses each republic suffered because of the programmes and the purges. These losses stunted everything from population growth to economic development for decades.

In the 1920s and 1930s tens of thousands of Central Asian people were deported to Siberia. Kazakhs and Kyrgyz nomads fled to China rather than surrender to the Red Army. More than half the livestock in Central Asia was destroyed, enormous tracts of land were rendered fallow by the killing of farmers, and the subsequent famines consumed much of the remaining population. The Basmachis reappeared in force in 1929, pushed out of semi-retirement in Afghanistan and Persia by the horrors inflicted upon their people by the collectivization programme. This programme was followed, between 1934 and 1938, by the Great Terror, the purges within the CPSU carried out by Stalin. Thousands of local communist leaders and cadres who had evolved from being Jadids, Basmachis or soldiers in the Red Army into becoming loyal communists were purged for being deviationists. Hundreds were put on trial and executed, with the result that the newly created Central Asian intelligentsia was decimated. Those communists suspected of promoting the interests of their nationality under the economic changes launched by Moscow were the first to be shot. Kazakhs and Kyrgyz were accused of being ultra-nationalists and having links with China; Tajiks were accused of being agents of British imperialism, while Turkomen were accused of promoting Pan-Islamism and Pan-Turkism.

The purges did not stop at the political elite. Writers and poets were executed. So were astronomers, biologists, scientists, doctors, engineers and military officers. People who had just struggled up the communist ladder by educating themselves were brought down, humiliated and executed. Of 700 writers, many of them from Central Asia, who met at the First Congress of the Union of Soviet Writers in 1934, only 50 survived to see the Second Congress in 1954.[25] Fewer than 2 per cent of the rank-and-file delegates to CPSU congresses in the 1920s still held their positions in 1939.

> The Red Terror gave the population to understand that under a regime that felt no hesitation in executing innocents, innocence was no guarantee of survival. The best hope of surviving lay in making oneself as inconspicuous as possible, which meant abandoning any thought of independent public activity, indeed any concern with public affairs, and withdrawing into one's private world.[26]

Thus it was that many Central Asian people in the private confines of their homes turned to Islam and the Sufi orders for spiritual sustenance.

Large parts of Kazakhstan, like Siberia, were turned into gulags. In 1937 in the vast Karlag complex of labour camps around Karaganda, there was a revolt by inmates which was forcibly put down after 440 prisoners were shot dead.[27] After the purges came World War Two, in which some 20 million Soviet citizens lost their lives, of whom again a large proportion were from Central Asia. Between 1920 and 1945 it is estimated that more than a quarter of the population of Central Asia died a violent death.

The war saw a relaxation of communist propaganda in Central Asia as Russian leaders mobilized the population on the basis of patriotism against the Germans. However, the end of the War saw a renewed tightening of communist control. Under Khrushchev in 1955, attacks against Islam in Central Asia intensified. Veil-burning ceremonies were given widespread publicity and Khrushchev revived the former Bolshevik 'Union of the Godless' in 1958, which shut down the few Islamic schools and mosques still open. Islamic weddings and funerals were banned, and in 1959 the end of the era of the veil was officially announced, with the ceremonial burning of the last veil in Bukhara.[28]

At the Twenty-second Party Congress in 1961, a declaration was passed that the nationalities problem in the Soviet Union had been solved with complete fusion between all ethnic groups and peoples.

Throughout the 1960s, however, nationalism amongst the constituent republics was a growing phenomenon that could not be ignored, even by the leadership of individual communist parties, who frequently issued warning shots across Moscow's bows. On 5 November 1969, to commemorate Lenin's address to the people of Turkestan, the five main Russian daily newspapers in each of the Central Asian republics published a joint editorial calling for the elimination of Great Russian chauvinism. At the universities a local cultural revival was under way and in the media local-language newspapers took a far more nationalist stance on issues vis-à-vis Moscow than the local Russian-language press. There was a rediscovery of Central Asia's Islamic heritage by a new generation of intellectuals which became quite evident in literature and language teaching, and the re-emergence of Sufi movements. Local communist leaders played a delicate balancing act, being ardent nationalists and good Muslims at home, whilst becoming internationalists and good communists when they visited Moscow.

Yet the myths continued to be propagated. At the Twenty-fourth Party Congress in 1971, President Brezhnev said that fifty years of Soviet rule had produced, 'a new historical community of people – the Soviet people had emerged', a people which was united.[29] Nothing could have been further from the truth. In the 1978 constitution even less formal independence and even fewer decision-making powers were given to the republics than before. (Brezhnev died in November 1982 and he was succeeded as general-secretary of the CPSU by Yuri Andropov, who died, in February 1984, and was succeeded by Konstantin Chernernko, who died after just thirteen months.)[30]

Gorbachev's accession to power in March 1985 coincided with the end of the long-running tenures of the first secretaries of the five Central Asian communist parties. By the end of 1986 all five had either died or been ousted: Jabar Rasulov of Tajikistan who had led the republic since 1961 and died of a heart attack in April 1982, Turdiakun Usubaliev who was forcibly retired in 1985 after running Kyrgyzstan since 1961, Mukhamednazar Gapurov of Turkmenistan who was retired in 1986 after running the republic since 1969, Dinmukhamed Kunayev of Kazakhstan who was replaced in December 1986, and Sharif Rashidov of Uzbekistan who was removed from office in October 1983 after corruption charges were brought against him.[31] These men had dominated Central Asia for nearly twenty years, through what was later called the 'era of stagnation'. They had built up a formidable party machine fuelled by patronage, corruption and clan loyalties.

Gorbachev now had the opportunity to introduce his new policies of *glasnost* and *perestroika* through a more enlightened leadership in Central Asia, which would be more sensitive to local conditions.

Instead, Gorbachev had no qualms in replacing some of them by Russians rather than by local leaders, thus creating considerable resentment at a time when national sensibilities were on the rise. He showed remarkable insensitivity to Central Asia and continued to treat the republics as colonies, which led to public resentment. The first unrest in Central Asia occurred in the most placid corner of the region – Alma Ata. In December 1986 Gorbachev removed the Kazakh party chief Dinmukhamed Kunayev, who had ruled the republic since 1964, and replaced him by an ethnic Chuvash from Russia, Gennady Kolbin. On 17 December 1986, a few days after Kolbin took over, anti-Russian riots against Kolbin's appointment broke out in Alma Ata. There is little doubt that the riots were partly engineered by Kunayev's supporters, but they fed on the strong Kazakh nationalist feeling in the streets.[32] At least seventeen people were killed and hundreds were injured as the riots spread to twelve other towns in Kazakhstan. Martial law had to be declared in many areas. The riots received immense publicity in the USSR and foreign press and shocked the ruling elite, as Gorbachev was just beginning to introduce his reforms in Moscow.

These riots nevertheless failed to make any real impact on the leadership's policies, which remained insensitive to the problems of the nationalities that erupted over the next two years. In January 1988 the issue of Nagorno Karabakh exploded into war between Armenia and Azerbaijan. The crisis in the three Baltic republics began and there was trouble in Georgia. Gorbachev considered these issues as security problems for the Soviet Union rather than as a failure of the CPSU policy on nationalities. He refused to admit that the CPSU had been wrong in the past and his first reaction to any unrest was to send in more troops and crack down hard. Invariably such actions backfired. During his political career Gorbachev had never served for any length of time outside Russia and he knew very little about the non-Russian republics or Central Asia. He had no idea of the anti-Russian resentment to be found in capitals like Tashkent and Dushanbe, the growing feelings of ethnic nationalism and the repression by the local communist governments.[33]

Central Asia continued to boil. In May 1988 there were riots in Ashkhabad because of the high level of unemployment amongst young people. In June 1989 dozens of people were killed and 1,000 were injured in the Ferghana valley of Uzbekistan during gun battles over land and housing between Uzbeks and Meskhetian Turks. Gorbachev was in West Germany at the time and tactlessly told journalists that 'Islamic fundamentalism had bared its teeth', which was inaccurate. In February 1990 dozens of people were killed in riots in Dushanbe and other Tajik cities over the proposed resettlement of Armenian refugees. In June 1990 gun battles between Uzbeks and Kyrgyz over land in the southern Kyrgyz city of Osh claimed dozens of lives and nearly led to war between the two republics. All the unrest that occurred was between ethnic groups and involved disputes over housing and land, the two most controversial issues in Central Asia.

The huge acclaim that Gorbachev's policies of *glasnost* and *perestroika* received in the western Soviet republics and in Europe was never duplicated in Central Asia. Every minor ethnic explosion appeared to set the stage for a larger explosion as all five communist parties refused to allow their populations to express themselves freely. They feared ethnic strife, economic strikes and an Islamic revival amongst their own people. Moreover, they feared Moscow's reaction if the Russian population in their republics were harmed in any way.[34] They relied on the well-tried tactics of repression, the police state and patronage to maintain themselves in power. Informal groups that tried to pressurize the regimes for change or to emulate the free speech and environmental movements in Russia were banned. *Perestroika* never effectively came to Central Asia except in the shape of small, semi-underground intellectual groups. The exceptions were Kazakhstan where a strong anti-nuclear movement developed, and Kyrgyzstan where the communists ran out of ideas and promoted Askar Akaev, a non-communist professor, to become president in October 1990.

Gorbachev's desire to pull out the 120,000 Soviet troops based in Afghanistan also worried the Central Asian leaders, who had benefited economically from the USSR's invasion of Afghanistan and were wary of the spread of Islamic fundamentalism by the Afghan Mujheddin. After coming to power Gorbachev ordered an impartial analysis of the situation in Kabul and by July 1987 he had summoned Afghan president Najibullah to Moscow to tell him, 'I hope you are ready in twelve months because we are leaving no matter what.'[35] In Moscow and Central Asia, protests by Soviet army veterans of the Afghan war had become an embarrassment for *glasnost*, but not for Central Asia's communist leaders. In November 1987, 2,000 veterans of the Afghan war held a meeting in Ashkhabad and decided to erect a monument for their dead. The meeting was broken up and as protests against the war multiplied in Central Asia in 1989, they were brutally suppressed by the police. Although the public was strongly against the war, the communist nomenklatura remained concerned about the domestic political fallout if the war ended in defeat for the Soviet Union, for it would signal a victory for Islam in the region.

The Central Asian leaders expressed their anger at Gorbachev for agreeing to the United Nations sponsored agreement signed in Geneva between Pakistan and Afghanistan in April 1988, which led to the withdrawal of Soviet troops. They complained bitterly that they were never consulted by Gorbachev on an issue that affected them directly.[36] By the time the last Soviet soldier had left Afghanistan, on 15 February 1989, the Central Asian leaders felt betrayed by Gorbachev – a factor that was to influence their negative attitudes towards him when the coup attempt took place in August 1991.

As power slipped from Gorbachev's hands through 1990 and 1991, Central Asian leaders hung on desperately to the old system, refusing to introduce economic reforms, liberalize the political system or open up their states to the outside world. Their conservatism was little more than self-preservation, for they feared a future which was uncertain and unpredictable. Many of them, like President Islam Karimov of Uzbekistan, adopted an increasingly nationalist rhetoric in order to silence their domestic opponents and ensure some modicum of popular support. In Moscow, however, their opinions hardly mattered and were not asked for. Out of twelve Politburo members in 1989–90 only two were non-Russian; Central Asia was represented neither in the Politburo nor the central committee of the CPSU. Only President Nursultan Nazarbayev had become close to President Gorbachev, and he was involved with Gorbachev's political moves to keep the old Soviet Union together.

The nationalities crisis worsened with the military crackdown in Lithuania in January 1991, after which the presidents of the Baltic republics asked for UN intervention. The nationalities issue had now become a major international issue, and scenarios about the fragmentation of the former Soviet Union came into vogue. The national question had become the mirror image of the painted Russian dolls – after opening the top doll, one finds successively smaller and smaller dolls inside. The breakdown of the communist structure had showed up the dormant ethnic tensions that existed down to the smallest district and even village level.[37] The Foreign Minister, Eduard Shevardnadze, resigned on 15 January 1991 warning the world of an impending military coup in Moscow. The economic crisis worsened and a country-wide coal miners' strike in March and April paralysed Kazakhstan, where some 70,000 miners went on strike. The miners' refusal to accept orders from the Supreme Soviet or to accept increased pay offers demonstrated the new militancy amongst the working class.

The growth of nationalism in Central Asia was mirrored in Russia itself, where intellectuals first began to voice the need to dump the Soviet empire if Russia was to make meaningful progress. Central Asia was seen not as the source of raw materials, but as an economic burden which was dragging Russia into backwardness. The Russian dissident Alexander Solzhenitsyn argued in a prophetic essay published in 1991 that Russia would only be strong 'once it has shed the onerous burden of the Central Asian underbelly'. He called for the break-up of the Soviet Union and rebuilding of Russian nationalism.

> We don't have the strength for the peripheries either economically or morally. We don't have the strength for sustaining an empire – and it is just as well. Let this burden fall from our shoulders, it is crushing us, sapping our energy and hastening our demise.[38]

Soon this had become a popular refrain with anti-communist politicians.

On 12 June 1991 Boris Yeltsin was elected president of Russia with 60 per cent of the vote, sending a chill through Central Asia. Yeltsin was seen as an ardent Russian nationalist, even a chauvinist, who had even less interest in Central Asia than Gorbachev and who would not hesitate to take Russia out of the Union if it helped his political career. If Gorbachev was considered weak and vacillating, then Yeltsin was seen as erratic, temperamental and unpredictable.[39] The growing tension between the two leaders was to undermine further what little political clout the Central Asian leaders could muster in Moscow, for international and domestic attention was almost entirely focused on Russia. Gorbachev spent the summer trying to negotiate a new Union treaty that would devolve powers from Moscow to the republics. On 24 July he announced that he and leaders of ten republics had agreed on a powersharing treaty. By 20 August 1991 the treaty was ready for signing, but a day earlier the coup makers made their bid to topple Gorbachev and scuttle the new Union treaty.

The reasons for the coup attempt and for its failure do not concern us here, except briefly. Before it took place, 20 per cent of the card-carrying members of the CPSU had already resigned, there was a crisis of political and economic confidence, and whereas communists saw the break-up of the Union as high treason, non-communists saw it as not progressing fast enough. Gorbachev could not satisfy either camp. The economic crisis worsened and the centre just ran out of money as the provinces refused to pay their taxes.[40]

The reaction in Central Asia to the coup was stunning. Only the non-communist leader Askar Akaev moved troops into the Kyrgyz capital Beshkek in order to prevent a communist coup taking place there. He immediately condemned the Moscow plotters. The Kazakh president, Nursultan Nazarbayev, who had stood by Gorbachev, said nothing for the first thirty-six hours as he watched which way the wind blew. Finally on day two of the coup he condemned it, but only after it became clear that the coup was failing. The leaders of Uzbekistan, Turkmenistan and Tajikistan openly supported the coup-makers and immediately used the coup to crack down on their own local dissidents.[41]

Yet within a few days, after the failure of the coup, these leaders had to relent. They were forced to dissolve their communist parties after Gorbachev banned the CPSU on 24 August, a decision upheld by the Supreme Soviet five days later. In Tajikistan a series of opposition rallies began in Dushanbe which on 7 September forced the first secretary, Kakhar Makhanov, to resign – the first political casualty of the end of communism in Central Asia. The conflict in Tajikistan between the communist hangovers from the past and a new alliance of Islamic and democratic forces was to spill over into civil war within six months. After the failed coup, Gorbachev failed to win the support of the republics for a new Union Treaty, and this deadlock prompted the three Slav republics to set up the Commonwealth of Independent States (CIS) without even consulting the Central Asian republics. Finally the newly enlarged CIS was formed on 21 December in Alma Ata, and four days later, on Christmas Day, Gorbachev resigned. Central Asia now had to cope on its own with the rising tide of nationalism and Islam. When Gorbachev had come to power in 1985, the position of official Islam, that Islam was tolerated by the communist system, was at its lowest level. There was only one madrasah operating in the whole of Central Asia – in Bukhara – which turned out a small number of Muslim clerics every year. The Mufti of Tashkent, chosen by the regime, was the official spokesman for Islam in the Soviet Union – a position that is inimical to the very spirit of Islam. Communist Party presses would publish a standard Muslim lunar calendar and a magazine for Muslims in different languages, but no Korans or other Islamic literature was available. A handful of nominated delegates would be allowed to perform the pilgrimage to Mecca every year. Muslim festivals such as Eid were officially frowned upon, and the ritual slaughter of animals on that day was forbidden. Instead, the faithful were told to make monetary payments to the mosques. Ramadan, the month of fasting, was strongly discouraged because it could reduce productivity; and it was described in the official media as a pre-Arab pagan custom that had nothing to do with the teachings of the Prophet Mohammed.

The drive against Islam after the 1917 Revolution had been unrelenting. The Islamic sharia courts were abolished in 1924, and this had been followed in 1928 by the closure of some 15,000 madrasahs across Central Asia. In the same year the veil was abolished and the Arabic script was replaced by a Latin alphabet. In 1930 Stalin requisitioned all *waqf* lands, those lands held by local mosques and religious endowments, which were often the only source of livelihood for local mullahs. Mosques were steadily closed down and the Union of Godless set up in 1925 to wipe out Islam was given permission by Stalin to turn mosques into social centres. In 1934 a government ban was placed on people performing *Haj* and printing presses were forbidden to publish the Koran.[42] A new communist-controlled Islamic establishment was set up to control and monitor the lives of Soviet Muslims. Of the four Islamic directorates, the largest, in Tashkent, covered the whole of Central Asia, another one in Ufa covered Russia, while there was a separate directorate for the Caucasus. Baku covered Azerbaijan, where the majority of the Muslim population were Shias rather than Sunni Muslim.

Yet right across the steppe Islam thrived in a semi-underground world. Marriages were registered at the local communist party office, but the mullah would also solemnize the marriage by a formal *nikka*, or betrothal ceremony. The marriage feast would be held at the crack of dawn, when the ceremonial *pilaf* was served to the whole collective farm along with other dishes. The dawn feast would be cooked all night with the guests dancing, singing songs and listening to professional musicians. Although in other Muslim countries these celebrations are held at night, in Central Asia they were held at dawn to hide from officials the ritual slaughter of sheep and the expenditure incurred, and to allow people to go to work in the morning.[43] The dowry and the bride price, officially banned under the communist regime, were still paid, though in goods such as jewellery and furniture as well as sheep and goats rather than in cash. Most people were still buried according to Islamic rites and every male child was circumcised in the traditional way by a mullah, after which a feast would be given by the boy's parents. Girls adhered to the conservative traditions common in most Muslim countries. They did not generally date boys and most girls did not sleep with any man before marriage.

Mixed marriages – that is, marriages with non-Muslims, were extremely rare and frowned upon. Muslim girls rarely married non-Muslims, for example Russians or Ukrainians, although a Muslim male would more often marry a Russian girl – still undergoing the Muslim marriage ceremony. The stability of the Muslim family, as well as local traditions, were the main reasons for the population explosion in Muslim Central Asia. On the collective farms most marriages were arranged, early marriages were frequent, and divorce was rare. Women were responsible for family cohesion, often looking after three generations under one roof. Alcoholism, a principal cause of divorce and broken homes in Russia, was rare in Central Asia, although most Muslims enjoyed drinking alcohol occasionally and even eating pork, which is not permitted under Islamic law. The enlarged family circle sustained itself with the private plots available to peasants on the collective farms, and with the bazaar economy, in which the private sector continued to play a major role in providing essential foodstuffs. Theft of state goods, corruption and favours to family and clan members were considered not a crime but an essential part of maintaining a decent standard of living.

Thus while an educated Uzbek or Kazakh might fail to observe many of the formal rituals such as prayer, Islam was still his religion and the defining circle of his cultural world. He knew that Islam gave him a distinct identity and made him what he was. A Christian or Jewish Uzbek, although they existed, remained unthinkable to most Uzbeks, and so children from mixed marriages were automatically presumed to be Muslim. Thus Islam became one of the defining factors of ethnicity. It helped to consolidate both the clan and the tribe as well as to create the much broader nationality. Islam reinforced ethnic solidarity and drove a wedge between Russians and non-Russian Muslims. The more the religion of Islam was driven underground by the communist regime, the more it prospered as a cultural phenomenon that linked people together in ethnic solidarity and togetherness against the non-Muslim races, particularly Russians. Moreover, the ethnic solidarity that Islam fostered cut across class divisions, since it united the family, the clan and the tribe rather than the class.

Thus Islam remained a direct challenge to the communist system for it did not allow the concept of the working or oppressed class to dominate the politics or social structure of Central Asia. Despite all the social, material and educational progress achieved by Central Asia, the people remained spiritually alienated from Russia because the gap between the Muslim and the non-Muslim world could not be bridged. The Soviet communists thought otherwise. They believed they had eliminated at least three major challenges that Islam presented to the communists in Central Asia: the *Jihad* or holy guerrilla wars launched by the Basmachis, the modernist Islamic trends represented by the Jadids, and the last vestiges of Pan-Turkism and Pan-Islamism. Moreover, the national communism espoused by Sultan Galiev had never been allowed to take root and the challenge posed by the populist Sufi brotherhoods amongst the people had been undermined.

The Soviet Union's leadership was to be proved wrong on all counts. The ideas of the Basmachis were to resurface in Afghanistan in the

1980s and in Tajikistan in the 1990s. The ideas of the Jadids returned in the pamphlets of new nationalist–Islamic parties in Uzbekistan, and the wider movements of Pan-Islamism and Pan-Turkism were to become lasting trends, the latter even taken up by former communist leaders. Moreover, it was the Sufi brotherhoods that kept religious ritual, prayer and the Muslim's inner life distinct and separate from the communist system. For the past thirty years writers like Alexandre Bennigsen and Enders Wimbush have claimed that Islam was being kept alive in Central Asia through Sufism, which was flourishing as an underground movement. Clearly they were right: the massive Islamic revival that took place during Gorbachev's *glasnost* could not have emerged from a vacuum.[44]

Sufism was the mystical trend of Islam that originated in Persia and Central Asia soon after the arrival of the Arabs. *Sufi* means 'wool' in Arabic and the name comes from the rough woollen coats worn by the early Sufi brethren. The Sufi orders or the 'Tariqah' which means 'the way', became secret societies under communism that taught people the rites of Islam as well as the methods of contemplation and prayer. Sufism had always been a reaction against authority, intellectualism and the mullah – thus making it ideally suited for ordinary people. Sufism had sustained Muslims before under just as trying circumstances, such as during the Mongol invasions when all the vestiges of Islam were wiped out, and later during tsarist days. For the people to fall back on Sufism during the communist era was nothing new. The Sufis practised the art of isolating themselves from their oppressors without necessarily trying to overthrow them, and their refusal to involve themselves in political parties or movements ensured that the KGB barely knew that they existed.[45]

There were four main Tariqahs, established centuries ago. The Kubrawwyah, which is the smallest order and named after Sheikh Najmuddin Kubral, is popular amongst the Turkomen and the Kara-Kalpaks in Uzbekistan. The oldest order is the Qaderiyrah, named after Abdul Qader Gilani who lived in Baghdad in the twelfth century, and it is today strongest in Bukhara, Kokand and large parts of Afghanistan. The Yassawiyah, named after Sheikh Ahad Yassawi, is most popular amongst the Kazakhs and Kyrgyz. Two branches of this order, called the Hairy Elders and the Lachis, organized guerrilla wars first against the Tsar and then the Bolsheviks in the Ferghana valley. The largest order is the Naqshbandiyah, founded in the fourteenth century and named after Sheikh Bahauddin Naqshbandi, which has followers throughout Central Asia, Persia and Afghanistan. These orders rarely come in conflict with each other, for they see themselves as 'paths leading to the summit of the same mountain'.[46]

The Sufis build their faith on ritual incantations, dances, music and sessions of physical shaking or whirling in a permanent quest for truth. These create an inner spiritual space within man that the communists could never hope to capture. No better description of the Sufis has emerged than that of the famous Arab traveller Ibn Battuta who described them some seven centuries ago.

> The mystics were grouped in congregations, called after some eminent Sheykh, who was regarded as the founder of the Tariqah or rule, including the ritual litany, which was one of the distinguishing marks of each congregation. Disciples of the order spread through the Muslim world and in most cases all the members looked up to the descendants or successors of the founder as their head … . The fundamental aim of the Sufi life was to pierce the veils of human sense which shut man off from the Divine and so to attain communion with and absorption into God. Their days and nights were spent in prayer and contemplation, in fasting and ascetic exercises. Members of the Tariqah met to celebrate the ritual litany, the zikr, according to their peculiar rites. The zikr was intended to produce a hypnotic effect on the participants and so allow them to taste momentarily the joys of reunion with the Divine.[47]

A much more political and militant Islam was introduced in the twentieth century by the Ikhwan ul Muslimeen or the Muslim Brotherhood, which originated in Egypt as a movement to bring about an Islamic revolution and the creation of an Islamic state. The brotherhood created a number of secret cells in Central Asian cities in the 1930s and although strictly underground, the movement has come out into the open and flourished since the advent of *perestroika*. The Islamic Renaissance Party (IRP) which exists in all five Central Asian republics is the direct heir to those early brotherhood groups.[48]

Wahabism, the strict puritanical sect that dominates life in Saudi Arabia, arrived in Central Asia around 1912, brought by Sayed Sharie Mohammed, a native of Medina. He set up Wahabi circles in Tashkent and the Ferghana valley. Today the Wahabis are seeing a major revival of their fortunes in the Ferghana valley where they are preaching Islamic revolution and the overthrow of the government of President Islam Karimov. They receive lavish funding from supporters in Saudi Arabia to build mosques and madrasahs. The Wahabis produced one of the first martyrs of Islam in the modern era when Bahauddin Vaisov, a Wahabi teacher in Ferghana, was sentenced to a prison term in 1950; he was placed in a lunatic asylum where he later died. Both the IRP and Wahabi movements are described in detail in later chapters.

It was ironic that Gorbachev's policies of openness did not lead to political liberalization in Central Asia, but instead had a dramatic impact in reviving Islam. Underground groups and private prayer circles emerged into the open and began to build mosques and criticize the establishment's Muslim hierarchy. Groups printed previously banned Islamic literature and simple pamphlets that described how to pray. Saudi Arabia sent one million Korans to Central Asia in 1990 and there was a boom in Koran publishing as the holy book was translated into local languages. The rise of nationalism in the republics coincided with this religious revival, and no nationalist party was without its programme to promote Islamic values and culture, as part of its wider nationalist and anti-Russian agenda. The more the communist system preached Soviet universalism, the more pressing became the demands of an Islamic revival and cultural particularism amongst the myriad of ethnic groups in Central Asia.

In February 1990, in an unprecedented show of defiance, Muslims demanded the resignation of Mufti Shamsuddin Khan Babakhan, the chairman of the Muslim Board for Central Asia in Tashkent. They accused him of womanizing and deviating from Islam, and he was forced to step down. At the same time the ambitious Qazi of Alma Ata, Radbek Nisanbai, had himself elected Grand Mufti of Kazakhstan, thus creating a separate Kazakh Muslim Board without consulting Moscow.[49] People were no longer satisfied that Moscow should determine who should be teaching them religion.

The first sign of this independent spirit in the Islamic revival was the building of new mosques. By October 1990 there were a total of 50 new mosques in Kyrgyzstan compared to 15 in 1989, 30 in Turkmenistan compared to 5 before, 40 in Tajikistan compared to 17 before, and 90 in Kazakhstan compared to 37 before. In Tashkent city there were 30 new mosques compared to just 2 in 1989.[50] A year later, by October 1991, there were over 1,000 new mosques in every republic and a new mosque was being opened every day. Converted homes, schools, social centres and even abandoned factories were turned into mosques, paid for largely by public donations from the local community. By October 1992 thousands of mosques had been set up in each republic.

For the conservative rulers of Central Asia the challenge of Islam is posing major problems. Most states, like Uzbekistan and Turkmenistan, have banned the IRP and other Muslim fundamentalist parties. Tajikistan was plunged into a bloody civil war in 1992 that has claimed some 50,000 casualties. The reactions of the various Central Asian regimes to the Islamic revival are explored in later chapters, but for each republic the key issue has been whether its leaders would allow the Islamic parties to work within the system or force them underground through banning orders, jail sentences and decrees. In the first few years the evidence pointed to repression and a refusal to accommodate the Islamic parties within the mainstream of parliamentary opposition. Democracy, thin on the ground in most parts of Central Asia, has suffered badly because of the regimes' unwillingness to open up the political system to a more varied opposition. The result has been that political parties barely exist and their future growth has been stunted.

The West has not helped matters by constantly pointing out the fear it has of an Islamic revival. During his tour of Central Asia in 1991, US Secretary of State James Baker warned every Central Asian leader of the dangers of Islamic fundamentalism and urged them to emulate Turkey's secular model rather than Iran's fundamentalism. Baker met not a single religious leader in Central Asia and made it clear that he thought fundamentalism was inimical to democracy and Western aid packages.[51] This has allowed a leader like Uzbek president Islam Karimov, to continue denying democratic rights to the Uzbek opposition under cover of halting the spread of fundamentalism. Western countries have thus been guilty of turning a blind eye to authoritarian governments and even rewarding them if they confronted Islamic fundamentalism. This has been a short-sighted policy, which has affected the credibility of these countries. The West's attitude was partly dictated by the nuclear arsenal that Kazakhstan had inherited from the former Soviet Union. Although the missiles were under the joint control of Russia, Kazakhstan and Byelorussia, President Nazarbayev was able to use them to extract further concessions from Moscow.

By December 1992, a year after gaining independence, the conservative regimes in Central Asia faced several common problems. The most pressing was the economic crisis, which built up a wave of public resentment as the rouble crashed, factories closed down and shops emptied of basic goods. But the vitally necessary debate over economic reform in many republics was superseded by growing political opposition from nationalist and Islamic fundamentalist parties. The kind of liberal, democratic lobbies that urged speedy economic reform in Russia were almost nonexistent in Central Asia. The nationalists and fundamentalists forced the regimes in Uzbekistan, Tajikistan and Turkmenistan onto the defensive, while in Kazakhstan and Kyrgyzstan the regimes managed to achieve some kind of equilibrium with the opposition. Each republic had its own peculiar set of political problems, but for all of them the coming economic crisis would determine their ability to build a future for their homeland.

Notes

1. H. Carrere d' Encausse (1988) *Islam and the Russian Empire: reform and revolution in Central Asia*, I.B. Taurus, London,
   2. Ibid.

3. A. Benningsen, 'Pan-Turkism and Pan-Islam in History and Today', *Central Asia Survey*, Vol. 3, No. 3.

4. A. Benningsen and E. Wimbush (1979) *Muslim National Communism in the Soviet Union: a revolutionary strategy for the colonial world*, University of Chicago Press, USA.

5. F. M. Bailey (1992) *Mission to Tashkent*, Oxford University Press, England.

6. S. Alvineri (1969) *Karl Marx on Colonialism and Modernization*, Anchor Books, USA.

7. J. Stalin (1975) *Marxism and the National Question*, Proletarian Publishers, USA.

8. H.B. Davis (1978) *Towards a Marxist Theory of Nationalism*, Monthly Review Press, USA.

9. H. B. Davis (ed.) *The National Question: selected writings by Rosa Lumemburg*, Monthly Review Press, USA.

10. Davis.

11. V. I. Lenin (1968) '*Address to the Communists in the East*', Selected Works, Progress Publishers, Moscow.

12. M. Lewin (1975) *Lenin's Last Struggle*, Pluto Press, London.

13. Bennigsen and Wimbush.

14. Ibid.

15. Ibid.

16. Ibid.

17. N. Bukahrin and E. Preobrazhensky (1969) *The ABC of Communism*, Penguin, London.

18. Stalin.

19. H. Carrere D'Encausse (1979) *Decline of an Empire: the Soviet Socialist Republics in revolt*, Newsweek Books, USA,

20. B. Nahaylo and V. Swohboda (1990) *Soviet Disunion: a history of the nationalities problem in the USSR*, Hamish Hamilton, London.

21. B. Brown 'The Public Role in *Perestroika* in Central Asia', *Central Asia Survey*, Vol. 9, No. 1.

22. Nahaylo and Swohboda.

23. Ibid.

24. R. Conquest (1988) *Harvest of Sorrow*, Arrow books, UK.

25. Ibid.

26. R. Pipes (1990) *The Russian Revolution*, Alfred Knopf, New York.

27. Ibid.

28. A. Taheri (1989) *Crescent in a Red Sky: the future of Islam in the Soviet Union*, Hutchinson, London.

29. Ibid.

30. G. Hosking (1990) *A History of the Soviet Union*, Fontana, London.

31. J. Critchlow (1991) *Nationalism in Uzbekistan: a Soviet republic's road to sovereignty*, Westview Books, USA.

32. Interviews by the author with Kazakh officials, 1990 and 1991.

33. H. Smith (1990) *The New Russians*, Vintage, USA. See also D. Doder and L. Branson (1990) *Gorbachev: heretic in the Kremlin*, Futura Books, London.

34. Brown.

35. Doder and Branson (1990).

36. Interviews with all the Central Asian presidents in December 1991 about their atttudes towards Afghanistan. See 'Central Asian Republics Must Be Con-

sulted', Ahmed Rashid (in Tashkent), *Nation*, (Lahore), 19 December 1991. Also Ahmed Rashid, 'Russia Launches Initiative for Afghanistan Peace', *Independent*, (London), 17 December 1991.

37. S. Crawshaw (1992) *Goodbye to the USSR: the collapse of Soviet power*, Bloomsbury, London.

38. A. Solzhenitsen (1991) *Rebuilding Russia*, Harvill, London

39. Interviews with government officials in Central Asian captials during 1990 and 1991.

40. Crawshaw.

41. Ahmed Rashid, 'Muslims' Chance to Seek More Power', *Independent*, 22 August 1991.

42. Hosking.

43. Information gathered by the writer during frequent visits to Central Asia and attendance at marriages and funerals.

44. Bennigsen and Wimbush.

45. Ahmed Rashid (in Uzbekistan), 'The Revival of Sufism', *Far Eastern Economic Review*, 17 December 1992.

46. Taheri. For a more detailed study see the numerous books on Sufism by Idries Shah, in particular, I. Shah (1990) *the Way of the Sufi*, Arkana Penguin, London.

47. I. Battuta (republished 1984) *Travels in Asia and Africa 1325–1354*, Routledge and Kegan Paul, London.

48. Ahmed Rashid (in Alma Ata), 'Bless Perestroika and send Korans', *Independent*, 4 June 1990.

49. Ibid.

50. 'The Islamic Challenge', *Far Eastern Economic Review*, 12 July 1990 (notes taken by author during travels in Central Asia in 1990).

51. Robin Wright, 'Islam, Democracy and the West', *Foreign Affairs*, Summer 1992.

3

Socialism along the Silk Road – Economy and Society in Central Asia

A few miles outside Beshkek, the bustling capital of Kyrgyzstan, nomads still follow traditions estabished some 3,000 years ago. Living alone in small yurts, tents made of felt, they tend flocks of goats and sheep in the high mountain passes for much of the summer months. In the winter they come down to the collective farms to overwinter, their flocks living off the fodder cultivated in the summer months. In the Karakum desert outside Ashkhabad, the capital of Turkmenistan, horsemen still spend their lives like their forefathers did, tending herds of horses and camels in the midst of a harsh scrubland and frequent sandstorms.

Over the centuries the greatest horsemen in the world have emerged from the Central Asian steppes to conquer lands in Europe, Asia and the Middle East. It is ironic that these great periodic outbursts of the nomads from their rolling grasslands were often a result of successive years of good rains, green pastures and abundant increase in the herds, which in turn led to a small population explosion, too many animals and land hunger. The economics of nomadism necessitated expansion and the conquest of new pasture lands until the conquering nomads themselves settled down and were conquered in turn by fresh waves of horsemen.

Marxism believed that nomadism was the first rung up the ladder towards the later development of agricultural and then industrial societies. But nomadism, from its earliest appearance in Central Asia when animals were first domesticated, cohabited with agricultural societies, who cultivated the fertile soil in oasis settlements. For centuries it was this palpable tension between the two very different economies and lifestyles of the herd and the harvest that differentiated the peoples of Central Asia. Over time one group often merged with the other creating a new tribe or a new social elite.

Thus within one generation the Golden Horde of Genghis Khan conquered, and ruled from the saddle, an area that stretched from Austria to the Sea of Japan and from Siberia to the Arabian Gulf. Wherever the nomadic conquerors appeared, they brought economic and social disaster to the agricultural peoples: because of mass slaughter, looting and the seizure of fodder and grain. Genghis Khan's first demand when he entered Bukhara in 1220 was the demand of all horsemen: 'The countryside is empty of fodder, fill our horses' bellies.' Farmers were often themselves turned into foraging nomads. Yet within a single generation the khans of the Golden Horde had become urbanized emperors, officiating over lavish courts that were sustained by a sophisticated agricultural base. Early Islamic philosophers and writers wrote continually about the 'perpetual oscillation between the sedentarization of the pastoral peoples and the qualified renomadization of the settled societies'. The sedentary peasant needed the nomads as much as the latter desired the agricultural products of a settled life.[1]

Likewise the great trading cities of the Silk Route depended on nomads to provide them with milk products and draught animals, whilst the caravan traders needed baggage animals, protection and guides. In turn the nomads depended on these caravans to exchange their wool, hides, carpets and animals for tea and textiles. The caravans carried stories of the rice and bread baskets of India and China, which held a vivid attraction for the Central Asian warriors. Traders and farmers were beholden to the nomads for the constant and sure supply of domesticated animals, especially the horse, which was the most valuable and prestigious animal whose speed, strength, endurance, stamina and sheer nobility created a horse culture in Central Asia. The first nomads rode on the dun-coloured horses of the Russian steppes, the *equus tarpanus* which was later cross-bred with the horses that the Persians, Greeks and Arabs brought with them. The famed horses of Badakshan, which could run over stony ground without metal hooves, the hardy Akhaltekian breed of the Turkomen, which could cross deserts, and the speedy mares of the Ferghana valley were all descendants of this horse.

If the horse was the currency of exchange, the price of which dominated the market much as house prices do today in European cities, then it was the Bactrian two-humped camel of Central Asia that determined the economic value of the Silk Route. Its thick woolly coat, its ability to traverse desert and mountains, its minimal requirements of fodder and water made it ideal for long caravan journeys though numerous climatic zones. These early travellers never considered Central Asia to be at the edge of the world or on the periphery. In the earliest Muslim maps, which placed Mecca at the centre of the world, Central Asia appears as just an extension of the land mass south of the Caspian Sea from Iraq and Persia. Central Asia was well integrated into the great Middle Eastern empires and economies. It was also well connected to India through the Pamirs and the Hindu Kush, and to China across the Tien Shan mountains. It was a vibrant part of the world economy because it occupied that crucial corridor that connected east to west and south to north.[2]

After 1917 the communists were to marginalize Central Asia, simply by determining that its trade and contacts with the outside world were henceforth to be through Moscow. Yet the process of marginalization had begun the day the great sea captains began to discover the sea routes to India and China. The sea routes opened a new and cheaper access to the Orient and spelt the end of the land route. In the fifteenth century as the Silk Route caravans diminished in size and importance, so too did the cities along the route. The nomadic tribes along the way broke up into squabbling, bickering entities while the nomadic respect for the safety of merchants and caravans dissipated into respect only for loot and plunder, and raids on richer rivals.

By the late eighteenth century Russia had built up considerable trade with the three weak and poor states of Bukhara, Khiva and Kokand. In exchange for finished goods such as textiles and tools, Russia imported raw materials, three quarters of which was raw cotton. Two thirds of this trade was with Bukhara and the rest with Khiva and Kokand.[3] For a time intense competition existed with the British in India who tried to sell their cotton goods to Central Asia through Afghanistan. The cotton boom did little for the people of Central Asia because the economies of these principalities were almost entirely personalized in the shape of their ruler. The amir of Bukhara personally profited from the astrakhan trade, which by 1870 amounted to some 15 million roubles, and controlled the export of cotton. He personally owned 12 per cent of the total cultivated land of Bukhara while 55 per cent belonged to the state. Only 7 per cent of fertile land actually belonged to the farmers. The ruler of Khiva owned the state's entire irrigation system, from which he could extract as many taxes as he liked.[4]

Between 1840 and 1860, Russian exports to Central Asia increased twelvefold and imports sixteenfold, and there was an economic imperative to expand trade even further. Russian merchants urged the Tsar to guarantee the safety of trade routes in Central Asia, and a powerful economic lobby demanded that the region be absorbed into the empire. The emancipation of the serfs in Russia freed a huge population. Between 1900 and 1914, when records were first kept, some 3.5 million Russians moved to Central Asia. Many of them became farmers and began to produce cotton. By 1913, 543,000 hectares under cultivation in Central Asia were producing some 646,000 tons of cotton, 87 per cent of Russia's total cotton production. Moreover, Central Asia offered Russian exporters the easiest market for their goods. Unable to compete in Europe because their goods were inferior, Russian merchants looked to Central Asia for markets where there was no competition.[5]

The conquest of Central Asia led to an even greater imperative to integrate this vast raw-material-producing region with Russia. In the age of railroad imperialism, the railway was the most logical means of integrating far-flung parts of the empire and connecting them to the hub of the wheel that lay in Moscow. Its advocates, who included the writers Tolstoy and Dostoevsky, saw the railroads as carrying out a great civilizing mission; romance about the railway was to become a part of Russian colonial history. Lord Curzon, who was to become Russia's mortal foe when he was later appointed Viceroy of India, described the importance of the Central Asian railway thus:

> A railway train, lit by electric light and speeding through the sand deserts of Central Asia, adds one more of the startling contrasts in which this extraordinary region abounds. This railway is a far more potent weapon to Russia in her subjection of Asia than half a dozen Goek Tepes. It marks a complete and bloodless absorption.[6]

Goek Tepe was the the crushing defeat of the Turkomen tribes by a Russian army in 1881 in which 6,000 horsemen were killed.

By World War One the Russians had built 4,300 kilometres of railways in Central Asia, including extensions to the Afghan and Persian borders which placed Tsarist forces just a few hundred miles from British forces in India. The railway decimated the nomads. Grazing grounds were handed over to Russian farmers from Moscow and Minsk, and the nomads were forced to take refuge in the mountains and poor scrublands of the steppes where large flocks and herds could not be maintained. They were beaten and killed much in the spirit of the early American settlers' attitude to the indigenous peoples. A continuous series of revolts by the nomads was ferociously suppressed by Russian armies. For farmers conditions were possibly even worse. The cotton economy dictated the terms of everything: housing, diet, clothing and work. Food crops were not encouraged and in many cases their cultivation forbidden, trees were cut down for miles around to facilitate cotton-growing, thus limiting building materials. Clothes imported from Russia flooded the markets, ruining the local handicrafts industry.

The economic crisis came to a head during World War One. Although the price of cotton in 1914–15 was fixed at 50 per cent higher than the price received by the farmer in 1913, the price of imported grain from Russia had risen by 100 per cent; in 1916 the grain price again doubled while cotton prices remained fixed.[7] During the winter of 1915–16 there was little snow, and a dry spring destroyed the crops. Productivity fell by up to 50 per cent in many areas. Nomads started to slaughter their animals at great loss in order to buy grain at vastly inflated prices. The tribulations of the Central Asian people during this period are described in greater detail in the following chapters, and their tragedy was not to end with the 1917 Revolution.

During the Civil War and the railway blockade by the White armies that began in early 1918, which cut off Russia from Central Asia, no grain and other imports could arrive and no cotton could be exported back to Russia. Famine gripped the whole region and was to last until 1920 when the railway was reopened by the Reds. By the time the Red Army had defeated the Whites, the economy of Central Asia was well and truly destroyed, its population dramatically reduced, and 50 per cent of the cultivated land lost. Between 1917 and 1920 the nomads lost an estimated 1 million horses and camels (two thirds of their stock), 7 million sheep and goats (three quarters of the total stock) and half their cattle. In settled areas peasants lost up to 60 per cent of their animals. In 1916 the population of Turkestan was estimated to be 7.3 million. By 1920 it had been reduced to 5.3 million despite the large-scale migration from Russia. The losses were catastrophic for many tribes. Tens of thousands of nomads fled to China, Persia and Afghanistan.[8] The communists thus inherited an almost nonexistent economy, a devastated infrastructure, ruined cities and a population that was seething with unrest and revolt.

Table 3.1 Population trends in Central Asia according to present republican borders (1,000's)

	1913	1939	1959	1970	1989
USSR	159,153	190,678	208,827	241,720	286,717
Uzbekistan	4,334	6,347	8,119	11,800	19,906
Kazakhstan	5,597	6,082	9,295	13,009	16,538
Kyrgyzstan	864	1,458	2,066	2,933	4,291
Tajikistan	1,034	1,485	1,981	2,900	5,112
Turkmenistan	1,042	1,252	1,516	2,159	3,534

Source: Carrere D'Encausse (1979) *Decline of an Empire: the Soviet Socialist Republics in revolt*, Newsweek Books, USA.

Before Central Asia had recovered from this devastation, it was to be subjected to forced collectivization, a process in which more than 1 million people died. According to Robert Conquest in his path-breaking book *Harvest of Sorrow*, if the deaths of the nomads, the kulaks (rich peasants) and urban dwellers are computed for the whole of the Soviet Union, the total deaths come to some 6.5 million people. Collectivization was to coincide with the devastating famine of 1932 –33 in which another 7 million people died across the Soviet Union. Table 3.1 demonstrates the slow growth of population in Central Asia between 1913 and 1939 because of these violent deaths as compared to the much faster growth after 1939. The collectivization campaign was made more brutal by the speed in which it was carried out. In 1923 the central committee of the CPSU declared in its Five Year Plan that 23 per cent of the sown area should be collectivized by 1930. Stalin cancelled the order and on 27 December 1929 he ordered the liquidation of the kulaks as a class.[9]

Between January and March 1930 10 million peasant holdings were brought into the collective farm system across the Soviet Union.[10] In Central Asia a rigid definition for kulaks was impossible and at times anyone who owned a cow was termed a kulak and killed or deported. In a few months, some 95,000 households were deported from Kazakhstan and Kyrgyzstan. From Turkmenistan some 2,000 house-holds were deported to Siberia, and in Uzbekistan 40,000 families were stripped of their farms and animals and forced to become col-lective farm workers.[11] Basmachi rebels restarted their guerrilla attacks and between 1930 and 1935 there were at least 160 recorded attempts at uprisings against the communists in Uzbekistan alone.[12] Nomads were forcibly collectivized in massive roundups by the Red Army that resembled cattle roundups. More Kyrgyz and Kazakhs fled to China, while the Turkmen migrated to Afghanistan and Persia.

Collectivization was followed by the beginnings of industrialization in Central Asia as enormous plants were set up in the major cities. Under the Soviet government the cities were to become industrial islands in a predominantly peasant culture. They were autonomous and hardly connected to the agricultural and nomadic economic base around them. Moreover, they were largely populated and governed by Russians, which further widened the rural–urban divide in Central Asia. Unlike other Third World countries, the main movement to the cities has not been by the rural peasantry but by migrants from outside Central Asia. This was partly because of the reluctance of the clans to move away from their lands and their lack of industrial skills, but also because of the unwillingness of Russian factory managers to give jobs and housing to local people.

World War Two had a dramatic and positive effect on Central Asia. The German invasion forced Stalin to move industries away from Russia. He did so in a remarkable but draconian fashion, in which factories were lifted in their entirety including the labour force and moved to locations east of the Ural mountains, in Central Asia and Siberia. Stalin also shifted entire ethnic groups eastward merely on the suspicion that they might fraternize with the advancing Germans. Between October 1943 and June 1944 people of seven small national groups were accused of treason and deported to Central Asia and Siberia. They included 1 million Volga Germans, 408,000 Chechens, 92,000 Ingush, 75,000 Karachays, 43,000 Balkars, 134,000 Kalmyks and 200,000 Crimean Tartars. Most of them were only allowed to return to their homelands after the 1957 Twentieth Party Congress in Moscow.[13] The arrival of these peoples increased ethnic tensions in Central Asia, which came to the surface during the Gorbachev era. The population surge between 1939 and 1959 shown in Table 3.1. is explained by the influx of these ethnic minorities and Russian migrants, during a period when thousands of soldiers from Central Asia died in World War Two.

Table 3.2 Urban population as a proportion of the total population of Central Asia (per cent).

	1939	1970
USSR	32	56
Russia	33	62
Uzbek	23	37
Kazakh	28	50
Kyrgyz	19	37
Tajik	17	37
Turkomen	33	48

Source: Carrere D'Encausse (1979) *Decline of an Empire: the Soviet Socialist Republics in revolt*, Newsweek Books, USA.

The enormous increase in migration to Central Asia from the western republics after World War Two is also highlighted in Table 3.3. Between 1959 and 1970 there was an increase of over 30 per cent in the number of Russians settling in Uzbekistan, Kazakhstan, Kyrgyzstan and Tajikistan. Many Russians settled in the cities and came to dominate key managerial and technical jobs. Tens of thousands of Russians arrived in Kazakhstan to become farmers during the 1950s as part of

Khrushchev's Virgin Lands Scheme to increase grain output from Kazakhstan. Even during the period of stagnation between 1979 and 1989 there was still an increase in Russian migration to Kazakhstan and Kyrgyzstan, whereas the other republics showed a small decline in migration. This enormous influx of Russians, carried out to alleviate population pressures in Russia and to produce a more homogeneous 'Soviet man', was to affect the attitude of the indigenous population when independence came in 1991. Ethnic nationalism, anti-Russian feeling and Islam as a cultural identifying factor against Russification were to increase.

Table 3.3 Increase in numbers of Russians in Central Asia, from 1959–1989 (1,000s)

	1959	1970	Change (%)	1979	1989	Change (%)
Uzbekistan	1,092	1,473	+35	1,665	1,652	-0.8
Kazakhstan	3,972	5,522	+39	5,991	6,226	+3.9
Kyrgyzstan	624	856	+37	911	916	+0.5
Tajikistan	263	344	+31	395	386	-2.3
Turkmenistan	263	313	+19	349	334	-4.3

Source: Carrere D'Encausse (1979) *Decline of an Empire: the Soviet Socialist Republics in revolt*, Newsweek Books, USA.

In the 1970s Soviet planners and Sovietologists abroad began to focus on the high birth rate of Muslims and the effect that this would have on the Soviet Union in the twenty-first century, as the Russian population declined. There was concern that the high birth rate of the Muslim regions could turn the Soviet Union into a majority-Muslim nation. In 1897 there had been 16 million Muslims in the Tsarist Empire. By 1970 there were 35.9 million Muslims in the Soviet Union and by 1982 the figure was 47.3 million or 17.8 per cent of the total population.[14] Although their numbers had increased, the Muslim share of economic and political power had remained much the same, as economic and political control was monopolized by Russians even as Central Asia's economy expanded. Soviet military writers feared that the Red Army could become predominantly Muslim, but there was little mention of the fact that 90 per cent of the senior officer corps came from non-Muslim regions. The truth remained that with a high birth rate, Central Asia would continue to provide the lumpen manpower for the Soviet economy and military, but little of the brains and leadership.

Between 1950 and 1989, while the rural population of the Soviet Union declined by 9.8 per cent or 10.7 million people, in Central Asia it actually increased by 13.7 million people, a staggering 149 per cent. This enormous growth outstripped the ability of the agricultural sector to absorb so much labour, while the people themselves were reluctant to leave their homes and go to the cities. The highest population growth was registered between 1959 and 1970 when it averaged a rate of 3.4 per cent a year. During this period the Uzbeks increased from 6 million to 12.4 million, an increase of 107 per cent, the Kazakhs increased from 3.6 million to 6.5 million, an increase of 81 per cent, the Tajiks increased from 1.3 million people to 2.9 million, an increase of 107 per cent while the Kyrgyz increased from 0.97 million to 1.3 million, an increase of 96 per cent.[15] In the past twenty-five years the population of Central Asia has doubled. Today 70 per cent of the population are under thirty years old, while 40 per cent are under fifteen years. These demographic changes have important political and economic implications for the leadership, which is still largely in the hands of much older and more conservative people.[16]

Table 3.4 Birth and infant mortality rates, 1980 (per 1,000)

	Birth rate	Infant mortality
USSR	20.0	27.3
Uzbek	37.8	47.0
Kazakh	23.0	?
Kyrgyz	32.6	43.3
Tajik	42.0	58.1
Turkomen	36.9	53.6

Source: O. Mirzayev and A. Kayumov (1992) 'The Demography of Soviet Central Asia and its Future Development'; in R. Lewis (ed.) Geographic Perspectives on Soviet Central Asia, Routledge, London; K. Watters, 'The Current Family Planning Debate in Soviet Central Asia', Central Asian Survey, Vol. 9, No. 4.

Table 3.4 shows the high birth rate for 1980, which was, apart from Kazakhstan, double that of the Soviet Union as a whole. However the table also shows another factor which partly negated this high birth rate – the high infant mortality rate, which in many republics was worse than in many Third World countries. In two republics, Turkmenistan and Tajikistan, the rate was more than double that of the Soviet Union. The high fatality rate amongst Muslim infants, which signified a lack of medical facilities, poor diet and polluted water, was rarely mentioned by Soviet writers, who concentrated solely on the implications of the high birth rate.

There is little doubt that the jump in the fertility rate in Central Asia was related to a greater sense of well-being, economic progress and better social amenities. Even though these did not compare with those of the western republics there was a marked improvement in the lives of Central Asians, who since the Russians first arrived in their region had suffered only social disasters. Table 3.5 demonstrates how the population increased in Central Asia as compared to Russia between 1979 and 1989. In Tajikistan, where it became common for mothers to produce as many as twelve babies in a lifetime, the population recorded an astonishing 45.5 per cent increase. The high birth rate was partly related to Muslim unwillingness to use birth control, and partly due to an important psychological factor. This related to the people's history of such enormous losses of population that there was an urge to ensure that the family line continued through the birth of many children. The wiping out of entire tribal and clan lines during the Civil War and collectivization made the survivors acutely conscious of their responsibility to continue their line of succession in an uncertain world.

Table 3.5 National composition of the population of the Soviet Union, 1979 and 1989 (1,000s)

Total population of	1979	1989	Increase (%)
Russians	137,397,089	145,071,550	5.6
Uzbeks	12,455,978	16,686,240	34.0
Kazak	6,556,442	8,137,878	24.1
Kyrgyz	1,906,271	2,530,998	32.8
Tajik	2,897,697	4,216,693	45.5
Turkomen	2,027,913	2,718,297	34.0

Source: Carrere D'Encausse (1979) *Decline of an Empire: the Soviet Socialist Republics in revolt*, Newsweek Books, USA.

Despite the growth in the Russian population, the pervasive influence of an educational system that emphasized the Russian language for upward mobility and a conscious policy of Russification, the Central Asian peoples remained intensely proud of their language and culture. Table 3.6. demonstrates that while the percentage of those knowing the national language remained fairly constant between 1979 and 1989, the percentage of those claiming to speak good Russian actually de-

creased in Uzbekistan by more than half and in Tajikistan by some 2
per cent. Those speaking good Russian increased only marginally in
other republics – the largest increase being registered in Kazakhstan
where nearly half the population was Russian anyway.

Table 3.6 is an important indicator for Central Asia's post-independence future because the figures demonstrate that despite decades
of communism, nationalism expressed through the local language
remains an important political factor. The figures also indicate that the
effort put into Russification and creating a new 'Soviet man', devoid
of ethnic prejudices, was markedly unsuccessful in Central Asia. The
dramatic increase in nationalist feeling and the revival of Islam in just
the first few months after independence demonstrated that nationalism and Islam remained important political and social factors in the
psychological make-up of the people even during the period of the
Soviet Union.

Table 3.6 Languages spoken in Central Asia, 1979 and 1989

	% regarding national language as their native tongue		% claiming to speak good Russian	
	1979	1989	1979	1989
Uzbeks	98.5	98.3	49.3	23.8
Kazak	97.5	97.0	52.3	60.4
Kyrgyz	97.9	97.8	29.3	35.2
Tajik	97.8	97.7	29.6	27.7
Turkomen	98.7	98.5	25.4	27.8

Source: Carrere D'Encausse (1979) *Decline of an Empire: the Soviet Socialist Republics
in revolt*, Newsweek Books, USA. Information supplied by Central Asian governments.

While the CPSU did a great deal to change the make-up of the
population and introduce universal literacy, it did little to diversify the
economy of Central Asia. There was an even greater intensification of
the cultivation of cotton than before. Much of the campaign of
modernization by the Soviet government in Central Asia was only
aimed at increasing cotton production. By the 1970s Central Asia
produced 95 per cent of the Soviet Union's cotton and 15 per cent of
its vegetable oil, derived from cotton seed. Yet Russia processed 70 per
cent of the nation's cotton yarn. One ton of raw cotton produces an
average of 3,400 metres of cloth and 94 kilograms of vegetable oil, but
Central Asia was prevented from profiting from the value added to

these end products and the taxes charged for them. There was an average tax of 400–600 roubles on one ton of raw cotton, while on the finished products the tax was in the region of 1,200–1,700 roubles.[17]

By the 1980s cotton constituted 65 per cent of the gross economic output of Uzbekistan, consumed 60 per cent of all of Uzbekistan's resources and employed 40 per cent of the Uzbek labour force. Yet Uzbekistan produced only 5 per cent of the Soviet Union's textiles, even though 70 per cent of the cotton grew there. 'The entire national economy and all of society was held hostage to cotton,' said an aide to President Islam Karimov. 'If factories were built in Tashkent, they were fertilizer factories to supply the cotton fields or machine tool factories to produce items for the harvesting of cotton, while the republic had to import basic foodstuffs and consumer goods from thousands of kilometres away,' he added.[18] During the economic stagnation of the 1980s, the volume of cotton exported abroad by the Soviet Union declined drastically. Between 1980 and 1985 cotton exports fell by 25 per cent and production also declined. As the yield declined so did the quality of the cotton fibre, as farm managers had little incentive to maintain quality. The one-crop economy had destroyed the farming patterns of centuries, the lack of crop rotation had weakened the soil and over-irrigation had increased salinity. The cotton monoculture had also eroded the nation's health, industry and finally even public morality as cotton scandals came to the surface, in which top officials had made piles of money.

The cotton monoculture also has had a dramatic effect in shortening the life span of Central Asia's meagre water resources. Central Asia is one of the most arid zones on the planet and the geographical division of its water resources is very unfavourable. Four fifths of the region's water resources originate in Tajikistan and Kyrgyzstan, the two most mountainous republics with the least amount of arable land. Meanwhile three quarters of the arable land is in Kazakhstan and Uzbekistan, which contain only meagre water resources. Attempts to correct this dichotomy led to the building of canals which has in turn created problems of salinization. In the past seventy years the area under cultivation has expanded dramatically and water consumption has risen accordingly. In Kazakhstan alone, farmland has increased from 2.9 million hectares in 1950 to 7.2 million hectares in 1980, and there is consequently a huge demand for water.

The whole of Central Asia is now suffering from a severe water shortage because of the water that is spent irrigating cotton fields. Some 23 per cent of the water that flows through irrigation channels to cotton fields is lost, which leads to severe shortages of drinking water in cities like Tashkent. Water shortages are leading to the desertification of farm and pasture land, whilst all the major rivers are highly polluted because of excessive use of pesticides and fertilizers for the cotton crop and by industrial wastes.[19] There is now acute salinization of the Amudarya river near its delta. In most years so much water is drained off the Amudarya and the Syrdarya rivers that their waters do not actually reach the Aral Sea. Some 46 per cent of the cultivated land in Turkmenistan is now suffering from severe salinization; the figure is 15 per cent in Uzbekistan and 16 per cent in Kyrgyzstan. One of the major reasons for the decline of cotton production has been the growing salinity.[20]

Despite the tragedy that was staring them in the face, Soviet planners still believed that rivers could be diverted, lakes emptied and canals cut through the desert without bringing any fundamental changes to the environment. The project of the century was a plan to divert the rivers in Siberia to Central Asia, thus increasing the flow of the Amudarya and Syrdarya, which in turn would fill the irrigation canals. The water of the Ob river in Siberia would be diverted through a 2,200-kilometre canal to the Amudarya. The canal would bisect the arid lands of Kazakhstan, bringing even more land under the plough. This plan was first advocated in the last century but taken up seriously from the 1950s onwards. In 1971 President Brezhnev even ordered that work should start on it, but later cancelled the order. President Gorbachev again looked at the scheme in 1986 but turned it down because of the huge costs involved. The water crisis has become even more serious because of the drying up of the Aral Sea – a tragedy that bore witness to how wrong Soviet planners were about grandiose and unnatural schemes.

The Aral Sea is a huge inland sea that has been fed by the waters of the Amudarya and Syrdarya for thousands of years. Under Stalin more and more of the water was diverted to irrigate cotton fields. During the past twenty-five years the sea has shrunk by 80 kilometres and its depth has decreased by 123 metres. It now contains only 31 per cent of its original volume of water. Whereas its surface area was once 66,000 square kilometres it is now reduced to just 40,000.[21] The sea is now divided into two bodies of water, the Large Sea and the Small Sea, with an island of sand that divides them. Where once fishing villages thrived on its shores, there are now vast beds of salt and the population has been forced to migrate. At the village of Mynak, fisherman once caught enormous catches that were tinned at a canning factory which employed 5,000 people. Now the sea is more than 20 miles away and the hulks of abandoned boats are rusting in the middle of town. When the canning factory closed down, Moscow bureaucrats had the bright idea of sending to the factory fish from other parts of Russia, a journey that took five days. This farce finally ended when the newly independent republics refused to send the factory any more fish.

Bird and fish life, flora and fauna have been devastated and the wind carries the salt for hundreds of kilometres in all directions, clogging rivers, the soil and people's lungs. The shrinking of the sea has raised summer temperatures, increased the dryness of the air and shortened the frost-free season – results that have badly affected the cotton crop across Central Asia.[22] The 3.5 million people living in the nearby Karakalpak region all now drink polluted water. In Karakalpak the infant mortality rate reaches as high as 100 for every 1,000 infants born, anaemia affects 80 per cent of all childbearing women, and cancer and hepatitis rates are well above the national average.[23] The Aral Sea region was also used for the testing of biological weapons by the Soviet military. In 1986, under pressure from Washington, the Soviet government named Vozrozhdeniye Island in the Aral Sea as a major testing site. Although it is believed to have been closed down in 1991, there is no record of the effect the experimentation has had on people.[24]

Water has become the essential resource base for Central Asia's agricultural economy. There are real fears that future conflict between the republics could be over water rights unless there is greater willingness for all states to tackle the problem together. Experts are only now beginning to understand the scale of the ecological damage carried out under communism in the Soviet Union and in Central Asia in particular. 'We have forfeited our earlier abundance, destroyed the peasant class together with its settlements, deprived the raising of crops of its whole purpose and the soil of its ability to yield a harvest, while flooding the land with man-made seas and swamps,' writes Alexander Solzhenitsyn.[25] The crisis defies the imagination – and all previous calculations. Lakes and forests are dying, marshes are turning into sandy wastes, and the cost of cleaning up the environmental damage could be astronomical – as much as $800 billion over a ten-year period according to one estimate. This expenditure would only deal with conventional pollution and still not tackle the nuclear pollution in Kazakhstan.[26]

Despite these problems the standard of living was greatly enhanced by the industrial development during World War Two. Machine tool manufacturing rose sixfold between 1939 and 1945 in the Central Asian region, while coal production rose tenfold and electricity output increased by 500 per cent.[27] After the war Moscow relaxed on the need to centralize every detail of the economy. For a brief period under Khrushchev local communist leaders were allowed to plan their industrial development according to their real needs. Decentralization increased industrial production in Central Asia, but immediately after Khrushchev's dismissal, centralization resumed with new-found vigour. In 1961 the central planners in Moscow created new economic regions, whose boundaries coincided with the division of the Soviet landmass into military districts by the Defence Ministry. The creation of military–economic districts based on the presumption of nuclear war with the USA further lessened the ability of local leaders to diversify and rationalize their economies. These became enmeshed with the strategic military doctrine of the Soviet Union.[28]

Table 3.7 Capital investment by sector during the 1980–85 plan

	Industry	Agriculture	Transport communications	Social sphere
Russia	38.9	11.9	15.2	30.0
Central Asia	28.5	33.2	8.3	26.8

Source: B. Rumer (1989) *Soviet Central Asia: a tragic experiment*, Unwin Hyman, London.

A prime example of how the Central Asian region suffered as a result of centralization was the inability of local leaders to exploit their huge oil and gas reserves. In 1970 Central Asia was only producing 4.5 per cent of the Soviet Union's total oil output, even though Kazakhstan and Turkmenistan had extensive oil and gas reserves. Only a small chemical industry and no other energy-intensive industry were established. On the other hand the Soviet state developed Central Asia's hydroelectric power, especially in Tajikistan and Kyrgyzstan, in order to supply European Russia with cheap electricity. Between 1960 and 1985 electricity production rose eightfold in Central Asia. Similarly, processed metals and steel were supplied to Central Asia even though the region contained plentiful mineral deposits that were not adequately exploited. In the classic colonial syndrome, Central Asia sold its raw materials cheaply while it was forced to pay higher prices for machinery and finished goods, even though they were often made of raw materials from Central Asia.

As the general economic crisis worsened during the 1980s, Central Asia received far less investment than other republics from the Soviet Union's exchequer. In the 1980 to 1985 Five Year Plan, investment in

Central Asia was less than in any other region of the USSR. While investment grew in the Soviet Union as a whole by 19 per cent and in the Baltic Republics by 34 per cent, it only rose by 16 per cent in Central Asia. Table 3.7 shows that while Russia received far more investment in industry, transport and the social sector than Central Asia, Russia received only one third the investment in the agricultural sector. This disparity ensured that the economic imbalance between the industrialized west and the agricultural east was only further accentuated. Through the period there was a significant decrease in the production of energy and consumer goods in Central Asia.

By 1989 with *perestroika* in full throttle in Russia, a litany of complaints arose from the communist parties in Central Asia. President Islam Karimov publicly complained that 45 per cent of all Uzbeks earned less than the subsistence wage of 75 roubles a month and that the reason was the republic's cotton monoculture. Kyrgyz leaders complained that fewer than 30 per cent of its industrial work-force were local people, while Kazakh leaders said that Kazakhstan's use as a nuclear testing ground had devastated an entire region of the republic. Tajikistan's leaders complained that there were 200,000 people unemployed in the republic.[29] President Gorbachev showed little sympathy and instead criticized Central Asian communists for falling behind in cotton production targets. The gulf between Moscow and the regimes in Central Asia was steadily growing.

Central Asia still offered a better way of life than many other regions of the Soviet Union. On collective farms much greater tolerance was shown towards the working of private plots than in Russia. In Tajikistan one quarter of the labour force was employed on private plots, and large flocks owned by individuals roamed the Pamirs. Although private plots constituted only 0.5 per cent of the total cultivated land, they contained 53 per cent of Tajikistan's cattle, and 37 per cent of its sheep, and produced 37 per cent of the meat consumed in the republic. In Uzbekistan private farms amounted to only 0.7 per cent of the total cultivated land, yet they contained 55 per cent of the republic's cattle produced 46 per cent of its meat and 40 per cent of its milk and vegetables. Basic food supplies, especially vegetables, fruit and milk, were obtainable in far greater abundance than in western Russia. In the smaller towns housewives cultivated every patch of soil in the gardens of their homes, growing melons, grapes and vegetables.

However, the enormous subsidies paid by the republics for foodstuffs were crippling local budgets. Retail prices of all the main foodstuffs had not risen since 1962, whilst money incomes began to rise steadily during the late 1980s. Meat in a state shop cost 1.75 roubles per kilogram, while production and distribution cost an estimated

4.70 roubles. The shortfall was made up by government subsidy, thus ensuring that the Soviet system paid the highest food subsidies in the world. Prior to the collapse of the Soviet Union, the prices of bread, sugar and oil had last been raised in 1955.[30] The bill for these subsidies was largely paid by Moscow in the shape of grants to the Central Asian republics.

In 1991, the last year of grants from the centre, between 20 per cent and 45 per cent of public spending in the republics was dependent on Moscow. Tajikistan received 45 per cent of its public spending budget from Moscow, Uzbekistan received 43 per cent, Kyrgyzstan received 35 per cent and Kazakhstan and Turkmenistan received 25 per cent each. In 1992 these subsidies suddenly stopped, ruining local government budgets. The overwhelming dependency on subsidies had meant that when prices were raised even an iota, there was an immediate impact on the population. After independence, when Russia slashed subsidies drastically and Central Asia had to follow suit, there was an overnight 100 to 500 per cent price rise in many basic foodstuffs. By May 1993 inflation was running at an annual 1,500 per cent.

The social services in Central Asia remained underdeveloped compared to those of the western republics. Sewerage and running water existed in fewer than 50 per cent of rural homes in Central Asia, and shortages of housing were a permanent problem in the larger cities which often led to disturbances. Whereas in the Soviet Union the average space for housing per capita was 14. 4 square metres, in Central Asia it was 10. 6 square metres per capita. Although there was universal literacy, there was still an acute shortage of skilled workers and technicians. In 1986 Tajikistan alone suffered from a shortage of 60,000 skilled workers, and the shortfall was only made up by encouraging Russians to come.[31]

Health care was also far worse than in the rest of the Soviet Union. Whereas in the 1980s in the Soviet Union there was an average of 41 doctors for every 10,000 inhabitants, in Central Asia the average was only 30.5 doctors. Although there were 128 hospital beds for every 10,000 people in the Soviet Union, in Central Asia the average was 111. Even capital cities such as Tashkent were chronically short of hospital beds. The inadequate conditions were worsened by ecological disasters such as the Aral Sea and the Semiplatinsk nuclear testing site, for which there were no special arrangements to treat victims. Infant mortality was two times the Soviet average. While Lithuania had an infant mortality rate of 11 per thousand, in Uzbekistan and Turkmenistan the rate was between 55 to 60 per thousand.[32]

When the Central Asian people compared themselves to the rest of the USSR they considered themselves worse off, but Muslim visitors praised the fact that at least there was universal literacy and a health service, which did not exist in other Muslim countries. Certainly more public amenities were available in Central Asia than existed in Pakistan, Iran or Afghanistan, and the USSR's educational system greatly enhanced the prestige of the communist system in the eyes of Muslim neighbours. In 1926 only about 7 per cent of Central Asian males and 1 per cent of the women were literate.[33] By 1939 universal literacy had been achieved, with most students learning Russian, their native language and at least one foreign language also.

The agricultural economies of Central Asia predetermined that the purchasing power of ordinary people was far less than in the rest of the Soviet Union. Thus in 1984, whereas an average of 29 television sets were sold for every 1,000 people in the Soviet Union, in Uzbekistan the average was 16 and in Kyrgyzstan the average was only 10. In the Soviet Union an average of 16 refrigerators were sold for every 1,000 people while in Uzbekistan the average was 9 and in Kyrgyzstan the average was 6. The shortage of consumer goods was far worse in Central Asia than in the western republics, as wages were much lower, savings were also low and there were more barter than cash transactions. Barter was just one aspect of a huge black economy which many experts said amounted to one third of the total economy in Central Asia. Clan and tribal loyalties made it much more difficult to stamp out corruption and the black economy, because clan members would protect each other from discovery. Moreover, family and clan solidarity were the only relief against the severe strains of centralization.

For the USSR economy as a whole, the average annual rate of industrial production declined from 7 per cent to 8 per cent for the 1970–80 period to just 4 per cent in the 1980–88 period. All the republics registered declines during this period but the losses in Central Asia were the largest. Part of the reason was that total investment in Central Asia had been steadily declining since 1970, in some republics more dramatically than others, as can be seen from Table 3.8. Tajikistan showed a drop in investment of as much as 20 per cent between the 1970s and 1980s, even as investment in Russia had been slowly increasing. The higher figures for Kazakhstan are related to the Virgin Lands Scheme in the 1950s and the industrial investment that followed Russian migration to the north of the republic.[34] The share for Central Asia, excluding Kazakhstan, in capital investment made by the Soviet Union between 1956 and 1985 amounted to an annual average of 6.26 per cent with Uzbekistan taking 3.8 per cent, Turkmenistan claiming 0.96 per cent, Tajikistan 0.73 per cent and Kyrgyzstan 0.76 per cent.

Table 3.8 Per capita investment 1960–85: USSR, Russia and Central Asia compared (USSR=100)

	1961–65	1971–75	1981–85
USSR	100	100	100
Russia	108	110	119
Uzbekistan	78	75	68
Kazakhstan	155	116	104
Kyrgyzia	68	67	54
Tajikistan	69	64	47
Turkmenistan	115	114	92

Source: R. Liebowitz (1992), 'Soviet Geographical Imbalances and Soviet Central Asia', in R. Lewis (ed.) *Geographical Perspectives in Central Asia*, Routledge, London.

Table 3.9 The USSR economy, 1990, various indices (%)

	Population	GNP	Production	
			Industry	Agriculture
Russia	51.3	58.7	66.4	46.2
Kazakh	5.8	5.3	3.5	6.9
Uzbek	7.0	4.0	1.7	4.6
Kyrgyz	1.5	0.9	0.5	1.3
Turkmen	1.2	0.9	0.4	1.1
Tajik	1.8	0.9	0.7	1.0

Source: R. Liebowitz (1992), 'Soviet Geographical Imbalances and Soviet Central Asia', in R.Lewis (ed.), *Geographical Perspectives on Soviet Central Asia*, Routledge, London.

Various indices for the Soviet economy in 1990 showed that although Uzbekistan had 7 per cent of the population it had only 1.7 per cent of the total industry of the Soviet Union, while no other Central Asian republic had more than 1.5 per cent. According to Soviet economists, simply to maintain the population at the current standard of living in Central Asia would necessitate a 250 per cent increase in investment from the centre by the year 2000 – an impossibility given the lack of resources. With its huge growth in population, Tajikistan alone would need 6–7 billion roubles over the next five years, though the republic's entire budget in 1987 was only 2 billion roubles.

As economic conditions worsened in 1990 in the Soviet Union as a whole, they became far worse in the Central Asian republics because of their inability to compete industrially and create value-added exports. Spare parts for industry and agricultural machinery from Russia became less and less available and the largely Russian technical workforce began to leave key industries and migrate back to Russia. It was clear well before the break-up of the Soviet Union that Central Asia was in rapid economic decline, with no hope of a recovery because of the falling rate of investment in the region. Independence only exacerbated what was already a miserable economic crisis.

After the August 1991 coup attempt there was a sudden rise in prices and growing uncertainty about the future. Despite the treaty of economic union signed on 18 October by eight Soviet republics, including those of Central Asia, the treaty's stabilizing effect was almost immediately washed away in massive price rises, the near collapse of the banking system and acute shortages of currency notes. The same month Central Asia faced a fiscal crisis when Moscow terminated its budget relief and subsidies from the centre, amounting to as much as 45 per cent of some republics' budgets.

In January 1992 President Boris Yeltsin of the Russian Federation abolished subsidies on key foodstuffs without consulting the Central Asian states. The subsequent food riots in Tashkent were a grim warning. The speed of the disintegration of the Soviet Union had caught everyone by surprise, but none more so than the nomenklatura of Central Asia, who were not prepared to cope with such radical economic changes. President Nazarbayev and others had been advocating the need for a new Central Asian common market which would make the region economically independent of Russia and increase local economic co-ordination. Such a common market would have pegged the rouble at a common exchange rate, ironed out shortages and gluts of goods among the republics, and above all presented a united front against Russia to demand better trade and monetary ties. All the leaders paid lip service to this idea, but there was little practical progress as the leaders disagreed so strongly about the extent of privatization in their own republics. None, moreover, were in a position to break the economic umbilical cord with Russia.

In a meeting of all the Central Asian leaders at Beshkek on 23 April 1992, the vastly differing approaches to the market economy and the reluctance of some states to legislate for privatization came to the surface. Turkmenistan refused to accept the conference documents on privatization, while Uzbekistan refused to consider a common pricing policy and wanted to retain large subsidies on foodstuffs because of the political fallout of the food riots. Apart from Turkmenistan, however, all the republics signed documents which increased their interstate co-operation in banking, transportation and trade. They all now faced one common problem: Russia was no longer bankrolling their budgets and they all needed to generate their own revenues through new taxation and exports. This could only be carried out by encouraging private enterprise and foreign investment.

Two states – Kazakhstan and Kyrgyzstan – had begun as far back as 1991 the process of enacting legislation that would allow a capitalist economy, private property and foreign investment with repatriation of profits. Other republics had taken no such steps when independence dawned and they continued to vacillate about such legislation through 1992. The legislative and economic changes made by each republic are discussed in later chapters, but the overall first experiences with privatization were not good. Even states advanced in legislation for privatization, like Kazakhstan, chose the most unprofitable state-owned companies or the farms with the poorest land to be sold off first to either workers, committees or groups of individual buyers. The results were open to easy criticism by communist hardliners, who continued to criticize any overhasty change to private enterprise.[35]

Thus in the first year after independence real economic change in Central Asia had been negligible. Some 98 per cent of the economy remained in the hands of the state. The state itself was becoming increasingly bankrupt as it bankrolled uneconomic and out-of-date factories, which in turn produced goods that nobody wanted any longer. Under the socialist system, industry was the very panacea for all backwardness and the symbol of progress and a bright future. Overnight industry then become a millstone around everyone's neck. Factories were overstaffed, badly managed, their machinery was old and a danger to the environment and public safety. Yet to do away with them by closing the factories would be to traumatize the people and create massive unemployment. Governments wanted, and still want, to avoid policies which promoted cost accounting, improved labour productivity, produced better technology and more efficient management but which would create massive job losses at a time when there was already a labour surplus of some 3 million people in Central Asia.

Widespread unemployment was already evident everywhere. By April 1993 new additions to the unemployed were coming from the tens of thousands of troops being demobbed by the CIS high command as it reduced the strength of the military. Many of these officers and soldiers were returning to their villages, where they had no jobs or income. Not surprisingly many of these well-trained men have become mercenaries for local warlords and criminal gangs. The dilemma for all the regimes had been how to balance economic development and the closing down of unprofitable factories without raising unemployment levels to a politically unacceptable level.

An additional impediment has been that despite *perestroika*, no real modern, capitalist business elite has emerged in Central Asia. Instead the old party bureaucrats have become business rather than state managers. They run their enterprises as they did in the past except that their rhetoric has changed from one of socialism to one of the market economy. Most of them have refused to sell off their enterprises, while others do so only at the cost of ensuring large payoffs for themselves and their families. This grip on industry by the old bureaucracy remains unshaken. In Russia these factory managers and their lobby in the Parliament led by the Speaker of the Parliament Ruslan Khasbulatov created a permanent crisis for President Boris Yeltsin in 1992 and 1993. As in Russia this problem needs to be tackled in a dynamic way.

The banking system has also protected this elite. The Central Asian republics still have to free the banks from being mere appendages to the central bank. In 1992 every republic set up a central bank which dealt with Moscow in monetary and trade matters and ruled over financial relations within the republic. Small, local banks were not run on a commercial basis but used by their respective central banks to funnel credit to the bankrupt state-owned enterprises. Even though banks were awash with credit after October 1992 when Moscow began to issue millions of new rouble notes, thus further fuelling inflation, banks were not able to give private entrepreneurs credit at any price, because they were not allowed to do so. There was no experience in dealing with risk evaluation, managers did not encourage private loans, and did not allow their banks to encourage entrepreneurs. Banks were incapable of allocating credit to foster private enterprise or mobilize savings because their interest rates were so low. Experts estimate that the savings rate in 1992 across the former Soviet Union dwindled from around 20 per cent to just 13 per cent.[36]

In late 1992 the growing economic crisis convinced hardline nationalists and communists to pressurize their leaders to leave the rouble zone and set up their own independent currencies. However presidents Nazarbayev and Akaev opposed this. At a CIS summit in October 1992, Nazarbayev was instrumental in persuading the CIS to rationalize the rouble zone by setting up an 'inter-Union bank' to create a unified financial system. 'It would be absurd for Kazakhstan or anyone else to leave the rouble zone and try and declare financial independence from Russia. This is still an interdependent economy. These are just the demands of sentimental nationalists who don't understand economics,' said Dr Chan Young Bang, the South Korean adviser on economic affairs to President Nazarbayev.[37] Across Central

Asia and Russia influential hardliners within the ruling circles were attacking the overhasty market reforms, the increasing role of the IMF in dictating monetary policies, and dependence on relief from the West. They also wanted to slow down privatization and the sale of natural resources to foreigners. 'Privatization has slowed down because it has become an intensely political issue,' admitted a Western diplomat in Alma Ata in December 1992.

With inflation running at an annual 1,500 per cent in early 1993, corruption, criminal gangs and the black market were more than just one way of life. They had become the only way of life through which people could actually raise their standard of living. To be receiving a dollar salary, to have access to saleable foreign goods or foreign travel, to be able to command large bribes, or to be able to run protection rackets were the only hedges against inflation ruining the family budget. Those who had to survive on meagre state pensions or government salaries quickly saw their life savings depleted and their standard of living slip down to the level where some had to scrimmage for food in local garbage heaps.

Every section of the community suffered under the staggering economic crisis. This can be judged by the near collapse of the newspaper industry within the space of a few months because of the rising cost of paper, which was all imported from Russia. The leading Kyrgyz daily newspaper, *Kyrgyzstan Tusu*, established in 1924, had a print run of 185,000 copies in 1991. In the first few weeks of 1992 the cost of newsprint rose from 830 to 22,000 roubles a ton. The newspaper was forced to restrict printing to 80,000 copies, laid off workers and asked the government for a subsidy to help defray the cost of newsprint. Journalists maintained that after the shortages of food and petroleum, the biggest shortage in Central Asia was that of paper. In 1991 the Writers' Union of Kyrgyzstan published over 150 new books. In 1992 it could not publish a single book, because of the cost of paper.

None of the Central Asian republics has even begun to tackle a crucial issue which will determine its future political stability and economic viability – the question of land distribution. Their failure to start breaking up the collective farms and allowing small private farms is already the major cause of food shortages in the cities, political unrest on the land and growing poverty. Lenin came to power on the strength of a single political slogan, 'peace, bread and land', and one of the first acts of the Bolsheviks was to distribute land to the peasants, even though a decade later the same land was to be collectivized in a bloody process. Yet Lenin was given a breathing space by taking that first historic decision. There is no breathing space for the leaders of Central Asia, where land hunger is growing amongst the 70 per cent of the population who live on the land. For this vast majority the communist system still continues in the shape of cotton quotas, communist managers and the lack of private land.

In Uzbekistan officials argue that there is too little arable land to be divided into viable farms amongst the 20 million population. They fear that any land distribution will lead to tribal and clan riots between the dozens of ethnic groups living in any single locality. At a few collective farms where there is a smaller workforce, district officials have formally handed over to peasants the private plots worked by them. No family can receive more than 10 *sotogs* or one tenth of a hectare, so these plots still allow only market gardening rather than farming. Officials point out that to privatize land will require billions of roubles of investment because the entire agricultural infrastructure will have to be both changed and improved, while small farmers will have to receive loans and subsidies to survive in the market.

Turkmenistan has already declared that agricultural land will not be privatized, while in Tajikistan reform is impossible due to civil war. More enlightened policies are being followed in Kazakhstan and Kyrgyzstan, but the problems remain the same. In the vast hinterland of Kazakhstan a bumper wheat crop was harvested in the summer of 1993 that would have touched 30 million tons, but up to one third of the crop was lost because of poor harvesting methods, nonexistent storage facilities and the shortage of transport.

Western countries and international finance agencies have still not earmarked even a portion of their aid packages to the CIS for helping land reform, while none of the regimes in Central Asia has the funds to do it alone. Governments need financial help to put together adequate packages to help farmers buy land and start farming. Unless loans are available to buy tractors, seed and fertilizer and to tide farmers over for the first few years, people will be reluctant to take on the burden of running a farm. Schemes in Kazakhstan to turn collective farms into joint stock companies are explored in Chapter 5, but even this scheme will need considerable financial support. The longer the land issue festers in Central Asia, the greater the fear that ethnic tensions, economic disparities and real poverty will only increase.

For economic planners the civil war in Tajikistan was a constant reminder of what could happen if ethnic, clan and ideological rivalries got out of hand. Tajikistan's economy had totally collapsed by January 1993 when a new pro-communist government took over. Gross domestic product was down by 50 per cent, many factories had been totally destroyed, others had ceased to function and became armed camps for roaming militias. The 1992 cotton harvest was left to rot in the fields, and food shortages were so chronic that there was starvation in many areas. The Regar smelter, 100 kilometres northwest of Dushanbe, which once produced 520,000 tons of aluminium annually, or 10 per cent of total Soviet aluminium production, had seen production drop to 370,000 tons in 1991 and 200,000 tons in 1992 until the plant was closed down in November because there was nobody left to run it. It may now never be reopened because the technical staff have fled and the machinery is so old that it would be dangerous to start it up again. Thus the civil war has destroyed some of the essential industry in the republic and the main hope of earning foreign exchange.

Rail links with the rest of the CIS were cut for much of 1992, so coal and oil could not be imported. This resulted in a 50 per cent cut in electricity generation and acute shortages of petrol. With transport off the roads, no heating in homes and no running water in major cities like Dushanbe, the future of modern life itself appeared under threat. Damage to the two main dams in the southeastern Kuliab region devastated irrigation systems in the valleys; as the Russian technical staff fled, there were fears of even greater catastrophes. Industry in the north around Khodjent, which had remained entirely peaceful and was responsible for two thirds of the industrial production of Tajikistan, had been bought to a virtual halt.

The high hopes held by the Central Asian regimes that foreign investment would come flooding into their states were entirely unrealistic, the consequence of gross political naïvety. In 1992 there was a world recession on, and for Western governments or multinational companies to show an interest in all fifteen of the newly independent states created out of the ashes of the former Soviet Union at the same time was impossible. (Central Asia's foreign relations and foreign investment potential are explored in detail in Chapter 9). The major investments carried out by the West during 1992–93 have been in the oil and gas industries in Turkmenistan and Kazakhstan, but surveys and negotiations had been going on over these oilfields for several years and the coming to fruition of these deals after independence did not signify any new investment initiative. In fact, in the first year after independence very few new investment deals were concluded between Western companies and Central Asia outside the oil industry.

In Central Asian capitals, finance ministers looked to the West and the Far East for investment, while they glanced only half-heartedly at the Muslim countries of Iran, Pakistan, Turkey and the Gulf region which were wooing them. But by 1993 the republics had realized that little was coming from the West and they had better seriously respond to offers from the Muslim south. This led to the first comprehensive economic plan to develop communications and other economic in-

frastructure in the region, agreed at the Foreign Ministers' meeting in
Quetta, Pakistan, of the Economic Coordination Organization (ECO),
which comprised ten countries of the region including five Central
Asian states.[38]

Those republics adjacent to China were also finding it expedient to
build up trade and political ties rapidly with Beijing, as China, fearing
the spread of Islamic fundamentalism, began to show much greater
interest in the economic development of Xinjiang and Central Asia.
Iran began providing some republics with cheap oil, while aid from
Turkey became a significant factor in helping the republics overhaul
their moribund infrastructure. However the major hindrance to expansion of ties and communications was the civil war in Afghanistan,
which continued into 1993 despite the fall of the Najibullah regime
in April 1992.

Central Asia's future lies in its vast agricultural, mineral and oil
wealth, which is still largely untapped. The exploitation of heavy industrial raw materials will need sustained investment for many years
but there are serious grounds for hoping that this will be forthcoming,
at least in the more stable states of Kazakhstan and Turkmenistan. An
intricate network of ties still binds the Central Asian states closely
together, including the power grid and the telephone system. The lack
of armed forces and the dependence on the CIS military and the CIS
market for their goods gives them common problems. Ethnic
intermarriages, the widespread ability to speak two or three local languages as well as Russian, and a cultural renaissance all point to a much
greater degree of economic and social unity in the region in the
future.

In fact, by 1993 all five states fully realized that unless there was
greater economic co-ordination between them, they would all fall by
the wayside. It is not viable for each state to set itself the same target
of economic national sovereignty by becoming self-sufficient in oil,
food or electricity. As happened in the former Soviet Union, electricity can be produced cheapest by those republics which have hydroelectric power, and can be sold to others who have oil or gas or more
food. What cannot continue is the old economic approach in which
a republic was made to produce nothing but electricity or cotton for
others to consume. To work out the mechanics of co-ordinated arrangements will take time and require a far better system of economic
data collection, diplomatic management and public involvement in
decision making than exists at the moment in any Central Asian state.
The old Soviet-style bureaucracy in these states cannot be expected
to work out co-operation agreements unless it is first overhauled and
modernized.

All the republics will face immense problems in doing away with the legacy of cotton monoculture and being forced to produce only one or two industrial items. Uzbekistan and Turkmenistan announced in 1992 that they would reduce cotton planting and grow more food crops on arable land, while they attempted to set up textile mills through foreign investment which would allow them to produce more finished cotton goods. However such efforts are extremely difficult when the entire use of land, irrigation systems, tractor stations and factories are geared to the needs of the cotton industry. It is in these republics' interests not to do away with cotton production, but rather to reduce it slowly and modernize what remains by improving the quality of the crop and producing finished cotton goods.

The leadership is also realizing that so far there has been no imaginative use or development of the intrinsic bazaar economy, which held sway even during the heyday of communism. Central Asia had a distinct advantage over the rest of the former Soviet Union because the bazaar remained a cornerstone for dynamic and productive private enterprise, ensuring that food shortages did not take place. In trade, banking, marketing and even production the bazaar mentality and methods that are already prevalent can become the main bridge to a fully fledged market economy. In Russia the idea of the market is being dictated from the top by new economic managers who are introducing what is essentially a foreign economic system to the Russian people. In Central Asia there is the need for economists to work from the bazaar upwards. By studying how private enterprise is already working through the bazaar, the black economy and the underground, and by bringing these operating systems into the mainstream through imaginative legislation, Central Asia could avoid the economic chaos and dislocation that will continue in Russia for many years to come. Despite the economic crisis and shortages, the fact that nobody has actually starved to death in Central Asia shows that the people are able to survive with the bazaar economy.

The key to economic success will be the acceptance of the notion that unless communications are improved to get goods in and out of landlocked Central Asia as quickly as possible, little progress can be made. Foreign investment will follow fax and telephone lines, access to ports in Pakistan or Iran and roads that lead somewhere, as surely as night follows day. Until that happens there will be little international interest in the region, but when it does Central Asia could be poised for an economic recovery that would far outstrip the old Silk Road in both its scope and its global connections.

Notes

1. K. N. Chauduri (1990) *Asia before Europe: economy and civilization of the Indian Ocean from the rise of Islam to 1750*, Cambridge University Press, England.

2. Ibid.

3. I. Spector (1959) *The Soviet Union and the Muslim World, 1917–58*, University of Washington Press, USA.

4. Ibid.

5. R. Lewis (1992) *Geographic Perspectives on Soviet Central Asia*, Routledge, London.

6. M. Hauner (1990) *What Is Asia to us? Russia's Asian heartland yesterday and today*, Unwin Hyman, London. Lord Curzon became Viceroy of India in 1898 at the height of the Great Game between Russia and England.

7. Spector.

8. M. Buttino, 'A Study of the Economic Crisis in Turkestan, 1917–20', *Central Asian Survey*, Vol. 9, No. 4.

9. R. Conquest (1988) *Harvest of Sorrow*, Arrow Books, London.

10. R. Conquest (1990) *The Great Terror: a reassessment*, Pimlico, London.

11. Ibid.

12. Ibid.

13. Conquest (1988).

14. M. A. Kettani (1986) *Muslim Minorities in the World Today*, Mansell Publishing, London.

15. Ibid.

16. P. Craumer (1992), 'Agricultural Change, Labour Supply and Rural Out-migration in Soviet Central Asia', in R. Lewis (ed.) *Geographic Pespectives on Soviet Central Asia*, Routledge, London.

17. B. Rumer (1989) *Soviet Central Asia: a tragic experiment*, Unwin Hyman, London.

18. Interview by the author with a senior Uzbek offficial in Tashkent, October 1992.

19. R. Mnatsakanian (1992), 'Environmental Legacy of the Former Soviet Union', Centre of Human Ecology, University of Edinburgh.

20. Craumer.

21. W. Fierman, 'Glasnost in Practice: the Uzbek experience', *Central Asian Survey*, Vol. 8, No. 2. See also Mnatsakanian.

22. J. Critchlow (1991) *Nationalism in Uzbekistan: a Soviet republic's road to sovereignty*, Westview Press, USA.

23. Mnatsakanian.

24. John Barry, 'Planning a Plague', *Newsweek*, 1 February 1993.

25. A. Solzhenitsyn (1991) *Rebuilding Russia*, Harvil, London.

26. Tony Barber, 'Republics Reel from an Ecological Disaster', *Independent*, 16 February 1993.

27. Rumer.

28. Ibid.

29. Ibid.

30. P. Cockburn (1989) *Getting Russia Wrong: the end of Kremlinology*, Verso, London.

31. Ibid.

32. P. Carley, 'The Price of the Plan', *Central Asian Survey*, Vol. 8, No. 4.

33. Craumer.

34. R. Liebowitz (1992), 'Soviet Geographical Imbalances and Soviet Central Asia', in R. Lewis (ed.) *Geographic Perspectives on Soviet Central Asia*, Routledge, London.

35. Much of the material for these and later paragraghs is based on my own notes and interviews made during my trip to Central Asia in November–December 1991.

36. Interviews with banking officials in Kazakhstan and Kurgyzstan, October 1992.

37. Interview in Alma Ata, October 1992. See Ahmed Rashid (in Alma Ata), 'The Next Frontier', *Far Eastern Economic Review,* 4 February 1993.

38. These were Iran, Pakistan, Turkey, Afghanistan, Azerbaijan, Kazakhstan, Kyrgyzstan, Tajikistan and Uzbekistan. The Quetta Declaration of 7 February 1993 set out the new economic plan. See Ahmed Rashid, (in Quetta), 'Linking up with Trade', *Far Eastern Economic Review*, 25 February 1993.

4

At the Centre of
the World – Uzbekistan

In the autumn of 1992 Imam Abdul Ahad, aged thirty-three, stood proudly in front of the mosque and madrasah complex he was building in the town of Namangan, in the Ferghana valley. A gaggle of inquisitive children surrounded the tower cranes and pulleys hauling up bricks and cement. It was the first major construction project in their poverty-stricken town for several years. With the cement barely dry, makeshift classrooms were set up for a hundred young boys studying Islamic law and the Koran. By the end of 1993 some two thousand boys and girls, segregated from each other, will have begun their studies in the Islamic faith. Education is free and so is their simple lunch, and the children are given free Islamic literature to distribute to their families. On weekends they join mullahs to propagate their message in local village mosques.[1]

Their message is deceptively simple: that the government of Uzbek president Islam Karimov is still communist and anti-Islamic and must be overthrown by an Islamic revolution, which will quickly engulf the whole of Central Asia. The Namangan project is costing 50 million roubles, or $200,000 at the rate of exchange of October 1992. The money comes from the Ahle Sunnah movement in Saudi Arabia, which is an organization for the propagation of Wahabism – the puritanical sectarian creed within mainstream Sunni Islam, which is practised in Saudi Arabia. Saudi believers, who have spent hundreds of millions of dollars supporting pro-Wahabi movements in Pakistan, Afghanistan and the Middle East, have moved into Central Asia at lightning speed.

The young imam, who speaks fluent Arabic, joined the Islamic underground during the Brezhnev era where he studied Islam in secret until 1989, when he led the first demonstration against the city authorities to demand a site for a new mosque. The Namangan mayor capitulated in 1991 after the militants occupied the Communist Party headquarters in the centre of town. The militants were given prime land in the centre of Namangan. 'The government had no choice but to allow us to promulgate Islam. For seventy-five years Uzbek people dropped away from religion. Now we are in a hurry to catch up those lost years,' said Imam Abdul Ahad.[2]

In the old quarter of Namangan the official government mosque is run by the increasingly frustrated Imam Bilal Khan. 'There were three mosques in the Namangan region during communist times, now there are 130, but everywhere the Wahabis are doing their propaganda. We do not have the funds like they do,' he said. 'People are pleased they can freely practise Islam now, but they do not want an Islamic revolution like the Wahabis say. We must go slowly and tackle other problems first like the economy,'

An intense struggle between revolutionary Islam and traditional Islam had begun in the Ferghana valley even before Uzbekistan achieved independence. It is not the only unrest the government faces. In the big cities, Uzbek nationalism is also on the rise. In Tashkent activists of Birlik, the ultra-nationalist Uzbek party that has been banned and battered by the government since it was founded in 1989, prepared to attend a human rights conference in Kyrgyzstan in December 1992. Birlik's leader, Abdulrahim Pulatov, was a famous professor of cybernetics at Tashkent University until he was thrown out of his job after being arrested for demanding democracy. Pulatov, a short, wiry, highly energetic person who has the capacity to be doing ten things at the same time, in the eyes of many Uzbeks has become a symbol of the struggle for democracy and human rights, a symbol of past Uzbek glories to others and a bitter thorn in the side of the government. In June 1992 Pulatov was badly beaten up by a gang of thugs who he says were agents of the Uzbek KGB. 'They hit me with an iron bar, cracked my skull and left me for dead. The hospital operated on me and looked after me for twenty days. Then the doctors told me they had been ordered to stop my treatment. I had to escape to Azerbaijan and Turkey,' he said.[3] President Karimov was so enraged that he cancelled all flights from Tashkent to Baku, the Azeri capital.

When Pulatov's brother Abdulmanab Pulatov arrived in Beshkek for a human rights conference on 6 December 1992, he was kidnapped by the Uzbek KGB, who shoved him into a van and drove him straight to prison in Tashkent. It was a crude manoeuvre, but fairly typical of the operating style of the still immensely powerful Uzbek security services. They appeared little concerned that the kidnapping occurred on the same day that the Uzbek government declared a national holiday to celebrate the passage of the country's new constitution through Parliament. The new constitution promises to respect human rights and democracy. A few days later Birlik was banned and Abdulmanab Pulatov was charged with insulting the president.[4]

The rising tide of Islamic militancy and Uzbek nationalism is the most serious challenge to the government of President Islam Karimov. A year after Uzbekistan declared independence, Islamic fundamentalists were preparing for an armed struggle to overthrow Karimov, while urbanized Uzbek nationalists, still unclear about their aims, were united in a common hatred of Karimov. Holding the middle ground were the majority of Uzbeks trying to make sense of their new country as runaway inflation, a crashing rouble and growing unemployment occupied their minds. Over the centuries the region that today encompasses Uzbekistan has always affected the whole of Central Asia, from the Urals to the Tien Shan and beyond into China. This is truer than ever today. The Uzbeks – the most numerous, the most aggressive and the most influential people of the region – occupy the Islamic heartland, the political nerve centre and the economic hub of Central Asia.

With a population of 22 million people, Uzbekistan is the largest Central Asian state. Some 14 million people in its territory, 71 per cent, are Uzbeks. Between 4 to 6 million Uzbeks live in the other Central Asian republics and they form substantial minorities in three of them: 23 per cent of the population in Tajikistan, 13 per cent in Turkmenistan and 12.9 per cent in Kyrgyzstan. In these republics, Uzbek aspirations have become important political factors that governments cannot ignore. This ethnic reality, and the fact that Moscow regards Karimov as an effective gendarme for Central Asia, has made him the most important political actor on the Central Asian stage. There is little doubt that the defeat suffered by Islamic fundamentalist parties in Tajikistan in December 1992 was partly engineered by Karimov's support for Tajik communist forces. In Kyrgyzstan, the powerful Uzbek minority has kept the nomadic Kyrgyz permanently unsettled and unsure of their future.

As many as 2 million Uzbeks live in northern Afghanistan, their presence the result of massive migrations southward during the Civil War in the 1920s when the Red Army forced out those Uzbek clans sympathetic to the rebel Basmachi movement. After the fall of Kabul in April 1992, the Afghan Uzbeks under their undisputed warlord, General Rashid Dostam, set up a parallel state to rival the traditional Pathan centre of Kabul. General Dostam, who is vehemently opposed to the Mujheddin, became a frequent visitor to Tashkent and a close friend of President Karimov, who viewed the Afghan Uzbek region as a buffer zone to prevent the spread of Islamic fundamentalism northwards. Some 25,000 more Uzbeks live in the Xinjiang province of China.

Uzbekistan covers 447,400 square kilometres and its landlocked borders touch all of Central Asia. To the north lies Kazakhstan, on the east Kyrgyzstan and Tajikistan, to the south Turkmenistan and Afghanistan. Uzbekistan lies between the two fabled rivers of Amudarya and Syrdarya, and some 70 per cent of its territory forms part of the massive Central Asian steppe, the vast plains that were home to so many nomadic invaders. In the southwest lie the foothills of the Pamirs and in the northeast is the lush and heavily populated Ferghana valley, considered the political barometer of Central Asia. In the south, the Uzbek steppe becomes one with the deserts of Turkmenistan, whilst in the west lies the ecological shatter zone of the Aral Sea.

Uzbekistan is the only republic that has played host to a variety of urban cultures for the past 2,500 years. The other capitals in Central Asia are relatively recent creations and they have few ancient palaces, ruined citadels or inspiring mosques to lure visitors. As nomadic conquerors swept through the lush valleys of Ferghana and Samarkand, they settled down to build enormous metropolises such as Samarkand. The monotony of the desert and steppe experienced by the nomadic tribes was broken by these oasis cities, which appeared to be paradises on earth. Kings and princes saw their cities as a vast theatrical stage on which new dramas could be constantly enacted. The building of a new mosque or madrasah was an attempt to outdo the former ruler by building even larger buildings and more ravishing interiors, on which imported craftsmen could experiment with the latest techniques. Recently Samarkand, Bukhara, Khiva and Kokand have become major tourist attractions, especially for Muslim visitors from Iran, Pakistan and Turkey, who are visiting the cities of their forefathers.

Tashkent, the bustling capital of Uzbekistan, is today the largest city in Central Asia with a population of 2.1 million people, many of whom are Russians. The city has a 2,000-year history although it was never a capital of the ancient world. As Tsarist Russia expanded, Tashkent became the local centre of governance, and tens of thousands of Russians were imported to man the Tsarist army and bureaucracy as well as to create what is still the largest industrial centre in Central Asia. Tashkent became the centre of the communist movement during the 1917 Revolution. When the Republic of Uzbekistan was created in 1924, the capital was temporarily shifted to Samarkand, but it reverted back to Tashkent, because it was the more modern city.[5] After the devastating earthquake of 25 April 1966, the city was completely rebuilt with earthquake-proof blocks of flats and a new underground railway system.

In recent times, Tashkent has become the urban weather vane for Central Asia, always the first to signal shifts in the public mood. In

1989 ethnic riots in Central Asia took place in Tashkent between Uzbeks and Meskhetian Turks – the harbinger of much worse ethnic riots across the republic. In January 1992 bread riots took place as students protested against the astronomical inflation. Central Asian leaders appealed promptly to President Boris Yeltsin to slow down the pace of reform and price liberalization in Russia.

The city's broad, tree-lined avenues, enormous wedding-cake government buildings in the style favoured by Stalin's architects, and the fashionable Russian elite that populate the parks and city centre are one side of Tashkent. Another, quieter side are the suburbs where many Uzbeks live, in one-storey clapboard homes built during Tsarist times. On the fringes of the city are the enormous industrial parks where tens of thousands of people live in appallingly built apartment blocks. For visitors there is little to see in Tashkent and the atmosphere is depressingly sanitized, lacking the atmosphere of either the great bazaar cities of the East or of the modern cultural metropolises of the West.

One of the oldest cities in the republic is the southern city of Termiz. Situated on the banks of the Amudarya river, which now forms the border with Afghanistan, the city has been the historical gateway south to Kabul and Delhi. A city was founded close to present-day Termiz by Alexander the Great in 329 BC, and Termiz itself was sacked by Genghis Khan in AD 1220. The city became an important crossroads on the ancient Silk Route. In 1894 the Tsar built a massive fortress, establishing the first Russian military post on the Afghan border. Termiz served as the gateway for Russian troops invading Afghanistan in December 1979.

Samarkand has excited the imagination of travellers for centuries. From prehistoric times people have lived in the valley of the Zeravshan river, on the banks of which Samarkand is built. Mythology says that the city was founded in the fifth century BC by the Sogdian king Afrasiab. The mounds that cover Afrasiab today have not all been dug up, but in the museum there are artifacts which show why even 2,500 years ago, Afrasiab was called the Centre of the Earth and The Glittering Summit of the World. Samarkand's real glory lies in the magnificent fourteenth-century monuments built by Tamerlane and his grandson Ulug Beg. When Tamerlane made it his capital in 1369, the city was already one of the largest in the world, with a population of 150,000 people.[6]

Tamerlane brought architects and builders from Persia, India, Afghanistan and Arabia to adorn his city; the Timurid style of architecture was in turn to influence the entire Muslim world. The Registan Square, built by Tamerlane and Ulug Beg, is a staggering but geometrically perfect complex of mosques and madrasahs, which stand in a huge square that dominates the city. The glazed bricks and blue ceramic tiles covered with Arabic inscriptions and the turquoise domes give a sense of both power and ethereal tranquillity. Close by is Ghori Emir, Tamerlane's own lavishly decorated mausoleum. His grave is a solid chunk of black jade where Uzbek families come and pray in the belief of his powers to bestow favours. A legend grew about Tamerlane's grave: that if it was disturbed, a catastrophe would befall the world. Stalin ordered his grave to be opened and Professor Gerasimov carried out the exhumation on 22 June 1941: the day Hitler invaded Russia. Samarkand became a major centre of Islamic learning, rivalling Baghdad and Cairo. The city maintained trade, intellectual and religious contacts with South Asia, the Middle East and Spain.

Medieval Bukhara contained 360 mosques and 113 madrasahs and followed Mecca as the second place of Islamic learning for Muslims. Even in 1900, there were 103 active madrasahs in Bukhara attended by some 10,000 students.[7] Many of these monuments are still standing. Old graveyards of saints, warriors and scholars show where they came from: Yemen, Arabia, Morocco, Spain, Persia and India. At the centre of the city is the Kalyan Mosque and its famous minaret, built of unbaked bricks. Opposite is the Miri Arab Madrasah, the only madrasah kept open and allowed to educate mullahs in the former Soviet Union. In a vast courtyard surrounded by two storeys of arches and blue-mosaic-covered walls, the students still study and live as they did six hundred years ago.

Khiva came into being in the tenth century as a fortress city to protect the caravans along the Silk Route and as one of the largest slave markets in Asia. In 1740 the Persian conqueror Nadir Shah, destroyed Khiva in an attempt to wipe out the slave trade. However the trade was quickly revived, to the extent that even in the nineteenth century more than 1 million slaves, largely abducted Persians and Russians, passed through Khiva's markets.

In all Uzbek cities the visitor is mesmerized by the bazaars, which are important reminders that communism was unable to destroy completely the entrepreneurial spirit of people who have been traders for centuries. While the variety of goods available is huge, the bazaar is also a study of human geography and ethnic affiliations. The faces – complexions, bone structures, eyes and features – of dozens of nationalities are mystifying in their variety. The staggering displays of clothes, hats, capes, boots and cheap jewellery distinguish one ethnic group from an other and emphasize how Central Asia is the great melting pot of the world.

The heart of Uzbekistan is still considered to be the Ferghana valley, some 300 kilometres long and 170 kilometres wide, bounded on three sides by high mountain ranges. Five large rivers flow through the valley, enabling widespread irrigation for extensive agriculture. Although most of the valley lies in Uzbekistan, in the northeast the valley extends into Kyrgyzstan and to the city of Osh. In the south the valley continues into Tajikistan and the city of Kanibadan. The valley is divided into three distinct regions around the towns of Ferghana, Namangan and Andizan. From earliest times it has supported the richest agricultural region of Central Asia. Its fruit and vegetables were famous throughout Asia and the valley still produces some four hundred varieties of grape. Ferghana horses were the favoured mounts for the nomadic tribes. The valley's strategic value was critical to early Central Asian rulers because it gave access in the north to Kashgar and Xinjiang, in the west to Bukhara and Samarkand, and in the south to the Pamirs and the land routes to Afghanistan and ancient India.

The earliest recorded inhabitants of present-day Uzbekistan were Persian tribes who migrated northwards and lived between the Amudarya and Syrdarya rivers from 1500 to 1000 BC. Later, Scythian nomad tribes from the north swept through Central Asia between 700 and 300 BC, until they were pushed aside by the growing Persian empire. The Persians created the province of Sogdiana and Bactria covering much of present-day Uzbekistan. Alexander the Great's invasion of Central Asia in 329 BC led to the founding of an Alexandria near Termiz and another city in the Ferghana valley called Alexandria-the-Farthest, which is present-day Khodjent. Alexander defeated the Persians, then the Scythians who lived north of the Syrdarya and finally the Sogdians. In Samarkand, Alexander killed his best friend Clitus during a drunken brawl and later married Roxana, daughter of a Sogdian chief.

A succession of nomadic invaders were to sweep through the region – the Sakas, the Parthians, the Persian Sassanids, the Arabs and the Ephthalite Huns – until the first Turkic tribes from Mongolia appeared in AD 400. The Turkic invasions, which continued until AD 1000, spelt the end of the Persian–Tajik cultural domination of Central Asia, which had been consolidated by the Samanids (874–999) from their capital of Bukhara. Despite the invasions of nomad tribes, the cities of Uzbekistan developed because they formed a crucial link in the Silk Road. Samarkand, Bukhara and Termiz were major trading cities and caravan resting places on the route. In 1220 the Mongols under Genghis Khan ravaged the region and it was left to Tamerlane in the fourteenth century to bring Turkestan together under one ruler again. Tamerlane was born near Samarkand in 1336 to a leading family of the Barlas Turks, who were once part of the Golden Horde of

Genghis Khan. Between 1382 and 1405, when he died, Tamerlane conquered from Delhi to Moscow and from Kashgar to Herat. He was the last of the great nomadic conquerors and his Turkic origins led to the replacement of the Persian language in Central Asia by the Jagatai dialect of Turkish.[8]

Tamerlane used the title 'Amir' or commander, and added 'Buzurg' or 'Kalan', which means great. These terms are still the mainstay of Uzbek clan structure. His principal achievement was to break down the tribal and clan system and create a supra-loyalty to the 'Leader'. Tribal autonomy was taken away and the tribal hierarchy was subordinated to the centralized command structure within the army. This tradition has continued even down to modern times as communist leaders presented themselves as supra-tribal leaders and claimed to be the successors of Tamerlane in order to gain the allegiance of all sections of society. Tamerlane was a Sufi, a follower of the Naqshbandi order, and during his reign the Sufis flourished at his court and in the countryside.

Tamerlane's grandson Ulug Beg was an outstanding scholar, mathematician, poet and ruler. His discoveries became a major part of the European Renaissance when science first established itself in the West. From his observatory in Samarkand, Ulug Beg plotted the course coordinates of 1,000 stars and measured the length of the year with amazing accuracy. He produced the first precise map of the heavens, which was used by Chinese and European scholars for the next four hundred years. The great-grandson of Tamerlane and heir of the Timurid dynasty, Prince Babar, became the ruler of Ferghana in June 1494 at the age of twelve. The Timurids had earlier lost Samarkand to a new and even more powerful tribal confederacy: the Uzbeks led by the Shaybani Khans. Babar fought long and hard to win back Samarkand but failed, and as a teenager he marched south to capture first Kabul and then Delhi. Under Babar, the Timurids were to give up their homeland in Ferghana but establish the Mughal dynasty that was to rule India for the next four centuries.[9]

The Uzbeks were the last of the great nomadic movements in the region. The earliest Uzbek clans were a component of the Turko–Mongolian Golden Horde under Genghis Khan. They traced their genealogy back to Uzbek Khan (1312–40), the son of Batu, who was the son of Genghis Khan. The Uzbek tribes, ruled by the Shaybani clan, established themselves between the Amudarya and Syrdarya rivers. Uzbek consolidation took place under Abdul Mohammed Shaybani Khan, who ruled from 1500 to 1510. In 1500 he captured Bukhara and established his capital, which the Uzbeks were not to lose until the arrival of the Russians. Shaybani Khan was helped in his task by the most famous of all early Uzbeks: Mir Alisher Navai (1441–1501), who is considered the father of the Uzbek language and the national poet. Navai created a written Turkic script and literature to replace Persian, and his masterpiece 'Farhad and Shireen', an original Persian epic poem, was transformed into an Uzbek epic. Navai was the Grand Vizir at the court for a decade.[10] Today Navai has been adopted as the national poet and the first Uzbek hero.

Mahmud ibn Wali, a sixteenth-century historian, describes the early Uzbeks as 'famed for their bad nature, swiftness, audacity and bold-ness', and writes that they revelled in their outlaw image.[11] They quickly cultivated a generosity of spirit and a hospitality that was unequalled anywhere in the Muslim world and much commented upon by for-eign visitors. Generosity is eulogized in Uzbek poetry as being the main feature of daily life, and the poet's image of the model prince was based on a leader who was 'pious, generous and brave'.[12] The main threat to Uzbek consolidation for the next two centuries came from their neighbours to the south, the Persians, who were Shias, unlike the Uzbeks who were Sunni Muslims.

By the eighteenth century, with the region marginalized by the end of trade on the Silk Road, three separate but weak Uzbek khanates had emerged in Khiva, Kokand and Bukhara. Nasrullah Khan, the amir of Bukhara from 1826 to 1860, consolidated the Bukhara state structure by creating a regular army that employed Turkomen merce-naries rather than Uzbek volunteers. He eliminated the feudal chiefs from the administration and replaced them with bureaucrats.[13] He was a ruthless ruler, who scorned religion and culture and ran a highly oppressive and totalitarian state that was to become a model for his neighbours. The khanates survived by imposing exorbitant taxes. Local chiefs, or *begs* were appointed by the amir to collect taxes, and as long as they delivered a set amount to the amir's coffers they were free to run riot in their own region. Many did, building palaces and setting up courts that often rivalled the amir's own court.[14]

Their rule was to create an image in Moscow of the Central Asian kingdoms as monstrous, medieval anachronisms with slave-based econo-mies, whose people were waiting for liberation by Russia. Even though in Europe tsarism was seen as a rapacious and backward political sys-tem, in Central Asia it was viewed by urban intellectuals as a progres-sive force in comparison to their local rulers. Russian troops under General von Kaufmann captured Tashkent in 1865 and Samarkand in 1868. Tashkent was made the capital for the new governor-generalship of Turkestan. In 1868 Bukhara became a vassal state of Russia. Many Uzbek chiefs refused, however, to accept this humiliation and fighting resumed, which led to another Uzbek defeat and an even more hu-

miliating settlement. In 1873 General Kaufmann signed separate treaties with the khan of Khiva and the amir of Bukhara, making their
states protectorates and abolishing slavery.

Even at the turn of the century the region was still considered
backward. The Danish traveller Olufsen, who visited the court of the
amir of Bukhara in 1911, described the city thus:

> The Amir of Bukhara still lives as in the days of yore, behind his high,
> crenelated walls, and his vassal kings, the Begs, still maintain their antiquated
> courts in gloomy romantic castles. The winding streets with their terraced
> houses of clay, the mosques and the madrasahs, are not yet disturbed by
> bourses in the European style. The mullahs, the dervishes, the qalandars and
> the divanas (beggar of feeble mind) still throng the sanctuaries as they did
> centuries ago. The mystique of enclosure prevails everywhere; the gates of
> the towns are shut at night, the doors of the houses are bolted against
> intruders and the aversion to intimate contact with those Christian dogs is
> the same as in the Middle Ages.[15]

Periodic revolts against the Russians continued as Uzbek anger
grew at the desecration of Islam, the seizure of their best land by
Russian settlers, and the worsening economic situation. In 1885 a
revolt gripped the towns of Osh, Margellan and Andizan in the Ferghana
valley. Led by a Sufi dervish, Khan Tura, it was brutally crushed by
Russian troops. The most serious of all the uprisings began in Andizan
in the Ferghana valley on 17 May 1898, where twenty-two Russian
soldiers were killed by Islamic militants. The revolt spread to other
cities before Russian reinforcements arrived from Tashkent. At its end
226 death sentences and 776 prison sentences were meted out to
Islamic militants by the Russians.[16] With Russia's defeat at the hands
of Japan in 1904 and the 1905 abortive revolution in Moscow, acts of
violence against Russian authority increased as did acts of banditry
against Russian farmers and traders. Significantly most of these rebellions were led by Islamic leaders from the Ferghana valley, who couched
their anti-Russian resentment in calls for a *Jihad*, or 'holy war'.

The Islamic revival in Turkestan and a growing nostalgia for the
wider unity of all Turkic peoples, or Pan-Turkism, were spurred on by
the Russian presence and encouraged by new ideas of political democracy and modern education in Europe, which now trickled through
to Central Asia. These impulses created the movement of Jadids or
Muslim reformers in Samarkand and Bukhara. The Jadids, or Young
Bukharians as they were also called, saw Turkey as a model for a
modern Muslim state. The father of the revival of Pan-Turkism was a
Tartar intellectual, Ismail Bay Gaprinski (1851–1914). In his newspaper *Tarjuman*, he advocated that people should unite under a common
Turkish literary language and a common culture and resist the ossifi-

cation of tsarism and the mullahs. Another Muslim reformer, Ahmad Makhdum Danish (1827–97), went even further by insisting that unless Central Asians learned the Russian language they could not progress. Another Muslim reformer, Jamal Din Afghani (1837–97), who gained prominence in India and Afghanistan, was also a major influence for the Jadids.[17]

The Jadids set up secret societies where they met to discuss the new ideas from Europe and Turkey. In public appeals to the amir in Bukhara and to the Russians, they demanded reform of the educational system and an end to the power of the mullahs. Young Jadids went to Istanbul to study and on their return many of them set up private schools in order to spread the ideas of modern education. By 1916, 40,000 pupils in Samarkand *oblast* (district) alone were studying in Jadid-run schools and some twenty-three newspapers and journals were being published by the Jadids in Central Asia. The Jadids were the first harbingers of political change in Muslim Central Asia for several centuries and their importance cannot be minimized. Similar movements began in British India.

For Muslims everywhere colonialism, whether under British or Russian masters, was a period of great frustration and humiliation. The Jadid reformers gave them an answer: that Muslims had failed to keep up with the times and allowed themselves to fall prey to their ossified power structures and their mullahs. Much of this early Jadid thinking is once again coming to the forefront in Uzbek politics as both Birlik and Erk, the major opposition parties, advocate similar Islamic and Pan-Turkic reforms in order to combat the remains of communism.

The acute economic crisis in Central Asia after World War One began led local Jadid groups to stage anti-Russian rebellions in many Uzbek cities. Russians were killed in Samarkand and Djizak in 1916 and the revolts were only crushed after troops were sent from Tashkent. As the revolution in Moscow began in the spring of 1917, the Jadids organized a conference of some 350 Muslim representatives from all of Turkestan to discuss the crisis, but the conference led to severe divisions, with some Jadids supporting the Bolsheviks while others were hostile to anything Russian.

The revolution came to Tashkent on 12 September 1917 when a soviet was set up, made up entirely of ethnic Russians belonging to rival Bolshevik and Menshevik factions. The Jadids, furious at being left out, cut off Tashkent from the rest of Uzbekistan. The Tashkent Soviet appealed for help from Alim Khan, the amir of Bukhara, who refused and instead persuaded White officers to join him for a struggle against the Reds and the Jadids. The Jadids, now furious with the amir's betrayal, began to gravitate towards the Tashkent Soviet, but they were to be once again betrayed, when the Bolsheviks signed a peace treaty with the amir in March 1918. They recognized the amir's authority and encouraged him to purge all Jadids from Bukhara's territory. The soviet set up an Autonomous Turkestan Republic on 30 April 1918, but its mandate barely extended beyond Tashkent. The uneasy peace between the Bolsheviks and the amir lasted until September 1920, when the Bolsheviks felt strong enough to take him on. General Frunze had arrived in Tashkent with fresh Red Army troops. He broke the siege, restored the rail link to Moscow and then attacked Bukhara, forcing the amir to flee to Afghanistan. A short-lived People's Republic of Bukhara was formed with an alliance of Jadids and Bolsheviks.

Like their truce with the amir, the Bolsheviks' temporary truce with the Jadids was only based on the fact that the Bolsheviks were hard pressed by the growing rebellion of tens of thousands of Uzbeks under the Basmachis. The Basmachi rebellion began in the Ferghana valley in 1918 where a local chief, Irgash, massacred Russian troops. Within the year local Basmachi commanders spread the revolt from Ashkhabad to Dushanbe, setting Central Asia aflame. (The details of the Basmachi revolt are covered more comprehensively in the chapters on Tajikistan and Turkmenistan.) Although ultimately defeated, the rebellion is still a source of national pride for the Uzbeks. Many Jadids supported the Bolsheviks during this time, believing the Basmachis were a reactionary force led by mullahs. This division within their ranks was to lead to the defeat of both the Basmachis and the Jadids, for after emerging victorious the Russian Bolsheviks ignored Jadid demands.

On 27 October 1924 the khanates of Bukhara and Khiva were dissolved and the Soviet Socialist Republic of Uzbekistan was created. The Ferghana valley was divided between Uzbekistan, Tajikistan and Kyrgyzstan, while the Tajiks were divided between the newly created Tajikistan and their homeland in Uzbekistan. The chaos this created in the lives of the majority of the people is still remembered. For those Uzbeks who had dreamed of creating a common Turkestan, Stalin's map makers had produced four separate states. In April 1923, at the CPSU Congress in Moscow, Stalin had termed Turkestan's backwardness 'the most unfavourable and the most disturbing of any in the national Republics. Turkestan was the weak link of Soviet power.'[18] Stalin was determined to prevent the Jadids or Muslim national communists under Sultan Galiev, or any other 'deviationists' from orthodox Marxism Leninism, establishing themselves in the power structure of the CPSU.

With the partition of Central Asia, Stalin ordered a purge of all local communist parties. Sultan Galiev and his supporters were arrested and, with the newly formed Uzbekistan Communist Party (CPU) just a few months old, 16,000 of its members were purged in 1924, leaving only 1,000 Uzbek cadres. For nearly a decade the CPU was devoid of Uzbek cadres who could counter the overwhelming influence of Moscow in reshaping the economy and the social structure. Tashkent became a Russian city in the heart of Central Asia, which was to direct the communist revolution. By the late 1920s the city had also become the centre of the Comintern's attempts to spread revolution to Asia. It served as the headquarters for Persian, Turkish, Chinese and Korean communists and a group of Indian revolutionaries under M. N. Roy. He was training Indians in sabotage and attempting to smuggle them into British India. But Tashkent, under tight Russian control, was a poor advertisement for self-determination for struggling Third World revolutionaries.

In the new republic, Moscow moved swiftly to dismantle the Islamic organizations. In 1924 Bukhara still boasted 100 working mosques and dozens of madrasahs where some 21,000 students still studied.[19] They were suddenly and without notice all closed down. The government expropriated the 'Waqf lands', the farmland endowed by former rulers to local mosques and madrasahs. Under the land reform launched in 1925, landlords, many of whom were local mullahs, had all their lands taken away. The tsarist regime had never attempted to carry out religious discrimination on such a large scale before, and it was something that the Uzbeks never forgot as Islam went underground and the secretive Sufi orders built up a following. At the same time the government carried out a massive literacy campaign. In 1923 the president of the executive of the CPU, Akhun Babaef, was still illiterate and so were 48 per cent of party members. In 1924 only 10 per cent of Uzbekistan's population was literate, but by 1932 literacy had jumped to 60 per cent – a major achievement that Moscow believed would finish the grip of religion on the people.[20] The script that was used for writing Uzbek, was changed from the Arabic to the Latin script in 1929 and then to Cyrillic in 1940.

From 1924 to 1937 Uzbekistan was led by the former Jadid and later communist Faizullah Kohjaev, but Russians headed most other important posts in the CPU. Under the slogan 'you cannot eat cotton' Kohjaev resisted the cotton monoculture being imposed by Moscow on the Uzbek economy – a position that was to earn him Stalin's wrath. He also resisted the further partition of Uzbekistan. The 1 million Karakalpak people who lived in western Uzbekistan were given autonomy within the USSR in March 1932, but in 1936 the region was finally transferred back to Uzbekistan. In 1938 Kohjaev and the first secretary of the CPU, Akmal Ikramov, were accused of treason in the last Moscow treason trial before World War Two. Kohjaev was charged with trying to contact British agents in Tajikistan while he had been president of the People's Republic of Bukhara nearly twenty years previously. Ikramov was accused of being a 'wrecker', trying to ruin the Uzbek cotton industry. The charges were absurd but both men were found guilty and shot after the trial.[21] Both are still remembered for their attempts to prevent the integration of the Uzbek economy with that of the Soviet Union and for their resistance to Stalin's desire to turn Uzbekistan into a mere cotton producer. Both men were rehabilitated in the 1960s on Khrushchev's orders.[22]

After Stalin's death in 1953, Nuriddun Akramovich Muhiddinov became first secretary of the CPU. He helped rally support for Khrushchev and in 1957 became the first Uzbek full member of the Politburo. Muhiddinov and his successor Sharif Rashidov, who headed the CPU from March 1959, began to promote Uzbeks to high office within the CPU. Rashidov created a most extensive apparatus of loyal officials, who built local fiefdoms oiled by corruption and patronage.[23] Before he was removed in October 1983, Rashidov was to perpetrate the scam of the century: the massive swindling of the Soviet exchequer by falsifying cotton production figures.

The cotton scandal was a direct result of the oversimplification of an idea by the central planners in Moscow. Under a command economy it was assumed that whatever the social, economic or ecological cost, cotton production would only rise and rise every year. Central Asia, and in particular Uzbekistan, was designated as a cotton producer and discouraged from growing anything else, even basic food crops. In the 1930s cultivation of rice, a staple food, was banned, grain had to be imported, and thousands of kilometres of irrigation channels were destroyed to create vast cotton fields where machine harvesters could operate.

Between 1940 and 1980 cotton production in Uzbekistan rose from 2.24 to 9.10 million tons. This fourfold increase was made possible by bringing more and more land under cotton cultivation; quality hardly increased, and the yield per acre in many areas actually decreased because of overcultivation. The rotation of cotton with other crops was abandoned, so soil erosion became worse, thereby increasing pests which led to greater use of pesticides. It was a constantly worsening cycle of ecological damage.[24] Meanwhile the Uzbek peasant never got to wear a cotton shirt. Such a shirt sold in Tashkent for thirty times more than the amount Uzbekistan received for its raw cotton when it was shipped to the western republics.

The in-built exploitation for this plantation economy travelled down the line. Whilst grain farmers in Russia received 60 kopeks an hour for their labour in the 1980s, cotton farmers in Uzbekistan received 16 kopeks an hour. The monthly wage for cotton pickers in Uzbekistan was 50 roubles, four times less than the national average. The use of insecticides and the lack of clean drinking water in poverty-stricken villages led to a higher mortality rate and an epidemic of diarrhoea, and diseases, which the inadequate health system could not cope with. A highly toxic defoliant called Butifos was used for decades until it was banned in 1987, after it had killed thousands of people.[25]

Nobody chose to see the danger that was looming on the horizon. In March 1982 President Brezhnev rebuked the Tashkent government for not increasing cotton production and for the decline in cotton quality. In 1986 President Gorbachev did the same, refusing to accept demands made by leading Uzbeks that Moscow reduce its demand for cotton so that Uzbekistan could grow more food. In such a situation it was not surprising that as Rashidov promised Moscow greater cotton output and he failed to meet the targets, he falsified figures. Only when Soviet satellites began to show that areas under cotton cultivation, as claimed by Tashkent, were not actually so, did an investigation begin. A KGB team arrived in Bukhara in 1983 and soon began to arrest low-level officials in connection with the scam.

The trail led to the top and the KGB investigators, Telman Gdlyan and Nikolay Ivanov, became instant celebrities in Moscow after Rashidov was dismissed in October 1983. They had discovered that between 1978 and 1983 the Soviet state was paying out more than one billion roubles annually for cotton that was never produced – a total of some 4.5 million tons. The scam is estimated to have earned Rashidov and his cronies the equivalent of some $2 billion. The minister for cotton production, Vakhobzhan Usmanov, was arrested and sentenced to death, ten first secretaries out of thirteen were jailed, while some 2,600 other officials were also jailed.[26] President Brezhnev's son-in-law, the Soviet Union's First Deputy Interior Minister Yuri Cherbanov, who went on trial in September 1988 on corruption charges, said that he had accepted the equivalent of $200,000 in a suitcase from Rashidov. Rashidov, who died before the investigation was completed, was stripped of all party honours in 1986 and his body was removed from its prominent burial place in Tashkent. By 1989 cotton production was down to 4.5 million tons. The after-effects of these policies were realized most disastrously in the drying up of the Aral Sea and acute water shortages across Uzbekistan.

Many Uzbeks viewed corruption within the CPU as legitimate because it was seen as a snub to Moscow rather than as depriving the republic of assets. Corruption was also a safety valve to keep the system running and allow clan networks to operate to alleviate local problems, food shortages and unemployment. Although Moscow used the media to accuse the CPU repeatedly of corrupt practices, such appeals increasingly fell on deaf ears. Rashidov realized that any slight criticism of Moscow was popular at home and thus he cultivated the vernacular press, which even local Russians did not bother to read. The Uzbek press became obliquely more anti-Russian in its editorial content. Similarly the elite discreetly practised Islamic rites at weddings and funerals, which made them popular at home but unpopular in Moscow. When Gorbachev came to power he railed against such practices and fifty-three members of the CPU were expelled for six months for performing Islamic rites.

Uzbek hostility to Moscow increased dramatically. Rashidov was hailed as a nationalist who defied Moscow; recently statues to his memory were erected in Djizak, his birthplace. Following Rashidov's fall from grace, Moscow had to appoint three leaders between 1983 and 1989 before the political situation in Uzbekistan stabilized.[27] The CPU's first secretary, Islam Karimov, was elected unopposed as president on 24 March 1990. A dour figure who rarely smiles, he was born in Samarkand in 1938 into a poor family. His mother was a Tajik and his father an Uzbek; both died young. He was raised in a state orphanage, the favourite recruiting ground for communist cadres, and struggled up the party ladder by being aggressively supportive of Moscow in his early years. He speaks Uzbek poorly and employed a language tutor when he began to give televised addresses to the nation. Those who have worked with him say he has little imagination and few ideas and has tended to surround himself with men of even less imagination.[28]

As the crisis in Moscow worsened in 1991, Islam Karimov was critical of Gorbachev's *glasnost* and refused to apply it in Uzbekistan. When the August 1991 coup attempt took place, Karimov openly declared his support for the coup makers, even as they were floundering. 'We have always been supporters of firm order and discipline. A leadership that abandons order and discipline can never return to power,' he said.[29] Among those arrested protesting against the coup attempt was Birlik leader Abdulrahim Pulatov who quipped, 'We have the honour of being the only people in the USSR arrested for violating the first order of the coup.' For several days the government tried to isolate the Uzbek population from events in Moscow by jamming Moscow television, while the government-controlled media dutifully reported every communiqué by the coup plotters.

Karimov faced acute embarrassment when the coup failed and Yeltsin became the powerhouse in Moscow. It was the single biggest mistake

of his career, and convinced both the Islamic and the nationalist oppositions that Karimov was essentially anti-democratic and could not
be trusted. On 31 August Karimov got Parliament to hastily declare
Uzbekistan's independence, hoping that this would stem the nationalist protest. Attempting to restore his credibility, Karimov banned the
CPU on 14 September, renaming it the National Democratic Party of
Uzbekistan (NDP). 'The government decided the best way to save
itself was to declare independence. The party changed its name but it
will not matter. Here is an island of communism,' said Birlik leader
Mir Alam Adilov.[30]

Karimov held presidential elections on 29 December, allowing
another candidate, Mohammed Salih, a poet and leader of Erk (a
breakaway faction of Birlik which was prepared to co-operate with the
regime). Birlik and the Islamic opposition remained banned parties
and could not put up candidates. Karimov won 85.9 per cent of the
votes cast, leaving Salih with just 12.4 per cent of the vote. The severe
economic crisis led to the first riots in Tashkent against rising prices,
in January 1992. Officially two students were shot dead by police, but
unofficial figures put those killed at between twenty and possibly fifty
students. Central Asian leaders were shaken by the riots and Karimov
cracked down hard on the opposition. A war of words developed
between the Moscow press, which rounded on Karimov for being too
harsh, and the local Tashkent press, which was heavily censored and
supported the government. Moscow's *Izvestia* published an article
entitled 'Don't Shoot at People in the Streets No Matter How Sharp
the Conflict,' which was immediately attacked by the Uzbek government. *Izvestia* was banned.[31]

Uzbekistan's one-crop economy made it extremely difficult for the
government to adapt to a market economy after independence. Any
expected move to a market economy was not helped by the extreme
conservatism of a leadership that was reluctant to endorse private
enterprise or encourage foreign investment, despite the fact that
Uzbekistan has a number of resources it can exploit. Uzbekistan has
a large natural gas industry, which produced 41 billion cubic metres
in 1991, much of it from the Mubarek gas fields. Uzbek gas is still
exported along a pipeline that stretches from Bukhara to the Urals.
Uzbekistan's petroleum production in 1990 was 2.8 million tons and
a large oilfield was discovered in the Ferghana valley in March 1992.

One third of the former Soviet Union's gold is produced in the
Kyzylkum desert, and Tashkent is a major producer of machinery and
chemicals for the cotton industry. During World War Two the enormous Chkalov aircraft production complex was set up in Tashkent,
while in Almalyk there is a complex of mining and metallurgical works.

Navoi, an industrial city created just thirty years ago, provides the republic with its fertilizers and chemicals.[32]

Much of Uzbekistan's industrial base is related to cotton production. Tashkent used to produce one out of every three cotton spindles made in the former Soviet Union. Under the Soviet regime, Uzbekistan's main industrial exports were building materials, automobiles, machinery for the oil and gas industry, and metals, while its major imports were electricity, timber and food. There were 1,600 factories linked by 3,480 kilometres of railway line, inland waterways of 1,100 kilometres and a road network of 80,300 kilometres. There is a huge manpower base of trained workers for potential future growth. In 1947 there were only 568 Uzbek technicians, but by 1975 their numbers had grown to 15,000, a key shift in policy by communist leaders like Rashidov, who trained and nurtured an indigenous elite.[33]

The republic has been hard hit, however, by the migration of some 1.7 million Russians. Some 200,000 Russians have left Uzbekistan every year since 1988, because of the rise of Islamic fundamentalism and discrimination in favour of Uzbeks. With a million Russians holding key technical and managerial posts having left by 1993, the economy suffered. Uzbek officials admit that the migration has been so massive that some plants have had to close because of a lack of trained personnel and spare parts, which Russian managers were always able to purchase.[34] In 1991 at the Syrdarya hydroelectric station, two power units were out of operation because of a shortage of trained technicians; the Navoi chemical complex was operating at half strength as was the strip-mining industry in Ferghana. Russian doctors were leaving in droves from all over the republic, crippling an already poor health service.[35]

Despite these problems, legislation favouring foreign investment has lagged far behind that of Kazakhstan or Kyrgyzstan, while legislation to enable Uzbeks to set up private factories, buy farms and own shops remains incomplete. By 1993 new laws were finally in place on privatization, foreign investment, trade, leasing, banking and currency and capital controls. However the new laws were frequently blocked by stubborn bureaucrats, and the continuing system of state orders, centralized distribution of inputs, and fixed prices killed off any private initiatives. 'The bureaucracy has put enormous hurdles in the way of privatization. It just does not want to see change and still wants to run a command economy,' said an Uzbek entrepreneur in Samarkand who was trying to set up a washing-machine factory.[36] At the end of 1992 the private sector only accounted for 5–9 per cent of gross national product. By 1993 there were about 570 registered joint ventures and subsidiaries of foreign companies, compared to 158 in 1991, but only one fifth had actually started operations.[37]

Agriculture remains the backbone of the Uzbek economy. Uzbekistan used to produce 65 per cent of the former Soviet Union's total cotton, 50 per cent of its rice and 60 per cent of its lucerne on some 856 collective and state farms. The area under crop had increased dramatically in the rush to grow more cotton. Some 2,189,000 hectares were farmed in 1913, and the area has now doubled to 4,400,000 hectares. In central and western Uzbekistan the steppe sustains some 4.1 million cattle, 9.3 million sheep and goats, and 700,000 pigs.[38] However the state farms remained inefficient; even when they were allowed to, they failed to produce sufficient food. In 1990 the small private plots belonging to farmers accounted for nearly half the local food production. To control prices, the government issued ration coupons in 1992 which allowed everyone to buy basic foodstuffs at partly subsidized prices. Some 30 per cent of government salaries are now paid in the shape of coupons.

There is large-scale unemployment in the countryside – estimated to be 22.8 per cent in 1990 – and widespread poverty.[39] In villages in the Ferghana valley and the Samarkand region, the two richest agricultural belts in the country, abject poverty is clearly visible. Uzbeks living in mud houses without toilets or running water depend on a single cotton harvest to see them through the year. Ragged children play around open drains and unemployed men loiter in the dirty, unpaved streets – scenes that are reminiscent of the chronic poverty in India or Pakistan.

President Karimov said for the first time in March 1992 that Uzbekistan would cut back cotton production by allocating 60,000 hectares less for cotton, so that wheat could be grown. In 1992 Uzbekistan produced 4.1 million tons of cotton and aimed to improve productivity so as to reduce the land area under cotton. In 1992 exports to countries outside the rouble zone doubled to $1.6 billion as Uzbekistan managed to put its cotton on the international market.

More than a year after independence there were still no plans for land reform or how to tackle the land hunger in such overpopulated regions as the Ferghana valley. 'The land issue is too sensitive, too complicated, too politically dangerous. Let's not talk about it,' said a senior bureaucrat.[40] At a collective farm near Djizak, independence had brought little change. One thousand poorly dressed workers toiled ten hours a day, seven days a week to bring in the 1992 cotton harvest. The farm manager, Omar Kulaka, a cousin of former communist boss Sharif Rashidov, uses a convoy of jeeps and shortwave radios to keep in touch with his foremen spread over the 5,000 hectares. He has a stud farm and a large, comfortable house. At the bottom of the scale is worker Qadir Kul, eighty-four years old, who was pensioned off twenty-four years ago but has returned to work to make two ends meet. His salary was 1,000 roubles a month, double what he received in 1991 but still not enough. 'Under Brezhnev potatoes were sixteen kopeks, now they are 16 roubles. I cannot live on even my pension and salary,' he said.

In 1991 the farm produced 5,500 tons of cotton and for the first time was allowed to keep 5 per cent of that to sell on the open market, but Omar Kulaka had no idea how to find foreign buyers to sell to. In 1992 the government purchased the best cotton at 18,000 roubles a ton and 3,960 roubles a ton for the poorest quality – a staggering amount compared to the 900 roubles a ton that the government paid in 1990 – but it was not enough. With inflation running at 1,500 per cent in 1992, 'Fertilizer, petrol, seed, wages, everything has gone through the roof and the government price is not enough,' said Kulaka. Many of the thirty-eight cotton-picking combines were lying in sheds because of a lack of spare parts, and a quarter of the thirty-six tractors were out of service.

The government has allowed farms to sell 50 per cent of their vegetables in the bazaar, but the irrigation network, the layout of the fields and the machinery available are only geared for cotton. Nobody knows how to grow anything else or has the means to do it. 'We do not have the storage, the freezers, the transport or the machinery to grow and sell more vegetables for the market,' said Kulaka. As a result, while 2,050 hectares is under cotton on his farm, only 100 hectares are under vegetables.

There is a deep desire among farm workers to acquire land. 'Every farmer is ready to take the land but the government is not giving,' said farmer Hakimov Mahmood. Yet there is also deep apprehension about actually taking the risk of owning land. 'Where will we get the inputs to grow crops?' Mahmood asks. How can tractors be divided and where will peasants get credit, seed, fertilizer or even fuel are common questions. Officials simply say there are too many people and too little land to be divided. Azad Jan, a farm manager in the Ferghana valley, feared that any land distribution would lead to fighting between the various ethnic groups living in any single locality. Unemployment is also fuelling ethnic unrest because farm workers belonging to ethnic minorities are always the first to be sacked.

Uzbeks have been involved in most of the recent ethnic violence in Central Asia, even when it has occurred in other republics. The larger Uzbek population and their greater social cohesion has led to many smaller ethnic groups becoming extremely frightened of a recharged Uzbek nationalism. On 3 June 1989 bloody riots broke out in Tashkent, and then in a dozen other towns, between Uzbeks and Meskhetian Turks who wanted to be returned to their homeland in Georgia. At least sixty-seven people were killed in Tashkent and another eighty died in Kokand. Some 15,000 Meskhetians were made homeless while others fled to Kazakhstan. In June 1990 there were even more violent Uzbek–Kyrgyz riots in Osh, just across the border in Kyrgyzstan, in which hundreds of people were killed.

The political opposition that has developed in Uzbekistan since 1989 is perhaps the most sophisticated and the strongest in Central Asia. Caught between the nationalists and the Islamic fundamentalists, the government is attempting to cajole and repress both sides at the same time. The strongest nationalist party is the Movement for the Preservation of Uzbekistan's Natural, Material and Spiritual Riches or Birlik, which means 'unity'. It was established in November 1988 by a group of eighteen prominent Uzbek intellectuals. At Birlik's founding congress on 28 May 1989 attended by three hundred delegates, the 45-year-old professor Abdulrahim Pulatov was elected chairman of the party's governing council. In October 1989 he led the first demonstration in Tashkent, of some 50,000 people, calling for Uzbek to become the republic's main language. One hundred people, including Pulatov, were arrested.[41]

For several years Birlik was housed in a tiny back room on the top floor of the Writers' Union building in central Tashkent. Its only assets appeared to be a table, a couple of chairs, a typewriter and a teapot. Over cups of black tea and numerous cigarettes, party leaders spent much of their time discussing how to take part in elections from which they were banned. During a congress of the party held in May 1990, dozens of squad cars roamed the streets and hundreds of police surrounded the building where delegates were gathering. Throughout the day tensions remained high as plainclothes security men took down details of anyone who entered the building, and interrogated foreign journalists. As I interviewed participants, my interpreter became increasingly nervous until he finally pleaded with me to leave. It was a bizarre introduction to Uzbek democracy.[42]

Birlik was finally registered as a movement, but not as a party, on 22 November 1991, three years after it was founded. Government repression continued unabated, however. In June 1992 as decribed above, Pulatov was badly beaten by four attackers wielding iron bars who were said to belong to the Uzbek KGB. Birlik claims 1 million supporters. It is a nationalist, broad-front organization, which is demanding a complete break from Moscow, democracy, the resignation of Karimov and a Pan-Turkic alliance of the peoples of Central Asia.

It also supports an Islamic cultural agenda and the use of the Arabic script for the written Uzbek language. Birlik is led by intellectuals, but also includes environmentalists, ultra Uzbek nationalists and Pan-Turkic and Islamic activists. However its core is Uzbek nationalism, which means that it adopts diverse and often contradictory political positions. The movement is confused and divided, but it commands respect amongst the people.

Pulatov has become a symbol for human rights activists for the whole of Central Asia. The US State Department's human rights report for 1992 condemned the repression against Pulatov and Birlik. The Western media has given intensive coverage to Karimov's methods of curbing the opposition, which has had serious repercussions in discouraging foreign investment. Birlik is virtually banned, its press has been closed down, its public meetings are not allowed, while its activists have been warned not to participate in human rights conferences abroad, at which President Karimov might be criticized.

Like so many new parties in Central Asia, Birlik is riven by factionalism and internal power struggles. The government's strategy has been based on keeping the opposition as divided as possible, which did not prove a difficult task. Birlik split in February 1990 and Erk was set up by Mohammed Salih. Erk adopted a more moderate stance on the national question and was prepared to work with the regime. A realist and at the same a mystic in his political philosophy, Salih is disliked by Birlik because he stood as a presidential candidate in the 1991 elections. However Erk has become increasingly opposed to Karimov and is now persecuted as much as Birlik. The day Parliament proclaimed Uzbekistan's independence, Salih composed a poignant poem which began, 'I am lying here and my head is empty. Just like the new declaration of independence.'

The Islamic opposition to the government has made equally dramatic strides since 1989. The official Islamic hierarchy sponsored by the government faced a crisis in July 1991, when the Mufti of Soviet Central Asia (later renamed the Mufti of Uzbekistan), Mohammed Yousuf Mohammed Sadik, was voted out of office and replaced by another mullah. Mufti Sadik was accused of corruption, of selling off free Korans from Saudi Arabia for a profit and of being too close to the government. He was reinstated two days later after the government intervened, but the affair demonstrated that proximity to the regime was viewed as treachery by many Uzbek Muslims.[43] Subsequently the pro-government Islamic hierarchy or official Islam, as it is called, faced severe challenges from the Wahabi movement in Ferghana, the Islamic Renaissance Party (IRP) and the aftershock of the civil war in Tajikistan.

The IRP, which was officially registered in Russia in the summer of 1990, remained banned in all of Central Asia except Tajikistan, where it lost out after a bloody power struggle. In Uzbekistan the IRP has considerable support in the Ferghana valley and the Samarkand region. The chairman of the Uzbekistan IRP, Abdullah Utayev, and his first deputy, Abdullah Yousuf, are based in the Ferghana valley. In August 1990 Uzbek intellectuals set up a rival Muslim party to the IRP. The Islamic Democratic Party led by Dadakhan Hassanov, a renowned composer and performer of traditional Uzbek music, also demands the imposition of sharia or Islamic law through a non-violent Islamic revolution in Uzbekistan, but it is willing to work with rather than against the regime.

It is the Wahabi movement in the Ferghana valley that is the most determined and best-organized of all the fundamentalist movements seeking the overthrow of the government. 'Ferghana can explode any time. People are just waiting for it to happen and nobody can do anything to stop it,' admitted a senior official of the Uzbek Interior Ministry in 1993. 'Everything has come at once, a new multi-party system, a poor economy and now the fundamentalists. We have no immediate answers'. Seven million people, one third of the total population of Uzbekistan, live in the valley, making it the most densely populated region in Central Asia. Overpopulated and with an acute land shortage, the valley now has an unemployment rate close to 35 per cent of the total workforce. The economic crisis in the valley has given the fundamentalists an effective political base.

Since 1991 militants have looked for confrontations with city authorities in order to seize prime ground in city centres to build mosques and madrasahs funded by the Saudi-backed Ahle Sunnah movement. By the end of 1994 the movement will have spent an estimated 500 million roubles, an astronomical sum in cash-strapped Central Asia; madrasahs will educate some 15,000 students.[44] A massive propaganda operation is under way in outlying villages in order to reconvert the population. 'First Ferghana, then Uzbekistan and then the whole of Central Asia will become an Islamic state,' said Imam Abdul Ahad in Namangan. Imams said their aim was to overthrow the 'communist government of Karimov' and spearhead an Islamic revolution throughout Central Asia.

Uzbek officials claim that the militants are creating a secret army, that students are undergoing weapons and martial arts training, and that in each city hit squads have been built up to strike at officials and create disturbances at an appropriate time. The crisis in Ferghana is compounded by the fact that local officials have no clear strategy to deal with the economic crisis and no idea how to curb the Islamic militants. The ruling NDP is an empty shell in the valley, unable to mobilize support against the militants. Officials themselves describe the NDP as rudderless, either without clear political goals or an ideology. The vacuum has forced many bureaucrats either to turn to Islam or to make contacts with the militants to ensure their own safety. However the militants have little influence in the capital Tashkent or in the vast southern regions of Uzbekistan, where Sufism and Uzbek nationalism are much stronger forces.

Islamic fundamentalists condemn the popular Sufi tradition in Central Asia claiming, quite wrongly, that it is 'nothing but a Zionist and Turkish conspiracy to undermine Islam'. They condemn Shias and other minority sects in Islam; meanwhile groups such as the Wahabis and the IRP are bitterly pitted against each other. In short, the militants maintain a narrow and highly sectarian view of Islam, which will bring them up against not only the government but other Islamic groups in the future. Much of this sectarianism has been imported from Asia and the Middle East as Arab, Pakistani and Afghan religious groups try to create new areas of influence. Cut off from the debates within the Islamic world for seventy years, the Central Asian militants have a naïve understanding of the principles of Islam and the rampant sectarianism that is prevalent beyond their borders, which is draining away Islamic solidarity. The growth of religious sectarianism in what was once a non-sectarian Central Asia is already dividing that society.

Uzbekistan's intense religious and political polarization is perhaps affecting women the most: some are being forced to conform to fundamentalist social mores, while others confront fundamentalism by taking up women's rights issues. Women who follow the Wahabis have abandoned their traditional colourful Uzbek costume for white veils that cover the body from head to toe. 'We have no tradition of the veil, this is something imported from Arabia. I have a girlfriend who has become a Wahabi and now she does not see me,' said a schoolteacher in Namangan.[45] In the larger cities *glasnost*, however, did create small opportunities for Uzbek intellectuals to promote women's rights. In 1990 the Uzbek press reported that some two hundred women immolated themselves with petrol, because of oppression by their husbands and in-laws. Uzbek film producer Shukhrat Makhmudov and his wife Raizeta made a number of documentary films about women – the pressures on housewives from male family members, prostitution and the lack of education amongst many women. These films were never shown on Uzbek television, but they had a wide private showing.

The more Westernized women in the cities who have regular boyfriends, wear short skirts and live away from their parents are invariably Russian or other non-Uzbek women. Most prostitutes in Tashkent are also of Russian origin. Thus many conservative Uzbek women tend to look down upon their Russian counterparts; this leads to ethnic prejudices, even within the women's movement and at the workplace. Uzbek women, like women in other Central Asian societies, remain essentially conservative because of Islamic and cultural traditions. Although many of them work, they perform only certain categories of jobs, such as nursing and teaching. They tend to agree to arranged marriages, rarely leave home before marriage and often have many children.

The nationalist and fundamentalist oppositions are at serious loggerheads with one another and so long as they do not unite, the government is relatively secure. Because of their differences, perhaps the most serious opposition to President Karimov comes from within his own NDP. The former Prime Minister, Shahrullah Mir Saidov, tried to oust Karimov in October 1991 but failed because he could not muster sufficient support within the party.[46] At least two major factions exist within the ruling elite. A conservative lobby around Karimov would like to halt all economic liberalization and stamp out the opposition. A younger and more liberal grouping would like to speed up economic liberalization and come to an understanding with Birlik so as better to combat the Islamic fundamentalists. Karimov maintains his position by balancing off the two factions and monitoring them closely. He has not hesitated to try and set up his own loyal opposition party. Usman Azimov, an adviser to Karimov, set up the Fatherland Development Party, which was quickly registered. Such self-serving creations enable Karimov to say that he has encouraged multi-party democracy in Uzbekistan.

Uzbekistan has retained the entire security apparatus from the Soviet era. The KGB, renamed the National Security Service, and the police are prominent everywhere and ordinary people are extremely reluctant and even scared to participate in public political debate. Karimov has created a National Guard of some seven hundred men and a new Ministry of Defence, staffed largely by Russian officers. The National Guard is being rapidly expanded. In early 1992 the government began to take over Russian military installations in agreement with Moscow, and in May all Uzbek soldiers serving outside Uzbekistan were recalled home to serve under a joint CIS–Uzbek military command which has 15,000 troops and 280 tanks as well as a large, modern air force. This command works closely with Moscow, as was seen by the military help given by Tashkent to pro-communist Tajik forces who defeated the Tajik Islamic opposition in December 1992.

While the civil war in Tajikistan preoccupied all Central Asian leaders, Karimov publicly proclaimed that he wanted Russia 'to be the guarantor of security in Central Asia'. He said that was in keeping with historical traditions and would ensure that Russia's interests coincided with Central Asia's interests. However he demanded that Uzbeks play a leading role in future security arrangements. It was already clear in Moscow in the summer of 1992 that both President Yeltsin and the right-wing opposition looked to Karimov to keep the peace in Central Asia. For the first time Moscow was relying on Karimov to take major initiatives to maintain security, rather than dictating the terms for such arrangements itself.

The passivity with which many Uzbeks have accepted the harsh measures by their government has been the result of the powers of the state security services and the dead weight of Uzbekistan's social and political history since 1917. If Tashkent was once the harbinger of revolution in Asia, it soon became the model for the communist status quo. Many people are genuinely apprehensive of change and say there has already been too much since the break-up of the Soviet Union. As in neighbouring Muslim societies, Uzbeks have relied upon strong personalities such as Karimov, who have little interest in promoting democracy and prefer to operate with weak state institutions. The government has successfully controlled prices after the January 1992 riots, but at a huge cost as this control still depends on heavy state subsidies.

There is a wide gulf between the public idiom and private discourse, which the leadership maintains by rigorous censorship of the media. Moreover, the gulf between city and countryside is enormous. The restless urban intelligentsia is largely ignored by the more placid farmers on the land, where expectations are low and thresholds of suffering very high. Thus the underlying political apathy nurtured by communism survives, though in new forms.

Intellectuals and reformers still hope for a peaceful transfer to more genuine democracy by means of a change of heart from within the elite. They point out that a more progressive and liberal elite is emerging in the ruling party, even though it is still uncritical of the president in public. Karimov has been slow to transform the economy precisely because he is aware that encouraging private enterprise will also encourage pressure for political change. He cites the aim of maintenance of stability at all costs, even at the cost of democratic reforms and economic changes. For many Uzbeks this is a self-defeating idea, as it brings more repression and shuts out modernizing influences.

The lack of direction or vision for the future makes Karimov a political chameleon, pretending to be all things to all peoples. He has visited Saudi Arabia and Iran in a bid to demonstrate his Islamic credentials. He opens his speeches with Koranic quotations and is shown on television praying at mosques. But these gestures towards Islamic piety do not convince the fundamentalists. Similarly he tries to drum up support from the nationalists by speaking of Uzbek history and the destiny of the Uzbek people. 'He is a man of no convictions. He can be a communist, or a nationalist or anything else. But when you take off the mask, there is nothing there and that is frightening,' says Mohammed Salih of the Erk party.[47] Karimov realizes that whatever happens in Tashkent will affect the whole of Central Asia. He is obsessed with maintaining the status quo because he feels that any over-hasty change will feed unrest and violence.

But change will have to come in Uzbekistan, if for no other reason than the fact that half the population is now under sixteen years old. Uzbek youth, like youth anywhere, are restless, uncertain and bored with the past. They are ready and willing to try out anything new. Despite the strident censorship, Uzbekistan is opening up to foreign ideas and goods as never before in its history. Youth make up the main congregation at prayer in the mosques, the crowd at Birlik rallies and also throng the discos and hotels frequented by foreign tourists. Change will be forthcoming because the majority of the population are demanding it.

Notes

1. Ahmed Rashid (in Namangan), 'With God on Their Side', *Far Eastern Economic Review*, 19 November 1992.

2. Ibid.

3. Hugh Pope, 'Uzbekistan: where democracy is forced to wait', *Independent* (London), 2 January 1992.

4. 'Uzbek Activists Seized', *The News*, Islamabad, 11 December 1992. Also interviews by the author with Birlik leaders, October 1992, in Tashkent.

5. E. H. Carr (1948) *Socialism in One Country, 1924–26*, Macmillan, London.

6. E. Maillart (1985) *Turkestan Solo*, Century Publishing, London.

7. M. Ispahani (1989) *Roads and Rivals: the politics of access in the borderlands of Asia*, I. B. Taurus, London.

8. B. F. Manz (1989) *The Rise and Rule of Tamerlane*, Cambridge University Press, Cambridge.

9. W. Erskine (1974) *A History of India under Babar*, Oxford University Press, New Delhi.

10. E. Allworth (1990) *The Modern Uzbeks from the 14th Century to the Present*, Hoover Institute Press, USA.

11. Ibid.

12. Ibid.

13. Ibid.

14. H. Carrere D'Encausse (1988) *Islam and the Russian Empire: reform and revolution in Central Asia*, I. B. Taurus, London. See also A. Vambrey (1873) *History of Bukhara*, reprinted by Indus Publications, Karachi.

15. Olufsen (1911) *The Amir of Bukhara and his Country*, Copenhagen.

16. G. Krist (1992) *Alone through the Forbidden Land: journeys in disguise through Soviet Central Asia*, Ian Faulkner Publishers, Cambridge.

17. Carrere D'Encausse.

18. E. H. Carr (1952) *The Bolshevik Revolution, 1917–23*, Macmillan, London.

19. Krist.

20. G. Hoskin (1990) *A History of the Soviet Union*, Fontana, London.

21. H. Carrere D'Encausse (1979) *Decline of an Empire: the Soviet Socialist Republics in revolt*, Newsweek Books, USA.

22. J. Critchlow, 'Did Faizulla Kohjaev Really Oppose Uzbekistan's Land Reform?', *Central Asia Survey*, Vol. 9, No. 3.

23. J. Critchlow (1991) *Nationalism in Uzbekistan: a Soviet republic's road to sovereignty*, Westview Press, USA.

24. Ibid.

25. W. Fireman, 'Glasnost in Practice: the Uzbek experience', *Central Asia Survey*, Vol. 8, No. 2.

26. D. Doder and L. Branson (1990) *Gorbachev: heretic in the Kremlin*, Futura Books, London. See also P. Cockburn (1989) *Getting Russia Wrong: the end of Kremlinology*, Verso Books, London.

27. Sharif Rashidov was replaced as CPU leader by Usman Khodzhaev, who in turn in January 1988 was replaced by Rafik Nishanov, who defended Moscow's demands for higher cotton production, and instantly became unpopular. He expelled some 18,000 CPU officials for corruption and demoted another 3,000.

28. Interviews wtith Uzbek officials, Western and Asian diplomats and Russians in Moscow who know Karimov. Interview with President Islam Karimov by the author, December 1991.

29. Edward Gargan (in Tashkent), 'Uzbekistan's Boiling Kettle', *International Herald Tribune*, 20 September 1991.

30. Kathy Evans (in Tashkent), 'Sausages and Democracy Are still the Stuff Dreams Are Made On', *Guardian* (London), 21 November 1991.

31. Peter Pringle, 'Time Not Right for Shooting in the Streets', *Independent* (London), 18 January 1992.

32. G. Sobratee (1987) *Uzbekistan*, Novosti Press, Moscow. Also Pakistan government figures and interviews by the author with Uzbek Officials.

33. Y. Roi (1984) *The USSR and the Muslim World*, George Allen and Unwin, London.

34. Interviews by the author with Russian and Uzbek officials in Tashkent, October 1992. See also Ahmed Rashid, 'Forced to Leave', *Far Eastern Economic Review*, November 1992.

35. Sophie Quinn Judge (in Moscow), 'Retreat from Empire', *Far Eastern Economic Review*, 25 October 1990.

36. Interview wth the author, December 1992.

37. World Bank, *Uzbekistan Economic Review*, May 1992. Also documents of the World Bank Group meeting for Uzbekstan, Paris 16 December 1992.

38. Pakistan government figures, Pakistan Foreign Office.

39. Interviews by the author with Uzbek officials, Tashkent, 1990.

40. Ahmed Rashid, 'Caught in a Cleft', *Far Eastern Economic Review*, 19 November 1992.

41. B. Brown, 'The Public Role in Perestroika in Central Asia', *Central Asia*

Survey, Vol. 9, No. 1. Also interviews with Birlik leaders by the author in Tashkent in 1990, 1991 and 1992.

42.   Ahmed Rashid (in Tashkent), 'Uzbek Opposition Demands Independence', *Nation*, (Lahore), 10 June 1990.

43.   Sophie Quinn Judge, 'Mufti Mutiny', *Far Eastern Economic Review*, 25 July 1991.

44.   Rashid, 'Caught in a Cleft'.

45.   Interview by the author in Namangan, October 1992.

46.   M. Brill Olcott, 'Central Asia's Post-Empire Politics', *Orbis*, Spring 1992.

47.   Caroll Bogert and Steven Levine, 'Where Old Soviet Habits Die Slowly', *Newsweek*, 8 February 1993.

5

Warriors of the Turquoise Hills – Kazakhstan

In the shadow of the snowclad Ala Tau, or Purple Mountains, grapes ripen in lush vineyards around the village of Isseyk, fifty miles from Alma Ata, the capital of Kazakhstan and just 150 miles from the Chinese border. A collective farm produces a rich madeira-type red wine and a delicate white wine that local farmers liken to a woman's caress. In a long hall built of logs, wine tasting is an elaborate ceremony, with fresh fruit and goat's cheese, homemade butter and warm bread. In 1990 the chronic food shortages in Moscow appeared a long way away.[1]

But behind this idyllic simplicity lies a formidably complex and tense social reality. The 10,000 hectares of the collective farm were worked by 1,500 workers, drawn from a staggering twenty-seven ethnic groups – and those who did not belong to Central Asia all wanted to go home. The nationalities crisis in Kazakhstan is on everyone's mind and crucial to the future stability of a republic that is almost as large as India.

The underpopulated Kazakh steppes were for Stalin a virgin dumping ground for ethnic groups whose loyalties to the Soviet state were in doubt. During my visit an elderly German couple working at the wine factory burst into emotional German greetings when seeing any foreigner. During 1989–90, two thousand German families from this district migrated to West Germany and by 1992 the rest had left too. A Chechen horseman herding fat-tailed sheep speaks of longing for his homeland in the Caucasus, while the Mesket Turks who see no future in returning to their Georgian homeland would prefer to move to Turkey if they had the chance. Despite seventy years of communism, ancient tribal and clan structures still flourish. Many collective farms are demarcated according to old tribal boundaries or into ethnic ghettos. Rudek Mnacakanyan, the Armenian farm manager and a deputy in the district soviet, speaks of the ethnic harmony in the past, but is deeply uncertain of the future as Kazakhstan approaches independence.

In Kazakhstan the ethnic problem is complicated by the fact that there are almost as many Russians in Kazakhstan as there are Kazakhs. Of the 17 million people, 42 per cent are Kazakh while 36 per cent are Russian. The statistics themselves have become a cause of controversy as Kazakh nationalism asserts itself. Russian demographer Maqash Tatimov reported that Russians and Kazakhs were equal at 39.5 per cent each of the total population in 1985 and that the Kazakh population would reach 42 per cent by 1990 – but these figures are disputed by the Kazakhs.[2] Nobody really knows the truth. The rest of the population comprises minorities from 100 different nationalities. There are 1 million each of Ukrainians and Germans, and nearly half a million each of Uzbeks, Tartars and Chinese nationalities. President Nursultan Nazarbayev knows that he is sitting on an ethnic powder keg. 'Our future policy must not be detrimental to any of the many, many nationalities in Kazakhstan,' says the concerned president.[3]

The Kazakhs themselves are scattered throughout Central Asia. Some 650,000 Kazakhs live in the bordering Xinjiang-Uighur Autonomous Region in China, largely as a result of mass migrations after the Bolshevik Revolution. Another 30,000 Kazakhs live in northern Afghanistan, while some 71,000 live in the People's Republic of Mongolia. A quarter of a million Kazakhs live in other former Soviet republics and there is a significant Kazakh population in Moscow.[4]

Kazakhstan is the largest of the Central Asian republics and the second largest of the fifteen former Soviet republics. Its massive landmass covers 2,717,300 square kilometres. It's territory stretches 3,000 kilometres from west to east and 2,000 kilometres north to south; it takes nearly five hours to fly from Moscow to Alma Ata – the same time it would take to fly from London to Ankara. For 5,000 kilometres its northern and western borders are contiguous with Russia, and it has a 1,700 kilometre eastern frontier with China. In the south it borders all the other Central Asian republics except Tajikistan. In the west it encompasses the northern shores of the Caspian Sea, the world's largest lake, and also much of the Aral Sea.

The Soviet state never included Kazakhstan in Central Asia because Moscow wanted to stress that its destiny was linked to Russia. The towns of northern Kazakhstan are so dominated by Russian settlers that its industries were never controlled by Alma Ata but instead directly by the Ministry of Industries in Moscow. This special relationship with Moscow and the sensitivity towards Russian settlers was reflected in the policies of President Nursultan Nazarbayev, who was the last communist leader to advocate the break-up of the Soviet

Union. Kazakhstan has found it most difficult to split with Russia and to distinguish its economic interests as separate from those of Moscow.

However, the break-up of the Soviet Union has also turned Kazakhstan into the first nuclear power in the Muslim world, ensuring that after December 1991 President Nazarbayev was the post-USSR politician most courted by the West after Boris Yeltsin. Kazakhstan has 104 SS-18 Satan Intercontinental ballistic missiles (ICBMs), with more than 1,000 warheads, making it the fourth-largest nuclear power in the world. (Tactical battlefield nuclear weapons were removed from the Central Asian republics soon after the break-up of the Soviet Union.) Although Kazakhstan's weapons come under the joint control of the four CIS nuclear republics – Russia, Ukraine, Belarus and Kazakhstan – President Nazarbayev is using the nuclear card to extract concessions from Russia and aid from the West. Kazakhstan owns the weapons but Russia controls them, and this dilemma has created political problems with peace activists wanting to give up the weapons and Kazakh nationalists demanding total control of them. The nuclear issue is dealt with in Chapter 10.

On Kazakh territory are to be found some of the most spectacular glories and horrors of the Cold War. The Baikonour cosmodrome in the northern Kazakh steppes was the Soviet Cape Canaveral, from where on 12 April 1961 Yuri Gagarin was launched in the rocket *Vostok* to become the first man in space. Also in the north are the nuclear testing grounds at Semipalatinsk – the USSR's equivalent to the Nevada desert testing range – where radiation pollution is still a living nightmare for local Kazakh nomads even though nuclear tests have been banned. In the west lies the Aral Sea, one of the greatest environmental disasters of the twentieth century.

The capital, Alma Ata, in the southeast corner of the republic, was founded by Russians in 1854 and was first called Vierny. It was a small village that traded in the most available local commodity, apples. The Bolsheviks renamed the city Alma Ata, or the City of Apples, and made it their capital only after they had first tried out Kzyl-Orda, an oasis south of the Aral Sea which was discovered to be far too hot.[5] In 1929 Alma Ata held only a few thousand people, but by 1940 the population had reached nearly one million people as Russian settlers arrived to staff the factories that provided goods for the farmlands. Although it has none of the monuments of other Muslim centres, Alma Ata is one of the most beautiful cities in Central Asia because of its green belt. Tree-lined streets, meticulously clean parks and gardens and numerous fountains, lakes and small canals give it a distinct European appearance. In winter the waterways become instant skating rings. Alma Ata's southern suburbs are situated on the steep slopes of the Ala-Tau mountain range, and the pride of the city is the massive Medeo skating ring and sports complex, which is ringed by pine-clad mountains. Children learn how to skate when they can barely walk.

The Kazakh language belongs to the Kipchak group of Turkic languages, all of which belong to the Altaic family. The Arabic script was used until 1928 when Moscow forced the Kazakhs to adopt the Latin script. They were in turn made to change to the Cyrillic script in 1940. There is no body of written classical literature, but lengthy oral epic poems from the past have been preserved by modern scholars.[6] From earliest times the Kazakh steppes were the grazing grounds for numerous nomadic empires which rose and fell in Central Asia. According to legend, the Kazakh tribes first called themselves the Alti Alash, named after their founder Alasha Khan, who united the Turkic tribes in southern Siberia and founded a neo-Kazakh state that flourished between the twelfth and sixth centuries BC. There is little evidence, however, of this early civilization or of the Alash people.

In 1218 the region was devastated by the Mongol hordes under Genghis Khan, and it was not until the fifteenth century that the Kazakhs emerged as the distinct people we know today. By then the Kazakh nomads had migrated southward with their flocks of sheep and goats and herds of yaks and camels.[7] In the fifteenth century the Shaybani khans united the Uzbek clans into the Shaybani Ulus, or 'gathering', which defeated the Timurids – the descendants of Tamerlane. A segment of the Shaybani Ulus later split away and sought refuge with the Chaghatai tribes on the Xinjiang–Kazakhstan border. These tribes, who lived beyond the pale of Shaybani control, came to be known by outsiders as 'Kazakh', possibly from the Arabic word qazac, which means 'outlaws'. However they preferred to call themselves 'Kyrgyz', while the Kyrgyz proper, as we know them today, were called the 'Kara Kyrgyz' for several centuries.[8] There is considerable debate on the origins of the word 'Kazakhs'.

As the Uzbek confederacy consolidated power in Bukhara and Samarkand, the Kazakhs or Kyrgyz as they were then called, took over the northern steppes. Under their first chiefs, Burunduk Khan (1488–1509) and Kasim Khan (1509–18), they achieved their distinct identity by fiercely resisting Uzbek advances. The Kazakh border with the Uzbeks was strung out along the Syrdarya river, with the Uzbeks to the south of the river and the Kazakhs to the north. In time the Kazakhs were divided into three *ordas*, or hordes. The Great Horde occupied eastern Turkestan, the Middle Horde lived in the central steppe region, and the Little Horde occupied the west bordering the Urals. Each orda was composed of tribal, clan and family units ruled by a khan. Together the khans demarcated distinct areas in which to graze their flocks and organize their military forces.

The Kazakh khanates frequently warred against each other. Although they united when faced with an external threat, they proved incapable of setting up a state system. They resisted the advances of the Uzbek khans from the south, attacks from the east by the khanate of Dzungaria based in northwestern China, and frequent raids from the west by the Kalmyks, who lived on the Volga river. But in the early seventeenth century the eastern Kazakhs were overrun by a Buddhist Mongolian tribal confederacy called the Qirots. The Kazakhs still refer to this period as 'the Great Disaster': the Kazakh ordas were forced to abandon their homes and migrate, until the Qirots were defeated by China's Manchu rulers in 1757. Around the same time the Kazakhs faced a new threat from the west and the north: the Russians.

The Russians had steadily extended their line of control southward from Siberia, building forts in Omsk in 1716, Semipalatinsk in 1718 and Orshk in 1735. From the Caspian Sea in the west the Russians steadily built forts penetrating deep into western Kazakhstan. The Kazakh khans, trapped between the Qirots and the Russians, finally acceded to Russian suzerainty and asked for Russian protection. The Little Horde signed a treaty with Moscow in 1731, the Middle Horde in 1740 and the Great Horde in 1742. During the next fifty years, the deterioration of their nomadic lifestyle caused by the devastation of the wars led to a series of revolts by Kazakh nomads against their own khans, the most far-reaching being the revolt of Batyr Srym in 1792. These revolts encouraged the Russians to abolish the khanates, and between 1822 and 1848 the entire Kazakh territory was incorporated into the Tsarist empire.

The new Russian rulers further squeezed the Kazakhs by importing Tartars and Cossacks to settle the best Kazakh grazing and farming lands. Between 1783 and 1870 there were at least eight major revolts by the Kazakh tribes against these Russian-backed settlers, but the Kazakhs were defeated with particular savagery by Russian armies sent from Siberia. Another period of great disasters had befallen the Kazakhs, which was not to end until well after the Bolshevik Revolution. By 1870 the Kazakhs had lost an estimated one million people, a quarter of their total population, in the wars, revolts, famines and land grabbing by the settlers.[9] Although they were late converts to Islam, having been converted only in the sixteenth century, the Russians attempted to control them further by importing Tartar mullahs, in the belief that Islam would make them more docile. Soviet historians rarely mention the deaths of so many Kazakhs, and they have always tried to prove that the early accession of the Kazakh khans to Russian sovereignty –

the first in Central Asia – demonstrated the general Kazakh desire to be joined with their elder Russian brothers.

Without any natural state formation, the Kazakhs were in no position to take on the Russians, although their subsequent revolts against Moscow's settler policy demonstrated that Kazakh nationalism was far from dead. Thus Kazakh history has been written in blood and the race has been close to extermination several times. The people's suffering over the centuries has determined their complex psychological make-up today. Still dominated by Russian settlers, they appear accommodating, docile and over-anxious to please the Russians – in appearance the most pro-Russian of all the Central Asian peoples. Beneath the surface, however, lie a bitter resentment and a keen sense of having been deeply wounded by history. Oppressed by both the Russians and their Uzbek neighbours, a strong latent nationalism persists which the new Kazakh rulers are now having to contend with.

In the late nineteenth century, in the most developed areas of Kazakhstan, rich Russian settler-farmers and Kazakh clan chiefs had developed an extensive semi-capitalist agricultural base that was similar to that of Russia itself. Absentee landlordism was rife and kulaks, or rich peasants, hired poor Kazakh nomads and Russian peasants to work their land. In 1891 1 million Russian peasants were shifted to northern Kazakhstan and the north has remained a strong Russian preserve ever since.[10] Central Asia faced famine and ruin during World War One and in 1916 the great revolt of the Kazakh–Kyrgyz nomads against Tsarist appropriations took place, which was brutally crushed by Russian troops. Thousands were killed and some 300,000 Kazakhs and Kyrgyz fled to Chinese Turkestan to avoid the crackdown.[11]

The political ferment created by the 1916 revolt pushed a small Kazakh nationalist party to the forefront. In 1905 a handful of Kazakh intellectuals had set up Alash Orda, an informal, underground party that was to be the first nationalist party calling for a free Turkestan in Central Asia. These intellectuals were to lay the first seeds of Kazakh nationalism and their writings today are playing an important part in the re-emergence of Kazakh identity.[12] The Alash leaders included Ali Khan Bukeykanov (1869–1932), a prince and descendant of Genghis Khan who became a Tsarist official. Ahmed Baytursun (1873–1937) was also a Kazakh aristocrat and a noted poet and educationalist, who was expelled from the region in 1909 for revolutionary activity but later returned to join Alash. Mir Yakub Dulatov (1885–1937), a Kazakh aristocrat who had studied at a Muslim madrasah, became a radical Muslim nationalist and was a founder member of Alash. Such men came from the numerically small, educated Kazakh aristocracy who entered politics at a time when the Kazakh nomads were leaderless.

All these nationalists were to die in the 1930s, victims of Stalin's purges.[13]

In 1917 Alash faced difficult if not impossible choices. Both the Whites and the Reds had little time for Kazakh nationalism although both sides were keen to enlist Kazakh help with false promises of freedom and autonomy. The Civil War was seen as a conflict between Russians in which the Kazakhs had little to gain no matter who won it. Alash remained crushed between these two forces and vacillated between them. Ahmed Baytursun wrote about the unpleasant choice facing the Kazakhs and Kyrgyz in 1918.

> The Kazakh–Kyrgyz received the first revolution (February 1917) with joy and the second with consternation and terror. It is easy to understand why. The first revolution had liberated them from the oppression of the Tsarist regime and reinforced their perennial eternal dream of autonomy, the second revolution was accompanied in the borderlands by violence, plundering and by the establishment of a dictatorial regime ... In the past a small group of Tsarist bureaucrats oppressed us; today the same group of people or others who cloak themselves in the name of Bolsheviks perpetuate in the borderlands the same regime.[14]

Alash Orda held its first official party congress in Orenburg in April 1917. The congress demanded that (1) all land seized by the Russians be returned to the Kazakhs, (2) Russian immigration into Turkestan be stopped, (3) education should be in the Kazakh language and (4) Kazakhs should stop helping the war effort. At the time these demands were the most radical nationalist demands put forward in Central Asia, and Alash Orda's moves towards greater autonomy or a free Turkestan were seen as a major threat by both the Reds and the Whites. Both sides were to court Alash but were consistently to deny them any political rights.[15]

As a result of the congress, Alash set up a government of the Eastern Alash Orda in Semipalatinsk in northeast Kazakhstan and elected Ali Khan Bukeykhanov as president. Because of the severe communications problems in the vast steppes, another centre of government was created in Zhambeitu in the Urals, which was called the Western Alash Orda government. For a time the Alash governments refused to join either the Reds or the Whites, resisting them both until January 1918, when the Bolsheviks captured Orenburg and disbanded the Alash Orda government. Many Alash leaders began to negotiate with the White armies. By the summer of 1918, the White armies under Admiral Kolchak had cut off Central Asia from Russia and were making rapid progress across the Kazakh steppes after defeating the Bolsheviks.[16]

The Civil War that raged across Kazakhstan for nearly five years devastated the population, the fragile economy and the land while it plunged Alash into fitful alliances as it debated which side to trust. After joining Admiral Kolchak, Alash leaders became quickly horrified at the cruelty of the White armies, while Kolchak himself refused to concede any of the Kazakh demands for autonomy. By 1919 Alash had rejoined the Bolsheviks, who by late 1920 defeated Kolchak, although sporadic fighting was to continue until 1923. In March 1920 the Bolsheviks called a Communist Party congress in Orenburg and invited the Alash leaders to participate.

Whilst the Bolsheviks could not afford to antagonize the Kazakh nationalists at a time when Red power was still so fragile in Central Asia, Alash leaders, encouraged by Lenin's statements on autonomy, hoped that they could achieve their aims through the Bolsheviks. Alash had little choice but to join the victors of the Civil War if it was to survive; its decision was also prompted by fears that the Russian settlers in the north might split Kazakh territory and enforce a union of northern Kazakhstan with Russia. Today, as Kazakh nationalism grows, similar fears still exercise the minds of the leaders of newly independent Kazakhstan.

By 1920 tens of thousands of Kazakhs had been killed and some 800,000 Kazakh–Kyrgyz nomads had fled into China. The poorer Russian settlers had also suffered horrendously in the Civil War. While the Russian kulaks in the countryside had largely joined the White armies, many Russian peasants and the urban proletariat in the towns fought with the Bolsheviks. The newly formed Communist Party of Kazakhstan (CPKZ) was to remain dominated by Russians for several decades. On 26 August 1920 the Kazakh Autonomous Soviet Socialist Republic was created and in October the first Constituent Congress of Soviets of the new republic was held with the participation of many Alash leaders.

Urged on by Stalin, however, the Russian communists soon began to purge Alash members, who were putting up stiff political resistance to the forced resettlement of the nomads and the collectivization of farms. In 1925 Ahmed Baytursun was the first to be purged from the CPKZ, and in April 1928 several other Alash leaders were denounced as ultra-nationalists and executed. Labour camps and gulags were set up in Kazakhstan to house former Alash members; they were soon filled with Stalin's victims from other republics. Kazakhstan soon began to equal Siberia in the notoriety of its gulags, where thousands of communists and nationalists disappeared without trace in the 1930s.[17]

After the forced collectivization of their livestock in 1930–31, tens of thousands more Kazakh nomads fled to China, while many Kazakh clans took up arms, only to be crushed by Red Army cavalry units.

According to one estimate, in the 1930s Kazakhstan lost through migrations, death, murder, prison, starvation and other causes 1.5 million people, or one third of the entire indigenous population.[18] Livestock losses were enormous as people killed their animals rather than see them appropriated by the state. The numbers of cattle shrank from 7.4 million head in 1929 to 1.6 million in 1933, and of sheep from 21.9 million head to 1.7 million.

It made little difference to the Bolsheviks that 80 per cent of the population depended on livestock rearing. 'The regime now undertook to turn a nomadic culture with centuries-old roots into a settled and collectivized agricultural society in a few years, against the deep-seated wishes of the population,' writes Robert Conquest.[19] The new collectives that were set up after 1929 were desperately poor. The nomads who were turned into farmers overnight had neither the tools, seed, housing nor the machinery to carry out even the basic tasks of farming. It was not surprising that out of the 400 agronomists listed as working on the collectivization process, only four were Kazakhs. In 1929 there were only 17,500 communists in the whole of Kazakhstan, the majority of them Russians. By the spring of 1932 famine was raging across Kazakhstan, and because it helped destroy local resistance to the communists, little help was forthcoming from Moscow.[20]

The Kazakhs have been a minority in their own homeland ever since the Civil War and have never recovered either their numbers or the ability to defy the Russians. The Kazakh holocaust – for it can be called by no other name – far exceeded that of any other Soviet nationality ruled by Stalin. The formation of Kazakh territory was even more disjointed. On 5 December 1936 the Kazakh Soviet Socialist Republic was formed. 'Kazakhstan's huge territory was stitched together by the communists in a completely haphazard fashion: wherever migrating herds made a yearly passage would be Kazakhstan,' wrote the Soviet dissident Alexander Solzhenitsyn.[21] At the Tenth Congress of Soviets of Kazakhstan in March 1937, a new constitution was adopted.

Hundreds of thousands more outsiders poured into the region during World War Two, further overwhelming the local Kazakh population; this was followed by yet another mass migration after the war. In order to boost agricultural production in the Soviet Union, Khrushchev announced his Virgin Lands Scheme in February 1954. The Kazakh steppes were declared virgin territory. Ignoring fears expressed by some experts that Kazakhstan would be turned into a dust bowl, the authorities allocated land to hundreds of thousands of 'volunteers' from Russia and the Ukraine and ordered them to farm it. For the Russians it was a new, empty frontier country like the Wild West to be 'civilized' and developed to meet grain production targets set by Moscow. For the Kazakhs it was another humiliating sign of the policy of colonization by Russia. In fact the scheme was unsuccessful. In widespread storms and wind erosion between 1960 and 1964, 4 million hectares of farmland were ruined and 12 million hectares were damaged. This was nearly half the land brought under cultivation in the scheme. Tselinograd, 960 kilometres northwest of Alma Ata, was the centre of the scheme and called the Virgin Lands City. Now it has reverted back to its old Kazakh name, Aqmola, or White Tombs, and the wheatfields have once again become infertile grasslands.

Khrushchev carried out another purge of the CPKZ, removing the secretary general Zhumabai Shaiakhmetov, a Kazakh, and his deputy and replacing them with two Russians, one of whom was Leonid Brezhnev. It was Brezhnev's ability to present the Virgin Lands Scheme as a modern economic miracle and his successful suppression of Kazakh protests against it that were later to bring him to prominence in Moscow. The growing political dissent in Kazakhstan was galvanized by the revolts in the gulags. After Stalin's death there were several uprisings in the camps, including hunger strikes at Ekibastuz, and in May 1954 in Kengir prisoners disarmed the guards and took over the camp to demand better living conditions.[22] The revolts were brutally suppressed, but they made the authorities realize that the camp system had to be slowly dismantled. So long as the inmates were docile, the camps were cheap and easy to run, but they created major headaches if they became centres of revolt and political dissent.

In 1964, Dinmukhamed Kunayev, a Kazakh and a Brezhnev loyalist, was promoted to the position of first secretary of the CPKZ. Becoming a member of the Politburo in 1971, he was to rule Kazakhstan for twenty-two years until December 1986. Standing over two metres tall, Kunayev was a giant who pampered Brezhnev, now first secretary of the CPSU, by arranging duck shoots for him around Alma Ata.[23] Under Kunayev, important party positions were still held by Russians, but this did not stop him from building his own power base by putting members of his Dzuze clan of the Great Orda into powerful bureaucratic positions.[24] A new Kazakh political mafia developed, owing complete allegiance to Moscow but at times pretending to take a nationalist position in order to ensure that Kazakh nationalism was not channelled into anti-Soviet feeling.

The rampant corruption of the Kunayev regime and protests by local Russians at the mafia-style politics of his entourage encouraged newly elected first secretary of the CPSU Mikhail Gorbachev to sack Kunayev in December 1986. He was replaced by an ethnic Chuvash from Russia, Gennady Koblin, fifty-nine years old and an outsider who was brought in to clean up the CPKZ. It was the first of many mistakes Gorbachev was to make in Central Asia. Gorbachev was totally insensitive to the growing nationalist aspirations in the region. By importing an outsider while practising *glasnost* at home, Moscow was once again signalling to the people that it did not trust a Kazakh.[25] On 17 December 1986, a few days after Kolbin took over, anti-Russian riots against Kolbin's appointment broke out in Alma Ata.

The riots sent shock waves through the Moscow establishment because they were the first to break out in Central Asia as the policy of *glasnost* got under way. Kazakhstan had always been pointed out as the finest example of inter-ethnic harmony in the Soviet Union. The riots also upset the communist elite in other Central Asian republics, who now feared similar expressions of anti-Soviet feeling and inter-ethnic strife. Coming at a time when Soviet troops were fighting the Mujheddin in Afghanistan, the riots raised fears that they might turn into a wider protest movement against the Soviet involvement in Afghanistan.

On 17 December some 10,000 people took to the streets in Alma Ata. The bewildered police forces, who were facing their first crowd control experience in more than fifty years, responded by opening fire on the demonstrators. Some two hundred people were injured in the firing and several people were killed. After a subsequent court of enquiry, some 1,200 police officers were fired from their jobs for overreacting. Within two days, the riots spread to twelve other cities in the republic. Troops were hurriedly brought in to control other towns, where martial law was declared until the demonstrations subsided. By that time at least seventeen people had been killed, including three members of the security forces. Chimkent and Jambnul, two of the worst-hit towns, were to remain under martial law until the end of 1987.

Kolbin tried to reassure the Kazakhs by setting up a commission of inquiry, but by the time the riots were brought under control Kolbin was a lame-duck leader. He had lost the support of the CPKZ and was defeated in the elections of March 1989, being replaced by Nursultan Nazarbayev as first secretary of the CPKZ. In the first direct elections, on 22 February 1990, Nazarbayev was re-elected as first secretary and became chairman of the Supreme Soviet. On 26 October 1990, Kazakhstan declared its sovereignty.

Nazarbayev was to emerge as the most important leader in Central Asia because of his adroit handling of the crises that were to follow in the Soviet Union and in Kazakhstan itself. He was born on 6 June 1940 in the village of Chemalgon in the Alma Ata region. His parents were peasant farmers and he won kudos at school as a wrestler rather than for any intellectual brilliance. In 1962 he joined the CPKZ, and he graduated in 1967 from the Karaganda Iron and Steel Complex Technical Institute.[26] Nazarbayev is married to Sara Alpysovna, who is an engineer, and they have three grownup daughters. Since independence, his wife has played an important role in encouraging charity work and raising money for children.

After the removal of Kunayev in 1986, Nazarbayev had been appointed chairman of the Council of Ministers of Kazakhstan – a job similar to being Prime Minister. He travelled extensively within Kazakhstan and got to know both the CPKZ members and the region's problems, which stood him in good stead when he emerged as the natural compromise choice as Kolbin's successor. He quickly grew close to Gorbachev, who in 1990 invited him to join the Politburo of the CPSU. According to a Kazakh journalist, 'Nazarbayev has been able to synthesize different political traditions: European reformism, adherence to democratic procedure and the hallmarks of the Asiatic leader – traditionalism, intuition and Oriental authoritarianism. He is a child of two worlds, in each of which he is a friend among friends.'[27] Moreover he played local politics skilfully, balancing Kazakh clan interests with Moscow's directives. Nazarbayev is from the Great Horde, but his first vice-president, Erik Asanbayev, was from the Middle Horde, while his first prime minister was from the Little Horde.

As the crisis grew in the Soviet Union, Nazarbayev remained intensely loyal to Gorbachev's dream of political and economic changes to be carried out without violent upheaval and without redrawing the map of the Soviet Union. He was Gorbachev's chief ally during the negotiations over the new Union treaty in 1991, and with Gorbachev argued fiercely against the break-up of the Soviet Union. Nazarbayev wanted a careful balance between the centre's respect for the sovereignty of individual republics and the republics' recognition of the strategic interdependence built into the Soviet state structure. Nazarbayev stressed the need for a 'single economic space' and a 'single strategic space', which required a centre with credible monetary and political authority. Nazarbayev was immensely popular at home, amongst both his fellow Kazakhs and Russians settlers. They trusted him because Nazarbayev knew that if the Soviet state broke up, Kazakhstan's Russian population would be irrevocably antagonized and peace in the region could be jeopardized.

The 20 August 1991 coup attempt was a testing time for Nazarbayev. He did not react for thirty-six hours because he was nervous of the reaction of local Russians, many of whom supported the coup. But once Nazarbayev heard that Yeltsin was resisting the coup, he threw his weight behind Yeltsin and condemned the plotters. Nazarbayev's delay was viewed as opportunism by some, but considering the possibilities of a Russian backlash in Kazakhstan, he was only being cautious.[28]

Once the coup was crushed Nazarbayev moved fast. At a special Congress of People's Deputies on 7 September, the CPKZ was renamed the Socialist Party, despite loud protestations by many communist deputies. Nazarbayev refused to head the new party, saying he had to be president of all the people. But Nazarbayev feared the worst as he watched Gorbachev's power ebb away, Ukraine become more inflexibly opposed to retaining the Soviet Union, and Yeltsin's immaturity as he rode the bandwagon of Russian chauvinism.

For Nazarbayev, 1 December 1991 was a day of mixed blessings. He was elected president in the first direct presidential elections in Kazakhstan, winning 99.8 per cent of the vote, but on the same day Ukraine voted for independence, thereby rejecting the Union. When the Slav republics formed the CIS without even bothering to consult Nazarbayev, he was furious. Yeltsin and the other two leaders feared that if Nazarbayev had been asked, he would have warned Gorbachev. Nazarbayev felt that Yeltsin had abandoned responsibilities to the Union which all the leaders of the republics were expected to maintain. 'We became independent by a process of elimination. We were the only ones left. They left us independent,' said a bitter vice-president Yerik Asanbayev.[29] On 16 December Kazakhstan announced its independence, the last of the Central Asian republics to do so. 'The majority of the Soviet people are against the disintegration of the Soviet Union. It will be kept intact but perhaps not in the same way as before,' Nazarbayev said.[30]

Finally the agreement that was to break up the Soviet Union and change the map of the world was agreed to by all the republics' leaders at Alma Ata on 21 December, with Nazarbayev presiding. The four nuclear republics – Russia, Ukraine, Byelorussia and Kazakhstan – signed an agreement for taking joint control of the nuclear weapons on their territories. In the next few months, Nazarbayev's latent bitterness towards the Russian leadership surfaced. He had been too frequently ignored, too often snubbed, rarely consulted and was now forced to react to events whose pace was being set by Yeltsin. Again in January 1992, when Russia announced that it was lifting price controls, Nazarbayev argued for more time so that other republics could implement such a step together with Russia. Yeltsin ignored his pleas.

Tensions between Nazarbayev and Yeltsin increased through the year as Yeltsin disregarded the Kazakh leader, even in such crucial matters as the future control of nuclear weapons. Yeltsin then hinted at a possible Russian move to redraw its borders with Kazakhstan that would demand inclusion of northern Kazakhstan in Russia. Nazarbayev was furious. In a harsh interview in April 1992, he directly blamed Russia for creating uncertainty about the future of the CIS. He said he had once supported the CIS, but there was an even more urgent need to form a Central Asian bloc that could stand on its own feet. 'My confidence in the stability of the CIS has decreased of late,' he admitted.[31]

Soon after, however, Moscow began to accommodate Nazarbayev. Russia and Kazakhstan signed an economic and military co-operation agreement on 26 May 1992, with both sides expressing hopes that this would set an example for other republics to follow. The agreement called for a single security zone between the two republics to be defended jointly, and for the common use of the Baikonour cosmodrome with its expenses to be met by all the CIS states. The agreement also set up the framework for a common market and open frontiers between the two states, but few of its terms were ever to be implemented by Moscow.[32]

Despite these problems Nazarbayev was reluctant to create a separate military force for Kazakhstan. In January 1991, as a gesture to nationalist demands he had set up a 2,000-strong Kazakh Republican Guard, drawn from former Kazakh conscripts and officers in the Soviet army, which was to be under direct presidential control. Although he continued to insist that the CIS armed forces remain united and control all of the former USSR's territory, there was strong opposition to his views from independent-minded republics such as the Baltics and Ukraine, as well as from hardline Russian nationalists within Russia. Finally, on 8 May 1992, he signed a decree setting up Kazakhstan's own armed forces and creating a defence ministry. But in a move to assuage the fears of Russian settlers, he appointed Lieutenant-General Ryabtsev, the Russian commander of the Fortieth Army, as the First Deputy Defence Minister and filled other posts with Russian officers. The new ministry continued to work with CIS forces to maintain the defence of Kazakhstan.

As Nazarbayev's prominence lessened in Moscow, it grew on the world diplomatic circuit, where he had become an international star. He visited the US, Canada, Britain, Switzerland, Turkey, China, India and Pakistan; numerous heads of states dropped in to see him in Alma Ata, and there were frequent visits by US Secretary of State James Baker. Foreign Minister Tuleutay Suleymenov visited several other countries in his own capacity. The first issue for every foreign visitor was what were Kazakhstan's plans for its nuclear weapons. Nazarbayev made it clear that so long as Russia kept its missiles so would he, but the missiles would be under joint CIS control.

The most significant development for Kazakhstan was its improved relations with China. Kazakhstan had been on the front line in the Soviet–Chinese cold war since the 1960s. Nazarbayev moved swiftly to rectify this situation. An economic and trade agreement was signed in January 1992, and in February another agreement allowed Chinese entrepreneurs to trade freely in Kazakhstan and set up manufacturing industries.[33] In May both countries announced a joint venture to build an electricity power plant in Xinjiang. The opening of the railway line between China's Xinjiang province and Alma Ata in early 1992 led to a dramatic increase in trade between the two countries. China quickly became Kazakhstan's largest trading partner outside the CIS. In 1992 Kazakhstan exported $228 million worth of goods to China and imported goods worth $204 million.

Since the creation of the CIS, Nazarbayev has maintained a three-pronged strategy – to preserve close links with Russia in order to pacify the local Russian population, to enhance Kazakhstan's historic and cultural identity in order to keep Kazakh nationalism in check and to strengthen links with other Central Asian states, for whom he has emerged as the leading spokesperson. It is a difficult balancing act when the political and ethnic opposition within Kazakhstan is growing.

Despite his popularity Nazarbayev runs an authoritarian regime, which like China does not allow serious political liberalization to take place but instead argues for economic liberalization and development first. Nazarbayev has learnt his lesson from Gorbachev, who allowed political liberalization to take place before he brought about any fundamental economic changes. Only three parties have been registered by the government and are therefore allowed to operate legally: the Socialist Party which is the renamed CPKZ, the Social Democratic Party which broke away from the Socialist Party, and the Azat party, the official Kazakh nationalist party. Azat, led by Ormantaev Kamal, was founded in 1991 as result of a merger between various Kazakh nationalist groups. It concedes a role for local Russians. However only a handful of the 360-member Supreme Soviet have declared their affiliation to any of the political parties, a fact that emphasizes the lack of party politics in the republic and the continuing loyalty to Nazarbayev.

But there is no shortage of opponents to President Nazarbayev. The first are the semi-underground and more extreme Kazakh nationalist groups. One such group, Adalat, which is strongly anti-Russian, was set up to commemorate the Kazakh victims of Stalin's purges and the deaths by famine in the 1930s. Alash, named after the first Kazakh nationalist party, is also the closest thing to an Islamic fundamentalist party in Kazakhstan. Zheltoksan or 'December', named in honour of the victims of the 1986 riots and led by Hasan Kozhakhmetov, who has spent a considerable time in prison, has adopted a strong nationalist platform. These are small urban-based parties within the Kazakh intelligentsia and youth, but they do not have a wide base of appeal largely because they are not allowed to propagate their ideas.

These parties opposed Nazarbayev in the 1991 elections, but Hasan Kozhakhmetov could not gather the 100,000 signatures needed to run as a presidential candidate, an indication of the party's wider lack of appeal. These parties promote an amalgam of demands, which include calls for a Greater Turkestan, closer ties with Turkey, and elements of Islamic fundamentalism. Alash held its first congress in Alma Ata in October 1991 but after a small anti-regime demonstration, security forces moved in and arrested several Alash members for allegedly insulting the President. The Islamic Renaissance Party (IRP) also has a small base in Kazakhstan, but it is mostly dominated by non-Kazakh Muslims, which does not make it attractive to Kazakhs.[34]

The most popular of the Kazakh opposition movements that spearheaded the growth of political parties have been the anti-nuclear and Green movements. The best known is the Nevada–Semipalatinsk Movement, or Nevada for short, which has subsequently developed into the People's Congress party, the most important political opposition. Nevada was founded in 1989 by two former Supreme Soviet deputies: Olzhas Suleimenov, an outstanding poet and writer, and Mukhtar Shakhanov, who headed the official commission that looked into the 1986 riots. The movement is named after the two nuclear test sites of the former Soviet Union and the USA. Nevada initially demanded an end to nuclear tests and the shutting down of the two test sites but its political platform has subsequently widened.[35] Nazarbayev has remained friendly with the leadership of Nevada, increasing speculation that he himself has encouraged Nevada in its activities. If this is true, then Nazarbayev has tried to channel Kazakh nationalism and anti-Russian resentment into a soft, semi-official party that confronts the heritage of Russian colonialism, not on the basis of ethnic chauvinism but on issues such as environmental damage, which have a wider domestic and even international appeal.

It is not surprising that environmental issues were to be the most important casting-off point for Kazakh intellectuals. Kazakhstan was a dumping ground not only for suspicious looking ethnic groups but also for heavily polluting industries such as lead and chemical plants, for nuclear tests and for agricultural experiments that drained the ground water. 'Kazakhstan was just a junk heap where Russia threw all its garbage,' said Olzhas Suleimenov.[36] In 1988 eight cities were

listed as overpolluted even by Soviet standards. The largest single cause
of pollution is the enormous Ekibastuz power plant in the northwest,
which runs on low-grade coal. The 450-kilometre-long Lake Balkhash,
west of Alma Ata, became heavily polluted after copper smelters were
set up on its shores in the 1930s. Bird and other lake life is practically
extinct, while the drawing of water supplies from the lake means that
40 per cent of Kazakhstan's population are drinking polluted water.
The region suffers from high levels of viral hepatitis, some 470 cases
per 100,000 people.[37]

The most dramatic issue for the Nevada movement has been the
nonchalant way that the Soviet armed forces used Semipalatinsk as
first an above-ground and then an underground nuclear testing site.
Since 1949 some 467 nuclear tests have been carried out at the site,
which is north of Lake Balkhash and east of Karganda. Above-ground
testing was finally banned by the 1963 Nuclear Test Ban Treaty. Olzas
Suleimenov gathered together a group of intellectuals and scientists on
28 February 1989 in Alma Ata to protest against two underground
nuclear tests in the same month, which had created huge shock waves
and a radioactive cloud over northern Kazakhstan. Within a few days
the movement collected over 1 million signatures in the streets for an
appeal that called for an end to all nuclear tests by both superpowers.
Following numerous demonstrations, the CPKZ was forced to pass a
resolution calling for the closure of the site. The Soviet army has not
conducted any tests at Semipalatinsk since October 1989.[38]

From 24 to 26 May 1990 Nevada organized the Soviet Union's first
international anti-nuclear conference. 'Brothers, citizens of the Earth,'
began the conference's main appeal. 'Our steppe is shaken by nuclear
explosions and we cannot keep silent any longer. There is forty years
of nuclear tests, which contained thousands of Hiroshimas. Fear for
the future poisons our consciousness. We are afraid of drinking water,
of taking food, of giving birth to our children.'[39] Alma Ata, the sleepy
Kazakh capital, had seen nothing like the May days of the conference.
Some four hundred nuclear scientists, doctors, experts and Green
activists from around the world arrived to participate and to congratu-
late the Soviet Union's first mass-based anti-nuclear movement. Since
the 1950s, Kazakh nomads herding their flocks around the Semipalatinsk
site had suffered massive doses of radioactive fallout. Children were
born blind, mute, deaf, without limbs or fingers and with other de-
fects. Hasen Alikenov, a nomad, said that since 1986 he had already
buried his wife, son, sister and nephew who had all died of cancer.
Doctors with Nevada said the mortality rate of the region is three
times higher than a decade ago. At least forty nomads are known to
have been used as guinea pigs to study the after-effects of a nuclear

explosion in the 1950s. Nevada claimed that 147 young Kazakhs had committed suicide because of their illnesses.[40]

On 28 August 1991, a week after the abortive coup attempt in Moscow, President Nazarbayev announced that the Semipalatinsk site would be closed down and compensation given for the victims of nuclear tests. In June 1992 the government declared the area around the site an ecological disaster zone, banned all agricultural activities and invited foreign specialists to help eradicate the effects of nuclear testing. By then the Nevada movement had developed into a bustling opposition party. On 5 October 1991 Nevada turned itself into the People's Congress of Kazakhstan at a large meeting in Alma Ata which was addressed by Nazarbayev himself. The new party, a broad front organization that now advocates speedy privatization, embraces many Asian nationalities living in Kazakhstan but few Russians.

An equally sensitive environmental and political issue is the future of the Baikonour cosmodrome. The home of the Soviet space programme and rocket testing facilities for the military, Baikonour was the most secret of all the Soviet Union's military installations. Situated on the Syrdarya river near the Aral Sea, even its real name, Leninsk, was never used and it is not marked on any map of the former Soviet Union. All Soviet space flights have taken off from Baikonour, where tens of thousands of people and more than twenty thousand troops live in an artificially created city on the steppe.[41]

The base is now controlled by CIS forces and is off limits to ordinary Kazakhs, who have been demanding more information as to what goes on there. The base costs 1 billion roubles a year to run and no single republic, not even Russia, is willing to foot the entire bill. Although there is now an agreement amongst all CIS states to maintain the base and share the cost, there is no agreement about whose jurisdiction the base should come under. The confusion about Baikonour was compounded on 20 December 1991 – on the eve of Gorbachev's resignation – when an SS-19 ICBM was launched from the base for a test flight. The Americans protested that the launch was a violation of arms control agreements, while many Kazakhs protested that such tests were being carried out from Kazakh soil by Russia without their government's approval.[42] In February 1992 Kazakh soldiers serving at Baikonour protested against the treatment being meted out by their Russian officers, and in the ensuing violence, three soldiers were killed and several barracks were set on fire.

With almost total disregard for the people or the environment, almost everything the Soviet Union did or touched in Kazakhstan has led to disaster. The tragedy is heightened by the fact that under wise management and efficient technology, the Soviet Union could have extracted far more from Kazakhstan than it ever did. Much Soviet investment in mining and heavy industry took place during World War Two. By the 1960s Kazakhstan had the third-largest gross national product of the Soviet Union's fifteen republics. Ninety different minerals were discovered in significant quantities in the region. By 1989 Kazakhstan supplied 25 per cent of the former Soviet Union's coal, 7 per cent of its gold, 50 per cent of its silver, 27 per cent of its electrical energy, 26 per cent of its agricultural products, 8 per cent of non-ferrous metals and 7 per cent of ferrous metals. Large quantities of chrome, zinc, cadmium, beryllium, copper, manganese and uranium were mined, while building materials and the raw materials for cement and other mineral-based products were also produced.

There are vast reserves of iron ore in the Kustanai Basin in the northwest of the republic that were discovered by chance in the 1950s when a pilot working for a prospecting party was amazed to see that the compass in his aeroplane began to whirl about for no apparent reason. It was later discovered that he had flown over some of the largest deposits of iron ore in the world. An enormous iron and steel industry was set up close to these deposits. In 1991 Kazakhstan produced 135 million tons of coal from the huge Karaganda and Ekibastuz coalfields north of Alma Ata, 26 million tons of oil from the Caspian Sea region, 8 million cubic metres of gas and 2,000 different items of machinery. In 1989 it supplied 27 per cent of the former Soviet Union's electricity through five thermal power stations built near the Ekibastuz coalfields. Transmission lines were constructed to transfer the electricity to Siberia, the Urals and European Russia.[43] The republic's main imports from other republics have been machine tools, timber and processed timber products.

The post-independence economic crisis hit industrial workers extremely hard, especially those in farflung regions. Food and consumer goods dried up as the transport network became ineffective and the dwindling central planning was not yet replaced by a market economy. In January 1992 tens of thousands of coal miners went on strike because of the shortages. Three quarters of the republic's coal mines were closed and the steel industry shut down, until the government agreed to allocate 10 billion in roubles as subsidies for bread and meat for the workers.

The government was unprepared for the break-up of the Soviet Union. Fixing exchange values was difficult when exports such as minerals had never been priced on the international market before. Moreover Kazakhstan was still tied to provide goods to other republics through a complex maze of treaties, and there was no law on the repatriation of profits by foreign companies. 'We are still paying for our goods with commodities. It is very complex to pay in dollars. We don't know how to convert our currency into dollars,' Prime Minister Sergei Tereshchenko said in December 1992.[44] The horrendous bureaucratic maze that still operated meant that even direct approval for a project by Nazarbayev himself could still lead to interminable delays. There was no housing available to rent to foreign businessmen, no decent hotels and a virtually complete lack of modern communications with the outside world. The only quick international telephone connection was in the Prime Minister's office. All other calls had to be routed through Moscow and booked a day in advance – all this in a country the size of India.

A month after independence, in Alma Ata, the shops were emptying fast and the prices of rotting cabbages in the free bazaar became astronomical. On the black market the dollar was king. Within ten minutes of foreigners checking into a hotel, well-dressed Kazakh women would be outside the door of their rooms with handbags stuffed full of roubles, wanting to buy dollars. Concierges demanded dollars for washing clothes, and the taxi drivers did not stop unless one waved dollar bills in the air. There was no faith in the economy or the rouble and an underground mafia was running a parallel dollar economy that was intensely resented by ordinary working people, who were still living on rouble salaries.

The economic crisis that existed all over Central Asia at the end of 1991 was short-lived in Kazakhstan: within a year there was a significant improvement. The difference was partly created by the spurt of Western interest in Kazakhstan's vast oil and gas fields. The Soviet Union had developed Kazakhstan's oil industry along the Caspian Sea, which produced some 26 million tons of oil in 1989 despite the backward technology that was being used. In the dry, blistering heat of Mangyshlak Oblast on the eastern Caspian shore, where the desert was long considered uninhabitable, an entirely new town – Shevchenko – was built twenty years ago to cope with the oil boom.

In recent years Kazakhstan has tried hard to lure foreign investment to develop the oil industry. After four years of negotiations with Chevron Corporation, the fourth-largest US oil company, Kazakhstan signed a letter of intent in May 1992 for a joint venture in the Tenghiz and Korelev oilfields near the Caspian Sea. A final agreement was signed a year later. The estimated oil reserves here are 25 billion barrels – equal to the size of Kuwait's oil reserves. Chevron would make an initial $1.5 billion investment to explore 4,000 square kilometres. Kazakhstan would receive some 80 per cent of the revenues. Initially, 60,000 barrels of oil a day would be extracted, and a new gas treatment plant is being built at Tenghiz to double the capacity of gas production.

Chevron may also build two more gas plants.[45] Oman announced that it would help Kazakhstan and Chevron to build an oil pipeline to either the Black Sea or the Gulf, making Kazakhstan independent of troublesome pipelines running through the former Soviet Union.

The Chevron deal triggered a sudden explosion of interest on the part of Western oil and gas companies. The release of enormous energy reserves after the break-up of the Soviet Union, relative political stability, and the most determined drive to privatize the economy of anywhere in Central Asia encouraged Western investors to see Kazakhstan as a new Asian tiger. 'Kazakhstan will see the highest level of Western investment in the energy sector for the next five to ten years – there is just much more stability here than anywhere else,' said Jack Van Wagner, external relations manager of British Gas.[46] In September British Gas and the Italian state-run oil firm Agip signed the deal of the century with Kazakhstan – to explore and exploit the massive Karachaganak oil and gas fields in the Urals in western Kazakhstan with a possible investment of up to $5 billion. Another deal was signed with the French oil firm Elf Aquataine to explore 19,000 square kilometres in central Kazakhstan.

'We are having very intensive negotiations with the oil industry all over the world. We need the experience of these countries,' said Uzakbai Karabalin, chief of the oil and gas department in the ministry of energy. 'We realize very well the difficulty of the transition period from socialism to a market economy, but we are moving fast.'[47] Kazakhstan's oil reserves were estimated by Western companies at 100 billion barrels, while gas reserves stood at 2.4 trillion cubic metres. The figures were being constantly revised upwards. Kazakhstan produced 28 million tons of oil in 1992 – 2 million tons more than the year before, a remarkable feat considering the economic slump across the former Soviet Union. With domestic consumption pegged at around 18 million tons and an annual domestic increase of 10–15 per cent, Kazakhstan had a large surplus to sell.

Suddenly Alma Ata hotel rooms were full of sharp-suited Houston oil executives. In their spare time they hired army helicopters to go skiing and bear hunting in the Tien Shan mountains. Negotiating with the Kazakhs was no walkover for the multinationals. Intensely conscious of public opinion, which suspected that the government was selling out cheaply to foreign oil companies, and the constant rumour of bribes and corruption at the top, the Kazakhstan government held out for the best deal through open tenders. In all joint ventures the government insisted on foreign companies investing in the social sector. Both Chevron and British Gas have had to offer large financial packages covering the environment, housing, water supplies, telecommunications and ensuring the training of a Kazakh technical workforce. No other republic has enforced such conditions and got away with them.

The potential bonanza in Kazakhstan has attracted numerous foreign companies. By the end of 1992 some three hundred joint venture agreements had been signed in mineral development, food processing and the oil industry. While no more than 10 per cent were expected to get off the ground, American companies, followed by the Germans, Turks, Koreans and Swiss, were showing keen investment interest. The International Monetary Fund (IMF) set up a permanent mission in Alma Ata and in 1992 began negotiations with the government for a $1.2 billion loan spread over three years – a massive investment for such a small population and a clear indication for Western businesses that the IMF considered the regime stable and willing to reform.

Kazakhstan's other principal attraction has been that it was the first CIS republic to implement wide-ranging market reforms. The basic privatization legislation was passed in December 1991. A voucher scheme was introduced, enabling citizens to buy their flats and shops, a year before such a scheme was introduced in Russia. Vouchers could also be used to buy shares in factories. By the end of 1992, some 40 per cent of Alma Ata dwellings had been sold to private owners. To contain the food crisis, the government ordered all food processing plants to be privatized by March 1993. Laws were steadily passed through parliament guaranteeing foreign investment and the repatriation of profits abroad, as well as comprehensive legislation regarding oil concessions, sub-soil reserves, taxation and other matters essential for developing the oil industry.

Kazakhstan's economy was still being dictated by Russia's downward spin. In 1992 inflation was running at 2,000 per cent, the same as in Russia, after the rouble had plunged from 250 to 400 to the dollar in October 1992 and on down to 800 in early 1993. Economists estimated that in 1992 GNP in the CIS as a whole and Kazakhstan had declined by 15 per cent and industrial production had declined by 33 per cent. Unemployment was rising rapidly, accounting for 25 per cent to 35 per cent of the labour force in Kazakhstan by 1993. '20 per cent of Kazakhstan's enterprises are non-profitable and every single one faces bankruptcy. Some three hundred enterprises have had to be closed down for short periods owing to shortages,' said Serik Akhanov, deputy director of the Supreme Economic Council.[48] Much of the present foreign investment in the oil industry will only start to give returns after several years. In the meantime Nazarbayev will have to hold the fort by curbing political dissent while retooling industry and agriculture to deliver more goods to the people.

The oil boom will also help to modernize agriculture. The total cultivated area of Kazakhstan is now 35.8 million hectares, compared to the 4.2 million hectares that were tilled in 1913 and the 6.8 million hectares tilled in 1940. Between 1954 and 1959, when the Virgin Lands Scheme was at its height, 23 million hectares of land were opened up and 544 state grain farms were established. In 1988 some 22 million tons of grain were produced, as well as large amounts of sugar beet, sunflower seed, vegetables, fruit and potatoes. In the 1950s the rural infrastructure was drastically modernized: 250,000 tractors were brought into use and some 5,000 small rural power stations were set up for generating electricity on the farms. Since then, however, agriculture has stagnated, cultivated land has reverted to grass, and crops are lost for the lack of storage and transportation.

A failure of the wheat harvest in 1991, in which only 11.9 million tons were produced, was turned into a bumper crop in 1992 with the production of 32 million tons, grown on 22 million hectares. The 15 million tons surplus could have earned the republic $1.5 billion. However, 8 million tons was earmarked for export to Russia, a large part of that sold at a fixed price in exchange for crucial machinery, spare parts and oil equipment. When Kazakhstan seriously enters the international wheat market it will affect world wheat prices in a big way. Not surprisingly US and Australian diplomats are closely monitoring international wheat sales from Kazakhstan. At present, however, the chronic state of storage facilities means that up to one third of the wheat crop is lost before it even reaches the market.

Some 70 per cent of Kazakhs still live in poor rural areas and many of them spend up to six months of the year away in the mountains with their flocks. With 9.2 million cattle, 35 million sheep and goats, 3 million pigs and 1.5 million horses, livestock rearing is still a vital part of the economy and allows many Kazakhs to continue a seminomadic lifestyle on the steppe.[49] Although Kazakh nomads may live for part of the year in flats on collective farms, in the mountains they still live in yurts. They stick closely to their clans, refrain from marrying outside the wider tribe and maintain traditions of hospitality and culture that are centuries old.

Individual ownership of farmland remains forbidden, but soon after independence the Kazakh government began a privatization experiment to allow farmers to rent land from collectives on fifty-year leases. This land can be inherited by future generations and rent is paid under a deferred system in cash or crops. Some 2,500 farms were rented, but the experiment has almost collapsed because there was no infrastructure to support private farmers. Seed, fertilizer, tractors and other machinery were unavailable and in some areas farmers could not even manage to buy diesel fuel. Outside Alma Ata, families have returned to their former collective farms and given up their leases because they could not raise loans. Old-style communist bureaucrats in the government are now using the failure to insist that private farms are an impossibility. Liberals are asking for a much bigger package of incentives, possibly with World Bank help, before further experiments are made.

In the meantime the government is encouraging collectives and co-operatives to become genuinely co-operative by distributing shares to the workers. Co-operatives existed in the communist system, but workers only held formal shares because the co-operatives were indivisible. Now the government is passing legislation to make the funds divisible for some 300 co-operatives in 1993. In October 1992 Rudek Mnacakanyan, the Armenian farm manager of the vineyard and collective farm who opened this chapter, hoped to change his farm into a co-operative by forming a joint stock company with shares for the workers. Pensioners would receive free shares; share distribution for others would depend on their length of service at the farm. Mnacakanyan, who had run the farm for twenty-four years, would remain manager and receive more shares than anyone else. The workers appeared enthusiastic about the idea, but the lack of legislation due to the political infighting in Alma Ata regarding the land issue was holding up the process. 'Since 1985 the government has been telling us we are in a transition period but this transition period is going on for ever. Real change has still to come,' said Mnacakanyan.[50]

The traumatic change from socialism to capitalism and the market has been most readily taken up by women, who envisage greater freedom and more alternative lifestyles being made available. The Kazakh nomadic culture ensured that women were never veiled, and out of all the Turkic-speaking women of Central Asia, Kazakh women are among the least restricted – by cultural traditions or by Islamic values. The Kazakh urban woman is more modern and cosmopolitan than her female Russian counterparts.

There has been an explosion of efforts by young women to learn English so that they can take up jobs in joint venture companies and work with foreigners. In 1991 there were two to three applicants for every seat in the republic's most prestigious language school, which has 2,000 students. In 1992 there were seven to eight candidates for every seat. 'The world is opening up. Never before have our students seen such opportunities for making money. Everyone wants to work for a foreign company,' said Zara Dashtamirova, head of the English philology department. The institute has begun offering English language courses for managers from local factories, farms and other state run organizations, so that in each at least one of their staff, many of whom are women, can converse in English.

Russians outnumber Kazakhs in Alma Ata, and the institute has more Russian pupils than any other nationality but there is growing resentment amongst them that the best jobs are now going to Kazakh women, even though their language skills may not be so good. Foreign embassies, for instance, prefer hiring Kazakh rather than Russian translators, to create a good impression in government offices. This element of reverse discrimination is a repudiation of seventy-five years of communist rule in which Russians were always favoured with the best jobs.[51]

What ordinary Kazakhs fear most of all after independence is the potential for ethnic strife. Without support from a strong centre in Moscow or the Soviet armed forces to maintain law and order, government officials are equally fearful of a minor ethnic dispute getting out of control. Meanwhile local Russians fear a Kazakh backlash. Although they still enjoy a better standing of living, jobs and housing than they would if they were to return to Russia, they have had to come to terms with the fact that they are no longer the master race in Kazakhstan. Many Russians are equally resentful of Boris Yeltsin, who by pushing for the break-up of the Soviet Union left them in the lurch, without any clear backing for their political and economic rights in the Asian republics. The one hundred other nationalities in Kazakhstan, many of them cooped up in ethnic ghettos on farms and on factory sites, also fear for the future. The smallest of inter-ethnic clashes have left many Kazakhs fearing the worst, such as a clash in October 1992 between Kazakhs and Chechens in which four Kazakhs were killed in the town of Ust-Kamenogorsk.[52]

Nazarbayev has always been supported by local Russians and other minorities because of his moderate views. However, a strong undercurrent of polarization between Kazakh nationalists and Russians is running through the republic, although Nazarbayev denies it. ('We are the only republic which people are not leaving. We are multi-national and the ethnic problem will only become acute if the commonwealth disintegrates and economic problems worsen,' he has said.[53]) A new movement amongst Russians in the north is also gaining ground. In December 1992 some 15,000 Russians demonstrated in Ust-Kamenogorsk demanding that Russian be recognized along with Kazakh as a state language and that dual citizenship with Russia be given to Russians. It was a sign of the new Russian belligerence and a result of the intense debate that had taken place over the language issue ever since a draft constitution was published in April 1992 and the public were encouraged to discuss it.

When the constitution was finally adopted on 29 January 1993, it endorsed Kazakh as the official language and made Russian the social language between people. It decreed that the president of the republic must have a command of Kazakh, a provision strongly objected to by Russian parliamentary deputies. According to them, this clause made it impossible for 60 per cent of the population to stand as president. Russian deputies also argued that the seeds of social and ethnic unrest and anti-Russian discrimination had been sown by the new constitution. Kazakh nationalists meanwhile insisted that not enough was being done to nurture a sense of Kazakh nationhood. The fear that the majority Russian population in the north could decide to opt out by seceding from Kazakhstan and joining up with Russia remains a constant anxiety for Nazarbayev.

No ethnic issue has been more sensitive for Europe than the fate of the Volga Germans. During World War Two, Stalin dissolved the Volga Republic and ordered the mass deportation of Germans to Central Asia. Between 300,000 to 600,000 died in prison trains and camps. There are some 2 million Germans in the former Soviet Union, of whom 960,000 live in Kazakhstan. Between 1989 and 1992, more than 400,000 Volga Germans resettled in Germany. Other, more militant Volga Germans are demanding the re-creation of the German Volga Republic – a cause supported by the German government, which is worried over the influx of refugees. The Bonn government has given $66 million to Russia to resettle the Germans in the Volga, but Russians living in the Volga are opposing this.[54] In any case, most ethnic Germans prefer to migrate from Kazakhstan to Germany.

The ethnic factor in the future stability of Kazakhstan is closely linked with the revival of Islam. Historically the Kazakhs are the least Islamicized of the Central Asian peoples, and they have undergone large-scale Russification. Islamic fundamentalism amongst Kazakhs is rare compared to Uzbekistan and Tajikistan. Nevertheless Islam now holds a fascination for Kazakhs, not just for religious reasons but because it is a part of their historical and national identity which they want to assert and which makes them decisively different from Russians. After the civil war in Tajikistan erupted, many Kazakhs expressed fears that the conflict would spread. 'Islamic parties and outside countries have played a disastrous role in Tajikistan. All this could degenerate into a very great calamity for the whole region,' said President Nazarbayev.[55]

Until January 1990 Kazakhstan's Muslims were governed by the pliant, Soviet-backed Muslim Religious Board based in Tashkent. However the ambitious Qazi of Alma Ata, Radbek Nisanbai, staged a minor coup on 12 January 1990, having himself elected grand mufti of Kazakhstan and setting up his own religious board, independent of

Tashkent. A short, round-faced man who is politically aggressive and intensely ambitious, he is also a deputy to the Kazakhstan Parliament and has begun to create an effective power base around himself.[56] He has played politics astutely, throwing his weight behind ecological and anti-nuclear movements, but has never crossed the limits to join the opposition. Nisanbai opened Kazakhstan's first madrasah in 1991, published his own translation of the Koran into the Kazakh language and began a monthly Islamic newspaper. At least 250 new mosques were built during 1990–91 through public subscriptions. 'Perestroika has been useful for Islam. Our people now want more Korans, mosques and Islamic schools. I will give that to them,' he said.[57] In 1992 Nisanbai set a target of building 300 more mosques.

Many of the faithful who come to pray every Friday at local mosques belong to non-Kazakh minorities, who see Islam as an effective means to distance themselves from both the Kazakhs and the Russians and as a means to assert their ethnic identity with their national homeland. These young men – Uzbeks, Tajiks, Chechen, Tartars, Uighurs or Mongols – are also the most energetic in distributing literature, in setting up study groups on the Koran and in forming an effective base for the Islamic Renaissance Party and other Islamic fundamentalist parties. Thus the revival of Islam has added to the ethnic complexity and tensions in Kazakhstan.

Kazakhstan is the centre of gravity in Central Asia, and when President Nursultan Nazarbayev speaks he has the political influence, the nuclear clout and the international standing to speak for all of Central Asia. At home, his political standing was temporarily damaged by the creation of the CIS and Russia's arrogant attitude towards him, but he has recovered from that sufficiently to assert once again his authority on a people who, seeing the turmoil all around them in Central Asia, view Nazarbayev as for the moment the only salvation. Kazakhstan faces immense problems: the potential for ethnic strife, a huge Russian population, environmental damage, nuclear weapons on its soil and long borders with other Central Asian states far more unstable than Kazakhstan. Nevertheless Nazarbayev's acumen and integrity has brought a level of stability to Kazakhstan that even the most optimistic could not have hoped for.

Notes

1. Ahmed Rashid, 'Ethnic Tensions Simmer in Stalin's Dumping Ground', *Independent* (London), 7 June 1990.

2. I. Svanberg (1990) 'The Kazakhs' in Graham Smith (ed.) *The Nationalities Question in the Soviet Union*, Longman, London.

3. Interview with President Nazarbayev, 8 December 1991.

4. R. Weekes (1978) *Muslim Peoples: a world ethnographic survey*, Greenwood Press, USA.

5. E. Maillart (1985) *Turkestan Solo*, Century, London.

6. Weekes.

7. I am extremely grateful for the research into ancient Kazakh history by Pakistan's ambassador to Russia, Ashraf Jahangir Qazi. Future reference to these reports will be under Qazi, Pakistan Foreign Office.

8. H. Oraltay, 'The Alash Movement in Turkestan', *Central Asian Survey*, Vol. 4, No. 2. For further details on the confusion between the two names Kazakh and Kyrgyz, see Chapter 6.

9. Maillart. These figures are also given by other historians.

10. Qazi, Pakistan Foreign Office.

11. See Chapter 6 for further details.

12. Oraltay.

13. A. Bennigsen and E. Wimbush (1979) *Muslim National Communism in the Soviet Union*, University of Chicago Press, USA. This book has excellent mini-biographies of these leaders.

14. Quoted in Ibid.

15. Oraltay.

16. Ibid. See also H. Carrere D'Encausse (1979) *Decline of an Empire: the Soviet Socialist Republics in revolt*, Newsweek Books, USA.

17. Bennigsen and Wimbush.

18. B. Nahaylo and V. Swohboda (1990) *Soviet Disunion: a history of the nationalities problem in the USSR*, Hamish Hamilton, London.

19. R. Conquest (1988) *Harvest of Sorrow*, Arrow Books, London.

20. Ibid.

21. A. Solzhenitsyn (1991) *Rebuilding Russia*, Harvill, London.

22. G. Hosking (1990) *A History of the Soviet Union*, Fontana, London.

23. David Remnick, 'Kazakhstan's Off Limits Hero', *Washington Post*, 29 December 1990.

24. D. Doder and L. Branson (1990) *Gorbachev: heretic in the Kremlin*, Futura Books, London.

25. David Remnick, 'Kazakhstan: a republic rebels', *Washington Post*, 1 November 1990.

26. Qazi, Pakistan Foreign Office.

27. Interview by the author with a Kazakh journalist who did not wish to be named.

28. Ahmed Rashid, 'Picking up the Pieces', *Far Eastern Economic Review*, 9 January 1992.

29. Andrew Higgins, 'Kazakhs in Thrall with a Colonial Past', *Sunday Independent*, 14 April 1992.

30. Interview with president Nazarbayev by the author, 8 December 1991.

31. Reuters, 'Kazakh Leader Losing Faith in CIS', *Dawn*, 24 April 1992.

32. Reuters, 'Russia, Kazakhstan Sign Military Pact', *Dawn*, 26 May 1992.

33. Agence France Press, 'China, Kazakhstan Sign Economic Accord', *Frontier Post*, 27 February 1992.

34. Personal notes from interviews with Kazakh officials, politicians and journalists.

35. B. Brown, 'The Public Role in Perestroika in Central Asia', *Central Asia Survey*, Vol. 9, No. 1.

36. Interview with Olzhas Suleimenov, May 1990, Alma Ata.

37. R. Mnatsakanian, (1992) *The Environmental Legacy of the Former Soviet Union*, Centre of Human Ecology, University of Edinburgh.

38. Interviews by the author with Nevada activists in Alma Ata in 1990 and 1992.

39. Nevada Appeal, 6 August 1990. This formed the basic document of the conference.

40. Notes taken at the conference and interviews with Nevada officials and victims of the nuclear tests.

41. Interviews with Kazakh officials, 1990 and 1991.

42. Jeffrey Smith, 'US Asks Russia to Explain Missile Test', *Dawn*, 23 January 1992.

43. A. Kekilbayev (1987) *Kazakhstan*, Novosti Press, Moscow. Many of the figures come from notes taken during interviews with Kazakh officials.

44. Rashid, 'Picking up the Pieces'.

45. Ahmed Rashid (in Alma Ata), 'The Next Frontier', *Far Eastern Economic Review*, 4 February 1993.

46. Ibid.

47. Ibid.

48. Ahmed Rashid (in Alma Ata), 'President Nazarbayev Still Faces Major Problems', *Nation* (Lahore), 24 October 1992.

49. Interviews with Kazakh officials during visits to Alma Ata.

50. Ahmed Rashid (in Tashkent), 'Toil and Trouble on the Land', *Far Eastern Economic Review*, 3 December 1992.

51. Interviews with students and teachers at the institute by the author, October 1992, Alma Ata.

52. Reuters, 'Four Kazakhs Die in a clash with Chechens', *News* (Islamabad), 19 October 1992.

53 Interview with President Nazarbayev, 8 December 1991.

54. Daniel Benjamin, 'Centuries Later, Homeward Bound', *Time*, 13 January 1992. Also personal interviews with Volga Germans in 1990 and 1991.

55. Sylie Kauffman, 'Kazakhs Plead Russia's Cause', *Guardian Weekly*, 27 September 1992.

56. Ahmed Rashid, 'Bless Perestroika and send Korans', *Independent*, 4 June 1990.

57. Ibid.

6

The Cradle of
the Earth – Kyrgyzstan

The Kyrgyz nomads, once part of Genghis Khan's Golden Horde, traditionally produced enough buttermilk, yogurt and cheese to feed the entire Soviet Union. Tucked away in a corner of Central Asia and surrounded on all sides by massive mountain ranges, they are the most isolated of all the former Soviet republics, with the least available resources to create an independent economy. Yet since 1990, well before the demise of the Soviet empire, the revamped Kyrgyz leadership has set in motion the most ambitious economic reforms in Central Asia – moves that could turn Kyrgyzstan into a Central Asian Switzerland.

The capital Beshkeh, formerly Frunze, is surrounded by some of the highest mountains in the world – the Tien Shan and the Alatau ranges. Covered in snow even in June, the mountains tower over the city giving a sense that one is living in a large bowl. During the long winter months, icy winds howl down the streets, which come to an abrupt end at the foot of the mountains. Thick mists that reduce visibility to zero and suspend air traffic can cover Beshkeh for days. When the sun does re-emerge it is a pale, cold shadow of its former self, which forces the locals to fasten more tightly their thick fur jackets.

The Kyrgyz have always called their land 'Altyn Beshik' – the Golden Cradle or Homeland. For two thousand years, from their mountaintop pastures, Kyrgyz shepherds have looked down upon a vast cradle made up of snow-covered mountains which they called the Wings of the Earth. Ninety-three per cent of the Republic's 198,500 square kilometres of territory is made up of mountains, and nowhere does the land surface fall below 500 metres above sea level. The highest mountain is Victory Peak (7,429 metres), which stands in the immense Mustag massif, one of the world's largest areas of glaciers, which covers 1,570 square kilometres, equivalent to the entire Caucasus. If all the ice in the republic's territory were melted, it would be under 3 metres of water.[1]

Water is everywhere. As a result of tens of thousands of years of glaciation, there are some 3,000 lakes, continuously filled by rivers flowing down from the mountains. Many of the lakes are more than 3,000 metres above sea level; others, such as Lake Maerzbacker, are so high that huge icebergs move from shore to shore within the lake. Those lakes below the tree line are surrounded by magnificent forests, which in summer climb up the mountain slopes in a profusion of colour. The slow-growing juniper tree is revered by the nomads and called the Queen of the Forest. It takes centuries for junipers to grow: some are 2,000 years old.

The population of Kyrgyzstan has always been vastly outnumbered by its livestock. Today 10 million sheep and goats, 2 million horses, yaks and cattle and half a million pigs feed on the lush grasslands, tended by shepherds and farmers whose lifestyle has changed little over the centuries. Nomadism is such an ingrained way of life that even the communist system proved incapable and eventually unwilling to break it down.

Kyrgyzstan is bordered on the east by China, while to the west lie Uzbekistan and Kazakhstan, whose capital Alma Ata is just a four-hour drive from Beshkeh across the steppe. To the south are Tajikistan and the Pamirs – another towering range of mountains. Landlocked Kyrgyzstan has always been one of the most inaccessible regions of the world. Few explorers dared to cross the forbidding Tien Shan mountains, and the first serious Russian expedition to map the region only arrived in 1856. So little was known of the region that even until the 1917 Revolution, Russians never bothered to differentiate between the Kazakhs and the Kyrgyz, calling them both 'Kyrgyz' and simply appending the word *kara* or 'black' to the ethnic Kyrgyz.[2] Ethnically there is little difference between the Kazakhs and the Kyrgyz. Coming from the same racial stock, the Kara-Kyrgyz were the mountain dwellers while the Kyrgyz (now Kazakh) were the inhabitants of the steppes. Kyrgyzstan itself was an artificial creation of Stalin's, founded in an attempt to divide the Kazakh nation into two separate entities. The Kyrgyz and Kazakh languages, customs and traditions are very similar.

Since the communist revolution the Kyrgyz have been swamped by Russian settlers who saw great opportunities for farming. Today the Kyrgyz number only 52.4 per cent of the 4.4 million population. Some 21.5 per cent of the people are Russian and 12.9 per cent are Uzbek; some eighty other ethnic groups also make their home here. The Kyrgyz are a Mongol people who speak a Turkic dialect called Kipchak which belongs to the Altaic family of languages. They number over 2 million people with 100,000 living in Chinese Xinjiang and some 35,000 living in the Wakhan corridor of Afghanistan who migrated to Turkey after the Afghan war began in 1979.[3] Another 200,000 Kyrgyz are scattered in the other Central Asian republics, where they are predominantly farm workers. In Kyrgyzstan itself, 85 per cent of the Kyrgyz live in the countryside.

The Kyrgyz are Sunni Muslims, but a strong streak of pre-Islamic Shamanism is still evident in much of their traditions and daily life. Shamans still thrive and are often called upon to intercede between the living and the spirits of the dead and they conduct funerals and other rituals. Pre-Islamic traditions continue, such as belief in the spiritual powers of mountains, rivers and the sun – beliefs that are passed on from generation to generation in the host of legends, epic poems and stories that are still part of Kyrgyz culture. Many nomads still keep a cradle made of juniper wood, considered to be the 'eternal tree', in the most prominent spot in their yurts.[4]

As with other tribal, nomadic people the history of the Kyrgyz has come down in the form of ballads and songs – none more famous than the *Manas* – a chronicle of the history of the ancient Kyrgyz people, which if recited in its entirety is longer than the *Iliad* and the *Odyssey* put together. Manas was a legendary hero who, mounted on a winged charger, performed incredible feats for the nation. The legends of Manas and the idea of a powerful avenger who can destroy the enemies of the Kyrgyz have sustained the tribes over the centuries in their bitter history at the hands of the Mongols, Russians and other conquerors. Frequently defeated and crushed by their enemies and repeatedly forced to take to their mountain fastnesses to avoid massacre, plague or famine, the Kyrgyz have created myths full of suffering and calamity.

The earliest recorded inhabitants of modern-day Kyrgyzstan were the Sakas, whose tribal confederacy established a kingdom in the region around the eighth century BC. The Sakas traded with China and Persia and remained defiant until they were conquered by Cyrus the Great of Persia, who employed them to fight in his armies against Alexander the Great. Defeated by the Greeks, the Sakas then joined Alexander in his invasion of India. The Sakas were pushed into Afghanistan and northwest India by subsequent tribal invasions from the north.[5] The first recorded evidence of the Kyrgyz people comes from Chinese chronicles dating back to the second millennium BC, which record the existence of some forty Turkic-speaking clans living along the River Yenisei in southern Siberia. One meaning of the word *kyrgyz* is 'forty clans'. The other meaning is 'indestructible'.[6]

Southern Siberia was one of the great breeding grounds of early Central Asian civilizations, and like other nomadic races the early Kyrgyz left behind rock paintings and stone idols in their nomadic

camps, which archaeologists have subsequently discovered both in
Siberia and along the route south that the Kyrgyz took. During their
migration south and in the Tien Shan, the Kyrgyz merged and inter-
married with other tribal clans: the Uzuns, the Sacae, the Huns and
the Orkhon Turks. An early description of the Kyrgyz was made by
the famous Chinese pilgrim and traveller Hiuan Tsang. Born in AD
602, Hiuan Tsang crossed the Tien Shan in 629, and described his
journey with the same sense of awe at the bleakness of the mountains,
the staggering fertility and beauty of the valleys and the great lakes that
filled the glacier-cut depressions as Russian travellers would feel 1,200
years later.[7] In AD 630 on the plain of Tokmak, northeast of present-
day Beshkeh, the Chinese traveller came across a gathering of the
ancient Kyrgyz clans under their great khan T'ong.

> The horses of these barbarians were exceedingly numerous. The Khan
> dwelt in a vast tent ornamented with flowers of gold, so bright they dazzled
> the eyes of the beholder. In front of his tent long mats had been stretched
> by order of his officers and there were seated in two rows, all clad in
> glittering habits of brocade, some 200 of his officers surrounded him ... the
> remainder of his forces was made up of cavalry mounted on camels or on
> horses, dressed in furs or fine wool and bearing long lances, banners and
> tall bows. So vast was their multitude, they stretched far out of sight.[8]

Six hundred years before Genghis Khan, the Kyrgyz were a formidable power in Central Asia, famous for their fighting prowess and their
hardiness and stamina in coping with living at high altitudes. They
developed fine pottery skills and made superb gold and silver vessels
that have been unearthed by Soviet archaeologists. The Mongol invasions were to change their destiny. It was on the plain of Tokmak in
1207 that Temeudjin routed his Mongol rival Gutchluk, and later
made himself Genghis Khan. The Kyrgyz first resisted the Mongols
but were badly defeated, suffering heavy casualties. Their autonomy
was shattered and the surviving branch of the Kyrgyz was later to join
Genghis Khan in his advance westward.[9]

At the end of the twelfth century the first European travellers
appeared in the region, Italian and French monks who visited Tokmak
and crossed over into China. Tokmak later became the seat of a
Nestorian archbishopric. Southeast of Tokmak is the other major site
of early Kyrgyz history, the great lake of Issyk-Kul where the Kyrgyz
tribes first built settlements after they arrived from southern Siberia.
Situated in a fold of the Tien Shan, the lake is a vast inland sea surrounded on two sides by some of the highest mountains of the world.
Some 182 kilometres long and 57 kilometres wide, the lake is in many
places more than 700 metres deep. Some seventy mountain streams
and rivers flow into it but none flow out of it.

The Mongols called it Iron Lake because of its icy black waters in winter that never froze over. Genghis Khan camped here, as did Tamerlane 150 years later. Legends about its origins and its history form a major part of Kyrgyz folklore. It is widely believed that at the bottom of the lake lie the ruins of an ancient city and civilization that are waiting to be discovered. Today the lake is a haven for fishing, tourism, and sailing and for artists who try to capture the stunning scenery around it on canvas. The lake waters are famous for their curative powers and falconers still come to the lakeside to train their golden eagles as they did centuries ago. Legend has it that falconry originated beside the waters of Issyk-Kul.[10]

The development of the Kyrgyz tribes demonstrates again how the great nomadic nationalities in Central Asia were formed less by the growth of their own numbers than by absorbing the fragments of tribes that floated around them. By the fifteenth century the Kyrgyz had assimilated smaller tribes such as the Kipchaks, the Comans and the Ghuz. Many such tribes were the victims of larger nomadic movements, hunger or defeat in battle. They came to the Kyrgyz for shelter and help, and later became part of their tribal structure.

After the demise of the Mongol empire and the appearance of Islam in the region, the focus of Central Asian history shifted to what is now Uzbekistan and the Ferghana valley. Stalin's division of Ferghana between three republics was to divide what was once a heterogeneous region. In the tenth century the city of Osh in Ferghana became a major centre of Islamic scholarship. Today Osh, populated largely by Uzbeks, is on the Kyrgyz–Uzbek border; in 1990 it was the scene of some of the worst ethnic riots in Central Asia. Archaeologists have discovered ancient irrigation systems and a mound dating to the time of Alexander the Great, which gives Osh a 3,000-year history. Legend has it that a mountain in the centre of the old town was blessed by King Solomon, and today it still bears the name Takht-e-Suleiman or 'the seat of Suleiman'.

For the Kyrgyz, Osh is a second Mecca. Thousands of pilgrims visit the city every year to pray on the mountain and at other Islamic shrines such as the mausoleum of Nabi Ayub (the Job of the Old Testament) and the mosque of the Mogul emperor Babar.[11] In the fourteenth century Zahir-ud Din Mohammed Babar (1483–1530), who founded the Mogul dynasty in India, built a hermitage on the Takht mountain, which overlooks the city. Here at the age of fourteen he retired to carry out *chilla* – the forty days of silent meditation with just bread and water to eat – that Sufis undergo every year. The Kyrgyz have revived Babar's memory and honour him as a Sufi saint. 'Stalin destroyed the shrine that was erected here to wipe out the memory of Babar and our spiritual forefathers. But nobody forgets their history,' said one local historian who helped to rebuild the shrine. At the shrine ageing Sufis sit and tell the story of Babar to pilgrims.

In the Middle Ages the Kyrgyz region produced renowned Islamic scholars. Yousuf (Jusup), a medieval encyclopaedist and philosopher, wrote the first book in the then Turkic language – the epic poem *Kutadgu Bilig* (Knowledge That Gives Happiness). Another Islamic scholar, Mahmud Kashgari, wrote the famous *Dictionary of Turkic Dialects*, which remains one of the original sources of the ancient Turkic languages.[12] But the geographical and political isolation of the region made Kyrgyz nomads peripheral to the empires that rose and fell in Central Asia. Unable to beat back conquerors such as the Uzbeks, they often hired themselves out as mercenaries for other empire builders or retreated into Chinese Turkestan when they wanted to avoid conscription and servitude.

As Russia extended its advance into Central Asia in the nineteenth century, building forts along the Orenburg line, the first Russian explorers reached the Tien Shan. Pyotr Semyonov, with an armed group of Cossacks, was the first to map Lake Issyk-Kul, in 1856. 'A blue emerald set in a frame of silvery mountains,' is how he later described it. Semyonov's exploration and study of the Tien Shan made him world-famous, and other Russia explorers quickly followed.[13]

In the 1850s the Kyrgyz achieved sudden notoriety in Moscow as a Kyrgyz bandit, Izzet Kutebar, threw the whole of Russian-controlled Turkestan into disarray. His band of hard-riding Kyrgyz nomads raided Russian-held towns from Orenburg to the Aral Sea between 1853 and 1858 and military expeditions were mounted to try and catch him. The process of fort building along the line of Russian control was speeded up.[14] In the unprecedented freezing winter of 1859–60, the Kyrgyz suffered a catastrophe, losing 80 per cent of their flocks. Thousands died in the snows of the Tien Shan as people tried to flee to Chinese Turkestan. In the next decade the Kyrgyz chiefs, depleted of resources and starving, had little choice but to accept Russian sovereignty in order to escape economic hardship and attacks by their neighbours.

With Russian control established, the Tsar ordered that millions of acres of prime Kazakh–Kyrgyz land should be given to Russian and Cossack settlers, who were to be exempted from taxes and military service. Every settler received 25 acres of the best grain-producing land and subsidies for fifteen years, as the first of many Russian migrations began into the region. Similar moves in Kazakhstan and other regions of Central Asia in the coming century were to fuel anti-Russian resentment.[15]

The Kyrgyz were forced deeper into the Tien Shan to avoid gangs of rapacious Russians out to steal both their land and their flocks. The last straw was the forced conscription of Kazakhs and Kyrgyz in 1916 for the war effort. The Kyrgyz rebelled and attacked Russian settlements and towns; a Cossack army led by General Aninekov was sent to crush the rebellion. The Cossacks carried out massive reprisals, slaughtering flocks and burning down Kyrgyz villages. Tens of thousands of Kyrgyz fled across the mountains into Chinese Turkestan, which for the Kyrgyz has always been a place of last refuge.[16] Even so, tens of thousands of people died at the hands of the Cossacks, Chinese border gangs and the snows of the Tien Shan.

In 1916 Manap Kendeur, the last great sage and patriarch of the Kyrgyz, who the tribal chiefs had consulted before they staged their rebellion, made a prophetic statement that is now part of clan lore. He took a handful of sand and as it ran through his fingers he said 'Now find the grains that were in my hands.' What he meant was that the Kyrgyz were now completely submerged by the Russians and there was nothing that could be done against them.[17] The Kyrgyz still term the 1916–17 repression the worst period in their entire history and local academics claim that the Kyrgyz may have lost up to one quarter of their population. The massive brutality they experienced at the hands of the Russians is one reason why the Kyrgyz have remained bitter but publicly uncritical of the Russians ever since. This bitterness has not lessened with the passage of time. Instead, within the nomadic traditions of storytelling and oral poetry the tales of those horrifying days have been kept alive and have become more magnified than ever before.

Kyrgyzstan remained outside the immediate orbit of the war between the White and Red armies after the 1917 Revolution. The huge Russian settler presence and the scattered and broken nature of the Kyrgyz nomads allowed the Russians quickly to establish a strong military presence to protect their fellow settlers and create the Communist Party of Kyrgyzstan (CPK), which was to remain dominated by Russian settlers. Many Kyrgyz joined the Basmachi Muslim rebels, but in 1919, after the offer of amnesty to the Basmachis, some 6,000 fighters including hundreds of Kyrgyz surrendered to the Red Army. However a prominent band of Basmachis under the Kyrgyz leader Khal Khodza continued fighting for the next three years.

On 30 April 1918, Kyrgyzstan became part of the Turkestan Autonomous Soviet Socialist Republic within the Russian Federation. A capital was established in the small market town of Beshkeh in 1925. The next year it was renamed Frunze in honour of the conquering Russian general Mikhail Frunze (1885–1925) and the town was connected to the railway line to Tashkent. In 1991 Frunze once again reverted to its original name.[18] In 1924 the Kyrgyz Autonomous Region was formed and then reorganized into the Kyrgyz Autonomous Soviet Socialist Republic on 1 February 1926. On 5 December 1936, Kyrgyzstan joined the USSR as a sovereign Union republic.

Throughout this period the CPK was dominated by local Russians, and the purges of the few Kyrgyz communists in the party began early. In 1925 a group of Kyrgyz communists who called themselves the Thirty complained to party chiefs about the over-extensive use of the Russian language. They were immediately purged from the CPK and their leader Abdurkarim Sydykov was exiled. The others were put on trial and imprisoned. Leaders from other nationalist groups such as the Kyrgyz Poor Peasants Union were also imprisoned.[19] Education in the mother tongue and use of the Arabic script were considered anti-revolutionary; Kyrgyz cadres were refused promotion in the party. In September 1940 a new Kyrgyz alphabet based on Cyrillic was introduced, further widening the gulf between the people and their own language. More purges of Kyrgyz communists took place during the Great Trials in 1937 and 1938 and Kyrgyzstan swiftly became a political backwater with Russians firmly in control of the CPK.

The purges were coupled with stiff but passive resistance by the Kyrgyz clans who fled their homes rather than participate in the 1924 census carried out by the Red Army and the collectivization of their flocks. Tens of thousands of animals were slaughtered to avoid their handover to the communists; caravans of nomads escaped across the mountains into China. A European witness, Gustav Krist, was later to record the flight of half a million Kyrgyz with their flocks of yaks, horses, camels and sheep as they were slowly squeezed by Red Army cavalry units.

> The sun had now risen and I looked back down the valley. To an enormous distance I could see camel train after camel train; the entire horde was on trek, flying from officials of the Soviets. The news of the Russian approach must have spread like a forest fire and by the time the officials reached the grazing grounds they found the land empty save for the herdsmen, who, when questioned as to the whereabouts of the owners of the herds, just shook their heads and answered: 'far away, far away' ... Hot tears filled my eyes, although I little suspected at the time that I had been the witness of the last march of the free Kyrgyz.[20]

Despite attempts to eradicate an entire cultural legacy, communism initially did little to change the lifestyle of the Kyrgyz nomads. It has remained the same for centuries largely because the harsh conditions of life have dictated the lifestyle far more than ideological or economic preferences. Krist wrote that shamans frequently used tricks like walking on burning coals or eating glass to impress their followers. Kyrgyz cattle thieves were highly honoured and buried like princes in mausoleums: robbery was considered a virtue by the hungry nomads. Tribal courts run by elders of the clans dispensed justice. The nomads slept periodically on a bed of dung to get rid of lice, whilst some of the richest clan chiefs had immense flocks of goats and camels. The main entertainment during the harsh winters was storytelling, by storytellers who would wander from camp to camp.[21]

For centuries and even today, the backbone of the economy has been sheep and yak breeding for wool, milk, meat and fat. For their felt tents, or yurts, a family needs to produce between 130 and 170 kilograms of wool, and must own a flock of at least thirty-three sheep a year for basic sustenance. In winter, sheep milk is used to make small balls of cheese or *korut*, the main source of protein and indeed food. Fermented mare's milk or *koumiss*, a strong and bitter drink, is still part of the staple Kyrgyz diet. It is stored in animal skins and is made in the traditional way. One third of yesterday's milk is mixed with the new milk and allowed to ferment in the warm temperature of the yurt. It is then churned and becomes alcoholic before turning into lactic acid.[22]

Even today yurts – circular, collapsible and transportable huts with a dome-like conical roof – are still visible just a few miles outside Beshkeh. A wooden frame is erected and a felt covering is put on and tied down with bands of rope. The white felt, which is bleached with crushed bone, is entwined with woven woollen bands and its walls are frequently lined with an embroidered reed fence. Thick bands of felt dyed red, purple and yellow circle the tent.[23] The yurt is used by all Turkic nomads in Central Asia, from Anatolia to Mongolia. Felt is the main staple cloth for clothes, tents, rugs and decoration, and it has been made in the same way for centuries. 'A circle of women first thrash the wool with whips, then lay it out in two long, thick layers on top of hessian. This is rolled into a bolt and soaked in water heated by a fire of dung.' The bolt of felt is then rolled back and forth to mat the fibres together.[24]

The small Kyrgyz horses became indispensible to shepherds for moving their flocks and herds the great distances they had to travel to find grazing. Horses and sheep were for centuries the main currency of exchange to buy goods, a wife or a weapon. Every encampment of yurts has a *manap* or clan chief, who makes the crucial decisions as to where the nomads should move to find better grazing. Kyrgyz camps are colourful sights with men dressed in baggy trousers and loose shirts, shod in high riding boots and wearing white felt hats to protect them from the biting cold and sharp sunlight. The women

wear enormous headdresses like huge white turbans. Even though
families now tend to live more sedentary lives on collective farms, the
men continue to travel long distances to graze their flocks.

Reluctant to give up their lifestyle, the Kyrgyz remained devoid of
a major political role in their own republic. After 1945 Moscow ensured that the first secretary of the CPK was usually of Kyrgyz origin,
but the second secretaryship and other important positions related to
internal security and the KGB were always held by Russians. In 1961
Turdakun Usubaliev was elected first secretary of the CPK and his
long-running compliance with the Russian-dominated party structure enabled him to keep the post until 1985.[25] The first sign of anti-
Russian resentment in an otherwise dormant republic surfaced in 1980,
when Prime Minister Sultan Ibraimov was assassinated by Muslim or
nationalist radicals who were never caught. His murder was hushed up
in the Soviet media but it came as a great shock to the CPK.

The Kyrgyz remained the least politicized of all the Central Asian
nationalities. This was reflected in the CPK, whose membership in the
1980s was still equally divided between 37 per cent Russian members
and 37 per cent Kyrgyz members, even though the Kyrgyz are a
majority of the population. The Russians were all-powerful, and from
1982 to 1987 over 80 per cent of Kyrgyz party leaders in the districts
were sacked.[26] A new constitution was adopted in 1978, and in the
1985 elections to the Supreme Soviet, 350 deputies representing one
for every 5,000 people were sworn in. The long-running first secretary
Turdakun Usubaliev was dismissed and replaced by Absamat Masaliyev,
who accused his predecessor of corruption and nepotism and then
proceeded to sack Usubaliev's allies in the party. Masaliyev was re-
elected as first secretary of the CPK on 10 April 1990, when a new
Supreme Soviet was also elected. By then, however, the political stale-
mate and the accumulated ethnic and economic tensions of years of
neglect were coming to a head.[27]

CPK politics revolved around three major political groupings, which
were divided according to their tribal and regional origins. Those from
Naryn in the east supported the former leader Turdakun Usubaliev,
and this Naryn bloc quickly swung around in 1990 to support the first
democratically elected president, Askar Akaev (see below), because he
too came from Naryn. The Naryn bloc has traditionally been the most
powerful in Kyrgyz politics. The Talas region in the west backed the
soon-to-be-deposed leader, Absamat Masaliyev, while the Osh region
in the south, which was dominated by Uzbeks, produced a powerful
economic lobby that resented not being part of the political power
structure in Beshkeh.[28]

The first sign of protest was in March 1989 when young Kyrgyz intellectuals organized an 'informal' opposition group called 'Ashar', or 'Solidarity'.[29] Ashar tried to resolve the acute housing shortage in Beshkeh – an issue that the CPK had failed to deal with. The demonstrators occupied land and began building temporary mud houses in the centre of the city. The city authorities capitulated and formally handed over land to Ashar to allow private houses to be built. On 4 February 1990 Ashar organized a rally in the main square of Beshkeh, again demanding better housing and that greater emphasis be given to the Kyrgyz language. They also demanded that a ban be placed on the entry into the republic of refugees from Azerbaijan, who were arriving in large numbers following the outbreak of war between Azerbaijan and Armenia.

The housing shortage was only the tip of the iceberg of economic stagnation in the republic. Unemployment in Beshkeh alone was reportedly running at 16 per cent.[30] Years of neglect of the infrastructure had led to acute shortages in transport, housing, education and essential consumer goods. The economic stagnation also fuelled ethnic resentment, especially in the south where the better-off Uzbeks controlled the best land and factories. On 3 June 1990 the economic discontent and latent ethnic hostility between Uzbeks and Kyrgyz in the south erupted like a volcano, the lava of which was to change the politics of Kyrgyzstan decisively.

Rioting erupted in Osh when a crowd of Uzbeks attacked policemen after local Kyrgyz had been awarded building plots on an Uzbek-dominated state farm outside the city. A wave of bloody revenge killings began as inter-ethnic rioting spread to other towns, including Beshkeh, and violent street clashes continued for several weeks. Soviet troops were hastily called in from Uzbekistan and Turkmenistan to restore order. In the first four days of rioting in Osh at least 48 people were killed and some 300 were injured. 'This is a mass disorder, a real catastrophe,' said a spokesman for the Kyrgyz Interior Ministry on 6 June.[31]

The border with Uzbekistan was sealed to prevent rioting spreading there, a state of emergency was declared in Beshkeh and a nighttime curfew was imposed in many cities. Police stations were burnt down after being stormed by rioters and thousands of Uzbeks began to leave for the safety of Uzbekistan. In Uzgen, north of Osh, the rioting was so bad that three quarters of the town's houses were burnt down. Video recordings made by local people showed Uzbek babies hanging on meat hooks in a butcher's shop after being killed.[32] Similar atrocities were being committed by Uzbeks. Horror stories of atrocities multiplied on both sides as the official death toll reached 200, although unofficial estimates put it at more than 1,000.

The newly formed Democratic Movement of Kyrgyzstan (DMK) demanded the resignation of the CPK leadership but first secretary Absamat Masaliyev refused to resign. Tribal and regional politics again came into play. The communists from the Naryn block saw a chance to revive the fortunes of their leader and former first secretary, Turdiakun Usubaliev. Outside Parliament they appeared to have the support of the DMK, which had a strong Naryn bias. However in the following months as resentment against the communists built up, the DMK refused to support a former communist and in the elections later that year it put up a non-communist candidate. He was a highly respected 46-year-old mathematician, Askar Akaev, the head of the Academy of Sciences. Under severe pressure because of the Osh disturbances and after intense political infighting, the government announced elections for October.

Askar Akaev was elected president by the Supreme Soviet on 28 October 1990, the first non-communist president to be elected in Central Asia. He was re-elected in full presidential elections in the autumn of 1991, when he ran unopposed. On 12 December 1990 Kyrgyzstan announced its sovereignty and immediately after the August 1991 coup attempt against President Gorbachev, Akaev declared full independence. Akaev vehemently opposed the coup attempt and he moved troops into Beshkeh to prevent local hardline communists from staging a coup of their own. On the first day of the coup, while other Central Asian leaders remained silent waiting to see the outcome, Akaev attacked the coup makers and threw his weight behind Boris Yeltsin. Once the coup was crushed in Moscow, Akaev banned the CPK.

Akaev's long-standing demands for a much looser grouping of republics within the old Soviet Union were quickly to be realized, but he was still faced with the growing economic and political crisis in the republic. In January 1992 student demonstrations broke out in Beshkeh for the first time since Akaev took over. The students demanded larger grants, and better accommodation and food. After the liberalization of prices in January, food prices had shot up by 400 per cent and even though the minimum wage was raised to 350 roubles a month and civil servants' pay was doubled, the population was hard hit by shortages and inflation. The situation was made worse during December and January 1992 by a chronic fuel shortage that stopped airline flights out of the republic and stranded most car owners. Kyrgyzstan had suddenly discovered that the break-up of the Soviet Union, although long desired, had exposed the fragility of its own economy and land-locked position.

Six months before the August coup attempt, President Akaev had been the first and only Central Asian leader to propose the idea of a British-style Commonwealth of nations rather than a confederation of states with a strong centre. The fact that he had enough faith in his economic reforms to deny Moscow a strong centrist role shocked other Central Asian communist leaders at the time. 'I have studied the British Commonwealth system and its principle is the best for the Soviet Union,' he said. His views were later endorsed by Boris Yeltsin and reluctantly by the other Central Asian leaders after they were faced with the break-up of the Soviet Union.[33]

Akaev has run against the grain of Gorbachev's *perestroika* and closely followed the Chinese model – first introducing economic reforms and promising greater political freedoms later. 'In agriculture and irrigation we perhaps follow the Indian model and in privatization the South Korean model. But we try not to follow any model. We should take the experience of everyone and transform it into our own experience. We need to establish our own model,' the president said. His policies appeared to have wide approval even though he has kept the lid on nationalist and Islamic opposition groups and the press remains under tight government control. The gravity of the crisis and the promise of quick economic reforms persuaded the intelligentsia to accept an authoritarian style of governance in which pro-market economic ideas were immediately accepted, but not ideas of real democracy. Akaev was helped by the fact that the communists had become largely discredited and unlike his counterparts in other Central Asian republics, he was able to push through economic reforms with little opposition.

The most rapid programme of privatization in all Central Asia was put into effect. A presidential decree passed in November 1991 ordered that farms with a profitability level below 15 per cent should be privatized. The first auction of state flats to individual owners in Beshkeh took place in December 1991. For the first time in over seventy years in Central Asia, thousands of apartments became the property of their surprised occupants. The physically handicapped and retired people received their homes free, while others paid through an intricate coupon system. After a sweeping round of new laws to encourage private enterprise and foreign investment, even foreigners could buy a four-roomed flat in the centre of Beshkeh, for 100,000 roubles or just $1,000 at the current black-market rates in December 1991. Some 4 per cent of state-owned farmland or 1.5 million hectares was privatized by January 1991 and by the end of 1992 another 15 per cent of urban and farm land was owned by individuals.[34] In January 1992 further laws were passed for the setting up of private enterprises and joint stock companies in which payments could be made in cash or through vouchers distributed to citizens on the basis of how long they had worked.

Akaev was not embarrassed to call upon foreigners to help him. After visiting Canada, he appointed Canadian businessman Boris Birstein as head of the Kyrgyz Commission for Reconstruction and Development. Arnold Saltzman, president of a New York firm and a former USA ambassador, was appointed as Kyrgyzstan's sole agent in the USA to sell its mineral and petroleum rights. He allowed the International Monetary Fund (IMF) virtually to draft the country's economic programme, which was approved by the government in June 1992. It called for accelerated privatization, lower government expenditures, tighter credit policy and the creation of a proper financial system. The IMF was expected to give a large loan to Kyrgyzstan in 1993.

President Akaev speaks with intellectual conviction of 'the need to create a society which people believe in'. In comparison to the other, overly cautious communist leaders in the region, Akaev is an unabashed capitalist. 'Of course we should give privileges and financial credit to those who do well in the private sector. We have to restore the private sector in the lives of ordinary people,' he has said.[35] Akaev has promised that eventually 70 per cent of all collective farms will be privatized – the only hindrance at the moment being the government's inability to provide enough seed and fertilizer to private farmers. 'We will quickly implement reforms so that farms are transferred to small farmers on an ownership basis and the land will be theirs for ever,' Akaev said. But bureaucratic incompetence and reluctance to carry out reforms have hindered the process of privatization and fostered a high degree of corruption, in which officials must be bribed to carry out the smallest procedures.

Cash- and resource-strapped Kyrgyzstan needed foreign exchange and Akaev hastened to cement ties with potential donors. Small industrial joint ventures were set up with China, South Korea and Turkey and it began to woo Iran and Pakistan for investment in industry and the infrastructure. In December 1991 Akaev visited Turkey and signed agreements for the supply of medicines and food, including 500,000 tons of wheat. By early 1992 Kyrgyzstan had obtained credits worth $350 million from the USA, South Korea, Spain and Italy. In May 1992 Akaev paid a crucial visit to China, where a number of economic deals were signed. Beshkeh became a favourite port of call for US Secretary of State James Baker, who pointed to Kyrgyzstan's economic plans as a model for other Central Asian republics to follow.[36]

The communist system did leave behind a strong economic base in agriculture, which the Kyrgyz could develop further through private farms. Over the years animal husbandry has vastly improved and a great deal of scientific research has gone into improving the quality of livestock. New breeds of yaks have been bred as meat, and new hybrids of ordinary cattle that can graze at the high altitudes produce twice as much milk and meat as ordinary cattle because they are much heavier. The quality of the small Kyrgyz horses has also improved, and horses are bred for meat as well as for transport. Milk, wool, cheese, butter and buttermilk are exported to other republics.

Some 1.3 million hectares are now under crop cultivation compared to just 640,000 hectares in 1913; 90 per cent of arable land is irrigated by water brought down from the mountains to the valleys. The republic is self-sufficient in wheat, beet, hemp, tobacco, rice, vegetables, sunflower oil and fruit. Beekeeping in the mountains provides some of the world's best honey. Agriculture is now highly mechanized and in 1990 there were 176 collective farms and 290 state farms with some 29,000 tractors. All the farms are connected to the electricity grid system. Agricultural production declined, however, in 1992 due to the political chaos. Production of wheat, a crucial crop for feeding the people, fell from 1.5 million tons in 1990 to 1.36 million tons in 1991. Potatoes, milk and meat production all registered severe declines. The harvests in 1992 also suffered because of an enormous shortage of fuel for harvesters. In 1992, 80 per cent of the argriculture budget was spent on buying fuel and lubricants and on their transportation to Beshkeh from other republics.

Under the Soviet system, extensive funds were put into agricultural research to develop new high-yield crop varieties and seeds for growing at high altitudes. Eight new wheat strains and seven varieties of barley have been developed for use at different altitudes and for planting in different seasons. Significant research has also been carried out on the medicinal wealth of the herbs and grasses of the mountains. The Institute of Organic Chemistry in Beshkeh has developed a number of drugs, especially drugs related to heart disease, from medicinal plants growing in the Tien Shan. A book called *The Medicinal Riches of Kyrgyzia* by leading academician Arstanbek Altmyshev, who heads the institute, has been translated into several foreign languages. 'All of Kyrgyzistan is my laboratory. Its relatively small territory encompasses all climatic zones of the world from sunscorched deserts to perpetual snow. The almost 4,000 species of plants growing here are an immensely rich Green pharmacy,' Altymyshev has said.

The Soviet system created a small industrialized sector which was extremely uneven in what it produced. Kyrgyzstan's main exports to the rest of the former Soviet Union were agricultural and dairy produce, electricity generated from dozens of dams in the Tien Shan, nonferrous metals and a small range of consumer goods. Its main imports were coal, building materials, chemicals, machine tools and a huge range of consumer goods.[37] Kyrgyzstan has three gold mines with estimated recoverable reserves of 400 tons.

There are some five hundred large industrial enterprises in the republic. Sugar refineries, tanneries, cotton and wool cleaning factories and flour mills, tobacco and timber processing factories have most of their raw materials at hand. There were, however, some Soviet-style absurdities such as the setting up of a sugar mill to process sugar cane imported from Cuba. Many factories faced temporary closures in 1992 as there were shortages of raw materials and inputs from other republics that were not delivered. Engineering enterprises, mainly producing items for electric power generation, registered a sharp decline. Huge hydroelectric stations had been built to export electricity to other parts of the former Soviet Union. Seven massive power stations were built on the 800-kilometre-long Naryn river which drops 3,000 metres from its source to its mouth and thus has a huge hydroelectricity generating capacity.[38]

Enormous potential still exists for development of the rich mineral resources of Kyrgyzstan, and several foreign companies are looking into the possibilities. A major problem, however, is transport of exports. Traffic is mainly by the tortuously winding roads cut through the mountains and there are only 370 kilometres of railway line in the entire republic. Exports have to be directed through either Kazakhstan and Russia to reach the Western seaboard or through Uzbekistan to the Black Sea. The distances are enormous and the problems have multiplied because every republic is now independent. In January 1992 Kyrgyzstan and Kazakhstan set up a working group with China and Pakistan to study the possibility of a new road network through Xinjiang that would link up with the Karakorum Highway in northern Pakistan to reach the port city of Karachi.

Akaev's mild manner and rush towards economic liberalization created a degree of domestic political consensus amongst the major opposition political parties that had sprung up. He made it a habit to meet every week in his office with the leadership of the seven main opposition parties. 'We have no major differences with the president, only that he should speed up privatization and liberalize prices faster,' said Kamalia Kenenbaieva, deputy chairman of the opposition Liberal Democratic Party and herself an academic turned full-time politician. 'Nobody is scared of the KGB any longer, but everyone is scared of economic reform because people don't know what it means. Therefore it must be done quickly.'[39]

Kyrgyzstan was the only Central Asian republic where both the government and the opposition's main agenda was how to liberalize the economy as fast as possible. It has been helped by the fact that a new political leadership has quickly emerged from intellectuals and academics who are respected both at home and abroad for their openness in considering new ideas and for their rejection of the old-style regional and tribal politics of the past. This has been a unique phenomenon in Central Asia, where either old-style communists or local power barons still dominate politics. Kamalia Kenenbaieva offered a simple explanation for the sudden commitment of intellectuals to enter politics. 'When I was teaching, my students asked me why are we all living so badly and I had no answers to give them, so a few of us decided to find the right answers by entering politics.'

The Islamic opposition has remained peripheral largely because of the tolerant attitude towards religion amongst the Kyrgyz and the fact that one quarter of its population are non-Muslims. Officials claim that there is no strong Islamic party because the government encouraged a multi-party system from the beginning. Moreover the mullahs in Kyrgyzstan have traditionally been outsiders, such as Tartar migrants, so there is no local ethnic Islamic leadership to play a political role as in Tajikistan. Where Islamic militancy has emerged, it has been quickly stamped on hard by the government. The Islamic Renaissance Party (IRP) has a base but it remains underground and is not widely popular. Although it may not be a political force as yet, Islam is still seen as a source of cultural inspiration and identification – a means to break with the communist past rather than a means to a new political future.

In 1992, however, the dramatic growth of the Wahabi movement in the Ferghana valley affected Osh and other southern towns. The Wahabis have begun to fund mosques and madrasahs to reconvert the Kyrgyz to Islam and to stop Western Christian fundamentalist groups, who are active in Beshkhe, converting the Kyrgyz to Christianity. The choice of Ferghana by the militants was largely due to the Islamic receptiveness of its people but also to its geographic location, which allows the militants to spread their message from there to Uzbekistan, Tajikistan and Kyrgyzstan.[40]

In summer 1992, the building of a large Wahabi mosque and madrasah began in Osh with a Saudi grant of 1 million roubles. By the end of the year the Wahabis were also funding a new mosque in Beshkhe. Imams at these mosques explained that they had been forced to turn to the Wahabis because no government funds were available for their mosque's expansion. President Akaev expressed his fears about the spread of Islamic fundamentalism due to the civil war in Tajikistan. 'The fundamentalists' only weapon is terror, they are stupid. They claim to be democratic, deny that they are setting out to establish an Islamic state, they say they are for peace and understanding. Yet all the time ... they want to seize power.'[41]

Despite the growth of fundamentalism, the nomadic origins of Kyrgyz society, which has sustained a much greater degree of freedom for women, make Islamic injunctions for women much less meaningful than elsewhere. In the past women had to work alongside their men to shepherd their flocks through the harsh terrain. The high infant mortality rate made it necessary for women to work, as child labour was not as available in the mountains as it was in the steppe. Today on collective farms women make up 60 per cent of the labour force and do most of the dairy work, while men do the herding and industrial work. One exception is the textile industry which is predominantly staffed by women workers.

Kyrgyz women do not normally wear the veil and often say their prayers alongside their men – which is not common in other Muslim cultures. However the Kyrgyz are still a highly structured patriarchal society where girls marry young and according to their parents' wishes, after an appropriate bride price has been paid. Although officially banned, the bride price is now paid in the form of gifts of animals or consumer goods rather than hard cash. Women rarely marry Russians or non-Muslims, and if they do they often are forced leave the region to avoid the social stigma.

Despite their physical isolation at the southern tip of the Soviet landmass, Kyrgyz intellectuals have produced some of the finest modern literature in the former Soviet Union. Former president Gorbachev's favorite author, whom he often quoted in his speeches, was the Kyrgyz writer Chingiz Aitmatov, who has written extensively about the cultural heritage of the Turkic people and how modernity is depriving man of his individuality.

Aitmatov's most famous novel, *And the Day Lasted Longer than an Age*, strongly alludes to the destruction of the past by the former Soviet regime. Aitmatov's heroes are the mankurts, who according to Kyrgyz legend were prisoners of war who were turned into slaves by having their heads wrapped in camel skin. Under a hot sun these skins dried tight as a steel band around their heads, thus enslaving them for ever. A mankurt did not recognize his name, family or tribe. 'A mankurt did not recognize himself as a human being,' the author wrote in a clear allusion to the dehumanizing aspect of communism. Another novel, *Execution Block*, was about the growing drugs culture among young people and a young man's search for God to save himself. The book caused a sensation when it was published in 1986 and there were demands by hardline communists that it be banned.

A reassessment of Islam and the Turkic past of Kyrgyzstan has been a recurring theme in modern Kyrgyz literature, and books that deal with these issues have been bestsellers. Murad Aliev's novel The *Cuckoo in the Month of May* is a paean to the Islamic past, whilst the poems of Qazibek Mambetiminov, a Kyrgyz Basmachi rebel who was killed by the Bolsheviks sixty-five years ago, have been republished after being banned, and are extremely popular.

As in other Central Asian republics, ethnic tensions dominate the political agenda. Many Kyrgyz fear that the troubles in Osh could be the tip of an ethnic volcano and much will depend on how quickly the government is able to satisfy economic and social shortages such as housing, which have fuelled ethnic unrest. Officials claim that the Osh troubles had their own peculiarities, which are now being rec- tified. 'There was a conflict in Osh between the Kyrgyz-dominated party authority and trade and business, which is in the hands of the Uzbeks who form 50 per cent of the population there,' said Foreign Minister Murat Imanaliev. In April 1991 an agreement was signed between local Uzbek and Kyrgyz leaders in Osh to give Uzbeks a share of the administration, while Uzbek schools were also opened.[42]

The agreements failed to take root on the ground. Two years after the riots, Osh was a city where ethnic apartheid was vehemently practised by both Uzbeks and Kyrgyz. Members of each community have their own schools, mosques, shops and cafés; there is little mixing between the two. Thousands of Uzbeks who feel discriminated against are returning to Uzbekistan. Umarjan Kasimov, the elected head of Uzbeks in Osh, has said that the Kyrgyz government has moved Uzbek districts out of the city limits and included outlying Kyrgyz villages within the city limits, so that the Kyrgyz can benefit from the city's amenities.[43]

But ethnic problems are not restricted to Osh alone. In Beshkeh, Russians are 50 per cent of the population and still hold the best jobs in government and industry. An estimated 100,000 Russians had left by the end of 1992, but their continued presence is fuelling Kyrgyz nationalism. The government is now attempting to implement reverse discrimination by promoting Kyrgyz bureaucrats to senior positions, but measures such as these and excluding Russians from places at university in favour of Kyrgyz students could also prompt a Russian backlash. 'For seventy-three years the Russians ruled us and still they have a psyche that everything belongs to them, but now there is a new situation where we are a majority and they are a minority. They will have to accept that or leave,' said one Kyrgyz intellectual.

There are eighty other ethnic groups including Koreans, Tibetans and Uighurs from the east, Tartars, Dungans, Chechens from the west as well as European ethnic groups such as Germans, Poles and Czechs. Overt expression of Kyrgyz nationalism has been kept in check by the government, but the potential for trouble is always there. President Akaev has so far avoided paying lip service to Kyrgyz nationalism as President Nazarbayev has done in Kazakhstan, but Akaev may well be forced to do so if there is a groundswell of nationalist feeling.

For much of 1992 former hardline communists and the new breed of Kyrgyz nationalists in Parliament blocked passage of the country's new constitution, which would have formalized the existing presidential system. Instead they pushed for a more powerful parliament and prime minister. Some fifty different groups and parties coalesced under the umbrella of the DMK, which demanded that Akaev's powers be reduced. After nearly a year's delay the new constitution was finally passed on 5 May 1993, in consequence of which Akaev was forced to concede some of his powers to Prime Minister Tursunbek Chengyshev. The 313-member Supreme Soviet was to become a 105-seat parliament after fresh elections.

A key factor in Kyrgyzstan's future will be its relationship with its powerful neighbour China, with which it shares a 1,000-kilometre border. Traditionally the Kyrgyz nomads have had close ties with Xinjiang, frequently crossing the border to escape persecution and hardship in their own region. But in recent years Chinese Muslims, especially Uighurs, have been escaping persecution in China by crossing into Kyrgyz territory with their flocks. This migration has worried the Chinese. Although the Beshkeh government is discouraging migration by Chinese Uighurs, it cannot afford to antagonize the Uighurs who are already living in Kyrgyzstan and are becoming more and more fervently anti-Chinese. The Uighurs have become important political players not only in Xinjiang, but also in Kazakhstan and Kyrgyzstan.

There is increasingly closer co-operation between China and Kyrgyzstan. When in August 1992 a powerful earthquake on the China–Kyrgyzstan border killed 50 people and injured 200, both countries launched a joint relief effort in the devastated region. The Kyrgyz are keen to encourage Chinese investment and in return are setting up transmission lines to provide China with electricity. 'We have opened up direct trade with Xinjiang and we want to establish trade and cultural links with all of northeast China,' said Foreign Minister Murat Imanaliev. China has welcomed President Akaev's determination to keep his country neutral and his promise that Kyrgyzstan would be the only Central Asian state that would not build its own army. 'The only acceptable model of foreign political relations for Kyrgyzstan is the model of permanent neutrality,' Akaev said.[44] Beshkeh was once one of the most important training centres for the Soviet Union's air force. In 1989 there were 2,300 foreign pilots training on Soviet aircraft at the Beshkeh air base, which was home for some 430 aircraft and helicopters. By February 1992 there were only 160 foreign pilots left.

Despite its intensive pro-capitalist legislation, Kyrgyzstan was still unable to attract major foreign investment in its first year of independence. The gross domestic product declined by 15 per cent in 1992 after a drop of 5 per cent the previous year. Industrial output declined by as much 25 per cent, while inflation was rampant. In January 1993 Akaev told workers that the country was facing a severe energy crisis because it was selling about one third of its hydroelectrically generated electricity to other republics at only 22–25 per cent of world prices. He admitted that Kyrgyzstan's economic performance was worse than that of Armenia and Tajikistan – two republics which faced war and economic devastation. To avoid being tied to the ever-falling rouble, the government became the first Central Asian state to introduce a new currency, the sum, on 10 May 1993.

Kyrgyzstan's lack of resources and industry means that there is relatively little for the government to privatize. Despite the sudden economic downturn in 1992 and the long-term problems of finding the resources to sustain an independent economy, the republic is hopeful that an IMF loan and increasing Japanese interest will help improve the economy. Moreover the country is almost self-sufficient in food and is taking the necessary steps to provide basic consumer goods for the population. The political and religious tolerance of the people is unmatched anywhere in Central Asia and this is Kyrgyzstan's greatest strength. If the government can overcome the serious ethnic problems it faces by greater integration, then it may succeed in calming the fears of the minorities and preventing a mass exodus of Russians. Kyrgyzstan faces a difficult future, but one which is not bleak by the standards of other Central Asian countries.

Notes

1. I. Cameron (1984) *Mountains of the Gods*, Facts on File, USA.

2. R. Weekes, *Muslim Peoples: a world ethnographic survey*, Greenwood Press, USA.

3. The Kyrgyz in the Wakhan corridor arrived as refugees in Pakistan after the Soviet invasion of Afghanistan in 1979. The Turkish government then helped them to resettle on a terrain which was similar to their own.

4. Interviews with Kyrgyz in Bashkek, December 1991.

5. T. Talbot Rice (1965) *Ancient Arts of Central Asia*, Praeger, USA. Rice gives a superb description of Saka civilization.

6. E, Maillart (1985) *Turkestan Solo*, Century Publishing, London.

7. Ibid.
8. Ibid.
9. Talbot Rice.
10. K. Omurkulov (1987) *Kyrgyzia*, Novosti Press, Moscow.
11. Notes by the author on a visit to Osh in October 1992.
12. Omurkulov.
13. Ibid.
14. H. Rawlinson (1875) *England and Russia in the East: the political and geographical condition of Central Asia*, Indus Publications, Pakistan.
15. Maillart.
16. Ibid. See also E. H. Carr (1952) *The Bolshevik Revolution, 1917–23*, Macmillan, London.
17. Ibid.
18. B. Nahalyo and V. Swohboda, (1990) *Soviet Disunion: a history of the nationalities problem in the USSR*, Hamish Hamilton, London.
19. Ibid.
20. G. Krist (1992) *Alone through the Forbidden Land: journeys in disguise through Soviet Central Asia*, Ian Falkner, Cambridge.
21. Ibid.
22. Interviews with Kyrgyz nomads, December 1991. Also Weekes.
23. Thomas Lowther, 'Pony Trekking on the Gengis Khan Trail', *Independent* (London), 21 November 1992.
24. Ibid.
25. A. Tahiri, (1989) *Crescent in a Red Sky: the future of Islam in the Soviet Union*, Hutchinson, London.
26. P. Cockburn (1989) *Getting Russia Wrong: the end of Kreminology*, Verso, London.
27. Interviews with Kyrgyz officials, December 1991 and October 1992.
28. M. Brill Olcott, 'Central Asia's Post-empire Politics', *Orbis*, Spring 1992.
29. An 'informal' was an informal organization made up of intellectuals and writers that sprung up after *perestroika*. Many informals later became political pressure groups or parties.
30. D. Doder and L. Branson (1990) *Gorbachev: heretic in the Kremlin*, Futura Books, London.
31. Francis Clines, '40 Die in Rioting in Soviet Kyrgyzia as Unrest Spreads', *International Herald Tribune*, 7 June 1990.
32. Vivien Morgan, 'Kyrgyzia Town Rebuilds after Untold Massacres', *Independent*, 19 July 1990.
33. Interview with President Askar Akaev, December 1991. Interviews with other senoir Kyrgyz officials in Beshkeh gave details of recent political history.
34. All figures were given by President Akaev and Foreign Minister Murat Imanaliev to the author, Beshkeh, December 1991 and October 1992.
35. Ibid.
36. Interviews with Kyrgyz officials, October 1992.
37. Pakistan Foreign Office figures.
38. Omurkulov.
39. Interview with the author in Beshkeh, December 1991.
40. Ahmed Rashid (in Ferghana), 'With God on Their Side', *Far Eastern Economic Review*, 19 November 1992.
41. Jan Krauze (in Beshkeh), 'Fear of Islamic Fundamentalism in Kyrgyzia', *Le Monde* (Paris), 14 October 1992.

42. Interview with the author, December 1991.
43. Interview with the author in Osh, October 1992.
44. Reuters, 'Kyrgyzstan Opposes Military Bloc', *Dawn* (Karachi), 18 March 1992.

7

The Mountains of
Islam – Tajikistan

The green flag of Islam, with the Crescent and Star and the Kalma or creed of Islam written in Arabic script, is the most potent symbol of the future in Dushanbe, the capital of landlocked Tadjikistan. Within nine months of independence a bloody civil war engulfed the republic and threatened to divide it along regional lines. Although it was ostensibly between pro-communist forces and Islamic fundamentalists, in fact the long-suppressed clan, regional and ethnic rivalries in the republic had quickly come to the surface after communism's demise. As Tajikistan faced the worst and longest-running political crisis of all the Central Asian republics, there were fears in early 1993 that the Tajik model of civil war, economic breakdown and ethnic conflict could spread to other republics.

'For seventy-five years the communists tried to wipe out the memory of Allah, but every Tajik today still remembers Allah and prays for the success of the party of Allah,' said Mohammed Sharif Himatzade, chairman of the Islamic Renaissance Party (IRP) as Tajikistan declared itself independent in December 1991.[1] Six months later Himatzade had left Dushanbe for a secret military base outside the capital where he was raising an 8,000-strong militia force for the IRP.[2] He returned to Dushanbe for ten weeks in the autumn of 1992 when the IRP was part of a coalition government, before it was overthrown and its leaders took to the mountains again. The IRP is riding the crest of an Islamic wave that has gripped many Tajik youth, who see an Islamic political system as the only way to revive past Tajik glories, as an expression of Tajik nationalism, and as the only hope for a more equitable economic system.

Himatzade is typical of the new breed of Tajik politicians. A forty-year-old mechanic and the son of a poor peasant, Himatzade is called by some of his followers 'the Gulbuddin of Central Asia' after the

Afghan Mujheddin leader Gulbuddin Hikmetyar. A charismatic figure who speaks so softly it is difficult to catch his words, Himatzade spent fifteen years in the political underground where he helped build up the IRP, which now has branches in all the Central Asian republics. He and other IRP leaders trained and fought with the Afghan Mujheddin. Tajik fundamentalists drew much of their inspiration from the Mujheddins' war against the Soviet Union's forces in Afghanistan, where Afghan Tajik guerrillas demonstrated their prowess against Soviet troops.

Landlocked Tajikistan, covering 143,100 square kilometres, is the southernmost republic of the former Soviet Union. In the south it shares a rugged, mountainous 1,030-kilometre border with Afghanistan, which in the east is separated from Pakistan by the thin wedge of the Wakhan corridor which in some places is only 10 kilometres wide. The corridor was mapped out by India's British rulers and the Tsar to ensure that the Russian empire was not contiguous with the British empire in India. In the east Tajikistan shares a 430-kilometres border with China's Xinjiang province. Its northern border adjoins Kyrgyzstan and to the west lies Uzbekistan.

Tajikistan has a population of 5.4 million people, of whom only 58.8 per cent are Tajiks, who are the original descendants of the Aryan population of Turkestan. Some 23 per cent of the present population are Uzbeks while 11 per cent are Russians, who live mainly in the cities. There are more than a dozen other nationalities including Kazakhs, Kyrgyz and Uighurs, and members of the Ismaeli sect of Islam. Tajikistan was the poorest of the fifteen republics of the former Soviet Union with the lowest per capita income, 25 per cent unemployment, a staggering 5 per cent annual growth in population, the lowest levels of educational attainment and the highest rate of infant mortality.[3] The Tajiks are mainly Sunnis of the Hannafi sect, the largest Muslim sect, but the Ismaelis are Shia.

More than 4 million Tajiks live in northern Afghanistan – at least 1.5 million more than in Tajikistan itself. Another 1 million Tajiks live in Uzbekistan; Tajiks are scattered throughout the other Central Asian republics. Some 20,000 continue to live in China's Xinjiang province. The Tajiks are the only major Central Asian nationality who do not speak a Turkic-based language. The area was once part of the Persian empire, and the various dialects of Tajik are related to Persian, or Farsi. The word 'Tajik' originates from *taj* or *taz*, used by the early Arab invaders to refer to those Central Asians who only spoke Persian. Physically the Tajiks are a classic example of miscegenation.[4] While the Afghan Tajiks display strong Caucasian features, as one travels further north Tajiks show strong Mongoloid characteristics. The mixture of

Greek blood from Alexander's invasion still produces Tajiks with blonde hair, blue eyes and Greek noses.

Many Tajiks consider their republic as an afterthought, carved out by the communists to divide and rule Central Asia. For centuries Tajiks and Uzbeks lived together in Turkestan – their common homeland – which comprises Uzbekistan and Tajikistan. Both ethnic groups were bilingual and shared a common history and culture. However in the arbitrary divisions carried out by Stalin's mapmakers these two ethnic groups were separated and the Ferghana valley was divided. While a thin lip of Tajikistan's territory, inhabited mostly by Uzbeks, juts into Uzbekistan, a sliver of Kyrgyz territory, which is inhabited by both Tajiks and Uzbeks, slices into western Tajikistan.

Stalin's mapmakers also handed over Samarkand and Bukhara, the two major centres of Tajik culture and history, to Uzbekistan. Dushanbe was built as a consolation prize. The loss of their cultural centres continue to hurt Tajiks, who see Dushanbe as a sterile modern city that reflects none of their cultural achievements. The Tajik claim that they were left with the rump of Central Asia – the uninhabited mountainous regions of the Pamirs and no rich agricultural region. These losses have sustained Tajikistan's tensions with Uzbekistan and fuelled fears that eventually the two republics may clash over their borders.

There are other ethnic and regional disputes, created by the communist system, which are helping push Tajikistan towards disintegration. In the north around Khodjent, where much of the population is Uzbek, there is a strong separatist movement. Khodjent was formerly part of the khanate of Kokand, and was incorporated into Russia as part of Ferghana in 1876. It developed industry and higher literacy levels than the areas to the south, which belonged to the emir of Bukhara and remained totally neglected until 1920. After 1917 Khodjent became a pro-communist region and was developed as the economic powerhouse of Tajikistan. An industrial infrastructure was created, tens of thousands of Russian settlers were brought in and strong links with Moscow and Tashkent developed. Invariably the leaders of the Communist Party of Tajikistan (CPTJ), such as Rakhmon Nabiev, came from Khodjent. Today these economic and political disparities have come to the surface with the north sympathetic to Uzbekistan and the former communists and strongly anti-fundamentalist.[5]

In the south there are longstanding economic and clan rivalries between the Kuliab district in the southeast and Kurgan Tube in the southwest. The Kuliab clans have always been closely linked with the Khodjent communist nomenklatura and have despised the neighbouring clans from Kurgan Tube, who are more overtly Islamic. By the summer of 1992 these rivalries, fuelled by the political polarization in the republic, erupted into an all-out civil war. The Kuliabi militia captured Kurgan Tube in fighting that left at least 2,000 people dead and the city destroyed.

Even greater ethnic complexities exist in the southeast. The Autonomous Region of Gorno-Badakshan, which shares its terrain, people and culture with northern Afghanistan, contains 44 per cent of the total land area of Tajikistan but only 3 per cent of the population. It is inhabited by seven different Pamiri ethnic groups including Ismaeli Muslims who are followers of the Agha Khan and have been victimized by both the communists and the fundamentalists. The Ismaelis have built up strong links with fellow Ismaelis across the border in Afghanistan, and the most militant among them are demanding a separate Ismaeli state. The Pamiri people live isolated lives, shepherding their flocks and tilling small patches of land. Their women wear bright silk pantaloons, brightly coloured floral scarves and long shirts. With their blue and green eyes, fine bone structure and long hair, Pamiri women are renowned for their beauty.

Around 93 per cent of Tajikistan's territory is covered in mountains – mostly by the Pamir range which until recently was one of the most inaccessible mountain ranges in the world. Even in its deepest valleys the Pamirs are never lower than 3,500 metres and not surprisingly they are still called the Roof of the World. Huge glaciers have created hundreds of river torrents that rush down the mountains and irrigate fields cut into the mountain side. This mosaic of small wheatfields is interspersed with apple, apricot and mulberry trees. In the Pamirs live the largest bear in the world, the *ursus torquatus*, which can weigh up to 225 kilograms, the largest yaks and the biggest sheep, whose horns Marco Polo described as being nearly two metres across.[7] During the summer the shepherds live alone in their yurts, or tents, seeking the best pasture as the snow recedes. Their yurts are formed of layers of felt that are tied around a wooden lattice made of willow that can easily be transported around the mountains.

One of the earliest recorded crossings of the Pamirs was by Marco Polo in 1273 as he headed east into Xinjiang and China.

> Ascending mountain after mountain, you at length arrive at a point, where you might suppose the surrounding summits to be the highest lands in the world ... you do not meet with any habitations, it is necessary to make provision at the outset accordingly. So great is the height of the mountains, that no birds are to be seen near their summits; and however extraordinary it may be thought, it was affirmed, that from the keenness of the air, fires when lighted do not give the same heat as in lower situations, nor produce the same effect in dressing victuals. Even amongst the highest of these

mountains, there lives a tribe of savage, ill-disposed and idolatrous people, who subsist upon the animals they can destroy, and clothe themselves with the skins.[8]

It was to be another six hundred years before Russian explorers were to map the Pamirs. In 1865 Alexis Fedchenko and his wife Olga became the first Russian explorers to cross the north face of the Pamirs and discover the largest glacier in the world, which is now named the Fedchenko Glacier. 'More is known about the moon than the Pamirs,' said Fedchenko when he began his travels.[9] His reports, which described the presence of large quantities of minerals such as coal, iron, gold and marble, ensured that in a few years the north would come under Russian suzerainty. The Pamirs are only one range in this veritable jungle of never-ending mountain peaks, which is the crossroads of some of the highest ranges in the world. To the east and north of the Pamirs run the Tien Shan and the Kun Lun ranges, to the west the Himalayas, while southward into Afghanistan stretch the Hindu Kush.

Dushanbe, the capital of Tajikistan, is in the heart of the mountains, surrounded by high peaks and lush orchards. It is situated in the Gissar valley on the banks of the Varzob river, and streams from nearby thawing glaciers run into the town watering parks and rows of trees. Before 1917 the village of Dushanbe was a small market town where every Monday a lively bazaar was held by the local population. The name Dushanbe, which means 'Monday' in Persian, stuck. For a brief period after the 1917 Revolution Dushanbe became the capital of the Basmachi rebels when the deposed emir of Bukhara, Said Alimkhan, took refuge in Dushanbe before he retreated to Afghanistan. In February 1921 Red Army troops entered the city and declared it the administrative centre of eastern Bukhara.

In 1925 Dushanbe held only 6,000 people. It had no railway connection with the rest of Central Asia, only one modern building and most Bolshevik offices were located in converted cattle sheds.[10] It grew rapidly as Russians moved in and by 1939 the population was 83,000; today it is over 600,000.[11] Dushanbe became a major industrial centre with textile, footwear and knitwear industries, and plants that served the metal and construction industries. In the old quarter, small houses are jammed close together as in any Muslim city, but the modern city built by the Soviets is featureless with monstrous concrete blocks that have little to do with local culture or tradition. Buildings in the city are generally not high, because Dushanbe sits atop a hazardous seismic zone. In this century alone, the city has been shaken by 500 earthquakes that have registered more than 5 points on the Richter scale. The three most catastrophic earthquakes have been in 1909, 1911 and 1949. The centre of the city is dominated by the huge Lenin

Square, now renamed Azadi (or Freedom) Square, which is surrounded by government buildings and the Parliament. It is here that the long-running public demonstrations have taken place. Lenin's statue was removed and replaced by one of Firdausi, the tenth-century Persian poet.

By the winter of 1992 Dushanbe had become a chaotic city tee-tering on the edge of collapse. A dusk-to-dawn curfew was imposed after some 1,500 armed men from Kuliab attempted a *coup d'état* against the government on 24–25 October. Foreign diplomats were evacuated and foreign businesspeople fled to Moscow. At dusk the police would disappear leaving the city in the hands of vigilantes who robbed cars and the homes of residents. Throughout the night shots would ring out from around the city, though nobody ever knew who was firing at whom. Armed mafias, political groups and ordinary criminal gangs controlled separate ares of Dushanbe and ran protection rackets target-ing traders.

The chronic shortage of fuel led to the city being virtually cut off from the outside world as airline flights were cancelled. People in their thousands began to flee the city. Russians sold their homes at throwa-way prices and were begging for airline seats to Moscow. By Decem-ber 1992 more than 200,000 Russians, one third of the Russian population, had fled Tajikistan. Food began to run out as there was no fuel for trucks to move farm produce to urban markets or to bring in consumer goods from neighbouring republics. Roads leading to Dushanbe were closed by armed gangs who demanded money from travellers. By the Tajiks, one of the oldest peoples of Central Asia, the humiliation and degradation was bitterly felt.

The forebears of the modern Tajiks were a sedentary people who controlled a key section of the ancient Silk Route. They dominated the cities of Central Asia even after they were ousted from political power by first the Turkic tribes and later the Mongols and Uzbeks. While the Arabs considered the Tajiks as Persian-speaking Muslims, the Turkic tribes considered them as Iranian and therefore outsiders. Tajik urban dwellers in Central Asia who spoke Turkic dialects were called by their ancient name, Sarts. Many of these Tajiks became a professional class of artisans and in time all urban artisans were called Sarts.[12]

Pastoral nomadism developed in the region now called Tajikistan between 1500 and 1000 BC, when Persian tribes moved northwards into Central Asia and Afghanistan. These tribes – variously called Tat, Tajik, Sart, Galsha and Farsiwan – settled between the Amudarya and Syrdarya rivers, before they were invaded from the north by the Scythians who swept through Central Asia between 700 and 300 BC.

The Scythians were later pushed back across the Syrdarya by the ever-expansive Persian empire, which ruled Central Asia for two hundred years.

The Persian kings ruled over Bactria, which covered southern Tajikistan and Afghanistan, and Sogdiana, which covered southern Uzbekistan and the western part of Tajikistan.[13] The ancestors of the Tajiks were the Sogdians, who inhabited the Pamirs when Alexander the Great left Kabul to invade Central Asia in 329 BC. After crossing the Amudarya he marched north founding a city Alexandria-the-Far-thest, which is today Khodjent. Capturing Samarkand he defeated the Scythians who lived north of the Syrdarya. He then turned south to defeat the Sogdians in one of his most famous battles: the storming of the Sogdian Rock, which the Sogdians considered impregnable. After defeating them, Alexander married Roxana (the daughter of the Sogdian king Oxyartes), who was considered the most beautiful woman in Central Asia.[14]

By the time Alexander died in 323 BC at the age of thirty-three, he had conquered much of the known world. His conquests were to be the first and last time for nearly 2,000 years that Europe and Asia were to be joined – until the Russian empire was extended into Central Asia in the nineteenth century. The Greeks and their successors ruled the kingdom of Bactria which extended as far west as Herat. The Bactrians, who ruled from 300 to 140 BC, were overthrown by the Sakas, whose culture was an exotic mix of Hellenism, Buddhism and Chinese influences. When the Sakas pushed south into India, a succession of nomadic invaders swept through Tajikistan: the Parthians, the Persian Sassanids and the Ephthalite Huns, who were in turn defeated by the first Turkic nomadic invasions in AD 400.

Unlike today, when Tajikistan and Afghanistan are on the periphery of Central Asia, in ancient times this region was the military and economic core of the region. Control of this gateway facilitated invasions westward into Iran and Europe or eastward into India. Moreover the region was an essential part of the Silk Route, from which would-be conquerors could collect extremely lucrative revenues. Events in Tajikistan reverberated quickly in political and trading circles in China, Afghanistan, India and even Europe. In the north of Tajikistan an ancient Buddhist city called Penjikent has been unearthed by archaeologists. Its ruins make it clear that it was a strategic crossroads of religious, cultural and trading influences for the whole of Central Asia.

Although Central Asia rapidly came under Turkic control, the Persian-speaking Tajiks remained major players in urban affairs, dominating the ruling bureaucracies of successive conquerors, controlling the bazaar, trade and the migration of artisans from Persia and India.

Culturally the people remained essentially Persian in outlook, and Tajik influence even spread back to the Persian heartland. The first Muslim rulers in Persia – the Samanids – were Tajik in origin. The Samanids had created a powerful kingdom in Central Asia with their capital at Bukhara. During their rule (874–999) an enormous intellectual flowering in the arts, sciences and literature took place that was to have a major influence in Europe a century later. Bukhara became one of the largest cities in the world with a population of 300,000 people.[15]

The end of the Samanid dynasty was caused by another spate of Turkic invasions: the Karahanid Turks, the Kara-Kitai nomads from Mongolia, the Seljuk Turks who swept down to modern-day Turkey, the Ghaznawid Turks who conquered what is now modern Afghanistan and the Khorezmshahs who set up an independent state at Khiva in 1077 and within one hundred years ruled all of Central Asia.[16] Tajikistan was to be devastated by the Mongol hordes in 1220 and then one hundred and fifty years later conquered by the Barlas Turks under Tamerlane. Until Tamerlane made his capital in Samarkand, he ruled from Balkh in northern Afghanistan and frequently marched through Tajikistan to conquer the rest of Central Asia. Tamerlane's successors were defeated by the Uzbeks, a defeat which spelt the end of Persian and Tajik influence in Central Asia.[17] The Tajiks became the vassals of first the Uzbek Shaybani khans and later, in the nineteenth century, the amirs of Bukhara and Kokand.

As Russia expanded into Central Asia, Moscow annexed the northern part of Tajikistan in 1868. Fears of British incursions from India prompted Moscow to annex the entire Pamirs; the region came under the governor-general of Turkestan based in Tashkent.[18] The rivalry with the British in India as the Russians advanced into Central Asia and began to covet Herat directly affected Tajikistan and placed the Pamirs at the centre of international attention. The Great Game between Russia and England over control of the land routes into India had begun in earnest and after much haggling both powers agreed to set up an Anglo-Russian Boundary Commission in March 1884, which eventually demarcated Afghanistan's highly porous northern borders with present-day Tajikistan. In order to prevent the new Russian frontier from being contiguous with India, the Wakhan corridor, which divides Tajikistan from present-day Pakistan, was created in the Pamirs.[19]

By annexing Tajikistan, Russia was also to inherit the problems of Afghanistan. For centuries Tajikistan and Afghanistan were considered one contiguous political region, with the amir of Bukhara ruling the now northern Afghan cities of Balkh and Kunduz. These ties were strengthened in the nineteenth century by successive amirs, who increased their influence in Kabul. In 1839 after the First Afghan War when the British drove the Afghan king Dost Mohammed from power in Kabul, he took refuge with the amir of Bukhara.[20] Persecuted tribal leaders, bandits, mullahs and merchants frequently took refuge in each other's territories; the army of the amir of Bukhara depended heavily on Afghan mercenaries. Moreover the amir of Bukhara was encouraged by the British to increase his influence in Kabul in the hope that this would reduce Russian influence. Today Islamic fundamentalists from Tajikistan are once again using Afghanistan as a base from which to launch attacks against the government in Dushanbe.

When the first Russian revolution deposed the tsar, a movement inspired by nationalism and Islam began in the Ferghana valley to throw off the Russian yoke. Tajik clan leaders played a prominent role in the first conference of the Ittefaq ul Muslimeen that was held in Kokand in November 1917. The conference set up a Provisional Kokand Autonomous Republic and demanded the promulgation of shariat Islamic law and the private ownership of land. The Bolsheviks refused to accept their demands and attacked Kokand in February 1918, razing it to the ground during three days of looting and immense slaughter.[21] By April almost every village in Ferghana and Tajikistan had set up Basmachi guerrilla groups to resist Soviet power. A landlord, Igash Bey, mobilized some 20,000 fighters in forty groups across Tajikistan and Ferghana. By the end of 1919 his forces had captured Osh and Andizan in the Ferghana valley. Across Central Asia similar revolts were being staged by the Basmachis.[22]

The Basmachi movement was born out of the Bolshevik's refusal to acknowledge the particularities of the Islamic tribal system of the region. The Russians took the derogative term 'Basmachi', from the Turkic language, in which it means 'robber' or 'bandit'. Locally, however, it was known as the movement of the 'bek' or freeman; later the Basmachis themselves were not averse to using the term, as it came to be associated with nationalism and Islam, as was the term 'Mujheddin' used by the Afghan rebels fifty years later.

The largely Russian Bolsheviks were totally alienated from the very people they were supposed to be leading and educating.[23] They made no attempt to understand the complex tribal and clan basis of the social structure, which they considered backward. In turn the Basmachis were helped by the British in India, who encouraged King Amanullah Khan of Afghanistan to send camel caravans loaded with arms and ammunition to Bukhara and Ferghana in 1919.[24] Initially the Red Army was overwhelmed by the Basmachis, until Marshal Frunze arrived in Tashkent in February 1920 to organize a new offensive.

Frunze attacked Bukhara forcing the amir to flee to Dushanbe and then to Kabul. Basmachi attacks on Frunze's forces delayed his advance but he finally entered Dushanbe in February 1921.

Frunze declared an amnesty for all Basmachis who surrendered and the 6,000 who did so in 1920 were instantly turned around and made to join the Red Army. Alongside brutal offensives in Ferghana and Tajikistan, Frunze also began to distribute food and money to local chiefs in a 'winning of hearts and minds' campaign.[25] The Civil War reaped a bitter harvest in Tajikistan, where the area under crops decreased by more than one half, three quarters of the livestock were destroyed, irrigation canals were damaged and entire villages were razed to the ground. All mosques were forcibly shut down or destroyed and land belonging to the madrasahs were redistributed to Bolshevik supporters. In 1923 a famine followed by a typhus and malaria epidemic swept through Tajikistan and Ferghana, wiping out an estimated half-million families.

Tajikistan now became the battleground for one of the strangest episodes of the Bolshevik revolution. A brilliant and ambitious Turkish army officer, Enver Pasha (1881–1922), arrived in Moscow and convinced Lenin to send him to Bukhara to raise an army to fight the Whites and the Basmachis. Pasha became the stuff of future Tajik legend when he joined the Basmachis instead. A charismatic figure who dreamed of reuniting the wider Turkish world in a Pan-Turkic Empire, Pasha had joined the Young Turks who overthrew the Ottoman empire and helped lead Turkey against the allies in World War One. He married a Turkish princess and was appointed minister of war at the age of thirty-two, but he was forced to flee Turkey after it was defeated by the Allies.[26]

Russia was still at war with Turkey when Pasha convinced Lenin that he could raise a Muslim army to defeat the Basmachis. So desperate was the Bolsheviks' position in Central Asia at the time that Lenin was willing to try anything and gave Pasha a free hand. However by the time Pasha arrived in Bukhara, Moscow had signed the Turco-Soviet Peace Treaty in March 1921. To fulfil his personal dream, Pasha decided to join the Basmachis instead and arrived near Dushanbe where he linked up with the most important Basmachi leader, Ibrahim Beg. In January 1922 they captured Dushanbe with just 2,000 men, but were forced to yield ground when a Russian relief force arrived.[27] Pasha tried to contact other Basmachi groups in present-day Kyrgyzstan, Uzbekistan and Junaid Khan in Turkmenistan as he fought running battles with pursuing Bolshevik troops. Pasha's forces were pushed back and on 4 August 1922 at the village of Baljuan near the Afghan border, the Bolsheviks finally caught up with him. With twenty-five of his bodyguards, Pasha rode full tilt into the ranks of the Red Army and died a hero's death. His dramatic death was eulogized in poems across Central Asia. Ibrahim Beg survived and fled to Afghanistan.

Pasha's tragic adventure was badly timed and ill judged. The Basmachis were small tribal groups unwilling to unite under local leaders, let alone willing to accept the orders of an outsider. In Tajikistan, Pasha was dealing with the only non-Turkish group in Central Asia and even though his main ally, Ibrahim Beg, was an Uzbek, none of the Basmachis fully trusted Pasha's intentions. Moreover by 1922 the Basmachis were being defeated everywhere, as the Bolshevik offensives gained momentum and famine destroyed the people's will to resist. Nevertheless Pasha's exploits gave the Basmachis an international significance that they had not had until then and his death became an inspiration for all Pan-Turkic movements in the future.

Although Basmachi resistance was wiped out in other regions, in Tajikistan it continued intermittently for several years. Thousands of Tajik Basmachis sought refuge in Afghanistan rather than surrender. Based in Mazar-e-Sharif, they launched attacks into Tajikistan in 1929. Encouraged by the British, Ibrahim Beg returned to Tajikistan from Afghanistan in 1931 but he was caught and executed by the Bolsheviks.[28] In a tragic repetition of history, in the winter of 1992 thousands of Tajik refugees from the civil war in Tajikistan took refuge in Mazar-e-Sharif.

The Basmachis went underground but their ideas and passion never fully disappeared. Fifty years later Azad Beg, a relative of Ibrahim Beg, revived the Basmachi ethos at the height of the Afghan war when he formed the Islamic Union to subvert communist Tajikistan. The Soviet Union said he was helped by the American CIA, Pakistan and Turkey to set up a Mujheddin group of former refugees from Tajikistan who lived in Kunduz province. However Azad Beg's efforts never matched those of the important Tajik Mujheddin leader Ahmad Shah Masud.

Throughout the 1920s the CPTJ, made up largely of Russian settlers and cadres sent from Moscow, remained insecure and unable to consolidate power. The threat from the Basmachis ensured that Tajikistan was the last republic to carry out socialist reforms such as collectivization. To consolidate further the division of nationalities in Central Asia, the Tajik Autonomous Soviet Socialist Republic was created as part of the Uzbek SSR in October 1924, even though several hundred thousand Tajiks continued to live in what was now Uzbekistan. In January 1925 the Gorno-Badakhshan Autonomous Region, with its capital at Khorog and inhabited largely by Ismaeli Muslims, was created. Finally on 15 October 1929 the Tajik Soviet Socialist Republic was established.

Although the Basmachi threat had diminished, Stalin never trusted the CPTJ, whose leaders he was to constantly accuse of ultra-nationalism and treason because of their alleged contacts with Britain. Between 1927 and 1931 there were several purges from the party so that by 1935, 66 per cent of the top party leaders who had begun their careers in the late 1920s had been purged. In the trials of 1937 the president, the secretary of the central committee and the chairman of the People's Congress of the CPTJ were purged and several leaders were executed.[29] In 1927 there were public protests when the Arabic script used for the Tajik language was discarded in favour of a newly created Latin script. This in turn was changed to Cyrillic in 1940, further confusing the language issue for most Tajiks. The legacy of the Basmachi revolt led Moscow constantly to ignore Tajikistan's cultural and economic development except for the northern region. This neglect was to exacerbate economic and political tensions between the various regions when independence came in 1991.

Industrial development in Tajikistan had begun in Khodjent under the Tsar. In 1913 the northern region produced 9,700 tons of oil, 28,000 tons of coal and 32,000 tons of cotton.[30] The rest of present-day Tajikistan had no industry until Stalin shifted factories to Central Asia during World War Two. By 1945 Tajikistan was producing ten times more coal and five times more machinery than in 1939. After the war the exploitation of the enormous mineral wealth of the Pamirs began, with the construction of the largest industrial complex in Central Asia. Built in stages, the South Tajik Territorial Production Complex near Dushanbe began to produce hydroelectricity, refined minerals, and manufactured aluminium while other plants produced a variety of chemicals. However bad planning and the poor quality of machinery had turned many plants into white elephants by the 1980s.

By 1989 Tajikistan was producing coal, zinc, uranium, radium, bismuth, asbestos, mica, lapis lazuli and other minerals. Eighty hydro and oil-fired generating stations produced some 15,700 million kilowatt hours of electricity, much of which was exported to other republics. The most ambitious project was to build eight huge power plants and dams on the Vaksh river, of which five had been built by 1989. Economic production has been falling rapidly since 1988, however, as the overall economic crisis in the Soviet Union has worsened. In 1989 Tajikistan produced 300,000 tons of oil, but output fell to just 90,000 tons in 1990 because of a shortage of spare parts, inefficient management and the migration of Russian experts.[31]

Agriculture remains the primary source of income for most Tajiks. Since the 1917 Revolution, the area under farm cultivation has nearly doubled, from 494,000 hectares to 803,000 hectares, while some 43,000

kilometres of irrigation canals have been built. Tunnels up to 12 kilometres long have been dug through the mountains to bring water
from the mountains to the valleys below, while 17 per cent of the
electricity produced is consumed by a network of pumping stations
that raise this water to the fields. Tajikistan's 157 collective farms produce fruit, sugar cane, barley, rice and millet; there is rich pastureland
in the Pamirs where in 1989 some 1.4 million cattle and 3.2 million
sheep and goats grazed. With five climatic zones the republic had the
potential to produce a vast variety of food crops, but as in other
Central Asian republics, Moscow's first demand was for cotton. Cotton cultivation, which yielded an average of 900,000 tons per year
before 1989, has ruined food production and created large-scale erosion and salinization of the soil. In 1992 much of the cotton remained
unharvested because of the civil war. Agriculture on the small private
plots has boomed and some 25 per cent of the labour force is now
employed on private plots.

Russian experts estimated in 1987 that simply to maintain the current
standard of living in Tajikistan, which was already the poorest republic,
would demand a 250 per cent increase in investment or another 6 to
7 billion roubles more. Considering that the entire budget in 1988 was
only 2.1 billion roubles, no such investment was possible.[32] Unemployment in 1989 was estimated at a staggering 25.7 per cent, the
highest in any of the former Soviet republics. Despite unemployment,
there was still a huge shortfall in skilled labour – some 60,000 skilled
workers were needed in 1986 while local technical colleges could only
provide 30 per cent of that. The import of skilled labour from Russia
and Uzbekistan only further fuelled ethnic tensions.

Tajikistan has the highest population growth rate in the former
Soviet Union. In 1940 the republic's population stood at 1.5 million
people and has risen to 5 million today. From 1979 to 1989 there was
an increase of 34 per cent in the population, an annual growth rate of
5 per cent. Infant mortality is also high and in Dushanbe, where
medical facilities are far better than in rural areas, it is estimated to be
51.8 deaths per thousand, compared to the Soviet national average of
25.6 per thousand.[33] With the present political chaos it is extremely
difficult to presume that future governments in Tajikistan will be able
to provide enough living space, agricultural land and industrial development for its ever-growing population. Due to the civil war, foreign
investment in Tajikistan has been zero, while its only effective trade has
been the bartering of goods with its immediate neighbours: Iran,
Pakistan and Afghanistan.

The economic misery suffered by the people and the political
polarization did not prevent a cultural revival in Tajikistan in the first

year after independence. The Tajiks have revived their literary past by once again popularizing the writings of Persian poets and philosophers such as Rudaki, Nasir-i Khusrau, Rumi, Saadi, Jami and of course the twelfth-century poet Firdausi, whose statue now stands in the centre of Dushanbe. This Persian heritage was largely ignored by the communists, who cut Tajikistan off from its language and cultural links with Iran. Some young Tajiks only realized for the first time in 1991 that their language, Farsi, is the same as that spoken in Iran.

No other writer has exemplified both the assimilation and the tensions between the Persian and the Russian literary heritages than Taimur Zulfikarov, who is Tajikistan's greatest writer. Novelist, poet, screenwriter and dramatist, he has tried his hand at every literary form and been eminently successful and popular. Russian literary critics have compared him to a modern-day Dante. Even though he writes in Russian rather than Persian, his style is distinctly Persian. 'I try to recreate the old Persian poetry and myths about the past, but bring them up to date with the present. I try and write as though I was reviving a long-lost language,' he has said.[34] His style is intensely philosophical and there is a strong strand of Sufism running through his novels. Russians too love his work because he combines the ancient myths of Russia with frequent digs at communism and Stalin.

This cultural revival did little to stem the political crisis. Tajikistan was always one of the backwaters of the Soviet empire and its problems barely reverberated in the corridors of power in Moscow. In 1979, however, Tajikistan was to be catapulted into the limelight as thousands of Soviet troops poured through Dushanbe on their way to invade Afghanistan. The city become one of the major bases for the Soviet supply line that stretched into Afghanistan. Thousands of Tajik troops took part in the initial invasion, but within six months a worried Red Army high command had withdrawn them as it became concerned about the growing fraternization between them and the Tajik Mujheddin. The influence of the Afghan war on Tajikistan was immeasurable as it intensified the growth of Islamic fundamentalism, Tajik nationalism and clan rivalries in the countryside.

Many Tajiks believe that the worst legacy of the Soviet Union was the Afghan war. Tajik Foreign Minister Lakim Kaqumov admitted this as early as December 1991. 'Afghanistan is the most difficult and complex problem we face, that we have ever faced, because we share a long border with it. The Mujheddin control most of the border region and there have been incursions into Tadjikistan. If Islamic fundamentalism is very high in Afghanistan then it is natural it will influence Tajikistan also'.[35]

The first major eruption in Central Asia after the 1986 Alma Ata riots occurred in Tajikistan. In February 1990 a state of emergency was declared in Dushanbe after riots broke out, just on the rumour that Armenians who had fled the fighting in Nagorno-Karabagh would be given apartments in Dushanbe. On 12 February Kakhar Makhamov, the first secretary of the CPTJ, tried to address the angry crowds outside the CPTJ headquarters, but he was shouted down and in the ensuing melée five people were killed and seventy were wounded. Another thirty-seven people were killed two days later as the riots spread across the city. Some 5,000 extra troops were brought into Dushanbe as demonstrations continued outside the Parliament building.

Public demands made during the demonstrations were the first signs of the growing influence of the IRP, whose movement had remained underground until now. People demanded better housing, the closure of pollution-spreading plants and of meat shops that sold pork, the opening of more mosques and an end to the Russification of Tajik names. A self-defence committee called Waadad, or Unity, was formed.[36] Until the February riots, there were only telltale signs of IRP activities. In 1989 five political cells run by Islamic militants had been broken up by the government and some fifty young mullahs were arrested. Some of those arrested, like Rajab Ali Shayev and Nureddin Saidov, were only in their early twenties.[37]

The February 1990 demonstrations were used by the now considerably frightened CPTJ as the excuse to ban opposition candidates for elections to the Supreme Soviet of Tajikistan in March. Thus 94 per cent of those elected were communists, who re-elected Kakhar Makhamov as president of the republic. The refusal of the communists to accommodate the opposition, at a time when other Soviet republics were liberalizing the political process, was to convince the IRP that there could be no compromise with the nomenklatura. Moreover the Tajik communists refused to contemplate any economic liberalization. All in all they were to remain the most unresponsive and unimaginative of all the communist parties in Central Asia who were trying to adjust with the trauma of change brought about by Gorbachev.

Not surprisingly president Makhamov supported the August 1991 coup attempt against Gorbachev. There was uproar in the streets and after demonstrations outside Parliament, Makhamov was forced to resign on 7 September. His replacement, acting president Kadriddin Aslonov from the liberal wing of the CPTJ, suspended the party and froze its assets. The hardline communists in the Tajik Parliament refused to accept this and staged a counter-coup on 23 September, replacing Aslonov with the 62-year-old Rakhmon Nabiev – who had been first secretary of the CPTJ from 1982 to 1985. Nabiev imposed a state of emergency and revoked the ban on the CPTJ.

Once again the opposition took to the streets in protest. For ten days thousands of people camped on Lenin Square, quickly renamed Azadi (or 'Freedom') Square, in front of the Parliament building. They prayed, chanted and sang while calling on the government to resign. A tent city mushroomed in the centre of Dushanbe as opposition groups bussed in more people, who began to live on the square. The good humour and lack of violence of these early demonstrations were to be in marked contrast to the later bloodletting in the civil war.

This, the first public demonstration in which IRP militants demonstrated their organizing skills, shocked other Central Asian leaders, and the scale of the protest forced president Nabiev to back down. He revoked the state of emergency and on 2 October once again banned the CPTJ. He also announced a date for elections and lifted the ban on the IRP and other opposition groups. A joint opposition alliance, made up of the IRP and two new democratic parties, chose Daulat Khudonazarov, a renowned film producer and an Ismaeli, as their candidate for the presidential elections.

New opposition groups had already emerged. The Rastokhez Popular Front founded in September 1989 by Tajik writers and intellectuals was sympathetic to an Islamic revival, but agitated for a parliamentary system and democracy. The Democratic Party of Tajikistan (DPTJ) was founded after the February 1990 crackdown by a 42-year-old professor of philosophy, Shodmon Yousuf. The party claimed a membership of 15,000 people and advocated a mixture of Islamic revivalism, Tajik nationalism and parliamentary democracy. In February another opposition party, the Popular Unity Front, was founded by a group of businessmen in order to push for a quicker transition to a market economy. Its chairman was Otakhon Latifi, a former journalist for *Pravda*.

The most important opposition figure, however, was one who did not belong to any of these parties. Qazi Akbar Turadzhon Zoda, forty years old, was the elected spiritual head of Tajikistan's Muslims. For several years he had been supported by the communists as the official spokesman for Islam in the republic, but as the political crisis deepened the qazi moved to endorse the demands of the Islamic fundamentalists. Trained in Tashkent and Jordan as a mullah, he is an enigmatic figure with a razor-sharp mind and a strong opportunistic bent to his politics. During the elections the qazi successfully shaped the opposition alliance but refused to stand as a candidate for the presidency. The qazi predictated the early demise of Nabiev. 'Nabiev cannot last. He does not have broad support and there are acute divisions within his own cabinet. People mistrust the communists while we are more united,' he said. 'Islam is strong. Two years ago there were only seventeen mosques in Tajikistan and nineteen churches. Today there are 2,870 mosques and still only nineteen churches,' he added proudly.[38]

The elections held on 24 November 1991 gave Nabiev a narrow and controversial victory, with only 58 per cent of the votes cast. He had defeated seven other candidates but the result that sent shock waves through all of Central Asia was that the IRP and opposition candidate won 34 per cent of the vote. The opposition cried foul and demanded fresh elections. Nabiev refused and once again revived the CPTJ on 4 January 1992. Battle lines were now drawn as the opposition realized that Nabiev was using his election victory to consolidate power for the communists rather than to accommodate the opposition. When US Secretary of State James Baker visited Tajikistan in February, Nabiev prevented him from meeting opposition leaders. His visit was followed by a widespread crackdown on the opposition.

In March 1992 the mayor of Dushanbe, Masud Ikramov, was arrested along with other members of the Dushanbe city council and leaders of Rastokhez and the DPTJ. Within days of the arrests massive street protests again gripped the capital. While tens of thousands of anti-government demonstrators camped at the 'Shaheed' or Martyrs' Square, Nabiev's supporters camped in a counterdemonstration in the Azadi Square.[39] Nabiev appeared to be blind to the impending crisis and on 1 May he persuaded Parliament to grant him sweeping emergency powers to deal with the crisis, even though opposition MPs boycotted the Parliament. In the next few days the protests swelled as over 100,000 people joined the movement against the government. Finally violence erupted. On 6 May three people were killed and eleven wounded in fighting between two groups of protestors. Nabiev introduced a dusk-to-dawn curfew in Dushanbe, but within a few hours the president himself was surrounded in his palace by protestors who took over key government buildings.

Nabiev's political hard-line and crackdown were backed by no forceful instruments of state or a mass base. There was no national army and only a demoralized and unarmed police force. Nabiev's National Guard of some 700 men, recruited partly from criminal elements from Kuliab, carried no credibility or military strength, while opposition parties were already creating their own militia units. The CIS troops based in Dushanbe were ordered not to get involved. On 7 May fourteen people were killed as the National Guard and the opposition's militias had numerous clashes across the city. The militias seized the palace after Major-General Bakhrom Rakhmonov, chief military adviser to Nabiev, surrendered it to avoid bloodshed. At night in pouring rain, gun battles raged across the city as opposition and pro-Nabiev groups set up roadblocks and fired upon each other. Civilians were paralysed with fear, as law and order broke down completely.[40]

The spread of the fighting and fears that the IRP was gaining an upper hand prompted Russian officers, commanding CIS military units in Dushanbe to organize talks between the opposition and Nabiev. After all-night talks on 7–8 May, an agreement was reached to set up a coalition government of national reconciliation, with the opposition promising to disarm its supporters and lift the blockade around the capital's main buildings. The agreement was signed by leading communist figures and Nabiev on the government's side, and from the opposition by Mohammed Sharif Himatzade, chairman of the IRP, Shodmon Yousuf, chairman of the DPTJ, Tahir Abdujabborov, chairman of Rastokhez, Daulat Khudonazarov, chairman of the Union of Cinematographers of Tajikistan, and Amirbek, chairman of the La'le Badakhshan organization (a political group made up of Ismaelis from the Pamirs).

Despite the agreement, armed clashes continued as the opposition insisted that Nabiev resign, while his supporters in Khodjent threatened they would declare their region independent if Nabiev was forced out. These threats from the pro-communist north were to multiply and lay the seeds of recurring fears of the partition of the republic. Clashes continued with at least eight people killed on 12 May, just hours before both sides met at a CIS military barracks and finally agreed to implement the 7 May agreement. The opposition agreed to Nabiev staying on as president while they received eight of the twenty-four ministries. General Rakhmanov was named as head of the republic's Defence Council while Daulat Usman, vice-chairman of the IRP, became deputy prime minister. Nabiev announced the creation of a transitional Majlis or national assembly, which would include all opposition groups, and he revoked the decree setting up the National Guard.

The tragedy of the past few months had been fuelled by the reluctance of the communists to share power or bring about economic reform and equally by the impatient opposition, particularly the IRP who wanted power immediately. The political struggle in Dushanbe created unrest everywhere as each region declared its autonomy and threatened to split away from the republic. In April the Gorno-Badakshan autonomous region, populated by Pamiris, transformed itself into an autonomous republic within Tajikistan. In May the communist leadership in Khodjent threatened to form the 'Northern Republic of Tajikistan' if Nabiev was removed from office. In another pro-Nabiev region – the southeastern city of Kuliab, the district authorities threatened to make the city independent rather than accept dictates from the new coalition government.

Tajikistan was in chaos. The president was helpless and unable to rule beyond the city limits of Dushanbe. The government now constituted both the ruling party and the opposition – a political duality which paralysed the administration. Both sides kept undermining each other and threatened to seize total power. Parliament existed but failed to meet. Moreover by the refusal of the communists in Khodjent and Kuliab to recognize the coalition government, Nabiev and his supporters were ensuring that the slide into civil war would be sooner rather than later. By June heavily armed communists from Kuliab were attacking collective farms around Kurgan Tube that supported the IRP.

On 28 June at least 100 people were killed on a state farm when Kuliabis stormed into villages, firing indiscriminately at the workers. With heavily armed Kuliabis attacking IRP strongholds throughout the Kurgan Tube region, tens of thousands of people began to flee their farms for the relative safety of Dushanbe. Anarchy spread as armed groups blocked highways, kidnapped travellers for ransom and stopped traffic along all main roads to Dushanbe. Bitter fighting continued around Kurgan Tube as arms flowed into Tajikistan from Afghanistan.

Mujheddin leader Gulbuddin Hikmetyar was said by KGB officials to have armed four hundred militants in Dushanbe alone, while his rival, Ahmad Shah Masoud, was also arming his supporters in the IRP. The IRP revered both the rival Mujheddin leaders, the Pathan Gulbuddin Hikmetyar and the Tajik Ahmad Shah Masoud, who after the fall of Kabul in April 1992 became the country's defence minister. Masoud was considered a national hero who had raised Tajik prestige by defeating the Soviet Union in Afghanistan. Both Masoud and Hikmetyar were helping arm and train factions of the IRP as the struggle for power intensified. Moreover within the IRP there was growing rivalry between the Muslim-Brotherhood-trained leadership of such figures as Himatzade and the charismatic Qazi Toradzhon Zoda, who was building up his own lobby within the party.

On 31 August 1992 students belonging to the Dushanbe Youth Movement – a body organised by the Qazi – stormed the Parliament building and took several government officials hostage. As protesters gathered outside Parliament, Prime Minister Akbar Mirzoyev and several other ministers resigned. Talks between the government and the opposition broke down and the Presidium of the Parliament declared Nabiev removed from office on 3 September, even though no vote was taken. Nabiev, hiding out in the CIS military headquarters, refused to go. An emergency meeting of Parliament to elect a new leader was called for 4 September, but members supporting Nabiev did not attend. Some thirty people were killed and several hundred were wounded in the fighting that went on around the city.[41]

President Boris Yeltsin and all Central Asian leaders declared that Tajikistan was on the verge of civil war and ordered CIS forces, which numbered some 10,000 in Tajikistan, to take control of the porous 1,300 kilometre border with Afghanistan. Finally on 7 September as Nabiev attempted to take a plane to Khodjent, he was stopped at the airport by IRP militants. There was a brief shootout in which three of Nabiev's bodyguards were wounded, after which Nabiev resigned. 'Nabiev understood that if he could not defend himself, he could not protect others,' said Aslidin Sakhidnazarov, a member of the parliament.[42] Parliamentary Speaker Akbarsho Iskandarov became acting president and asked the opposition to continue working with the communists in the coalition government, appealing for a ceasefire.

Nabiev's forced resignation was the worst possible nightmare scenario for other Central Asian leaders. Not only was he the first communist leader to be deposed, but the manner of his ousting was a naked *coup d'état* and an abrogation of the constitutional norms that these leaders were desperately keen to preserve in such uncertain times. President Islam Karimov of Uzbekistan wrote to the UN Secretary-General Boutrous Boutrous-Ghali saying 'the threat of anarchy and chaos looms on the entire region' and he warned that 'our region must not become the next hot spot and the object of geo-political games'. The Russian and Kazakh foreign ministries warned other countries not to interfere and spoke about the danger of the conflict spreading and destabilizing the entire region. 'Such a development would threaten the security not only of the Central Asian states but also of Russia,' said a Russian Foreign Ministry spokesperson.[43]

Russian troops belonging to the 201 Motorized Rifle Division were deployed along the border with Afghanistan and at the strategic Nurek hydroelectric plant, which provides electricity to the whole of Central Asia. However Tajik conscripts deserted with their weapons leaving only Russian officers covering their bases. Continuous fighting around Kurgan Tube claimed hundreds of casualties. On 27 September the Kuliabis seized four tanks and took control of the centre of Kurgan Tube, forcing hundreds of Kurgan Tube militiamen to retreat and thousands of civilian refugees to flee to Dushanbe. Some three hundred prisoners were released from the jail in Kurgan Tube and these criminals joined the Kuliabi forces.

It was apparent that despite the influx of arms from Afghanistan, most of the weaponry being used in the conflict in the south had been seized from local troops and policemen. The interior ministry said that some 18,000 weapons had been captured illegally, while dozens of military vehicles had been seized by both sides. With the lives of CIS officers in jeopardy, Moscow ordered 2,000 additional troops to fly to Dushanbe on 28 September. 'The Tajik soldiers are taking sides in the conflict according to their clan origins,' said the Russian Deputy Foreign Minister Georgi Kunadze. He feared that the desertion of Tajik soldiers of the 201 division, could lead to an unprecedented collapse of military discipline which could shatter army morale in Russia itself.[44] 'We do not have the money or the men to send a larger peacekeeping force,' he said.

Moscow appeared helpless as Tajikistan drifted towards partition and civil war. CIS troops took over the airport and other key installations in the city to preserve some semblance of normality as Russian officers swore they would stay to protect Russian citizens. But in a clear sign of Moscow's panic, the Russian Foreign Ministry opened an office in a Dushanbe hotel to organize the mass evacuation of Russian settlers because they could no longer be protected. 'This is the real end of the Soviet empire. Russia can no longer protect its own citizens,' said a disgruntled Russian journalist as he watched swarms of Russians crowd around the reception area for evacuees to Moscow. Most of the nearly 1 million settlers of European descent – Russians, Germans and Ukrainians – were preparing to leave. Some 200,000 Russians and others had fled Tajikistan in the first nine months of 1992. With flights out of Dushanbe cancelled because of fuel shortages, many people were becoming desperate. The office of the director of Tajik Air was peppered with bullet holes after two young Russians held him hostage in September. They were demanding an aeroplane to fly to Russia.

Meanwhile IRP leaders in the coalition government condemned Russia for sending more troops to Tajikistan and accused them of fanning the conflict by helping the Kuliabi forces. 'I have no faith in the CIS or in Russia and no foreign forces can restore peace. The Russian army has been the main source of supply of weapons to the warring sides,' said Deputy Prime Minister and IRP leader Daulat Usman.[45] With acting president Iskandarov committed to call in Russian troops and the IRP determined to protest against their presence, the government was itself divided and became even more incapable of offering a political solution.

As the guerrilla war in the south became more and more brutal, tens of thousands of Tajiks were forced to migrate to Dushanbe. In a block of flats in the centre of the city, a grandmother, Ziadullova Uduzkhan, clutched her nine grandchildren and wept uncontrollably while telling the story of how her daughter, the children's mother, was raped and then skinned alive in Kurgan Tube. Atrocity stories from the south multiplied as the Kuliabi forces and the Islamic militia around Kurgan Tube slaughtered each other and any civilians they could find. By mid-October 126,000 refugees had arrived in Dushanbe, where there was no refugee relief organization and the government was incapable of providing for them.[46]

Even amongst ordinary Tajiks, anyone who had the money or the connections was trying to leave for a safer republic. A massive shift of population, not seen in Central Asia since collectivization in the 1930s, was under way. The family of Zarina Muhammadieva, a young English interpreter, was part of the well-to-do Tajik business elite, but the entire family was migrating to Samarkand. Many of Zarina's classmates, both Russians and Tajiks, at the prestigious Foreign Languages Institute had already left Tajikistan. Nozigul Zamanova, a widow with two daughters who held a good job but belonged to the Ismaeli sect, was trying to emigrate with help from Ismaeli friends.[47] In the north around Khodjent, thousands of Uzbeks were packing up, selling their homes and crossing the border into Uzbekistan, fearing that the civil war could soon turn against them.

The civil war gave outside powers, especially Iran, an unprecedented opportunity to establish their influence in Tajikistan. By the end of 1992 Iran was backing a wide range of political parties with money, food and military supplies while Afghan Mujheddin groups and Pakistan's Jamaat-e-Islami were also active in training and supplying Islamic fundamentalists in Dushanbe. In October, when the entire foreign diplomatic corps from six countries resident in Dushanbe numbered around twenty diplomats, the Iranian mission alone comprised twenty-one official diplomats and some fifty unofficial diplomats.[48]

Iran backed the government of president Iskandarov with money, fuel and goods but also backed other parties. At the headquarters of the DPTJ military wing, Commander Nazarudin Zuberdulla admitted: 'Iran is helping the DPTJ with funding, food and other supplies. We are forming a National Guard of four thousand men and our women are selling their jewellery to buy guns.' At Dushanbe's central mosque, teachers at the new madrasah built by Qazi Toradzhon Zoda proudly claimed that the building has been built with Iranian funds, that their salaries were paid by Teheran and that the qazi was creating his own militia force of some 8,000 men outside the city. The qazi was a little more enigmatic about foreign aid. 'The only help I want is from Allah, but if some of our neighbours are really Muslim and they help us for Allah's sake, then that is fine,' he said.[49] Foreign diplomats claimed that the IRP was receiving air drops of weapons from Iranian aircraft.

Diplomats said that Iranian intelligence officials played a major role in encouraging the opposition to topple Nabiev in September. Unlike in the past, when Iran backed only Shia fundamentalists, in Dushanbe it was following a more broadly based policy of backing all sides, as no one party had either the mandate or the military clout to assert itself across the country. Iran was also trying to outdo the growing funding and support from Saudi Arabia, Pakistan and the Afghan Mujheddin. Iran's role was greatly reduced after the coalition government was ousted by the Khodjent and Kuliabi forces.

As divisions within the coalition cabinet further weakened the government, an extraordinary coup attempt took place on the weekend of 24–25 October 1992. Some 1,500 armed men infiltrated the city and seized the parliament building. These forces were from Kuliab and they demanded the reinstatement of Nabiev as president. At least 100 people died in street fighting before militia units loyal to the IRP put the rebellion down. Russian troops stationed in the capital took no part in the fighting, but they took control of the airport and other strategic centres in the capital. Anarchy was now rampant and the crisis had reached such proportions that a few hundred armed men could attempt to take over the entire country.

The government, riven by factionalism, had now lost all credibility and was forced to accept the demand for a meeting of Parliament in Khodjent, where its pro-communist members could dominate the proceedings. As a prelude, on 10 November president Iskandarov and his cabinet resigned. At the extraordinary two-week session of Parliament, Imam Ali Rakhmanov, a communist leader from Kuliab, was elected president and Abdulmalek Abduljanov from Khodjent became prime minister. The Parliament also voted to scrap the country's presidential system and replace it with a parliamentary system. It announced a ceasefire and reconciliation between warlords from opposing factions. The Tajik interior ministry announced that 50,000 people had died in the fighting since the previous June and some 500,000 people, or one tenth of the total population, were now homeless refugees in the republic.[50] Rakhmanov's election signalled a severe defeat for the Islamicists and the democratic opposition as the members of the Khodjent faction proved that they retained their grip on Parliament. They attempted to revert back to the communist power sharing arrangements in Tajikistan, when the two top posts were usually shared between leaders from Khodjent and Kuliab.

But there was no reconciliation and no ceasefire as fighting continued. There were some eight hundred casualties when Kuliabis attacked refugees camped in the south. Thousands of Tajiks began to flee to northern Afghanistan – a tragic irony as that country was itself in the midst of a civil war. Around 70,000 refugees who had fled the communist militias near Shartuz arrived on the north bank of the Amudarya river, separating Afghanistan from Tajikistan. Lacking adequate food or clothing in the bitter winter snows, hundreds of men, women and children died. Others tried to swim across the river using rafts and logs, but more than 200 died, shot dead by Kuliabi militiamen or swept away by the raging waters. Those who managed to cross over found an empty wasteland, until the International Red Cross arrived to move them to Mazar-e-Sharif and take care of them. In the rest of Tajikistan some 537,000 people were internal refugees with no prospect of being looked after.[51]

In Dushanbe, IRP militia units set up barricades and resisted attempts by the new president to take up office in the capital. Militias from Kuliab and Khodjent retaliated with a full-scale attack on the city on 5 December; in heavy fighting over several days hundreds of people were killed. On 11 December Dushanbe fell to the pro-communist forces and the new president and prime minister flew in from Khodjent. As the Islamic militants took up positions outside the city and fighting continued, it became clear that both CIS troops and Uzbek soldiers from Uzbekistan were helping the government militias. Uzbek jets and helicopter gunships bombed and rocketed the town of Kofirnikhon, where the Islamic rebels held out. On 19 December an Uzbek helicopter gunship was shot down and at least 150 people were killed in fighting around the town. When Kofirnikhon fell three days later, Islamic militants fled east to the Pamirs and south to the Afghan border from where they vowed to launch guerrilla attacks.

The worst was yet to come. In Dushanbe the Kuliabi militia under their ruthless commander Sanjak Safarov, a 65-year-old criminal who had spent twenty-three years in jail for murder, went on the rampage against supporters of the opposition. People were dragged out of their beds at night and shot in the streets, hundreds of women were raped and children saw their parents being shot before their eyes. Most of the victims were supporters of the DPTJ and the IRP, but hundreds of Ismaelis were also wantonly killed even though many had no political connections. Perhaps as many as five thousand people were killed in this Tajik-style ethnic cleansing to which neighbours like Russia and Uzbekistan turned a blind eye. The USA later castigated the Rakhmanov government for terrible atrocities, human rights violations, 'summary executions, hostage taking, torture, rape and looting.'[52]

IRP leaders including Himatzade and Qazi Toradzon Zoda fled to Afghanistan. Leaders of the DPTJ fled to Moscow and the Baltic republics as death sentences were passed on them by the government.

At President Karimov's urging, Russia agreed to send 3,000 more CIS troops in January 1993 to patrol the Afghan–Tajik border, where a state of emergency was declared. In February Russian Defence Minister, General Pavel Grachev visited Dushanbe and formally ordered the 201 division to help the government. A Russian general was appointed as the new defence minister of Tajikistan. He raised officers' salaries to 50,000 roubles a month, an unprecedented sum for a soldier.

The government was preoccupied with stopping the infiltration of IRP militants from northern Afghanistan with arms and other supplies. The militants used the Tajik refugees around Kunduz and Mazar-e-Sharif to help them carry weapons back into Tajikistan and they received considerable help from Hikmetyar's Hizbe Islami forces, who refused to allow the Red Cross near their bases on the Afghan–Tajik border. It was clear that given the uncertainty in Afghanistan, the IRP would use Afghan bases to launch attacks into Tajikistan, a policy that was all too familiar to the communists from the Basmachi rebellion. In February and March heavy fighting continued around Dushanbe as the IRP launched guerrilla attacks on government positions. In the Rumit gorge outside the city, the 201 division joined government militias to drive back the Islamic fighters. The Islamic militants celebrated on 30 March when they heard that the Kuliabi leader Sanjak Safarov had been killed in an internal dispute with his deputy.

Six months after it had come to power the government had made no attempt to reconcile the warring factions inside Tajikistan. Instead it had gone on the offensive against Islamic fundamentalism and the opposition as it tried to consolidate the former Soviet-style nomenklatura in power. The government was only able to carry out such pogroms because of unconditional support from Moscow and Tashkent. With the tacit approval of all the Central Asian states, Uzbekistan had now become the gendarme of the region and dictated strategy to the Rakhmanov government. Tashkent became the main provider of fuel and food supplies to Dushanbe. Moscow's greater interventionist role in Central Asia was a significant shift from its earlier refusal to get involved in the region. (This is detailed in Chapter 9.)

The government's policies ensured that clan warfare would continue unabated in the republic. Entire districts such as the Garm, where the Qazi came from, and Badakshan were designated as the strongholds of the opposition. In military offensives to create a *cordon sanitaire*, civilians from these areas were driven out of their villages and collective farms. The ideological battle in Tajikistan had always been a veneer for the district and clan rivalries between Kurgan Tube and Garm on the one hand and the Kuliab and Khodjent regions on the other. This only intensified during the summer of 1993.

Tajikistan has become the linchpin of future stability in Central Asia. Despite the formation of a new government, many people across Central Asia still fear that Tajikistan could break up along regional lines, with the communist southeast linking up with the northern Khodjent region and separating from the anti-communist southwest. As Afghanistan itself disintegrates into warring fiefdoms run by war-lords, a seismic fissure of partition seems to be spreading northwards. The repercussions of events in Tajikistan are already affecting the populations of Uzbekistan and Kyrgyzstan. At present no single party appears strong enough to keep the country united and the danger is that as in Afghanistan, a multi-sided civil war will continue for years, which will once again suck in outside powers. Clandestine help from Afghanistan, Iran and Pakistan for the fundamentalists and support from Russia and Uzbekistan for the government will ensure that local differences will be augmented as regional powers fight an Afghan-style proxy war over the territory of Tajikistan.

Notes

1. Ahmed Rashid, 'The Crescent of Islam Rises in Tajikistan', *Nation* (Lahore), 25 December 1991.

2. Ahmed Rashid, 'Stoking the Furnace', *Far Eastern Economic Review*, 5 November 1992.

3. R. Weekes (1978) *'Muslim Peoples: a world ethnographic survey'*, Greenwood Press, USA. Also Ahmed Rashid, 'Dominion of Dominoes', *Far Eastern Economic Review*, 24 Sepetember 1992.

4. Weekes.

5. Ahmed Rashid, 'The Tajik Time Bomb', *Far Eastern Economic Review*, 15 October 1992.

6. The Ismaelis are a branch of Shia Islam and follow the leadership of the Aga Khan. Interviews by the author with Ismaeli militants in Dushanbe in December 1991 and in Kabul in October 1991 and April 1992. See also, Ahmed Rashid, 'Forced to Flee', *Far Eastern Economic Review*, 12 November 1992.

7. I. Cameron (1984) *Mountains of the Gods*, Facts on File, USA.

8. M. Polo (1961) *The Travels of Marco Polo* (with an introduction by F.W. Mote), Dell Publishing, USA.

9. Cameron.

10. R. Sikorski (1988) *Dust of the Saints: a journey to Herat in time of war*, Chatto and Windus, London.

11. M. Asimov (1987) *Tajikistan*, Novosti Press, Moscow.

12. M. Ispahani (1989) *Roads and Rivals: the politics of access in the borderlands of Asia*, I. B. Taurus, London.

13. T. Talbot Rice (1965) *Ancient Arts of Central Asia*, Praeger, USA.

14. J.W. Mcrindle (1896) *The Invasion of India by Alexander the Great*, reprinted by Indus Publications, Pakistan.

15. Ispahani.

16. Ibid. See also B. Forbes Manz (1989) *The Rise and Fall of Tamerlane*, Cambridge University Press, Cambridge.

17. Forbes Manz.

18. Asimov.

19. Ibid.

20. H. Rawlinson (1875) *England and Russia in the East: the political and geographical condition of Central Asia*, London, reprinted by Indus Publications, Pakistan, 1980.

21. F. R. K. Marwat (1985) *The Basmachi Movement in Soviet Central Asia*, Emjay Books, Pakistan.

22. H. Carrere D'Encausse (1979) *Decline of an Empire: the Soviet Socialist Republics in revolt*, Newsweek Books, USA.

23. A similar situation arose in Afghanistan after the communist coup in 1978 when Afghan communists, who had a minuscule social base, tried to enforce communism on a tribal and Islamic people.

24. Marwat.

25. Ibid.

26. Carrere D'Encausse.

27. Marwat.

28. Ibid.

29. R. Conquest (1990) *The Great Terror: a reassessment*, Pimlico Press, London.

30. Asimov.

31. Interviews with Tajik officials, Dushanbe, October 1992.

32. Government of Pakistan figures.

33. Ibid.

34. Interview with the author, Dushanbe, October 1992. See also Special Report on Tajikistan (by Ahmed Rashid) in *Herald*, (Karachi), November 1992.

35. Interview with the author, Dushanbe, December 1991.

36. M. B. Olcott, 'Central Asia's Post-empire Politics', *Orbis*, Spring 1992.

37. A. Taheri (1989) *Crescent in a Red Sky: the future of Islam in the Soviet Union*, Hutchinson, London.

38. Rashid, 'The Crescent of Islam Rises in Tajikistan'.

39. Reuters, 'Demonstrators Hold Protests in Tajikistan', *Dawn* (Karachi), 30 April 1992.

40. Reuters, 'Tajik Leader Calls for Support', *Independent* (London), 7 May 1992.

41. Daily Reuter Reports, *News* (Islamabad), 1–7 September 1992.

42. Reuters, 'Tajik President Steps Down', *Dawn* (Karachi), 7 September 1992.

43. Reuters, 'No Policy Change Following Nabiev Ouster', *News* (Islamabad), 8 September 1992.

44. Interview by the author in Moscow, 30 September.

45. Rashid, 'Stoking the Furnace'.

46. Ahmed Rashid (in Dushanbe), 'Refugees Flee Tajikistan', *Nation* (Lahore), 9 November 1992.

47. Ahmed Rashid (in Dushanbe), 'Forced to Flee', *Far Eastern Economic Review*, 12 November 1992.

48. Ahmed Rashid (in Dushanbe), 'Outside Powers Destabilising Tajikistan', *Nation* (Lahore), 8 November 1992.

49. Ibid.

50. Agence France Press, '50,000 Killed in Tajik Fighting', *Nation* (Lahore), 24 November 1992.

51. US State Department (1992) *1992 Human Rights Report for Tajikistan*, Washington, DC.

52. Ibid. Also interviews over the telephone with victims of these purges, December − January 1993.

8

The Desert Horsemen – Turkmenistan

Behind the office desk of Muradov Nepesovich, president of the Majlis (formerly the Supreme Soviet of Turkmenistan), there hangs an enormous and priceless carpet. In the traditional, intricate Turkman style and with a staggering half-million knots to the square yard, Lenin's image glares down at the onlooker. In the anteroom there are more priceless carpets depicting Marx and Engels.[1] After the break-up of the Soviet Union, Lenin's statues were easy to smash in other Central Asian republics, but Turkmenistan's conservative leaders appeared to have no intention of taking down such an important link with the past. In Ashkhabad, the capital, little changed despite the end of communism, the break-up of the Soviet Union, and independence for Turkmenistan.

On 13 December 1991, the day that the five presidents of the Central Asian republics met in Ashkhabad and decided to join Boris Yeltsin's Commonwealth, Turkmen officials were in a state of shock. When jokingly asked if the independence they had now won would be celebrated with parties or fireworks, they merely scowled and their long faces drooped even further. The former Communist Party of Turkmenistan (CPT) is now the Democratic Party of Turkmenistan (DPT), but despite an election no opposition parties are allowed, the same communists hold office and they still run a police state. President Saparmurad Niyazov is the chairman of the DPT and he is proud of the fact that out of its 52,000 members, 48,000 are former communists.

Ashkhabad, just 40 kilometres from the Iranian border, is set in some of the most desolate landscape in the world. The city sits on the bleak rollercoaster foothills of the Kopet Dagh mountains and beyond it lies the Karakum, or Black Sand, desert – a howling wilderness of red sand and shifting dunes over which sandstorms blow salt from the ecologically devastated Aral Sea into the city.[2] The sand dunes, which grow to enormous heights, blow across oases and water holes and smother them. Areas of dry clay soil or *takyrs* that form enormous cracked surfaces, hard as concrete, stretch for hundreds of kilometres, rendering even the grazing of flocks impossible.

Ashkhabad with a population of 400,000 people is the most southern and the hottest city in the former Soviet Union and is situated on an unstable seismic zone. First in 1929 and then again on 6 October 1948 Ashkhabad was struck by severe earthquakes. The latter measured 9 points on the Richter scale and destroyed the entire city, killing 110,000 people, or two thirds of the entire population. News of the earthquake was never released and when foreign countries tried to offer aid, Stalin refused to even acknowledge that the earthquake had occurred. Turkmen still relate the backwardness and the intellectual poverty of their republic to that earthquake, for it wiped out the entire intelligentsia and the educated middle class in the city – the potential leadership that could have given hope for the future. President Saparmurad Niyazov himself was orphaned – the earthquake killed both his parents.[3]

Turkmenistan, which covers the territory of the former Transcaspian region of Turkestan, was one of the poorest and most isolated of the former Soviet Union's fifteen republics. At independence it carried the unenviable burden of having one of the highest unemployment rates, the highest infant mortality rate, the lowest level of literacy and the most polluted agricultural land in the entire Soviet Union. Despite seventy years of communism, the majority of its 4.2 million people still define themselves according to their tribal loyalties and few were prepared to break their economic dependence on Moscow, which appeared the only guarantee of survival.

For centuries Turkmenistan was a desolate land, inhabited only by the nomadic warrior Turkmen tribes who fiercely resisted, but eventually succumbed to the Persians, the Turks and later the Russians. Around 350,000 square kilometres of the republic's 488,000 square kilometres is occupied by the waterless wastes of the Karakum desert, where only the hardy Turkmen nomads with their small flocks could survive the rigours of extreme temperatures. Rainfall in these regions is so rare that people remember single rainstorms that occurred years ago; acute water shortages are the biggest problem the population faces. Only 2.5 per cent of the land area is arable and the only significant agriculture is along the banks of the Amudarya river, which runs along the eastern edge of the Karakum. Along the 1,100-kilometre-long, Lenin Canal, water is carried from the Amudarya to Ashkhabad but its unprotected banks have caused massive waterlogging and salinization of the surrounding land. The arable land is also heavily polluted because of the overuse of pesticides and fertilizers.[4]

Of the population, 72 per cent are Turkmen, 13 per cent are Uzbeks and 12.6 per cent are Russians who have settled in urban centres over the past fifty years. The republic shares its southern border with Iran where some 313,000 Turkmen live and its eastern border with Afghanistan where another 390,000 Turkmen live.[5] The Afghan Turkmen are largely from the Ersari tribe who migrated in the nineteenth century, while the Tekke tribespeople, who led the revolt against the Bolsheviks, arrived as refugees in Afghanistan in the 1920s. For the Turkmen, borders were meaningless until the Bolshevik Revolution, for they considered Iran and Afghanistan as much a part of their homeland as modern Turkmenistan is. Later the huge Soviet military cantonments built in southern Turkmenistan demonstrated how strategically important these international borders became to the Red Army. Turkmenistan's western shores are washed by the Caspian Sea and in the north it adjoins Uzbekistan and Kazakhstan.

In the eighteenth and nineteenth centuries many Turkmen migrated into Mesopotamia and Anatolia. There are still 170,000 Turkmen living in Iraq and another 80,000 in Syria. Tens of thousands more Turkmen live in Turkey. The Turkmen of Central Asia have remained Sunni Muslims, but many of the Middle Eastern Turkmen have become Shias. Although they have assimilated with the predominant local culture, they still identify themselves as Turkmen. The original Turkmen language belongs to the Oghuz group of Turkic languages and is close to modern Turkish and Azeri. The small body of Turkmen poetry and history was written in the Arabic script, but in the twentieth century Stalin forced the people to adopt the Cyrillic alphabet.

The Turkmen region has been inhabited ever since the fifth millennium BC, according to Soviet archaeologists who have unearthed the remains of agricultural settlements in the south.[6] From the sixth century BC, the region was part of the Persian empire; two centuries later it was conquered by Alexander the Great after he defeated the Persians. The Parthian kings, who ruled a vast empire across Central Asia after the Greek conquests, built their capital at Nyssa, 18 kilometres from present-day Ashkhabad. The remains of Nyssa have been unearthed and bear testimony to the building and cultural skills of the Parthians. From the second century BC to around AD 10, the Parthians built a flourishing civilization with a high standard of art, pottery and weapons production influenced by both China and Persia. Its wealth was based on the Silk Route: Nyssa became a city that linked China with Europe. Traffic on the Silk Route created oasis towns in ancient Turkmenistan and allowed the region to flourish until the Middle Ages.[7]

The present-day Turkmen migrated from the Altai region, in eastern Turkestan, to the Caspian Sea in the tenth and eleventh centuries, as part of the larger migration of the Oghuz Turks. They built up a formidable reputation as raiders and warriors, who attacked caravans along the Silk Route and raided settled areas in Persia, Afghanistan and Central Asia. The loot from these raids comprised mostly slaves, whom the Turkmen traded with the Arabs and later with the khanates of Khiva and Bukhara. Even in the nineteenth century the Turkmen captured an estimated 1 million slaves from raids into Persia. The Persians failed to subdue this trade despite frequent military expeditions.

Much of early Turkman history concerns either resistance to the Persians and the khanates of Khiva and Bukhara or fighting on their behalf. Unable to build an empire of their own from their desert wastes, the Turkmen frequently helped others to build theirs. Persian kings tried to keep the Turkmen in check with punitive military expeditions, but they rarely managed to penetrate or control the Karakum desert, to which the Turkmen would immediately retreat when faced with an external threat. When the Persian king Nadir Shah invaded Central Asia in 1741, the Turkmen tribes first put up fierce resistance, but once they were defeated they joined Nadir Shah's armies.

The Turkmen first came into contact with Russians in the early part of the sixteenth century when Russian caravans trading with Central Asia passed through Turkmen territory. After the Russians captured Astrakhan, on the western shores of the Caspian Sea, Russian caravans used the city as a base from which to trade with Central Asia.[8] The defeat of Persia by Russian armies in 1813 positioned the Russians on the borders of Turkmen territory for the first time. The Treaty of Gulistan of 1813 gave the Russians control of all Persian dominions in the Caucasus and the Russian navy the sole control of the Caspian Sea. From 1834, under the pretext of securing their trade routes, the tsars built a series of forts on the eastern shores of the Caspian, slowly encroaching into Turkmen areas.

The largest and most powerful of the Turkmen tribes, the Tekkes, resisted the new Russian forts which frequently sent out military expeditions to harass the nomads and seize their flocks. In 1870 the two great Tekke chiefs, Khushid Khan and Nur Verdi, began to attack these expeditions in a guerrilla war that went on intermittently until the end of the century. Russian generals suffered their worst defeat in 1881 when they tried to capture the Tekke fortress of Geok Tepe and an entire Russian army was decimated. In a retaliatory expedition, the Russians at last captured the fort and massacred 6,000 of its defenders. Facing artillery and machine gun fire for the first time, the Turkmen horsemen retreated into the desert and carried out scorched-earth tactics in order to deny the advancing Russians their villages and water wells.

In 1870 there were some 200,000 Turkmen tents, holding an estimated 1 million people, divided into some twenty-four tribes, scattered across the desert. The Tekkes, the Yomut and Goklan lived in the south and east of the region. General Kaufman, who finally subdued the region for the tsar, called these tribes the most formidable light cavalry in the world and the greatest marauders in Asia. After conquering Bukhara and Samarkand, in 1873 General Kaufman moved against Khiva, the largest city in the Turkmen region.[9]

The Turkmen had taken part in Khiva's affairs either as mercenaries or as part of a complex power struggle waged by successive khans with the local Uzbeks. The Turkmen were often used by the khans as a security force to keep marauding Kazakh and Kyrgyz nomads away from the city and to keep the ambitious Uzbeks off balance. In return for military services the khan granted many Turkmen, particularly the Yomut, land, cash and exemptions from taxes.[10] The khans of Khiva were notorious for their backwardness and their attempts to keep their people poor and uneducated. Even after Khiva became a Russian protectorate, the then khan, Mohammed Khan (1865–1910), refused to allow schools, electricity or a telephone system to be introduced in his domain. The Russian excuse for its 'liberation' of Khiva was to free the hundreds of white Russian slaves captured by the Turkmen and now serving the khan.

Two Russian military expeditions set out for Khiva in 1873, one from Tashkent and the other from Orenburg. The Yomuts who dominated the region around Khiva put up fierce resistance, fighting street to street even after the khan had surrendered. The Russians carried out horrible retributions in Khiva which are still remembered today. 'This expedition does not spare either sex or age. Kill all of them,' were the orders Kaufman gave to his officers. Almost every inhabitant was slaughtered and the Yomuts were saddled with huge indemnities, which impoverished them for decades.[11]

Capitalizing on their victory, the Russians created a Transcaspian government in 1874 under General Lomakin, which was based at Krasnovodsk, the main Russian base on the eastern Caspian shore and in the heart of Turkman territory. Persia quietly gave its agreement that the Russians could subdue the Turkmen tribes. In their endeavours the Russians were helped by the fact that the Turkmen tribes refused to unite. The long-standing rivalry between the two largest tribes, the Tekkes and the Yomut, were played up by the new rulers, allowing them to annex the entire Turkmen territory by 1886.

Russian administrators, soldiers and traders arrived in the territory to run the new protectorate. Russian workers were moved in to build ports and the Transcaspian railway along the Caspian Sea, where there was a large Russian naval presence. Working conditions for the Russians worsened in the most isolated, hottest and poorest region of the empire. In 1900 Russian workers in Ashkhabad began a series of strikes and protest movements demanding higher pay and better living conditions. They were brutally suppressed. During the 1905 Revolution against the Tsar, strike committees were set up in all the stations along the Trans Caspian railway line and a Bolshevik committee was formed in Ashkhabad which set up a secret printing press – the first in Central Asia.[12]

Local Russian protests against the Tsar were seldom joined by the Turkmen, amongst whom a renewed anti-Russian resentment was growing. The huge indemnities forced upon the tribes for their revolts, the decapitation of the tribal elite, the frequent looting of their flocks and herds and the redistribution of the best land to Russian farmers all contributed to the anti-Russian feeling. The Russians had introduced extensive cotton cultivation and the karakul sheep to the Turkman region precisely so that the tribal cultivators could pay back the huge fines imposed on them from the past.[13]

For the first time in Turkman history an undisputed leader emerged from the tribes. He was Mohammed Qurban Junaid Khan, a wealthy Yomut landlord and local Islamic judge, who characteristically for a nomadic society first gained local prominence as a successful bandit against Russian settlers. He was to use the growing chaos in Central Asia to attempt to throw out the Russians. In 1916 Junaid Khan led an attack on Khiva after accusing the khan of co-operating with the Russians. Junaid Khan captured the city and the khan, and proclaimed himself Khan of Khiva – a position he held for only a few days until he was pushed out. Junaid Khan then moved south and captured Ashkhabad, executing several Russian officials. When the Russians sent a punitive expedition to crush the revolt, Junaid Khan retreated into the Karakum and eventually sought refuge in Persia.[14]

By 1918 when the civil war broke out after the Bolshevik Revolution, Junaid Khan was accepted as the paramount leader of all the Turkmen tribes – a hero who had the capacity to organize armies, command the respect of the tribes and put the fear of God into both the Reds and the Whites. Initially the Turkmen joined neither side in the Civil War and instead demanded their freedom from Russia. Junaid Khan's popularity was finally recognized by the khan of Khiva, who asked him to head his army after the Russians abandoned Khiva in 1918.

Based in Khiva, Junaid Khan was now courted by both the Red and

the White armies and he eventually signed a peace treaty with the
Reds, which guaranteed the independence of Khiva. However the
Bolsheviks were only buying time and in 1919, having crushed local
White armies, they attacked Khiva. Once again Junaid Khan fled to
the desert; some of his Turkmen allies were co-opted by the new
Bolshevik regime until 1920, when they too were killed. For a brief
period British troops based in northern Persia invaded Turkmenistan
in support of the White armies. The East Persian Cordon force, with
its headquarters in Meshad and under the command of Major-General
Wilfred Malleson, drove north, captured Ashkhabad and then seized
Baku and the oil wells on the Caspian. The force had moved 1,200
kilometres inland, cut off the Central Asian railway and thrown the
Bolshevik armies into total disarray. International pressure forced the
British to retreat, however, as other European powers feared British
control of the strategic Baku oil wells.

Junaid Khan was condemned by the Bolsheviks as a Basmachi rebel
and a tool of British imperialism, but this did not stop him leading
another uprising in 1920. Again there was a ceasefire, which was to
last until 1924 when Junaid Khan staged a fresh rebellion. He attacked
Khiva with some 15,000 men but was forced to retreat after the Red
Army arrived. He retired to the desert from where he continued
sniping at Russian convoys. Finally in 1927, aged seventy, he led his
final rebellion against the Bolsheviks. In a raid on a Red Army camp
he lost two of his sons and his force was badly mauled. Again he
retreated into the desert – later he crossed the border into Persia,
finally settling in Afghanistan where he died in 1938. Today Junaid
Khan's exploits are being pieced together by nationalist Turkmen who
have been denied any written account of his exploits since the 1920s.

Despite his nationalist spirit and desire for independence, Junaid
Khan's revolts lacked political organization and clear direction. Although he successfully united the tribes in the heat of battle, tribal
fissures always re-emerged after defeat. Continuing long-standing
Turkman prejudices, he failed to win over the powerful Uzbek tribes
and the small urban trading class, with whom there were constant
tensions which were fully exploited by the Bolsheviks. The very make-
up of nomadic Turkman society was unable to create the political
structures for a lasting basis for change. Few of the new ideas of the
progressive Jadids in Uzbekistan penetrated the desert wastes of
Turkmenistan, which helped to ensure that the frequent revolts would
remain only the expression of fierce Muslim tribal resistance rather
than an alternative to Soviet society.

The intermittent revolts of the Turkmen nomads from 1870 to 1927
was the most sustained and bloody confrontation with Russian expan-

sionism in Central Asia. Few Central Asian nationalities fought so fiercely or suffered such retribution as the Turkmen tribes. For decades famine, the destruction of their flocks, the poisoning of their waterholes and their isolation from other resistance movements in Central Asia did not deter them. The bloodletting and destruction have soured Russo–Turkmen relations ever since and will continue to be a major factor in determining the future of an independent Turkmenistan's relations with Russia. This factor has much to do with recent statements by President Niyazov, that Turkmenistan would not co-operate with the CIS or with any Central Asian economic union.

A European traveller, who journeyed through Turkman areas in 1924 described the plight of the tribes as desperate but proud. More than 1 million Turkmen had retreated into the desert to escape the Red Army, which had formed a camel corps of troops to chase them and finish their resistance. Even after they were forced to settle on collective farms in great poverty, the Turkmen retained their traditional tribal customs. Guests were welcomed with tremendous hospitality, the slaughter of sheep and displays of Turkmen horsemanship. Travellers still commented that the Turkmen loved their horses more than their women. The Dab, or tribal law, was still adhered to by the young generation and administered by the elders; they paid only lip service to Soviet laws.[15]

Bolshevik suspicions of the Turkmen only helped to perpetuate previous tsarist policies. In a series of purges in the 1920s the local Bolsheviks, who were almost entirely of Russian origin, eliminated the tribal hierarchy through imprisonment and executions, while attempting to create new centres of loyalty through a system of patronage and favours. The region was absorbed into the Turkestan Autonomous republic after 1918. On 14 February 1925 the Soviet Socialist Republic of Turkmenistan was created, but there were very few local cadres to implement the policies of the CPT and the republic was effectively run by Russians for decades.

Industrialization and the collectivization of private farms began in 1928, later than in other Central Asian republics, because of Moscow's fears that any radical measures could lead to fresh rebellions. Without engineers or technicians Turkmenistan was dependent on Moscow for everything from investment to technical help and communist cadres. Textile and food processing industries were set up in Ashkhabad early on and Turkmen workers were sent to other factories in the Soviet Union to learn how to operate machinery. The Soviet army sealed the borders with Iran and Afghanistan after setting up large military bases in the south and east to contain the threat of infiltration by Basmachi Turkmen rebels who had taken refuge in these countries. When the

Soviet army invaded Afghanistan in 1979, these military bases were to provide crucial logistical support for the maintenance of troops in Herat.

The few Turkmen who aspired to climb up the ladder of the CPT faced purges and retributions. During Stalin's purges in the 1930s, leading Turkmen communists were charged with being British agents and secret supporters of the Basmachis and were arrested and shot. Nederbai Aitakov, the chairman of the Turkman Supreme Soviet, was tried and executed during the purge of 1937, along with dozens of other senior Turkmen communists. The Turkman Arabic alphabet was changed to Latin in 1926 and then to Cyrillic in 1938, creating further resentment both amongst the population and within the CPT. The purges were accompanied by waves of Russian migration to Turkmen cities such as Ashkhabad where they took over the best housing and jobs available. Between 1926 and 1939, the population of Turkmenistan grew by 200 per cent because of this influx of Russians. Today Turkmen still only constitute 41 per cent of the population of Ashkhabad.[16]

After the catastrophic earthquake in 1948, Moscow's indifferent attitude increased bitterness against the Russians. When, in the 1950s, CPT leader Suhan Babaev tried to promote Turkmen cadres over the heads of Russians, he was purged and expelled from the CPT by Khrushchev, who accused him of promoting ultra-nationalism. Mukhamednazar Gapurov, a pliant Turkman first secretary, ran the party from 1962 to 1977, but Russians continued to hold the most powerful positions in the government and the party. Gapurov was later accused by Moscow of corruption and nepotism. 'Under him cadres were often promoted to leading posts on grounds of personal loyalty, family ties or birthplace,' said a 1986 report to the CPT Congress. 'He had created a breeding ground for nepotism, flattery and careerism,' it continued.[17] In fact Gapurov was later praised by Turkmen nationalists for promoting Turkmen up the party ladder and resisting orders from Moscow.

The Brezhnev era saw greater emphasis being placed on promoting Turkmen to high office, but these officials could only command respect from Moscow if they were prepared to crack down on any form of local dissent. Such policies ensured that social and economic development in the republic remained stunted as local initiative never developed. In one of the most appalling human rights cases in 1971, the poet Annasultan Kekilova was locked up in a mental asylum after criticizing local officials in her poetry. She died in the asylum. Today her poems have once again become widely popular.

President Gorbachev's reforms barely penetrated Turkmenistan, and even though in Moscow Turkmen leaders repeatedly voted for *perestroika*

in the Supreme Soviet, they never applied reforms at home.'Our deputies voted for Gorbachev and *perestroika* in Moscow but they were
tyrants at home,' said a female computer worker in Ashkabad.[18] But
the news of changes in Moscow slowly penetrated into the region
despite attempts by the government-controlled press to ignore them.
The first protest movement was sparked off by veterans from the war
in Afghanistan, who on their return home found that the government
refused to acknowledge the deaths of Turkmen soldiers or help in the
rehabilitation of the wounded. In November 1987, two thousand
veterans held a protest rally in Ashkhabad – the first in the city for
more than fifty years. They strongly condemned the cover-up by the
authorities and decided to erect a monument for their dead without
government help.[19]

In the autumn of 1989 some six hundred academics and intellectuals formed the first 'informal' group, named 'Agzybirlik' or 'Unity'.
They called for a memorial day for the massacre at Geok Tepe in 1881
but the government declared the meeting illegal and denounced the
group as ultra-nationalist. Further meetings, which discussed health
and ecological problems, were broken up by police as the government-controlled press went on a verbal rampage against them. Turkmen
intellectuals who gave interviews in the Moscow press calling for
glasnost to be applied in Ashkhabad were run out of their jobs. A storm
erupted in Parliament in late 1989 after an article was published in the
English-language *Moscow News* describing how the cotton monoculture
in Turkmenistan had ruined the health of children. Officials furiously
denied the charges of poverty and mismanagement and purged several
journalists who were thought responsible for the article.[20]

Niyazov supported the August 1991 coup attempt against Moscow
but hurriedly backed down after the coup was defeated. The government had declared the sovereignty of Turkmenistan on 22 August 1990,
but refused to allow any opposition group to meet, leave alone reg-
ister itself as a party. In October 1991, the newly formed Democratic
Front Party of Turkmenistan was forced to hold its first congress in
Moscow because the meeting had been banned in Ashkhabad. Its
leader, Mohammed Durdu Murad, advocates a union of all Turkic
people, but he cannot get his message to the people because of censorship and bans on meetings. The Islamic opposition remains minimal, with the Islamic Renaissance Party and other groups banned.
After years of state control and isolation from the Muslim world,
Turkmenistan has witnessed the mushrooming of mosques and
madrasahs as in other Central Asian republics, but Islamic fundamentalist groups remain underground. At the social level, however, Islam
is widely adhered to and practiced, especially by the young.

The collapse of the Soviet Union came as a major shock to the government of President Saparmurad Niyazov. He had become first secretary of the CPT in 1985 and consolidated his grip by proving unswervingly loyal to Moscow and promoting those Turkmen communists who supported him. In November, a month before the collapse, Turkmenistan's myopic leaders rejected the privatization of land and denounced foreign investment that was not controlled by the state. Six weeks later, left stranded by Moscow, they were to become overnight advocates of foreign investment. Government ministers scrambled around trying to set prices of gas and other exports in dollars and then to market them internationally, while also trying to secure food shipments from other republics. 'We do not know much about markets and have to educate ourselves first,' admitted a worried-looking Foreign Minister Avde Kuliyev, who had only twenty officials in his ministry in December 1991 – none of whom had any experience of dealing with the outside world.[21]

For several months there was economic chaos as the leadership refused to carry out privatization programmes at home even though other Central Asian republics had already begun to do so. Hastily, the minimum wage was raised to 350 roubles from a previous minimum of 200 roubles, and all government controls on wage rises were abolished as the rouble crashed against the dollar. By January 1992 prices of foodstuffs had shot up by 500 per cent in the markets, despite weekly government statements that it was trying to control prices. The prices of imported foodstuffs were freed to encourage entrepreneurs to bring in food whatever the price. In March 1992 a privatization law was finally passed, but it gave the state the right to hold the largest stake in all property to be sold, so as to avoid what officials called speculation and hasty transformation.[22]

Having such long borders with Iran and Afghanistan, the republic faced serious security problems. In January 1992 a new defence ministry was set up headed by Danatar Kopkov, the former KGB chief of Turkmenistan. Conflicting statements were issued for several months: officials said that Turkmenistan would not create its own armed forces but would sign a defence agreement with Russia, while other officials said an independent army would be created. However the government was keen to retain its military links with Moscow.[23] In June 1992 an agreement with Russia was signed creating a joint military command structure in which Russian officers and soldiers would oversee a local Turkmen army. This agreement would still allow CIS troops to guard Turkmenistan's borders with Iran and Afghanistan. Some 30,000 CIS troops with 700 tanks and a Corps Headquarters were based in Turkmenistan in 1992, but this number was being rapidly depleted as the CIS cut back its overall troop strength.

The press remains under state control and muzzled under the Committee for Preservation of State Secrets in the Mass Media. Reports in Russian newspapers and films from Moscow television are pre-censored and the tight political control remains unflinching. A new draft constitution based on a strong presidential system was released for public discussion in March 1992 but after a minimum of debate in the press, all of it favourable, it was adopted on 18 May. It renamed Parliament the Turkmen Majlis, *majlis* being the Persian word for Assembly. It gave President Niyazov increased powers and stripped Parliament of considerable legislative powers. Although the new constitution guaranteed the private ownership of land and property, it did not define how it could be obtained.

At first the government insisted that fresh elections were not needed because 98 per cent of the population had cast their votes for President Niyazov on 26 October 1990. However as free presidential elections took place throughout Central Asia in 1991–92, Niyazov changed his mind. In June 1992 he ran unopposed in Turkmenistan's first general elections, on a platform of nationalist rhetoric stating that with Turkmenistan's gas and oil wealth his government would turn the republic into another Kuwait.[24] A month earlier he had raised pensions and allowances for large families, whilst he improved his Islamic credentials by taking part in the annual pilgrimage to Mecca. On 22 June Niyazov was re-elected president with 99. 5 per cent of the votes in his favour, according to the government. No other political party was allowed to take part in the campaign.

Despite this, for most Turkmen the crucial legacy of the Soviet system was not the lack of political freedom, but the poverty and ecological disasters that have dominated their lives. The facts are simply appalling. Unemployment in Turkmenistan stood at 18.8 per cent in 1989, one of the highest in Central Asia. The inadequate health system had led to a 62 per cent increase in jaundice, hepatitis and gastro-intestinal diseases during the 1980s; these usually curable diseases accounted for 80 per cent of all fatal illnesses. In 1992, 127 hospitals and clinics were without running water, many had no electricity, and postoperative infections were rampant because of the poor sanitary conditions. 'We work like doctors did in the Middle Ages,' one local doctor has said.[25] In 1989 the infant mortality rate was 54 per thousand, one of the highest in the Soviet Union, ten times higher than in Western Europe and on a par with Cameroon. In the poorest regions in the north such as Tashauz, the rate soars to 111 deaths per thousand according to official statistics, which are generally considered to be underestimated. Child labour in the cotton fields, widespread infant malnutrition, and continued inbreeding resulting from the tribal traditions of cross-cousin marriage worsened the situation.

The poverty on collective farms outside Ashkhabad is stark – comparable to the worst poverty in South Asia. Semi-naked children without shoes run through dirty alleys that have no sewerage; they work on the chemical-and-fertilizer-infected land, which creates large sores on their feet. Women give birth at home because of the lack of maternity care. Families have little furniture and share their living rooms with animals because no animal sheds are built. Many houses are tin shacks that leak when it rains. This poverty is self-perpetuating as the ruling party appears reluctant to initiate any social programme. And the collapse of the Union dramatically worsened the overall economic crisis. Turkmenistan grows little food and 70 per cent of its total imports from other republics are basic foodstuffs and consumer goods. The republic produced only 4.47 million tons of grain in 1991. (Farmers were given increased rates for grain – raised from 3.4 roubles per kilogram to 6 roubles per kilogram to encourage them to grow more grain.)

Food shortages have increased over several decades as Moscow set larger and larger quotas for cotton production. Turkman cotton yields were extremely low compared to other regions of Central Asia because of the huge investment required and the shortage of water. In 1991 some 1.4 million tons of cotton were produced, twenty times more than the output sixty years ago. The region provided 14 per cent of the former Soviet Union's cotton fibre, but only 3 per cent of its cotton was processed within the republic. There is still a chronic shortage of textile plants which the government is now trying to rectify. But the effects of trying to produce cotton in what are essentially an unsuitable soil and climate have been devastating. Huge irrigation projects bringing water from the Amudarya have bought water to parched lands but drastically depleted the water input into the Aral Sea, creating an ecological disaster there. Inadequate drainage has increased salinization, making once-arable land incapable of growing any crops.[26]

The 1,100-kilometre Karakum Canal, which was begun in the 1950s and only completed in 1990, brings water from eastern Turkmenistan to Ashkhabad. Along its shores huge cotton plantations have sprung up, but collective farms were forbidden to grow food crops. Another 200-kilometre canal was being built in the north in order further to expand irrigated land for cotton. On the 350 collective farms there is considerable mechanization, with some 41,200 tractors and mechanised harvesting of cotton.[27]

Animal husbandry, the traditional economic base and lifestyle of the nomads, has continued under the collective farm system. Camel raising has steadily declined, even though camels are still the main form of transport in the desert and provide much-needed milk, meat and wool. Although some 4.7 million sheep and goats, 700,000 cattle and 200,000 pigs are still reared, these numbers are considered too little for the population's own needs. The Russians introduced the money-making karakul sheep for their expensive wool, which is now a major export. Along the Caspian Sea there is extensive fishing, but the lack of refrigerated storage facilities does not allow the fish to be transported inland. Horse raising, once the backbone of the Turkmen tribes, has declined. The Turkman breed of Akhalteke horses is one of the oldest and most revered horse breeds in the world. After conquering the Parthians, Alexander the Great entered the Parthian capital of Nyssa, near present-day Ashkhabad, riding an Akhalteke horse called Bucephalus, which became famous throughout the world and was the only horse to have a city named after it.

Outside the cities Turkmen peasants and nomads continue their lives as they have done for centuries. Marco Polo described the Turkman lifestyle seven centuries ago.

> The Turkmen roam over the mountains and the plains, wherever is good pasturage, for they live off their flocks. They have clothing made of skins and dwellings of felt or of skins. They weave the choicest and most beautiful carpets in the world. They also weave silk fabrics of crimson and other colours of great beauty and richness and many other kinds of cloth.[28]

Many nomads still live part of the year in yurts as they graze their flocks in the desert shrub.[29] According to traditional practice, men still buy their wives after paying a *kalim* or bride price, which can be as much as 40,000 roubles or the equivalent in sheep and camels.

The tribal system remains strong, with individual loyalties first given to the extended family, the clan and then the tribe rather than to the state. Clans still live together and practise extensive intermarriage. In rural areas female seclusion is carried out quite extensively. Women cover their heads and do not talk to strangers who may be visiting the family yurt. The tenets of Islam, prayer and fasting are strictly observed in the desert; having enough money to perform the *Haj* is still the strongest wish of most nomads. The Turkman military tactic of retreating into the desert when confronted with a larger invasion force is still a psychological tactic for many people – except this time the retreat is carried out because of the overwhelming economic and social problems in the cities.

While Turkmenistan is famous for its carpets and karakul wool,

which is stitched into coats and hats, the real money-earning export
of the republic was the 85 billion cubic metres of natural gas produced
in 1989 at twenty-eight gas fields. 47 per cent of the economy's turnover came from industry, and the bulk of that was dependent on gas.
'The problem is that after the collapse of the Soviet Union we have
no idea who will now buy our gas. We were once the centre of world
trade because of the ancient Silk Route, but now we have to start
again,' said Foreign Minister Avde Kuliyev in December 1991.[30] Gas
still flowed along the massive pipelines to Russia and the Ukraine,
who now had to pay higher prices for it, but Turkmenistan received
none of the subsidized food and consumer goods once provided by
the centre. The government did not have the dollars to buy these
goods elsewhere and the economic crisis rapidly worsened after December 1991 as prices went up by five hundred per cent.

Moscow's pricing system was much to blame for the post-independence crisis. Under the communist system the republic received
just 5 or 6 roubles for 1,000 cubic metres of gas – a totally unrealistic
price. After declaring sovereignty Ashkhabad raised the price to 34
roubles, and in 1992 raised it to 870 roubles, which still left Turkmenistan's natural gas the cheapest in the world. (By the end of 1992
the government raised the price to 8,000 roubles, which was on par
with international prices.[31]) Ninety per cent of the gas was sold to
other republics and whether they would still buy such huge quantities
at the new prices was doubtful. A major crisis erupted in March 1992
when Ukraine refused to pay the new prices. The Turkman government promptly closed down the pipeline and refused to ship any more
gas to the Ukraine. A few days later gas was cut off to Armenia because it also refused to pay the new prices, and disputes developed
with Georgia and Azerbaijan. Finally these republics came to an understanding with Turkmenistan after agreeing to provide consumer
goods and food in barter deals which were priced at world prices.

In 1991 natural gas production fell to 80.4 billion cubic metres and
then to 55 billion cubic metres the following year as the cutback in
exports and a severe shortage of spare parts, technicians and other
problems mounted up. But Turkmenistan has a phenomenal 8.1 trillion cubic metres of natural gas reserves, and President Niyazov is
basing his country's economic recovery on the sale of this gas abroad.
Having got over its initial confusion, the government began assiduously to court foreign companies and neighbouring states for investment. Turkey, Iran and Pakistan expressed keen interest in building gas
pipelines to their countries and in providing Turkmenistan an outlet
to the sea for gas exports.

In April 1992 Turkey, Iran and Turkmenistan reached an agreement to build a gas pipeline to Europe costing $2.5 billion dollars, which would be paid for by Saudi credits. In the first phase of construction the pipeline would have the capacity to carry 28 billion cubic metres of gas.[32] The government is also trying to attract foreign investment to build a petrochemical plant which would add value to the natural gas by producing liquified natural gas and other chemicals. The centre of the gas industry is Mary (formerly Merv) in eastern Turkmenistan. Here huge gas-fired electricity generating plants allow the republic to export some 3,000 million kilowatts of power to other republics, but the price it has received for this product so far has been very low.

Turkmenistan also has some 700 million tonnes of proven petroleum reserves. In 1989 it produced 5.4 million tons of oil, but output dropped to 5.2 million tons in 1992. The largest oilfields are in the western region of Nebit Dagh; new wells have recently been opened in Mum Dagh. Krasnovodsk, the Russian fort built in 1869 on the Caspian Sea, is now the republic's main port and the centre of the oil-exporting industry; a large refinery is located there. However, as with its gas, the government faced the problem of receiving low prices from other republics for its oil, which was initially priced at 15 to 70 roubles a ton when world prices were $150 a ton. The government raised the price for oil in stages through 1992. In June 1992 an Italian oil company signed a letter of intent to build an oil refinery some 300 kilometres northeast of Ashkhabad. Six months later the government asked for bids from foreign companies to explore oil in two onshore and two offshore blocks. An Argentinian firm gained one block of some 10,000 square kilometres, but Western interest in oil exploration in Turkmenistan has so far been limited.

Turkmenistan's other main exports are astrakhan furs, which in 1989 were sold for only 15 to 20 roubles a fur to Moscow for processing and turning into coats and hats. On the international market a single finished coat earned Moscow thousands of US dollars. Cardzou, in the northeast of the republic with a population of 162,000 people, has developed into the second-largest city in the republic, with large-scale industry including cotton mills and sulphur, super-phosphate and other chemical processing plants. A French company signed a contract in 1992 to build a $250 million textile plant, which will allow Turkmenistan to add value to the cotton it produces. Turkmenistan is also rich in mineral deposits, but they were barely exploited in the past because other former Soviet republics were producing similar minerals. Turkmenistan will need considerable foreign investment to unearth these minerals, while exporting beyond the republic remains a major problem.

The 20,000 kilometres of roads and 2,120 kilometres of railways are inadequate even for local trade in the vast territory of Turkmenistan, while the only sea outlet is to the landlocked Caspian Sea. The export of oil, gas and minerals needs access to the sea and until that is made possible through Iran, these products are still exported through neighbouring republics. In October 1991 Iranian Foreign Minister Akbar Ali Velyati signed a memorandum in Ashkhabad to pay for a road and rail link from Askhabad to Meshad which will give Turkman exports access to the Persian Gulf, but this will take several years to build. In the meantime, Iran promised to buy up to 3 billion cubic metres of gas and 150,000 tons of diesel fuel from Turkmenistan for onward sale abroad during 1992. In exchange it would provide 6.5 million tonnes of refined petroleum products to Ashkhabad, set up a refinery to produce lubricants, and help in the further exploration of oil and gas.[33]

In November 1991 the border with Iran was opened for the first time since it was closed after the Iranian Revolution. Although Turkmen citizens are not allowed to travel more than 40 miles inside Iran, barter trade between northern Iran and Turkmenistan has started, which has led to a sudden increase in the smuggling of consumer goods, fuelling the already large black market in Ashkhabad. Teheran gave Turkmenistan $50 million in credits to buy Iranian goods; Pakistan has provided another $10 million of credits. Considerable barter trade and smuggling are being carried on with Herat in Afghanistan. Turkmenistan provided the regime of President Najibullah with diesel fuel until Kabul fell to the Mujheddin in April 1992. Meanwhile a Pakistani delegation visiting Ashkhabad in December 1991 showed a keen interest in building a gas pipeline across Iran and Afghanistan to Pakistan (but with the continuing instability in Kabul, this project is still on hold). In May 1993 several Turkish companies announced that they would invest some $800 million over the next few years in tourism, food processing and textiles, as the rivalry between Iran and Turkey for influence in the region increased.

Turkmenistan was initially the most ill prepared and the most reluctant of the Central Asian republics to deal with the problems of independence. There was no programme for privatization, creating a market economy or encouraging joint ventures with foreign partners. In June 1992, when other republics had opened their doors to property privatization, President Niyazov said there could be no privatization of flats or houses for another ten years. The government also remained insistent on offering concessions to foreign companies only as long as it remained a majority share holder. However by the end of the year it had changed its tune. To encourage foreign investment the government announced a tax exemption for three years for any foreign company investing 30 per cent of the value of any new project

in the republic. President Niyazov insisted that Turkmenistan's oil and
gas would be sufficient to provide it an income, no less than that of
Kuwait's in a few years' time.

But the president sees his oil and mineral resources as a means to
raise the standard of living without undergoing any of the necessary
economic changes required to move to a market system. He views
investment and development not as means to open up the economy
but as means to retain even tighter political control over the people.
Niyazov refused to join various economic forums proposed by the
CIS and the other Central Asian states. At the May 1992 summit of
the Economic Co-operation Organization (which comprises Pakistan,
Iran, Turkey, Azerbaijan and the five Central Asian states), he took a
strong anti-integrationist position, declaring that states should rely on
bilateral agreements and not on any economic union. He said that
countries should not live off each other but develop their own economies independent of each other – a slap in the face for the ECO.

At the Tashkent summit of Central Asian republics in January 1993,
Niyazov said that the CIS should only be a consultative body and not
co-ordinate economic development. He again strongly rejected all
CIS or Central Asian involvement in Turkmenistan's development plans.
This go-it-alone policy has been fuelled by his belief that Turkmenistan's
oil and gas will provide a quick solution to the country's economic
problems. It also reflects the problems he has had with other republics
in getting a fair price for the country's exports.

This attitude has also been strengthened by Niyazov's desire to keep
Turkmenistan as isolated as possible and free of the political turmoil
in Russia and other republics. He has created a crude Stalinist per-
sonality cult around himself, creating an entire government department that only disseminates pictures of him. His portrait is everywhere
and in parades columns of students march arm in arm with his portrait emblazoned on their T-shirts. There is no hint of political *glasnost*
or of allowing democracy to flourish; political parties have remained
banned. 'The communists are stronger than ever. Lenin created a dictatorship of the proletariat. Niyazov is building his own dictatorship
and independence is only for the regime and the mafia,' said Durdu
Murad, leader of the underground opposition party Democratic
Front.[34]

Opposition to the government is still muted, but anti-Russian feeling is growing and there is stronger criticism as opponents maintain
a steady attack on the regime through the Moscow press. In December 1992 the government was harshly criticized by international human rights groups when it refused the leaders of the nationalist party,
Agzybirlik, permission to travel to Beshkek, capital of Kyrgyzstan, for

a human rights conference. The government placed those wanting to go under house arrest. Turkman nationalism has been fuelled by the underground printing of prose and poetry by former nationalist literary figures. The Pan-Turkism espoused by many nationalists has a genuine international connection, for tens of thousands of Turkmen live in Turkey, Iran and Afghanistan. In the future it is these reopened links with their ethnic family abroad that are most likely to fuel greater political consciousness inside Turkmenistan. The republic's international borders have been opened and no matter how hard the regime tries to control the flow of ideas and people, the cross-border flow will generate its own momentum.

As it celebrated its first year of independence, the government proudly pointed out that the country was stable and had experienced none of the upheavals or the threat of Islamic fundamentalism that other Central Asian states were subject to. Yet in the long term Turkmenistan remains one of the most potentially unstable states in Central Asia, because the political repression exerted by the state is coupled with its inability to open up the economy sufficiently to attract foreign investment. The dream of becoming self-sufficient and as rich as Kuwait on the basis of oil and gas exports cannot be realized unless foreigners are convinced that the country is politically stable and capable of guaranteeing their investments. Turkmenistan's exposure to the outside world of competition has been very limited, and until the government's tunnel vision regarding development and democracy changes, it is unlikely to achieve an economic take-off.

Notes

1. Ahmed Rashid, 'Reluctant Turkmenistan Caught in a Dictatorial Time-warp', *Independent*, 28 December 1991.

2. P. Hopkirk (1990) *Setting The East Ablaze*, John Murray, London, for a description of the region during the 1917 Revolution.

3. M. Brill Olcott, 'Central Asia's Post-empire Politics', *Orbis*, Spring 1992.

4. R. Mnatsakania (1992) *Ecology of the Former Soviet Union*, Centre of Human Ecology, University of Edinburgh.

5. R. Weekes (1979) *Muslim Peoples: a world ethnographic survey*, Greenwood Press, USA.

6. B. Yazkuliev (1987) *Turkmenia*, Novosti Press, Moscow.

7. A. Taheri (1989) *Crescent in a Red Sky: the future of Islam in the Soviet Union*, Hutchinson, London. For the early art of the Parthians and the growth of Nyssa see T. Talbot Rice (1965) *Ancient Arts of Central Asia*, Praeger, USA.

8. M. Saray 'Russo-Turkmen Relations up to 1874', *Central Asia Survey*, Vol. 3, No. 4.

9. H. Rawlinson (1875) *England and Russia in the East*, republished by Indus Publications, Pakistan, 1980.

10. Y. Ros (1984) *The USSR and the Muslim World*, George Allen and Unwin, London.

11. Saray.

12. Ibid.

13. F. R. K. Marwat (1985) *The Basmachi Movement in Soviet Central Asia*, Emjay Books, Pakistan.

14. Ibid.

15. G. Krist (1992) *Alone Through the Forbidden Land: journeys in disguise through Soviet Central Asia*, Ian Faulkner Publishing, Cambridge.

16. M. Hauner (1990) *What is Asia to Us: Russia's Asian heartland yesterday and today*, Unwin Hyman, London.

17. P. Cockburn (1989) *Getting Russia Wrong: the end of Kremlinology*, Verso Books, London.

18. Interviews by the author in Ashkhabad, December 1991.

19. D. Doder and L. Branson (1990) *Gorbachev: heretic in the Kremlin*, Futura Books, London.

20. Interviews by the author with Turkmen journalists in Ashkhabad.

21. Interviews with government officials Ashkhabad, December 1991.

22. Reuters report, 23 March 1992.

23. The debate is detailed in *Central Asia Significants*, compiled by the Centre of Central Asia in Islamabad, March 1992.

24. Reuters, 'Turkmenistan Polls Today', *Muslim* (Islamabad), 20 June 1992.

25. David Remnick, 'In Soviet Central Asia, Death Stalks the Children', *Washington Post*, 21 May 1990. Figures are from B. Rumer (1989) *Soviet Central Asia: a tragic experiment'*, Unwin Hyman, London.

26. Rumer.

27. See Chapter 3 for further details.

28. T. Severin (1984) *Tracking Marco Polo*, Zenith Books, London.

29. See Chapter 6 for details of the nomadic lifestyle.

30. Interviews in Ashkhabad, December 1990.

31. Interview with Vice Prime Minister Nazar Soyunov, published in *Central Asia Significants*, March 1992.

32. Central Asia Significants, June 1992.

33. Reuters report, 24 January 1992.

34. Reuters report, 23 March 1992.

The Great Game Revisited – Central Asia's Foreign Policy

In those fateful December days in 1991 as the Soviet Union broke up, the old communist party bosses of the five Central Asian republics scurried around to put together Foreign Ministries and find diplomats who could deal with the outside world. There were few Central Asian diplomats in the old Soviet Foreign Office who were either of ambassadorial rank or spoke foreign languages or had served in Western capitals. Career diplomats of Central Asian origin were usually relegated to Soviet embassies in Africa or Asia and served at junior levels.

Moreover with Central Asia having been cut off from the outside world for so long, there was an acute lack of information about foreign countries, and only a handful of experienced academics or officials, who could guide their governments through the global diplomatic minefield. From the standpoint of the outside world, five new countries were coming into being, the names of which most people could not even spell.

After President Yeltsin reorganized the Soviet Foreign Ministry into the Russian Foreign Ministry, Kazakhstan could only muster some twenty diplomats from Moscow, none of whom had had any experience in the West. No more than a dozen diplomats opted for Turkmenistan, while Tajikistan had even fewer. Party secretaries from the provinces were roped in to perform diplomatic duties. Yet telephone and telex communications, air travel, mail and diplomatic pouches still had to be routed via Moscow. Russia was to continue issuing visas for visitors to Central Asia, and Central Asian diplomats travelling abroad had first to travel to Moscow to receive their visas and often their instructions. Each republic set up a liaison office in Moscow, which became almost as important as the Foreign Ministry at home.

The irony of the situation was not lost upon the heirs of the great Turkic and Mongol conquerors, whose couriers rode from China to Europe carrying messages and threats that were often enough to create a political crisis thousands of miles away. Even in the nineteenth century, as the Great Game between Russia and England was played out and Central Asia had been considerably weakened by divisions, the region still appeared awesome to outsiders. 'Turkestan, Afghanistan, Transcaspia, Persia – to many these words breathe only a sense of utter remoteness, or a memory of strange vicissitudes and of moribund romance. To me, I confess they are pieces on a chess board upon which is being played out a game for the domination of the world,' said Lord Curzon.[1] Only the Bolsheviks were to push Central Asia into a diplomatic limbo where the outside world could only be viewed through Moscow's eyes.

In Central Asian capitals the communist elite had grown up learning foreign languages and perhaps even praying to Mecca, but they had never met a foreigner, travelled abroad or met a Muslim outside of the region. Ignorance of the outside world was so enormous, the lack of experience so obvious, the shortage of expertise so dehabilitating, that Asian diplomats described their initial handling of foreign affairs as childlike. Moreover they had little time to catch up as the outside world caught up with them first. Even before the Soviet Union broke up, high-level Iranian, Turkish and Pakistani delegations were touring Central Asia in fierce competition with each other to woo the new governments. Central Asian presidents would come out of party meetings to discuss the latest step taken by Moscow and then have to face Iranian Foreign Minister Akbar Ali Velyati or some other dignitary who wanted answers to crucial questions. What will your foreign policy be, who will you befriend, what will be your policy on Afghanistan, Islam, your neighbours or Russia and do you accept our offers of aid?' It was enough to set their heads spinning. 'For a time we thought we must be the most important people in the world,' said one Turkoman diplomat.[2]

Not surprisingly, the emergence of five new states in Central Asia had affected the whole world. For the USA and Europe, who had been out of touch with the region for seventy-five years with the exception of a handful of academics and travel writers, it was a case of general ignorance and limited interest, because of the momentous events in Moscow. With the collapse of the Soviet Union, India had lost its major ally and it had few ties with the new Central Asian states. China, realizing that economics had brought about the Soviet collapse, quickened its own economic reforms. Japan and its neighbours faced an enormous political vacuum in the Far East and a year later, still could not decide how to fill it. The west Asian Muslim countries dreamed of dominating their new neighbours. The anti-American Arab states and the Palestinians had lost their most powerful backer in the Soviet Union, while for the Muslim Brotherhood Central Asia was a challenge where the banner of Islamic fundamentalism could be raised on virgin territory. Everywhere in Africa, Asia, Central and Latin America, proxy wars between the former Soviet Union and the USA ground to a halt. For all these countries, Central Asia was an old idea taking on a new life.

For the Russians the trauma of losing an empire and having to live with fourteen new states was even more bewildering. A new phrase was quickly coined, 'the near abroad', to distinguish between former republics and foreign countries. For those 25 million Russians who lived outside Russia, life had suddenly become unpredictable, uncertain and full of fear for the future, especially in Central Asia. Over the past few years, many Russians had already migrated back to Russia, but after independence the trickle became first a torrent and then, as Tajikistan erupted into civil war, a flood. But these Russians were returning to no homes, no jobs, hyper-inflation and shortages of everything. Thus most Russians in Central Asia were caught between two stools, fearing to stay because of the uncertainty, yet fearing to leave because of the unknown that lay back home.

The speed with which independence came gave no time to Central Asian leaders to formulate polices towards their neighbours. Thus their relations with the rest of the world were dominated not so much by what they wanted, but by what the rest of the world desired to do with Central Asia. The first to leap into the region in competition with each other for influence and leverage were Turkey, Iran and Pakistan.

Central Asia gave Turkey unprecedented international importance. The languages of four of the new states, and of Azerbaijan, are Turkic dialects, their peoples come from Turkic stock and their leaders looked first to Turkey for political inspiration and economic aid. Turkish intellectuals proudly boasted that, from the Balkans to China, a Turk could now travel freely meeting his own people and communicating in Turkish. Central Asian scholars were even more eulogistic. 'There is one cultural world based on the Turkic languages. Turkey, having achieved nationhood, is the head of this world. The Crimean Tartars and the Azeris are the neck and shoulders. The Kazakhs are the heart. The Uzbeks and Turkomen, with their nomadic traditions, are the legs. Though the body is torn apart, the old roots and language are still there,' said Kazakh scholar Almaz Estekov.[3] Turkey's membership of NATO, its role as a base for the US military during the Gulf War and its self-avowed secularism made it the pre-eminent favourite of the

Western powers, through which their own relations with Central Asia could be expedited. Washington was especially keen for Turkey to play a major role to counter Iranian influence.

With Turkey having a population of 57 million people and another estimated 95 million people of Turkic stock in former Soviet and Chinese Central Asia and the Caucasus, the idea of Pan-Turkism suddenly took root again. Ever since Kemal Ataturk turned Turkey into a secular state in 1924, Turkey has been looking westward rather than to the east, but while the business and political elite looked to joining the European Common Market, Pan-Turkism was kept alive by nationalist and Islamic fundamentalist groups. As Central Asian leaders arrived in Ankara praising Turkey to the skies, there was a popular ground swell of demand for a Pan-Turkic foreign policy which no Turkish government could ignore.

The West pushed Turkey to play a modernizing and moderate role in Central Asia. NATO chief Manfred Woerner said in Moscow in February 1992 that Islamic fundamentalists were becoming increasingly strong in the Muslim republics and that this did not conform to NATO interests. NATO looked to Turkey to redress the balance. After a meeting in Washington on 13 February 1992, President George Bush and Turkish Prime Minister Suleyman Demirel pledged to expand aid and other help to Central Asia. Bush pointed to Turkey as the model of a democratic, secular state which could be emulated by Central Asia. 'In a region of changing tides, Turkey endures as a beacon of stability,' Bush said.[4] US companies were encouraged to find Turkish partners with whom to do business in Central Asia, and US diplomats encouraged Central Asian politicians and bureaucrats to travel to Turkey to see a modern country at work.

In recent years Turkey has been a dream country for the Central Asian elite. Rich, secular, westernized, close to the Americans yet Islamic and Turkic, it appeared to offer exactly what the nomenklatura wanted. Ankara became the first foreign port of call for Central Asian leaders who wanted aid, political support and access to the West, which they believed Turkey would provide. They also wanted to use the Turkish card to demonstrate to Moscow that they had a powerful foreign patron, even as President Yeltsin ignored them and took major decisions without consulting them. Being well received in Turkey also went down well at home, for it legitimized their power base in the eyes of the growing nationalist movements in the respective republics.

In the autumn of 1991 Turkish president Turgut Ozal invited the presidents of all five republics and Azerbaijan to Ankara, where the seeds for future co-operation were planted. He pledged to support their declarations of sovereignty and spoke enthusiastically of the re-emergence of a Pan-Turkic world. It was the first major international gathering of the Central Asian leaders and it immediately alerted Iran, Pakistan and the Arab countries to Turkey's efforts. Prime Minister Demirel visited all five republics in April 1992 and discreetly informed his hosts that they should steer clear of Iran if they wanted Turkish and Western help. He made available $500 million worth of loans and tied credits to Azerbaijan and Central Asia. In Alma Ata he told an audience of delirious Kazakhs that a great Turkic world had emerged, stretching from the Adriatic to the Pacific Rim.'This place is our fatherland. Both our history and our culture begins from here,' he said.

Ankara moved swiftly to build its influence in the region. Some 10,000 students from Azerbaijan and Central Asia were offered scholarships at Turkish universities, technical colleges and business schools. Turkish television began to broadcast via satellite to Central Asia. A programme costing some $300,000 to send Turkish technicians and professionals as volunteers to Central Asia took shape under the auspices of the United Nations Development Programme. Turkey's Religious Affairs Directorate sponsored Islamic affairs councillors in Central Asia, who pledged to build a mosque and a madrasah in every capital. Some 480 Islamic scholars came to study at Turkish madrasahs. Ankara set up a training course for diplomats and helped build their foreign ministries from scratch. On 30 October 1992, President Ozal opened another summit in Ankara of the leaders of the five Central Asian states and Azerbaijan, at which he appealed to those present to 'make the Twenty-first century that of the Turks,' and said that such a summit would now take place every year. When Turgut Ozal died in April 1993 during a tour of Central Asia, he was mourned by tens of thousands of people from Alma Ata to Baku.

The Turks also moved quickly however to stabilize relations with Moscow, not wishing to upset President Yeltsin with their very obvious bid for political influence in Central Asia. Turkey and Russia had been traditional enemies for centuries, and since 1950 Turkey's role in NATO had been that of a pro-Western base for monitoring the former Soviet Union's southern rim. For Turkey the break-up of the Soviet empire came as an unexpected bonus, an outright victory after centuries of rivalry, but Turkey realized that it could not rub Russia's nose in the dust. In May 1992 on a visit to Moscow, Prime Minister Demirel tied up a $300 million deal to continue buying gas from Moscow. The Soviet-Turkish trade in 1990 was worth $1.7 billion and neither country could afford such trade links to collapse.

It was partly to placate Russia that Turkey negotiated with nine countries neighbouring the Black Sea the formation of a Black Sea

Economic Organization. The countries – Turkey, Russia, Azerbaijan, Ukraine, Bulgaria, Rumania, Armenia, Georgia and Moldova – signed the accord on 25 June 1992 in Istanbul. The accord gave Turkey a pre-eminent role in the region, which was now not restricted merely to Central Asia. Turkey also tried to play a role in negotiating an end to the conflict between Azerbaijan and Armenia, but its military and economic assistance to Azerbaijan made such a role dubious in many eyes.

By December 1992 Turkey had pledged some $1.2 billion in loans and trade credits to Central Asia and Azerbaijan, more than any international agency or neighbouring country. Yet despite the cultural and political influence that Turkey had attained, its economic clout remained negligible. In the midst of a deep recession, Turkish companies did not have the funds for serious investment in Central Asia. Turkey also proved unable to provide the bridgehead into Central Asia for Western companies. US and European oil and gas companies that were investing in Kazakhstan and Turkmenistan were doing so under their own steam.

It was Turkey's geographical inability to offer a port and access to the sea that allowed Iran to become a serious economic rival to it and also forced Central Asian leaders to rethink their love affair with Turkey. By 1993 many leaders were highly sceptical that Turkey could deliver economic benefits. Turkish investment in industry was not forthcoming, Turkish television programmes were not widely popular, and Islamic fundamentalists promoted the idea that Turkey was just a stalking horse for the Americans, who wanted to deprive Central Asia of its Islamic heritage. People realized that much of Turkey's interest was galvanized by its attempts to keep Iran out of the region. From first naïvely thinking that whatever was in Turkey's interests was also in their interests, Central Asian leaders quickly realized that what might be in Turkey's and the West's interests was not necessarily in Central Asia's best interests.

During 1992 the rivalry between Turkey and Iran grew enormously as Turkey tried to block every Iranian move in Central Asia – stopping attempts to build oil and gas pipelines through Iran, accusing Teheran of exporting fundamentalism, and criticizing Iran at Central Asian forums. Then, in March 1993, power-strapped Armenia asked Iran to supply it with gas, a move that was clearly supported by Russia in order to thwart the Turkish influence in Azerbaijan. 'We think Russia would benefit from expanded Armenian–Iranian relations. We realize that Turkey is trying to penetrate the Republics of the former Soviet Union. This Turkish penetration has to be limited,' said Vladimir Starikov, a Russian diplomat in Armenia.[5] In April 1993 a major Armenian offensive against Azeri forces ensured that Turkish–Iranian rivalry intensified. Russia also encouraged Turkmenistan to build closer ties with Iran.

Iran had moved swiftly into Central Asia as the Soviet Union hovered on the verge of break-up. In November 1991 Iranian Foreign Minister Akbar Ali Velyati travelled to all five republics. Velyati reaped the most benefit in Persian-speaking Tajikistan, which was trying to offset Uzbek–Turkish influence, and in Turkmenistan which borders Iran and needed to find a sea outlet for its exports. Teheran agreed to build a rail link from Ashkhabad to Meshad in Iran, which would give Turkman trade access to the port of Bandar Abbas. It also proposed building an oil pipeline from Ashkhabad to the Persian Gulf. Velyati insisted that Iran had no political interest in supporting Islamic groups or in becoming involved in these states' domestic politics. Iran, he said, only desired normal trade and economic ties.

The initial Central Asian reaction was benign because Teheran and Moscow were already on good terms. Russia needed Iran to offset Turkish influence. In turn Teheran had rebuilt its military arsenal after the war with Iraq by purchasing Soviet weapons worth $10 billion between 1989 and 1993. Russia and the Central Asian states also considered that in Afghanistan, more of an Islamic threat existed from the Saudi-backed fundamentalist Mujheddin led by Gulbuddin Hikmetyar than from the Iranian-backed Shia Mujheddin. At the same time Iran played an adroit diplomatic game by establishing close ties with all the non-Muslim republics. Teheran signed deals to provide oil to Ukraine, Georgia, Armenia and Russia, and smaller trade deals with the Baltic republics. It is estimated that Iran has given Central Asia some $700 million in various forms of aid, but exactly how much remains a mystery. Oil and trade deals are shrouded in secrecy, trade credits are not disclosed and neither are contributions to political parties, mosques and other projects.[6]

As the Turks were setting up the Black Sea Economic Organization, Iran set up the Association of Persian Languages on 19 February 1992 with Tajikistan, the Afghan Mujheddin and any other state that wished to join. Iran then sponsored the Caspian Sea Organization comprising Iran, Russia, Turkmenistan, Azerbaijan and Kazakhstan – a move that elicited the dry comment from President Ozal that 'this was one organization too many'.[7] However Teheran refused to be drawn into a slanging match with Turkey and held back its criticism of the USA, which it claimed was denying Iran its rightful role in Central Asia.

Iran's benign image in early 1992 was to take a severe battering by the end of the year because of its involvement in Tajikistan. Iran funded numerous political parties and militias including the IRP, but when they were defeated by neo-communists, Iran was vilified by all the neighbouring states, especially Uzbekistan. Only Turkmenistan persisted in enlarging trade ties with Teheran. The crisis highlighted Iran's biggest problem – the fissures within its own revolutionary politics. There are acute divisions on policy towards Central Asia between the Foreign Ministry under Velyati, which believes in wooing the republics by acting responsibly, and the Revolutionary Guards, who want to support radical Islamic groups. Even though Iran lost out in Tajikistan, that has not ended its ambitions to radicalize Central Asia and bring about an Islamic revolution.

Iran has had its fingers burnt in Central Asia and its influence has been reduced for the time being. But Iran cannot be ignored because of its access to the sea, its role as a communications hub, its influence in Afghanistan and its oil wealth and oil technology. Moreover, it has befriended Russia, which is still influential in Central Asia. Teheran is certain to continue playing a major role in Central Asia, despite setbacks like Tajikistan, because it considers the region as its historical area of influence.

Pakistan is the third important Muslim neighbour that is eager to influence Central Asia. Pakistanis are fascinated with the region because many of their tribes and clans are descended from the Moguls and other invaders who arrived from Central Asia to conquer India. Sufism, inherited from Central Asia, thrives in Pakistan's rural areas, whilst the border city of Peshawar was a centre of trade in goods and weapons for the Central Asian khanates before the communist era. With the winding down of the Afghan war and Islamabad's growing problems with Washington over its nuclear weapons programme, Pakistan hoped to revive its fortunes in the West by selling its new geostrategic importance as the gateway to Central Asia for Western business. Karachi is the nearest port city for the Central Asian states and by air Islamabad is closer to Tashkent than it is to Karachi. Dushanbe is only an hour's flight from Islamabad, and by road through Afghanistan the distance from Dushanbe to Karachi is 2,720 kilometres. In contrast the Iranian port of Bandar Abbas is 3,400 kilometres, Vladivostock 9,500 kilometres and Rostov on the Don 4,200 kilometres away.

Although Pakistan does not have money to invest in Central Asia, it hoped to market its short route to the sea and provide services such as transport, banking, insurance and business training programmes. It could also provide expertise and international contacts to help develop the textile industry in Central Asia. There was only one precondition to this and that was peace in Afghanistan, because Kabul controlled Pakistan's land access to Central Asia. In 1988 the all-powerful military and President Ghulam Ishaq Khan still believed in a Mujheddin victory, that would bring a pro-Pakistan Mujheddin government to power in Kabul. The Foreign Ministry and to some extent two successive prime ministers, Benazir Bhutto and Nawaz Sharif, preferred a negotiated settlement that would allow Pakistan to open up trade links with Central Asia, but their views did not prevail until 1992 when Kabul was captured by the Mujheddin. This dichotomy of views within the Pakistani ruling establishment on Afghanistan was duplicated in its policy towards Central Asia. While the business elite looked for markets in a politically stable Central Asia, the fundamentalist Jamaat-e-Islami wanted an Islamic revolution in Central Asia.

The Jamaat chief Qazi Hussain Ahmad called on the government to confront 'US imperialism and the new world order by using the Central Asian Republics for a combined fight', saying that Pakistan must provide Central Asia with 'Islamic guidance rather than economic aid'.[8] This kind of rhetoric disturbed Central Asian leaders. In March 1993 the foreign ministers of Uzbekistan and Tajikistan directly accused the Jamaat of arming and training Muslims radicals from their republics. During the Afghan war, the Jamaat had trained Muslim fundamentalists from Central Asia and encouraged them to fight alongside the Mujheddin. By 1992 the Jamaat was helping these radicals in their own countries together with its main Afghan ally, Gulbuddin Hikmetyar. The Jamaat also helped IRP leaders in Uzbekistan and Tajikistan to establish links with Arab Islamic groups.

Pakistan's policy makers were clearly divided as to what the country wanted out of Central Asia. One of the moderate and secular cabinet ministers, the Minister of State for Economic Affairs, Sardar Asif Ali, led a large Pakistani delegation on a month-long trip to Central Asia and Azerbaijan as the Soviet Union broke up in 1991. He received a mixed reception: the Central Asian leaders were extremely wary of Pakistan because of its long involvement in the Afghan war and its open backing for the Mujheddin.

Pakistan offered the republics and Azerbaijan $10 million each in credits to buy light engineering goods and medicines, and sent food and medicines as gifts. Uzbekistan was offered $30 million. Pakistan also initiated various training programmes for Central Asian officials in banking, insurance, business studies and other fields. It quickly opened embassies in Alma Ata and Tashkent; Pakistan International Airlines began a weekly flight from Islamabad to Tashkent. In March 1992 Pakistan tied up a $500 million deal with Tajikistan in which Pakistan would provide food and consumer goods for five years, the profits of which Tajikistan would use to finish construction of a dam that would produce electricity to be supplied to Pakistan. The transmission line would cross the Pamirs and the Wakhan corridor. The deal, negotiated by finance minister Sartaj Aziz, came under considerable criticism when Tajikistan disintegrated into civil war.

In May 1992 Pakistan's Prime Minister Nawaz Sharif attended the economic summit of the Central Asian states in Ashkhabad which set up a highway council to look into establishing better road links between the republics and Pakistan. All the Central Asian leaders visited Islamabad as part of attempts to improve ties with both India and Pakistan, but there was no further aid that Pakistan could provide them with and Islamabad remained extremely slow in following up even its earlier promises.[9]

Pakistan's relations with Moscow remained tense because of the Afghan war. Russian leaders were convinced that Pakistan could have done much more to free an estimated eighty Soviet prisoners of war still in Mujheddin hands. Russian suspicions were well known to Central Asian leaders. Nevertheless Moscow had continued helping Pakistan through the 1980s, first helping set up a steel mill in Karachi and then providing technicians and loans for its further expansion. By 1989 Pakistan owed the former Soviet Union some $533 million.

Unlike Iran and Turkey, however, the Pakistanis made little effort to improve relations with Moscow during 1992. Russian suspicions of Pakistan increased when Prime Minister Nawaz Sharif made no attempt to control the activities of the Jamaat in Central Asia, while he himself proved incapable of setting an agenda for relations with the region. Pakistan's initial good will in Central Asia was eroded as its foreign policy appeared to have no clear objective. However Pakistan remains an important player in the region, if for no other reason than it can provide the nearest access for Central Asia to the sea. Its geostrategic position makes it impossible for Central Asia to ignore Pakistan.

The fierce competition between Turkey, Iran and Pakistan for influence in Central Asia was coupled with their attempts at co-operation in a regional organization. The Economic Co-operation Organization (ECO), set up by the three countries to facilitate trade and communications, had been moribund for more than a decade. In February 1992 at the ECO summit in Teheran, the Central Asian states applied for observer status; soon after Azerbaijan, Turkmenistan and Uzbekistan accepted full membership. Tajikistan, Kazakhstan and Kyrgystan became full members later in the year, as did Afghanistan after the Mujheddin victory. Initially the Central Asian states approached the ECO cautiously. They were not sure whether it was an Islamic or a secular organization and they did not want to antagonize Russia, which was suspicious of the ECO because it was a Muslim grouping. Nevertheless, the ECO had suddenly become a ten-member organization with a very viable potential.

Iran, Pakistan and Turkey had wooed the Central Asian republics assiduously since 1991, but had been treated as economic lightweights as the republics looked to the West and the Far East for real economic aid. By 1993, however, they had been decisively snubbed by a recession-hit West, while investment from Turkey was slow. They had nowhere to turn to except the ECO, which was the only bloc prepared to help them, especially in the vital field of communications. In a sudden reversal of policy, the five republics responded enthusiastically at the ECO meeting of foreign ministers in Quetta, Pakistan, in February 1993.

Whereas a year earlier Central Asian diplomats could barely find Karachi or Bandar Abbas on the map, in Quetta they arrived with detailed feasibility reports to discuss how to open up routes to the sea. At Quetta, foreign and finance ministers of all ten ECO countries thrashed out a comprehensive plan for the economic integration and development of the entire region.'The Quetta Plan of Action for ECO' called for the setting up of road, rail and air links and the development of ports so that trucks and railway wagons can 'travel from one end of the region to the other at internationally acceptable standards' by the year 2000. Air links would be established between all capitals and an ECO airline and transport company would eventually be formed. Tourist visas, tariffs, customs duties and other restrictions on the free flow of people and goods would be made uniform. A new ECO Trade and Development Bank was set up.

Although the plan was highly ambitious and there was little indication of where the money was going to come from, officials stressed that the infrastructure for communications already existed. What was needed was linking the national infrastructure properly with those of their neighbours.'We are at the starting post of a new era in this region. The funds will be forthcoming once the world sees the economic potential that can be harnessed here,' said Pakistan's Foreign Secretary, Shehreyar Khan.[10] Afghanistan and Tajikistan, the two countries at the heart of the ECO and through which communications would have to pass, were in the throes of bloody civil wars. Despite these setbacks, the republics were now obsessed with finding the shortest possible route to the sea.

There will probably always be intense competition between Turkey, Iran and Pakistan to provide the republics with the necessary communications links, but there is also a strong possibility that they could unite under the ECO to co-ordinate their competition. For Turkmenistan and southern Uzbekistan the shortest route to the sea lies through Iran, but for all other states the shortest route is through Afghanistan and Pakistan. In order to avoid the troubled city of Kabul, there was a proposal to rebuild the road from Termiz to Mazar-e-Sharif in northern Afghanistan and take the westerly road through Herat on to Quetta in Baluchistan province. From Quetta goods could easily reach Karachi, while a new Pakistani port is being built at Gawadar on the Makran coast. Pakistan also proposed to Kazakhstan and Kyrgyzstan a new route from Alma Ata to Xinjiang to link up with the Karakorum Highway which runs from the Chinese border to Islamabad. This route would only be passable in the summer months but it would link Central Asia with China and Pakistan, thus opening up the old Turkestan to the sea for the first time in history.

The key to communications routes and future stability will be the region's relations with war-torn Afghanistan. Kabul's close historical links with Central Asia have been explored in Chapter 7. Afghanistan remains part of the heart of Central Asia, but natural north–south communication links were curtailed by the tsars and completely blocked by the Soviet authorities. New east–west links to Moscow were established, which are now proving inadequate. To re-establish the north–south link needs peace, which has eluded the Afghans for the past fifteen years.

The Soviet Union first took Afghanistan seriously when the Basmachis restarted their raids into Central Asia from bases in northern Afghanistan in 1929. This led to a new Soviet strategic doctrine of the need to protect its southern flank from pro-American Muslim states, the Islamic world and capitalism. The doctrine depended on the Soviet Union retaining Afghanistan in its sphere of influence. Moscow was also sensitive to the fact that eight of Afghanistan's nine northern provinces were populated by Central Asian peoples, many of whom were Soviet citizens who had fled to northern Afghanistan in the 1920s. Today these peoples include 4 million Tajiks, 1.5 million Uzbeks, 500,000 Turkomen and several thousand Kyrgyz nomads and Pamiri Ismaelis.

The Soviet invasion of Afghanistan in 1979 was the ultimate extension of its strategic doctrine, but the political fallout was to be a burden for Central Asia. Brezhnev never consulted Central Asian leaders about the need for an invasion, nor did Gorbachev consult them when he ordered the pullout of Soviet troops. Nobody asked for their opinions as the Najibullah regime, the Mujheddin, Moscow and Islamabad tried to work out a political settlement for Afghanistan between 1989 and 1992. Central Asia had no role in the Soviet decision-making process after 1979, and this created much bitterness, which fuelled anti-Afghan feeling. Moreover, the military brunt of the war fell on

Central Asia. The 'limited contingent of Soviet Forces in Afghanistan' of some 120,000 men of the Fortieth Army had its headquarters in Termiz. The manpower, the supplies, the air bombardments and finally the coffins for the 13,000 Soviet soldiers that were killed all originated in Central Asia.

A major outcome of the war has been that the political border between Central Asia and South Asia, or between the Turkic world and the Pathan milieu, which traditionally ran along the northern steppe of Mazar-e-Sharif and the Amudarya river, was *de facto* shifted southward to the Hindu Kush mountains and Kabul. The Soviet invaders devastated the eastern Pathan tribal belt, but dealt with Afghanistan's northern provinces comparatively benignly. This discrimination during the war was to fuel ethnic tensions between those of Turkic origins and the Pathans inside Afghanistan. The 1992 revolt of the Uzbek warlord General Rashid Dostam against his mentor President Najibullah sealed the fate of the Kabul regime and established the north as a separate Turkic political entity controlled by Uzbeks. The Uzbeks now had less in common with their Pathan brothers than ever before.

The *de facto* partition of Afghanistan by 1993 led to new fears for Central Asian leaders. General Dostam's secular Uzbeks were a convenient buffer zone to prevent the spread of Islamic fundamentalism northwards by the Pathans. However the war had created a power vacuum in Kabul and the south. Kabul was rapidly filled with warring militias, Islamic fundamentalists, drug traffickers and a plethora of arms – all of which trickled into Tajikistan. Kalashnikovs and Korans were being smuggled into Central Asia even during the war with the Soviets, but once Soviet troops left the trickle became a deluge. In Tajikistan in 1993 the CIS forces could not plug the border effectively because General Dostam did not control the entire Afghan–Central Asian border.

Along with weapons came drugs. A UN report stated that 5 to 7 million CIS citizens, the majority of them in Central Asia, had become addicted to drugs during the 1980s. Central Asia became a major drug-trafficking route to Europe for the Afghan and Pakistani heroin mafias. The region began to grow its own drugs. Cannabis is now grown on 140,000 hectares in Kazakhstan, 60,000 hectares in Kyrgyzstan and large areas of Uzbekistan and Tajikistan.

In South Asia India was hit hardest by the break-up of the Soviet Union and the independence of Central Asia. New Delhi had built up excellent political, military and trade ties with the former Soviet Union. Some 70 per cent of India's armaments were of Soviet origin and its armament factories depended on Soviet weapon parts. There was a high turnover in Indian exports of consumer goods to the former Soviet Union. But now Indian trade in the undervalued rouble with the newly born Russia ceased overnight, and a chronic shortage developed of spare parts for weapons and Soviet-built factories in India. According to one estimate in October 1992, 50 per cent of India's fighter planes had been grounded, one third of its tanks had been mothballed and an assembly line for tanks had been shut down.[11]

Although India had had a consulate in Tashkent for years, Indian Airlines had operated a weekly service to Tashkent, and thousands of Indian students had studied at Central Asian universities, New Delhi's relations with Central Asia had been dependent on Moscow. India had few direct ties with the new leaderships in Central Asia. Indian deputy commerce minister Salman Khurshid visited Central Asia in the summer of 1992 and announced credits of $10 million each to Uzbekistan and Kazakhstan and $5 million to the other republics. India would also help Iran build the railway link between Ashkhabad and Meshed. Despite a desire to counter its main rival Pakistan's growing influence in Central Asia, Delhi's major priority was to re-establish military and trade links with Russia. These efforts culminated in President Yeltsin's visit to Delhi from 27 to 29 January 1993, when a new Treaty of Peace and Friendship was signed along with a defence co-operation agreement whereby India agreed to pay for all military spare parts in hard currency.

India delayed opening embassies in Central Asia and there was considerable disappointment amongst the region's leaders that India was not playing a larger role. They valued India for being a secular state with a large Muslim population and an old friend of the former Soviet Union. But India still sees Russia as the real political power in the region. When India does decide to improve ties with Central Asia, it will not be that difficult. The tens of thousands of Indian students who have studied there will form a hard core of experienced business professionals. Its huge manufacturing base can supply consumer goods, whilst its factories can absorb many of the raw materials from Central Asia. India's constraint is the lack of a direct land route to Central Asia. Unless it is prepared to make peace with its old enemy Pakistan, its trade with the region will remain negligible.

Arab Muslim states responded enthusiastically to the opening up of Central Asia. Saudi Arabia launched a major initiative to woo Central Asia back into the Islamic fold as early as 1990, when it sent 1 million Korans to the region and funded projects to translate the Koran into local languages. The arrival of the Korans created massive public excitement and led to a number of scandals concerning local mullahs who sold the free Korans for profit. King Fahd invited hundreds of prominent Central Asians to perform Haj in 1991 and again in 1992. And in August 1991 the Saudis dramatically improved their image in Moscow by signing a $1.5 billion loan to the Soviet Union in recognition of Moscow's support during the Gulf War. However Arab interest has remained at an emotional and religious level rather than at a practical level. In February 1992 Saudi Foreign Minister Prince Saud al-Faisal visited Central Asia, but a year after that visit there was still no Saudi diplomatic mission in any Central Asian capital.

The Saudis have neglected state-to-state relations in favour of the funding of Islamic groups, mosques and madrasahs. Islamic charities backed by the Saudi government have been lavish in their donations for scholarships, Islamic literature and schools, while other charities have funded the revival of Wahabism (dealt with in Chapter 4). The Saudis see their mission as winning back the people to Islam rather than cultivating economic or trade relations. Even though the first foreign bank to set up shop in Alma Ata was the Saudi bank 'Al Baraka Kazakhstan', there has been little Saudi investment in the region. Central Asia's rulers have been disappointed at the lack of Saudi investment in their countries, and they remain suspicious of Saudi and Gulf States funding for the fundamentalists.

In the future Central Asia's relations with China could become even more important than its relations with the Muslim world. Three states, Kazakhstan, Kyrgyzstan and Tajikistan, share a 5,000 kilometre border with China. The same Turkic peoples live on either side and there have been large-scale cross-border migrations since 1917. Nomads entered Xinjiang with their flocks during the Civil War and the collectivization campaign, and there were similar migrations from Xinjiang to Soviet territory during Mao's Great Leap Forward in the 1950s and the Cultural Revolution in the 1960s. The Sino-Soviet split in the 1960s cut off all official contacts between Central Asia and Xinjiang and escalated military tensions in the region. One third of the Soviet Army was moved from Europe to face China, and billions of roubles invested in new airfields, barracks and roads along the border.[12]

The thaw in relations between Moscow and Beijing in the 1980s released a flurry of activity as leaders on both sides of the border restarted trade and other links. President Nazarbayev took the initiative by agreeing with China to build a railway line linking Alma Ata with Urumqi, the capital of Xinjiang. 'We want to improve our relations with foreign countries and especially China, free of control from the conditions of dictatorship from the centre,' he said in 1990.[13] The 1,350-kilometre railway line was opened to passenger traffic in June 1992. Northeast of Alma Ata the line cuts through the gorges of the snowclad Ala Tau mountains to Aktogay and Druzhba, where the

Kazakh builders met a Chinese-built line constructed through the Gobi desert. The new line linked Beijing to Alma Ata, Tashkent and Ashkhabad and once the railway extension is extended to Meshed, it will continue to Teheran, Istanbul and Europe. With the opening of the line, Alma Ata's hotels were quickly filled with Chinese trade delegations, concluding deals for Chinese consumer goods in return for Kazakh chemicals, wheat and minerals.

In February 1992 Kazakhstan signed an economic and trade agreement with China which allowed Chinese concerns to set up factories in Kazakhstan. In March Uzbek President Islam Karimov visited Beijing and signed fourteen agreements with the Chinese. By the end of the year all the Central Asian leaders had visited Beijing. Chinese Prime Minister Li Peng arrived in Moscow on 22 April 1992 for the first visit of a high-ranking Chinese leader since 1964: Beijing signed a ten-year economic co-operation agreement with Russia. Accompanying Li Peng was Governor Tomur of Xinjiang province and his presence explained a great deal of China's concerns in Central Asia.

On 5 April 1992 there had been an abortive uprising in the town of Baren in Xinjiang, in which at least twenty-two people were killed and some fifty wounded. The uprising was led by Abdul Kasim, an Islamic fundamentalist and leader of the Free East Turkestan Movement. The Chinese authorities said the group, made up of Uighurs and Kyrgyz, had acquired arms and training from the Afghan Mujheddin. A widespread crackdown followed in which Islamic leaders were rounded up. 'We should effectively intensify supervision over religious activities and the venues for such activities,' Governor Tomur said at the time.[14] The Chinese took the event very seriously. The Khunjerab pass and the Karakorum Highway which crosses into northern Pakistan were closed and relations worsened between China and Pakistan and the Afghan Mujheddin. Pakistan was warned by China that it would question its relationship with Pakistan if Islamabad did not control the activities of fundamentalists based on its territory.

In fact hundreds of Xinjiang Islamic militants, sponsored by Pakistan's Jamaat-e-Islami, had been trained by Afghan Mujheddin and had taken part in battles against the Kabul regime.[15] The Muslim unrest in Baren was a tiny incident, but for the Chinese it was the thin edge of a potential Islamic wedge. It brought Xinjiang and the leaders of Central Asia together for they now faced a common threat. Xinjiang co-ordinated security with Central Asia and Moscow. Joint military patrols were organized on borders and the Chinese began to take a keen interest in events in Tajikistan.

China's suppression of its own Muslim population had led to severe economic deprivation in Xinjiang: the region had been badly neglected for decades. In a clear reversal of that policy, in April 1992 Beijing announced that it would invest $370 million in some forty infrastructure projects, notably oil production and communications in Xinjiang. This was an increase of 23 per cent compared to the investment made in 1991 which in turn was double the investment made the previous year. China was now anxious to develop the region to stave off the appeal of fundamentalism and Uighur nationalism. Uighur nationalists settled in Kazakhstan have formed the Uighurstan Liberation Front, which aims to liberate the Uighur motherland from Chinese rule, but they are kept under tight control by the Kazakh authorities.

Following Kazakhstan's example of opening up the steppe for oil and gas exploration, China's state oil company announced that the Tarim Basin in the Taklamakan desert would be opened to foreign oil companies for exploration. In March 1993 bidding for a 72,000-square-kilometre block was opened and another eleven blocks in Xinjiang were to be on offer by 1994. The total oil reserves in the region are estimated at 74 billion barrels. By 1993 Xinjiang, Kazakhstan and Kyrgyzstan were following closely co-ordinated policies on many issues. The dramatic increase in trade, Chinese investment in these two republics, common policies on oil and gas exploration and common security concerns were bringing the entire region closer together. Thus China and Central Asia have become natural economic and political partners. It is a relationship that holds enormous potential for the future and one which is dependent on neither the West nor the Islamic world. For Central Asia the relationship is also an essential balance to offset pressures from Russia and Muslim neighbours to the south.

The USA and Europe have been slow to take initiatives in Central Asia, as they have been preoccupied with establishing relations with the western republics. US Secretary of State James Baker's tour of the region in the spring of 1992 was followed by those of European foreign ministers, whose main interest was in getting to know President Nazarbayev as he held onto nuclear weapons. The pace of their diplomatic presence has been set not by governments but by the large oil and gas multinationals. A diplomatic presence generally followed the multinationals. International lending agencies such as the IMF and the World Bank also set up offices in Central Asia as the republics began negotiations for loans. These agencies quickly found that evaluating the republics' economic potential would take much longer than expected, the reasons being a lack of data, the unpredictable rouble and their collapsing economies.

All the republics except Turkmenistan, which decided to ignore the

IMF, co-operated closely with the agencies, but by early 1993 only Kyrgyzstan had been certified by the IMF as assistance-worthy.[16] The IMF spent most of 1992 negotiating with the Kazakh government for a $1.2 billion loan spread over three years – a massive investment for such a small population and a clear indication for Western businessmen that the IMF considers the regime stable and willing to reform. In May 1993 the International Bank for Reconstruction and Development approved a $60 million loan for Kyrgyzstan.

There was considerable concern in the Muslim world at Israel's growing involvement in Central Asia. Some eighteen Israeli companies were active in Kazakhstan by 1993, offering the republic new irrigation techniques and modern technology to improve cotton and vegetable production, whilst taking commodities as payment instead of cash. In Kyrgyzstan, Israeli firms won contracts to improve food processing, cigarette production and the use of drip irrigation. In Uzbekistan Israeli companies planned to set up textile plants. Israel's efforts were closely backed by the USA as both countries were keen to offset Iranian influence. Israel was also keen to get a foothold in Central Asia because of its vast mineral and oil resources that Israel's resource-strapped economy needs so badly. Central Asian leaders saw their relations with Israel as highly productive and a signal to the West that they were secular and not dependent on the Muslim world. Moreover they were also aware of the positive effect this would have on Jewish American businessmen.

Of the Far Eastern countries South Korea showed the most interest immediately after independence. There are large Korean minorities in Uzbekistan and Kazakhstan, and South Korean entrepreneurs arrived in Tashkent and Alma Ata and set up some projects, largely in the restaurant and food processing businesses. Later South Korean electronic companies began to set up small factories in the region because of Central Asia's cheap but well-trained labour force. Japan appeared to show little interest in Central Asia until the end of 1992, when five separate Japanese economic and financial teams arrived to study Central Asia. The Kazakhs were hopeful that the Japanese would begin major investment in the region by the end of 1993.

However the most crucial foreign policy factor for Central Asia has been its relations with a country much closer to home and well known to all of them – Russia. Apart from Turkmenistan, all the republics favoured a closely knit CIS, which they presumed would take on overall security responsibilities, create a common rouble zone and ensure a united response to major economic issues that everyone faced. The strongest proponent of this view was President Nazarbayev, who championed the cause of the CIS at every summit meeting. But any move to strengthen the CIS was strongly opposed by Ukraine, while Georgia and the Baltic republics refused to join it. Obsessed with building a relationship with the West and unable to antagonize the other republics, Moscow had no coherent policy towards Central Asia in the first year of independence. Moscow's passivity created a geopolitical vacuum which worried Central Asian leaders.[17]

Russia itself was searching for a foreign policy. While the liberals under Foreign Minister Andrei Kozyrev desired closer ties with the West and a loosening of ties with the 'near abroad' or other republics, nationalists and communists wanted to reassert Russian authority in the other republics even though the CIS armed forces were in total disarray. Hardline leaders such as Vice-President Alexander Rutskoi still believed Russia should act as a bridge between Europe and Asia and that because of the presence in Central Asia of millions of Russian settlers, Russia could not abandon a role in that region's security.'A sacred principle for me personally is that once the Russian flag has been raised it should never be lowered. The same applies to people. Every state should be aware of the inevitability of punishment for what is perpetrated against Russian citizens. One cannot permit people to wipe their feet on Russia and its citizens,' Rutskoi said in a hard-hitting statement aimed at the liberals.[18]

This view was a reflection of the old communist attitude also advocated by former President Gorbachev, who in July 1986 in a famous speech made in Vladivostok waxed lyrical about the common Asian and Pacific home that Russia shared in the east. In the same year at Delhi he spoke about a common Indian Ocean home that Russia shared, and in October 1987 at Murmansk he addressed Canadians and Scandinavians about a common Arctic home. Yeltsin's advisers had no time for this grandiose image of a Mother Russia responsible for so many 'homes' spanning vast continents and cultures. Instead they wanted to anchor Russia firmly in Europe. Other intellectuals argued that Russia must not get stuck in a new global North–South divide by backing only the North, but must try to be a member of both worlds.[19]

Russia's lack of interest forced the republics to assert their own independent foreign policies. Thus Tajikistan became closer to Iran, Azerbaijan to Turkey and all five republics joined the ECO despite Russia's reservations. Russia only began to realize how dangerous its apathy was to its own security when the civil war in Tajikistan began. Urged on by President Islam Karimov, Russia committed itself to helping overthrow the coalition government in Dushanbe, and CIS forces began to play a major role in trying to stop the spread of fundamentalism.

At the summit meeting of Central Asian states in Tashkent in January 1993, the presidents took a tough line towards Moscow. They expressed their anger at Moscow's attitude and threatened to delink themselves from the rouble zone and set up their own currencies. For the first time Kazakhstan accepted that it was a part of Central Asia and the region officially changed its former Soviet name of 'Kazakhstan and Middle Asia' to 'Central Asia'. President Nazarbayev proposed an economic union like the Association of South East Asian Nations (ASEAN), a common newspaper, airline and TV station, and co-ordination on prices for energy and other basic goods. Moreover the presidents criticized Russia for allowing political dissenters from their republics to set up political offices in Moscow. Later that month at the CIS summit in Minsk, President Yeltsin committed Russia to encourage greater co-operation between CIS member states. 'We cannot allow a situation where a Central Asian bloc led by Kazakhstan goes off on its own,' said Yeltsin.[20] A new draft charter was signed by seven republics to set up an inter-states bank to facilitate trade and clear payments between member states. Only Turkmenistan did not sign the agreement.

President Yeltsin now began to advocate that Russia should play a more forceful security role in Central Asia. 'I think the moment has come when responsible international organizations including the UN should grant Russia special powers as a guarantor of peace and stability in the region of the former Soviet Union. Russia has a heartfelt interest in stopping all armed conflicts on the territory of the former Soviet Union,' Yeltsin said.[21] The statement angered opposition leaders in Central Asia, who said Russia was preparing to interfere by backing dictatorial regimes in the region. But Central Asian leaders were pleased about Yeltsin's commitment, as they all felt the need for a CIS security umbrella.

Eighteen months after independence the Central Asian states could claim that they formulated their own relations with foreign countries, but their leaderships were still in two minds about this. On the one hand, to placate their own domestic public opinion they wanted to appear independent of Russia and free to set their own foreign policy goals. On the other hand they wanted the CIS armed forces to play a larger security role in Central Asia. It was the experience of the Tajik civil war that had brought about this changed perception. In the future Russia's policy towards Central Asia will alternate between intervention and non-intervention, depending on the state of Moscow's troubled political scene, but most of Russia's leaders now feel that they do not want to abandon Central Asia to the influence of outside powers.

At the core of this policy is Russia's high regard for President Islam

Karimov. Uzbekistan has become the linchpin of Russia's security aims for the region, but with the dramatic difference that Moscow is no longer dictating terms to Tashkent. Rather President Karimov is now advising Moscow where, when and how it should intervene to stabilize the regimes in Central Asia. 'Karimov's authority is not questioned by any group in Russia. He is a resolute man and a strong political leader much admired in Moscow,' said Deputy Foreign Minister Georgi Kunadze.[22] But Moscow's close ties with Karimov are exacerbating tensions between Uzbekistan and the other republics, especially Kazakhstan, which is its main rival. The threat that other republics feel from Uzbekistan because of its large population and the substantial Uzbek minorities in all their national territories has been explored in detail in Chapter 4. This perceived threat will grow, the more Moscow is seen to be backing Tashkent.

President Karimov did not hesitate to use the Uzbek minority in the Khodjent and Kuliab regions of Tajikistan to act as a fifth column to topple the government in Dushanbe. Even as the other Central Asian states applauded his actions, they feared the dangerous precedent that had been set. They realized that in future Karimov could use the Uzbek minorities in Kyrgyzstan or Turkmenistan to act as pressure groups to affect policies in these states also. Moreover, after receiving Karimov's military help, the new Tajik government became totally dependent on Karimov's good will for the opening up of roads and the supply of petroleum and basic foodstuffs to Dushanbe. Politicians now speak of Tashkent's 'sphere of influence' and even of a 'Greater Uzbekistan' that could endanger the equilibrium in Central Asia.

Most of all, Uzbekistan's growing regional role has challenged Kazakhstan, which sees itself as the rightful leader of Central Asia. Even though it has a small population spread over a vast territory, Kazakhstan's mineral and oil wealth will make it the economic powerhouse of Central Asia in the future. Uzbekistan is jealous of the wealth of Kazakhstan and could claim some share to it in the future as the political rivalry between them grows. In May 1993 Uzbek newspapers openly criticized President Nazarbayev – a reflection of growing Uzbek envy at Kazakhstan's economic successes. If Kazakh and Kyrgyz leaders further liberalize their societies, allowing multi-party elections, then tensions with a dictatorial Uzbekistan will increase. That is why President Nazarbayev does not want to be dependent on a Russian–Uzbek axis for future security in Central Asia. What is at stake is more than just strategic rivalries, but ideological differences about how these states will map out their political and economic futures.

Despite these problems there are also points of agreement. For the time being both Kazakhstan and Uzbekistan want a strengthened CIS – it is ironic that the most powerful voices for a more integrated CIS are coming from Central Asia. Thus the leaders of the region do not envisage a Central Asian common market soon. Their threats to Moscow about expanding ties with the ECO or China are little more than attempts to blackmail Moscow, to convince it of the need for a more equitable relationship.

Kazakhstan, though, is rapidly opening up to Western companies who want to develop its oil and gas resources. The government has already enacted legislation that will allow foreign investment, the repatriation of profits abroad and the privatization of state-owned companies. Uzbekistan has resisted any headlong shift towards privatization, kept a tight control on all foreign investment and restricted local efforts to create an entrepreneur class. Western companies will naturally gravitate to Kazakhstan and to a lesser extent Kyrgystan, where foreign investment is encouraged but resources are few.

The danger in all this is that Central Asia itself may divide along a north–south axis. The more resource-rich, more prosperous and liberal Kazakhstan and Kyrgystan will be adopted by the West and Japan and eventually become economically self-sufficient. The more authoritarian and resource-poor Uzbekistan and Tajikistan could become the Third World of Central Asia, beset by long-term political and economic problems that will force foreign investors to ignore them, thereby increasing internal authoritarian trends. Ignored by the West, both republics could become more dependent on the Islamic states to the south, which would bring some economic benefits but would also encourage the spread of Islamic fundamentalism which would further polarize Central Asia.

The growing Russian–Uzbek alliance, the rivalry between Uzbekistan and Kazakhstan, the wealth of the 'north' versus the growing impoverishment of the 'south', as well as a host of local ethnic and political problems, could divide Central Asia before it is able to reach a consensus on forming a stronger economic union on the ASEAN model. Moreover, Stalin's borders in Central Asia are potential causes of future conflicts at both a political and an ethnic level. There are Russian claims on northern Kazakhstan, Tajiks demand the return of their cultural centres of Samarkand and Bukhara from Uzbekistan, Turkmenistan has disputes with Uzbekistan over water rights while Uzbekistan demands the return of the Uzbek-majority regions of Khodjent from Tajikistan and Osh from Kyrgyzstan. There are an estimated eighty potential border disputes simmering in the former Soviet Union and there is no mechanism for resolving them.

The odd one out is Turkmenistan, which has decided to take its own path, rejecting all initiatives about Central Asian economic or political union. It has imposed a harsh, authoritarian political system and it is reluctant to privatize its economy. President Niyazov is convinced that oil and gas wealth will lure in Western companies, under whatever terms he offers them, and that this will allow him to rebuild the economy. Such a strategy may well fail because of the prevailing tensions within Turkman society and the fact that economic prosperity will itself trigger off demands for greater political freedom. For the time being, without Turkmenistan, talk of a Central Asian union at any level is not entirely feasible, because the republic is a major communications hub and will soon have access to the sea through Iran.

Any future Central Asian union will need help from the outside world before it can be achieved. To maintain genuine stability Russia will have to pursue a more evenhanded policy in Central Asia than it has done so far. Russian leaders cannot allow democracy to flourish in Russia but back dictatorships in Central Asia. Nor can they ignore the need for Central Asian governments to begin a dialogue with Islamic fundamentalism. However Moscow will have to encourage Central Asia to break its economic dependence on Russia so that a Central Asian common market can emerge. This appears unlikely so long as Russia is beset by economic chaos and still needs cheap Central Asian raw materials. Russia's policy will fluctuate until there is political stability in Russia itself.

The ECO could help mould Central Asia into an economic union by providing communications and other infrastructure developments that would link Central Asia to the outside world. But the ECO is plagued with internal rivalries, lacks resources, and will be unable to mobilize the finances from the West to revamp communications on the major scale needed. The West fears a new Islamic bloc emerging in Asia and will do nothing to help finance or build up the ECO. Moreover, the policies of the recession-hit West are set less by their governments than by the multinationals, who will go only where the profits are highest and political stability is guaranteed. The rich Pacific Rim countries such Japan and South Korea will follow much the same policies. This will only encourage the economic polarization of Central Asia into rich and poor nations. Central Asia will also have to accept that no single foreign country can be its saviour and provide its aid or be a role model. Rather, an overlapping of influences and role models will take place with perhaps Turkey providing a cultural model to some republics and South Korea and China providing an economic model to others. Foreign policies cannot be bound by any single vision, but will have to remain orientated towards specific issues as they emerge.

Any Central Asian union can only come about when these states first settle their myriad of inter-ethnic problems and border disputes, and stop using minorities in each other's territories as political pawns in complex power games. There has to be a wider local debate on foreign policy options, and decision making will have to become a more public affair, rather than a matter of a handful of leaders taking decisions in secret in presidential palaces and at summit meetings. Nowhere in Central Asia have the people been empowered through the ballot box: until this takes place, policies cannot take root.

Eventually the key to the future has to be greater economic union and cohesion. Mineral-, oil- and energy-rich states will have to create a rational development policy in which they provide other republics with what they produce in exchange for goods they are short of. Only unprecedented good will between them will encourage a rational basis for economic exchange, in which for example Kazakhstan provides Central Asia with oil and wheat, Tajikistan provides electricity, and Uzbekistan provides cotton. At the heart of Central Asia's future foreign policy and its attempt to secure a viable economic union will be the terms of its future security, which are explored in Chapter 10. How national and regional security is determined will be crucial to Central Asia's future stability.

Notes

1. A. Verrier (1991) *Francis Younghusband and the Great Game*, Johnathan Cape, London.

2. Comment made to the author in Ashkhabad, December 1991.

3. Robert Kaplan, 'Shatter Zone', *Atlantic Monthly*, April 1992.

4. John Yang, 'US, Turkey to Expand Aid to Central Asia', *Dawn*, 13 February 1992.

5. James Dorsey, 'Iran Moves to Offset Turkish Influence', *Dawn*, 28 March 1993.

6. Estimated by the author after conversations with Central Asian officials and Iranian diplomats.

7. Agence France Press report, 'Caspian Grouping Formed', 19 February 1992.

8. 'Central Asian Muslims Looking Towads Ummah', *Nation* (Lahore), 18 September 1991.

9. Ahmed Rashid (in Tashkent), 'Government Fails to Follow up on Major Initiatives in Central Asia', *Nation*, 26 November 1992.

10. Ahmed Rashid (in Quetta), 'Linking up for Trade', *Far Eastern Economic Review*, 25 February 1993.

11. Molly Moore (in New Delhi), 'Has Soviet Collapse Hit India Militarily?', *Dawn*, 7 October 1992.

12. M. Hauner (1990) *What is Asia to Us: Russia's Asian heartland yesterday and today*, Unwin Hyman, London.

13. Interview with the author in Alma Ata, 1990.

14. Reuters, 'Afghan Arms Linked to China's Unrest', *International Herald Tribune*, 10 May 1990.

15. Interviews by the author with Pakistani civilian and military officials. See Ahmed Rashid (in Islamabad), 'Pakistan Prepared to Evict Radicals', *Nation*, 22 March 1992.

16. M. Brill Olcott 'Central Asia on its Own', *Journal of Democracy*, Winter 1993.

17. B. Rumer, 'The Gathering Storm in Central Asia', *Orbis*, Winter 1993.

18. Interview with Rutskoi, *Frontier Post*, 8 July 1992.

19. Jonathan Steele (in Moscow), 'The Bear's Necessities', *Guardian*, 4 January 1993.

20. Reuters report on Minsk summit, 22 January 1993.

21. Reuters report, *Dawn*, 28 February 1993.

22. Interview with the author in Moscow, 30 September 1992.

10

Uncertain Homelands – Security, Islam and Nationalism

Some countries that gained their independence from colonial powers in the twentieth century created their own guerrilla forces and liberation armies, that were ultimately turned into regular armies to defend the new state and secure its borders. The destabilizing feature of the five new states in Central Asia was that none of them could guarantee their own security. With no armed forces of their own, they were forced to depend on the military forces of the former colonial power, Russia, and on the good will of their neighbours not to stake claims on their borders.

Central Asia became a region of stark military contrasts. One state, Kazakhstan, became a *de facto* nuclear power, affecting the world's nuclear balance of power. In another, Tajikistan, the growth of medieval-style warlords and local militias led to a bloody civil war. A third, Uzbekistan, projected itself militarily in the region not through its own force of arms, but by borrowing its military clout from Russia. Kyrgyzstan meanwhile forswore forever the building of an army and declared its neutrality. If the process of independence for Central Asia was one of the strangest ever witnessed, then even more confusing and complicated was how these new states were to tackle the problem of their security. Their leaders themselves were at a loss as to what to do.

They were faced with borders that had been carved out of the map by Stalin and which bore little relation to ethnic realities on the ground, with a Russia that saw itself as the ultimate guardian of their territories, and with the bewildering mushrooming of ethnic nationalism and Islamic fundamentalism at home which they had no experience of and no legitimate security apparatus to deal with. On an overnight train journey from Samarkand to Bukhara, a young Uzbek and practising Sufi described his country as an uncertain homeland. 'After centuries of struggle the peoples of Central Asia may have gained a homeland but they are deeply uncertain of the future. Independence has come to us too quickly and too easily,' he said.

For a decade after the 1917 Revolution, Central Asia was a cauldron of men at war. White and Red armies, Basmachi militias, bandit gangs, mercenary nomadic cavalry units and foreign-funded saboteurs roamed the steppe at will. It was the traditional nomadic way, with every tribal chief making his own claim to power through the barrel of a gun and no Genghis Khan or Tamerlane to unite them. Seventy years later in Tajikistan that fearful scenario appeared to be repeating itself; there were indications that this anarchy could spread northwards.

When the Red Army had emerged triumphant from the Civil War, it had established the Turkestan Military District (TMD) with headquarters in Tashkent. Starting from scratch Stalin built an enormous military infrastructure to keep the peace in Central Asia. Roads, railways, telecommunications, depots, workshops and factories were built to help control one of the most volatile regions of the Soviet Union. Entire cities were constructed to house the military and then cordoned off from civilians. Later, rocket factories and nuclear testing sites were added.

The TMD was responsible for preventing the Muslim east from penetrating Soviet territory and for containing the American encirclement of the Soviet Union from the south as the USA built bases in Turkey, Iran and Pakistan. When Beijing became the enemy, these Soviet forces were turned around to face the Chinese border. The TMD organized the invasion of Afghanistan in 1979 and kept the 120,000 Soviet forces stationed there supplied for a decade. The Red Army became the crucible where race and religion were supposedly melted down to produce the new Soviet man.

With the collapse of the Soviet Union, the Red Army was stripped of its numbers: tens of thousands of soldiers were demobbed as the new CIS armed forces took shape. The TMD was severely affected and lost many of its men. Even in 1992 there were considerable CIS forces in Central Asia, nominally under the joint command of Russia and the respective republics in which they were stationed. Tajikistan had 6,000 soldiers, Kyrgyzstan 8,000, Uzbekistan 16,000, Turkmenistan 34,000 and Kazakhstan 63,000. In each of these republics the majority of the conscripts were drawn from the republic, but many of the officers were Russians who had volunteered to stay on and serve in Central Asia. Some of them were to form the basis of the new republican armies.

Some 4,000 tanks, 10,000 armoured personnel carriers, 3,200 artillery pieces, 220 aircraft, millions of small arms and huge underground ammunition dumps lay in the hands of these republics.[1] Chaos or the collapse of the centre could lead to these weapons falling into the wrong hands. Many did as soldiers sold their weapons to local militia and mafia chiefs. The real threat did not, however, come from these weapons, but from the far more deadly reality that Kazakhstan had been left with a hefty portion of the Soviet nuclear strike force.

The problems raised by Kazakhstan's acquisition of nuclear weapons dominated Western and Asian strategic reactions to the Central Asian republics immediately after their independence. Kazakhstan had 104 SS-18 intercontinental ballistic missiles (ICBMs) with a total of 1,400 warheads on its soil. Each ICBM could travel up to 11,200 kilometres and carried ten independently targeted warheads, each of which was equivalent to half a million tons of TNT. The two main missile bases were in the north, in areas dominated by Russian settlers. Overnight, Kazakhstan had become the fourth-largest nuclear power in the world. It was an awesome responsibility for President Nursultan Nazarbayev and immensely disturbing for a world that barely knew him or his policies.

After the failed August 1991 coup, US Secretary of State James Baker rushed to Alma Ata, where Nazarbayev told him that so long as Russia maintained its nuclear capability, Kazakhstan would retain its nuclear weapons. 'I am absolutely against having any single republic control all nuclear weapons by itself, irrespective of how large that republic might be. I say that in the Soviet Union, defence should be unitary and all nuclear weapons should be under the control of the central government,' Nazarbayev told Baker.[2] In December, as the Soviet Union was on the verge of break-up, Nazarbayev told Baker in another meeting that the joint control of all nuclear weapons should be shared by the nuclear inheritors of the Soviet state – Russia, Ukraine, Belarus and Kazakhstan.

At the meeting in Alma Ata on 21 December at which the formation of the CIS was formally announced, all four nuclear states agreed to keep the Soviet strategic arsenal under collective central command, to accept US expertise in moving nuclear weapons from outlying republics to Russia by 1994 and in carrying out plans for the destruction of nuclear weapons. The only part of this agreement that was ever fulfilled was that by July 1992 all tactical nuclear weapons had been moved to Russia. The US Congress sanctioned payment of $400 million to the four nuclear states for the destruction of their surplus nuclear weapons.

The nuclear issue quickly became a political football for Ukraine and Kazakhstan, as they tried to extract more concessions from Russia and greater financial aid from the USA by playing their nuclear cards.

Nazarbayev continued to blow hot and cold on the nuclear issue, now appearing immensely amenable to US suggestions, now threatening to procrastinate. On 28 January 1992 he declared that he would not transfer his weapons to Russia. 'It is not our fault that we have become a nuclear power,' he told the French Foreign Minister Roland Dumas.[3] Rumours abounded in the Western press that Kazakhstan had sold an SS-18 to Iran and that it was about to provide Teheran with uranium. None of these reports was ever proved but they kept Western intelligence agencies on their toes for much of the year.

President Nazarbayev travelled to Washington in May 1992, where he met President George Bush and signed a protocol in which Kazakhstan agreed to sign the first Strategic Arms Reduction Treaty (START I), which would eventually allow the elimination of one third of Soviet and US nuclear weapons. Ukraine and Belarus had also signed such a protocol with the USA, so that all three states had guaranteed that they would either destroy their missiles or move them to Russia within seven years. All three states also pledged to sign the Nuclear Non-Proliferation Treaty (NPT) in the shortest possible time. Russia was officially designated as the successor nuclear state to the former Soviet Union.

However Nazarbayev again appeared to backtrack on his commitments. 'Our neighbour China is a nuclear power. Pakistan and India are nuclear powers. That is why we have a clear position. It will take at least fifteen years to destroy these missiles if work progresses well. It would be desirable for these countries to join us.' he said.[4] It appeared that he was now demanding that all Kazakhstan's neighbours abandon their nuclear weapons before Kazakhstan did so.

In June 1992 the US and Russia agreed to START I, which would eliminate all land-based multiple warhead missiles, leading to an eventual ceiling of each side fielding 3,000 to 3,500 warheads by the year 2000. The first missiles to be eliminated would be the SS-18s, the very missiles on Kazakh soil. Ukraine, with 1,650 nuclear warheads on its soil, refused to fall in and began a lengthy process of threats, blackmail and ultimatums to Washington and Moscow in a bid to obtain security guarantees from the USA and more than the $175 million earmarked by Washington for Kiev for the elimination of its missiles. In January 1993, after three days of talks in Washington, Ukrainian leaders agreed to accept US security guarantees after Russia had agreed to compensate Ukraine for giving up its nuclear weapons.

Another crisis erupted in May 1993 when Ukraine again reneged on its earlier pledges and now demanded $3 billion from the USA for dismantling its weapons. The crisis was only averted when US Defense Secretary Les Aspin visited Kiev in June and proposed that Ukraine's nuclear warheads be placed in storage under international supervision and that the US would help modernize Ukraine's conventional weapons systems.[5]

Ukraine, in the words of one US official, just kept moving the goalposts to extract the maximum concessions from the USA. But both Ukraine and Kazakhstan had legitimate fears of Russian domination, which could only increase if Russia was to become the only nuclear weapon state in the former Soviet Union. There were justifiable fears that the political uncertainty in Russia could bring a xenophobic leader to power, or even a military coup, which might lead Russia to use nuclear blackmail to redraw its borders or even to reestablishing the old Soviet Union. Nazarbayev played a skilful game, never appearing as stubborn as Ukraine, but using Ukraine's positions as a stalking horse for his own policies.

Nazarbayev held back from signing the NPT or stating categorically when he would return his nuclear missiles to Russia or destroy them. Although appearing to be more reasonable than Ukraine, in reality he was just as ambivalent about his intentions. Nazarbayev's real aim was to keep Moscow in a state of uncertainty, to retain a strong negotiating position for other issues by maintaining his nuclear ambivalence and at the same time to force Western countries to come up with more aid before he yielded to their demands. In short, until there was greater stability in Russia and in relations between the West and the former Soviet republics, Kazakhstan would not surrender its nuclear weapons.

Nazarbayev knew that for Washington the nuclear issue was of paramount concern. The new Clinton administration had placed nonproliferation at the top of its foreign policy agenda and could not afford to lose face at the hands of small republics whose international clout was at best minimal. CIA chief James Woolsey told a Senate committee, 'Non-proliferation poses one of the most complex challenges the intelligence community will face for the remainder of the century.' He said that twenty-five countries were now developing nuclear, biological and chemical weapons and that some countries were trying clandestinely to obtain nuclear material from the former Soviet republics.[6]

The West was indeed worried. Speculative media reports in 1992 spoke of Tajikistan selling enriched uranium to potential Third World customers at the rate of $100,000 for one kilogram. The Tajik government was now running a secret uranium enrichment plant near Khodjent, but officials strongly denied that the plant was involved in illegal sales. The plant had been built in the 1940s to provide fuel for the first Soviet atom bomb and produced 3 per cent of the former

Soviet Union's total uranium.[7] In 1993 the US and Germany asked Kazakhstan to look into the possible smuggling and sale of low-grade nuclear fuel and metals such as beryllium and zirconium which are used in nuclear weapons. A report prepared by Russia's Foreign Intelligence Service and made public in the USA in 1993 cited 'the growing interest of international organised crime structures in conducting illegal trade in fissionable and other especially dangerous material'.[8] But despite such reports it appears that the Central Asian republics acted responsibly with their nuclear materials and were not tempted to sell fissile materials to countries like Iran.

Other Central Asian republics publicly pretended to ignore the nuclear tussle between Russia, Kazakhstan and the USA, but it remained a major source of friction between Uzbekistan and Kazakhstan. President Karimov both envied and feared Kazakhstan's nuclear clout because it affected his bid to become the *de facto* leader of Central Asia. He disliked the fact that Western leaders visited Alma Ata more frequently than they did Tashkent and were more willing to provide economic aid to Kazakhstan.

In the first year of independence, however, all the republics faced immediate problems of how to evolve effective security measures for their states. Immediately after the break-up of the Soviet Union a Joint Military Command was set up in a bid to save the Soviet armed forces from disintegration. The six signatories of the agreement were Russia, Kazakhstan, Uzbekistan, Tajikistan, Kyrgyzstan and Armenia. Interminable negotiations began between Russia and these republics about their future military relationship. The crisis in the CIS military was acute. An eight-year restructuring plan was begun, and troops were demobbed; many faced return to Russia where housing, goods and money were in short supply. Morale amongst officers and men plummeted.

All this made it impossible for the CIS high command to formulate any new military doctrine. Without knowing how far their mandate stretched, it was difficult for generals to commit themselves to Central Asia. Initially CIS troops in Central Asia were designated as part of CIS forces but given a loose national status as they came under the joint command of officers from Russia and the respective republic. Even this arrangement was not entirely clear. Each republic negotiated for itself rather than following a joint Central Asian strategy. This only increased the chaos in the negotiations and delayed decisions.

The situation became more complicated in March 1992 when Russia said it would create its own army and defence ministry rather than rely on a united CIS force. For many Central Asian leaders this was a major blow, and forced even those leaders reluctant to do so to think about creating their own national forces. Almost immediately Nazarbayev announced the setting up of a Kazakh National Guard. Uzbekistan said it would build a national army of 25,000 men, while Turkmenistan said it wanted no more than 2,000 men and would rely entirely on CIS forces.

At a meeting of Central Asian leaders in Beshkek in April 1992, President Nazarbayev proposed a common defence agreement amongst all the republics which could then be part of a larger defence pact with Moscow. President Karimov shot the plan down and proposed instead NATO-style local armies that would co-ordinate for a common defence. Turkmenistan refused to co-operate with other Central Asian states. Other leaders expressed their disillusionment with the CIS and said no military agreements could be made unless it was clear what the Russian army's role would be. Discussions on collective security arrangements quickly collapsed; no headway was made despite a number of Central Asian summits.

In June 1993 the CIS formally abandoned the Joint Military Command set up in 1991 by Russia, Armenia and four of the Central Asian states. Russia, which would have had to bear the cost of such a command, refused to do so and the Central Asian states were left with the options of discussing a looser co-ordinating military body to be set up by 1994, or relying entirely on their own forces. The basic issues of defence thus remained unresolved, as it was still not known how such co-ordination would be achieved. What was to be the relationship between CIS forces and national forces, how were effective command-and-control structures to function and how would the division and maintenance of military hardware and facilities be made?

Clearly, two military doctrines needed to be meshed together: one based on the specific needs of each republic and one for the CIS as a whole, where Russian strategy would dominate. With Central Asian states in their infancy and Russia in turmoil, neither military doctrine could be created. A system of collective security was not workable because of the diverging security interests of the member states. Leaders still feared that the new CIS forces would only be a euphemism for the Russian army playing a colonial role in their republics. But in the first year after independence Russia appeared to withdraw from the region, not wanting to get sucked into the hypernationalism, Islamic fundamentalism and economic breakdown that were prevalent.

The Tajik civil war changed all that. Russia was soon providing help to Uzbekistan and the Tajik neo-communists to defeat the Islamic opposition. Russian military officers also realized that a landslide migration of Russians from Central Asia could trigger off a bloody reaction against Muslims in Russia itself and thus increase instability in the small autonomous Muslim republics in Russia. And with its still significant Muslim population, Russia did not want to see the spread of Islamic fundamentalism into its territory. By 1993 the need to contain the spread of fundamentalism from the south – implying Iran, Afghanistan and Pakistan – had become a truism in the CIS high command. Russia's defence minister, General Pavel Grachev, paid repeated visits to Tajikistan, raised the salaries of officers serving there and promoted many of them in the field.

The threat from Tajikistan was treated as a one-off event and did not bring the five republics closer in co-ordinating their military strategy. On the contrary, events in Tajikistan moved them further apart because the three smaller states became even more fearful than previously of Uzbekistan's political and military ambitions. All the states except Kyrgyzstan, which refused to create an army, wanted their own national forces but the expense involved in creating these was prohibitive and international lending agencies were in no mood to give loans to countries that would use already scarce funds to build armies. This problem must remain unresolved for the foreseeable future, although in the meantime Central Asian states have gone ahead in trying to form small national forces.

It would be only common sense for the Central Asian states to pool their resources and set up common defence forces. But political, economic and ethnic differences have spilled over into the military sphere and now appear to make this impossible. At best the Central Asian states can co-ordinate their efforts when there is a perceived external threat, such as the infiltration from Afghanistan of Islamic militants into Tajikistan. In late 1992 all the states committed troops to guard the Afghan–Tajik border under CIS command, but when the next regional crisis comes, political differences between the states may be so acute that even such agreements may be impossible. Another dampener is that for the time being neither Russia nor the West is keen to see a common Central Asian defence strategy evolve. They would like to see the region kept militarily weak and thus non-expansionist and non-belligerent. But this could create a political and military vacuum that might in the future be filled by outside powers such as Iran, Turkey or Pakistan.

In 1992 Turkey quietly committed officers, men and equipment to Azerbaijan in its fight against Armenia. Iran could do the same if there is an appeal from some future pro-Islamic government in Tajikistan, while some officers in the Pakistan military openly advocate a common defence pact between Pakistan and Central Asian states as a bulwark against India. If Central Asia is not helped by major outside powers such as Russia and the USA to evolve a common defence strategy, it may in the future be forced to look to its more powerful neighbours for military help and this could create much wider regional tensions and even conflicts.

Long-term national security will depend on how these states tackle the two main political movements in Central Asia: ethnic nationalism and Islamic fundamentalism. In the past, independence or national liberation struggles were processes in which leaders and elites proved themselves and gained experience, the goals of the elite and the masses became welded together and local differences were resolved. These struggles also released enormous energy, commitment and self-sacrificing attitudes towards the building of the nation. It is this process that has helped new nations get through the difficult transition period after independence. Such was the case in India, Pakistan and Indonesia or more recently in Vietnam and Zimbabwe.

Central Asia experienced no such political process, its peoples were barely touched by political events and the enormous gap between the rulers and the ruled only grew wider. Even that initial euphoric welding of people and nation that takes place immediately after independence was totally missing. Central Asian republics did not go through any of the natural pangs of state-building and thus their identity is at best confused. Under communism, the people were largely alienated from the political structure and decision-making. After independence this alienation only increased as many regimes bunkered down to survive and paid little heed to democratizing society, devolving power to the regions or involving the people in the political process. The underlying factor behind the ethnic, religious and political opposition to these regimes is the public's sense of its growing alienation. There are few signs that the regimes are aware of this or are trying to rectify it.

After independence there was not even the usual clear sense of public outrage against the former colonial power. The blurring of the empire and the colonies and the fact that Russians have lived for nearly 150 years in Central Asia have created a shadowy acceptance rather than a clear distinction between colonizer and the colonized. There is a grudging admission by many that, despite the huge cost in Central Asian lives, Russia did 'civilize' Central Asia and drag it into the modern world. Russian culture proved to be a window to European culture, and even local reformers of the nineteenth century such as the Jadids were, after all, Russian-educated.

This mixture of fact and ignorance, anger and apology makes it more difficult for nationalist ideas to gel a society together. Strident nationalism sounds slightly false, especially when it is being intoned through speeches made in Russian and when Russian is the only common language of communication across Central Asia. Some 10 million Russians lived in Central Asia. Once the elite, they are they are now an unwelcome but still powerful minority, even though one fifth, or 2 million people, had fled Central Asia by the end of 1992. Those left behind do not speak the local languages and will increasingly come to live in Russian ghettos cut off from the mainstream. Yet their very presence will be a constant reminder to hardline nationalists that a Central Asia without Russians is inconceivable for the time being. The Russians will have to be accommodated, and this fact alone will force the nationalists to soften their strident tones and be more pragmatic.

An even more complicated problem for the nationalists is that dozens of minorities live in each state. The break-up of the Soviet empire has spawned minorities within minorities. Any nationalist revival will have to ensure a programme watered down enough so that it includes distant cousins from different tribes; otherwise the nationalists will be unable to gain support from all strata of society. In the past five years the region has already witnessed many ethnic bloodbaths; these should act as warning signals for the future if the majority should become too demanding.

Since the end of the Cold War nationalism has shown two faces across the world: a reactionary face looking backwards to past glories, racism and fascism; and a modernizing face that looks to the future in the building of a wider ethnic community. In Central Asia something different has happened. Communist parties have tried to turn themselves into nationalist parties and this has created strange political creatures. There is a high degree of intolerance, violence and ugly undemocratic rule, but also a rush to embrace democracy, capitalism, Western culture, Islam, foreign languages, and a family of all the Central Asian peoples. The leadership has turned nationalism on its head, by promising not a single identifiable goal but everything and nothing, the best and the worst from the outside world.

This has only led to greater confusion, and a counter-reaction could follow.

> A wounded nationalism is like a bent twig, forced down so severely that when released, it lashes back with fury. Nationalism ... in the former Soviet Empire seems today to be one vast, open wound. After years of oppression and humiliation, there is liable to occur a violent counter-reaction, an outburst of national pride, often aggressive self-assertion by liberated nations and their leaders.[9]

Under communism, people had come to believe that if the government was strong and brutal it must be obeyed, but if it was weak it could conveniently be ignored. These are the principles that still guide many people and allow leaders like Islam Karimov and Saparmurad

Niyazov to continue ruling in the old way without too much public protest. Despite all the pretence of nationalism, no Central Asian leader has given a sense of citizenship to his people as yet, a concept that was also completely alien to Soviet society. Before, people tended to withdraw into private worlds if the state became too strident in its demands. People still do so today, leaving politics to the politicians as they react to the political and economic chaos around them.

Nothing exposed this confused attitude more clearly than the failed August 1991 coup in Moscow. Most Central Asian leaders first applauded the coup, then denounced it but suppressed any opposition protest against the coup. Then they declared independence and promised democracy, yet demanded the creation of a new type of Union and kept a ban on all opposition parties – all this within the space of one week. Nationalism in Central Asia is thus an amalgam of modernism and reaction, of democratic intentions and totalitarianism, state control over industry yet half-hearted attempts at privatization.

These are states with very little knowledge about how the outside world works, whilst their leaders have only borrowed ideas as to how to bring about change. Thus there is a constant conjuring up of ideal models: the Turkish model of secularism and capitalism favoured by Karimov; the Chinese model of the market economy, leadership worship and little democracy favoured by Niyazov; the South Korean model of economic development and consumerism at the cost of political freedoms favoured by Nazarbayev. Nobody has yet devised a Central Asian model, based on Central Asian history and society, which could be meaningful to their own people. Nationalism thus finds it difficult to put down roots.

Another major deterrent to nationalism acting as a modernizing force is the continuing grip of tribal and clan politics, which the Soviet system did not destroy but sustained and solidified within the various communist parties. 'The leaders are hostages to the clans, which offer conditional assistance and manipulate situations to serve their own narrow interests' rather than creating broad national support through a party system.[10] Thus the managers of the *kolkhoz* or collective farms, have the same relationship to farm workers as the khans did before 1917, and many of them come from the same elite families. It is not surprising that Nazarbayev and Akaev, who both come from traditional elite families within the Kazakh and Kyrgyz clan systems, are more politically secure, and more popular – and can afford to have a more open view of reform – than Karimov or Niyazov, who were bought up as orphans and can lay claim to no genuine regional or clan base.

The growth of 'localism' has been demonstrated most devastatingly in Tajikistan. The Tajiks felt historically deprived after they lost their cultural centres of Samarkand and Bukhara to Uzbekistan because they considered themselves the original inhabitants of Central Asia and the guardians of its cultural traditions. As a result Tajiks have perhaps the least sense of national pride and identity of all the peoples of Central Asia. Under communist rule in Tajikistan, clan politics, localism and patronage flourished, creating one of the most corrupt and inefficient political systems in the former Soviet Union.

Clan divisions became so enshrined in the communist party that leadership positions were openly divided amongst the clans. This division of the spoils of power led to the present civil war. Political parties still have to take root in Central Asia, political debate around issues rather than personalities and clan loyalties is only in its infancy, and economic reforms at the local level are still geared towards helping one's clan rather than the district or the country.

Yet Central Asia can never revert to what it was before 1917 or to what it was before December 1991. Before 1917 Turkestan was simply divided between the settled areas of what is now northern Tajikistan and Uzbekistan and the nomadic areas of Turkmenistan, Kazakhstan and Kyrgyzstan. Later the Soviets divided Central Asia into separate ethnic homelands, but built a universal economic and political system that refused to recognize the very differences between ethnic groups that the Soviet system had itself created. A single value system of socialist industrial society was imposed on very diverse peoples. This contradiction, of allowing territorial diversity but disallowing real cultural and social diversity, still acts as a dampener on nation-building today.

Neither the pre-1917 nor the pre-1991 system worked, but the tragedy is that the new generation is faced with the task of building a future without any real knowledge of its past. The communists managed to wipe out the history and economic and political traditions of the people. Today's ruling elite has a far better knowledge of Soviet goals than of their own national goals, far more experience of socialism than capitalism, and they feel far more comfortable talking Russian than Kazakh or Uzbek. Moreover, the majority nation is often a minority in its own cities; in some states, for example Kazakhstan, there are almost as many Russians as there are Kazakhs. How relevant in such a situation is Kazakh nationalism if it is only to put ethnic groups at each other's throats? All these problems will do much to reduce the ability of nationalism as the only cohesive force to keep society together.

Nationalism and the crisis of identity it generated affected another major factor in Central Asia – that of Islam. The Islamic revival has been quite extraordinary, an unprecedented phenomenon in the history of the Islamic world and a clear rejection of the Soviet system. Nowhere in the world has religious feeling been suppressed for so long and with such brutality and yet been revived with such enthusiasm. There have been a number of distinct phases in this revival, which has spanned just five short years.

The floodgates of the Islamic revival opened in 1989. It was a cultural, social and religious phenomenon, as people publicly wanted to demonstrate their separateness from the communist system and Slavic culture. Yet popular knowledge of the religion of Islam was minimal and information on political activism, ideas and debates in the Islamic world beyond Central Asia was almost nonexistent.

Yet by 1992 in some areas such as Tajikistan and the Ferghana valley, the politics of Islam generated in the Middle East and South Asia were already being fought over with guns. Both the liberating aspects of the religion and culture of Islam and the unfortunate sectarianism that has plagued the Islamic world in the twentieth century arrived like a tornado in Central Asia. The revival was exacerbated by the violent reaction to Islam of the ruling elites, who refused to understand what was happening or to accommodate it as part of their political agendas.

Gorbachev's *perestroika* and the loosening of communist control allowed the revival to take place. The impact of the Afghan Mujheddin's defeat of the Soviet army through a *jihad* – something the Basmachis had not achieved – created an even greater sense of awe and curiosity about Islam than might otherwise have developed. Above all, what emerged was a historical and cultural memory of the past, even though its details were somewhat hazy: that Central Asia had been the home of vast Islamic empires that once ruled Russia and the world. At their own expense people rushed to build mosques and hire young mullahs to teach them the tenets of Islam. The bureaucratic structure of official Islam, that is, Islam sponsored by the state, was swamped by a public hunger for guidance and help in this revival. But the political leaders in Central Asia ignored these demands and failed to modernize, fund or support the official Islamic bureaucracy. There were a series of revolts by the public against the Islamic hierarchy and a number of Islamic clerics were thrown out of office after being accused of being communists, alcoholics or womanizers.

People learned to bypass official Islam as they set up their own mosques and other structures, while the arrival of funds, Korans, literature and mullahs from Saudi Arabia, Iran and Pakistan spread these countries' particular versions of Islam. The fundamentalist Muslim Brotherhood had long run a small underground movement through the Islamic Renaissance Party (IRP). The IRP was legalized in 1990 in Russia, but it remained banned in Central Asia. The IRP and other Islamic groups had no compunctions in declaring their intention to create an Islamic system in each republic which, they said, would lead to greater Central Asian unity. They considered both the ruling elite and the secular nationalists to be equal threats to this task.

The vacuum created by the lack of leadership from the official Islamic hierarchy allowed fundamentalist groups to proliferate. The growing involvement of outside powers increased as Wahabi groups from Saudi Arabia, Iranian Revolutionary Guards and some Sunni fundamentalist parties in Pakistan took advantage of the unprecedented political opportunities. The refusal of Central Asian governments to allow Islamic education in government schools resulted in the spread of unofficial Islamic schools.

Like the governments of Central Asia, the West, particularly the USA, also became unnecessarily hostile. During the Cold War the Western powers had always used Islam as a means to undermine communism in Central Asia. In the 1920s the British in India supported the Basmachis with guns and money; again in 1939 the British infiltrated agents from Afghanistan and India to whip up Islamic feeling in Central Asia. Fitzroy Maclean, a British diplomat and secret agent, advised his government in a secret memorandum in October 1939 that Britain should help destabilize Central Asia using its mullahs in order to prevent Russia invading Turkey and Iran as Germany fought Britain.[11] In 1979 the USA used the Afghan war to spread Islam in Central Asia and undermine communism. The CIA funded the Afghan Mujheddin to smuggle in Korans, tape recordings, money and weapons to Islamic groups in Uzbekistan and Tajikistan.

Yet after 1991 the West suddenly changed tack. US Secretary of State James Baker publicly warned Central Asian leaders to stay clear of radical Islam and the influence of Iran. This only encouraged Central Asian leaders to increase their rhetoric against fundamentalism, in order to gain an audience in Western capitals and international lending agencies. Thus, instead of supporting moderate Islam and legalizing Islamic parties, the rulers drove political Islam further to the wall, giving Islamic militants a propaganda coup and every reason to accuse the rulers of being crypto-communists and unbelievers.

The spread of Islamic fundamentalism in Central Asia became a popular bogey in the Western media after the Tajik civil war began. However as we have seen in Chapter 7, Tajik Islamicists were driven as much by clan rivalries, the growth of localism and economic deprivation as by their desire to set up an Islamic state. Local people saw the IRP in Tajikistan as a political party first, representing the group interests of particular regions and clans, and an Islamic party second.

The fact that the IRP was allied to secular nationalist and democratic parties against the neo-communist forces appears to prove this. Similarly, in the Ferghana valley, it is the particular history of the valley and the present economic and political vacuum that has allowed fundamentalism to flourish there.

The popularization of Islamic fundamentalism in Central Asia faces major obstacles. The majority of the population are Sunni Muslims belonging to the Hanafi tradition, and inculcating sectarian beliefs and dividing society along such lines will be difficult. Ethnic minorities will not join a movement led by an ethnic majority or vice versa, making it difficult for Islamic parties to build a movement that crosses ethnic lines. Moreover, ethnic divisions and rivalries, which are increasing across Central Asia, will militate against the unitary form of fundamentalism. High literacy levels, the continuing impact of Slavic and now Western cultural influences, the growth of a free-market economy and the chaos that Tajikistan and Afghanistan have descended into under Islamic regimes will remain important factors in dissuading people from joining such movements.

There is also a major spiritual obstacle to fundamentalism and that is Sufism. Along with the overall religious revival, there has been a tremendous revival in Sufism, the mystical trend of Islam that originated in Central Asia. For centuries Sufism has been the most tolerant expression of Islam, incorporating Buddhist, Shaman and even Christian beliefs and it has helped mould the tolerance towards all religions that exists in Central Asia. 'There were Sufis here before Islam. These mountains generated a feeling of being one with the One God – Allah,' said Sheikha Safaroper, an 86-year-old woman who is the guardian of a Sufi shrine in the Pamirs.[12]

Everywhere in Central Asian tens of thousands of people are once again visiting the shrines of old Sufi saints, many of them long abandoned because of the refusal of the former communists to maintain them or allow people to pray at them. Collective farms are rebuilding shrines at their own expense, as clans and families 'go on retreat' to the shrines for weekends to meditate, picnic, play and gossip. Pilgrims travel great distances to shrines, where they pray for a cure for illness, for a job, a baby or a good marriage. Once deserted, such shrines are now alive with people, especially the young, who are told stories about the lives of the mystics and their miraculous powers and taught Sufi rituals by their elders. Beside small lakes, in wooded grottoes, caves and hidden valleys in the mountains, Sufis are once again coming to perform the centuries-old rite of *chilla* – the forty days of solitary meditation undertaken every year with just bread and water as sustenance.

The private world inhabited by Sufis kept Islam alive in Central

Asia during the worst communist repression, for Sufism is a deeply personal, silent expression of faith which does not need the trappings of mosques, formal prayers and mullahs to retain its essential spirit. Now Sufism, with its belief in the power of saints, has once again gripped people's imaginations and provides spiritual sustenance at a time of enormous political and economic turmoil. Fundamentalist leaders attack the Sufis for being overly tolerant of non-Islamic influences, for their belief in saints and miracles, for their superstitions and their divergence from the strict commands of the Koran and puritanical Islam, but these criticisms have little influence over ordinary people. Many people resent this criticism for they see Sufism as being an ancient part of Central Asian culture, which has existed far longer than fundamentalism.

But there is no organized Sufi response to the threat of fundamentalism, because Sufis do not believe in political parties. They have no messianic mission or desire to preach a political cause, but their belief in tolerance and moderation is winning them converts everywhere, at a time when many people have had enough of ideologies. Sufis are playing a prominent role in reviving the ancient skills of martial arts, healing through herbal medicine, education, publishing ancient poetry and literature, meditation and yoga. Part of the cultural revival in Central Asia, which is also supported by the nationalists, is closely linked to Sufism. In contrast the fundamentalists have little to offer in terms of promoting old cultural skills and knowledge, and they instead promote a puritanism that is alien to Central Asia. 'People may be initially lured by the fundamentalists because of their vast funds and their message of revolution, but the beauty of Islam in Central Asia is that it is rooted in culture and philosophy and above all tolerance. This cannot be wiped out in a hurry,' according to Safarbai Kushkarov, a 38-year-old prominent Sufi and renowned herbalist in Djizak, Uzbekistan.

The political problems for Central Asia's leadership will continue to be further compounded by the chronic economic situation. The differing approaches to the market economy and privatization demonstrate the inherent confusion and lack of ideas and experience of the rulers at present. Between January and May 1992, after Russia lifted price subsidies and Central Asia was forced to follow suit, the prices of basic consumer goods rose 23-fold in most Central Asian cities. The debt of state-run enterprises increased 47-fold and 80 per cent of state-run enterprises faced bankruptcy. Industrial and agricultural output was 25 per cent lower in 1992 than in 1990 and the average rate of consumption had returned to what it was in the 1950s. The economy of many of these states was simply imploding.

The public assumption in Russia that the lifting of price controls and the creation of a free market would miraculously solve economic problems proved to be naïve. Even pro-market Central Asian leaders learned their lessons fast and slowed down the pace of reform. There was a severe backlash from diehard communists who rejected reform economics. State intervention was still seen as necessary to prevent the total collapse of production of essential goods. Consequently hopes that an economic union could be created in Central Asia proved to be premature. The republics' ties to Russia, their competing products, political and ethnic differences and above all the scarcity of funds and resources made any immediate economic union impossible, even though Central Asia holds great economic promise. Self-sufficient in food, cotton, oil, gas and electricity it has far more going for it than many countries in Asia or Africa who became independent earlier on. However the economic legacy of communism remains an immense burden that will not be shed easily.

The situation for some republics worsened even further in 1993. Kyrgyzstan, the most liberal reformer and the strongest advocate of greater regional co-ordination, was forced to deal a mortal blow to economic and monetary union, when it abandoned the rouble zone and set up its own currency. Plagued by hyperinflation, President Askar Akaev shocked his own people on 10 May 1993 when he introduced the sum and cancelled all trading in roubles or dollars. Central Asian leaders were furious and President Karimov ordered the Uzbek–Kyrgyz common border to be closed, Uzbek gas supplies to Beshkek to be shut down and the supply of petroleum and foodstuffs to be stopped. 'I perceive this as political subversion against Uzbekistan. Akaev's policy is trying to drive a wedge between the Central Asian countries,' he fumed. Akaev's action was seen as a betrayal by other Central Asian states, which feared a flood of roubles from Kyrgyzstan into their republics.[13]

The move appeared to be encouraged by the West and international lending agencies. This further angered Central Asian leaders and it allowed hardline communists to step up their propaganda against IMF-sponsored economic reform programmes. Because of the plummeting rate of the rouble, the IMF had recently abandoned its advice to Central Asian states to stay within the rouble zone, and it was now encouraging the republics to establish their own currencies as the first step towards gaining IMF financial support. Just before Beshkek abandoned the rouble, the World Bank had given Kyrgyzstan a credit of $60 million, while later Washington pledged $100 million in aid, Japan pledged $60 million and Switzerland $10 million. There was criticism that the West was deliberately trying to undermine Central Asian unity.

Kyrgyzstan's move prompted fears that every republic would now pursue its own economic and monetary course creating further tensions and disparities in the region and dampening foreign investment. Hopes that the five states would in future co-ordinate their defence and foreign policies now looked even less likely. Kyrgyzstan set a trend that other Central Asian states can do little to stop.

Russia tried to stem the tide as more and more republics considered abandoning the rouble. In September 1993 Russia formulated a 'Common Rouble Zone' with several Central Asian republics, but the exorbitant demands Moscow made forced the republics to set up their currencies even sooner than expected. On October 29, Turkmenistan introduced the *manat* with new currency notes stamped with the portrait of President Niyazov. US$300 million of the republic's US$800 million hard currency reserves were pledged to back the new currency. On November 14, Uzbekistan introduced the sum currency that would operate in tandem with the rouble for an unspecified time. The rouble crashed against the dollar in Tashkent reaching R18,000 to US$1, compared to R4,000 to the US$1 just two weeks earlier. In Kazakhstan President Nazarbayev publicly blamed Russia for ruining the rouble zone and received authority from the Kazakh parliament to introduce a national currency. Kazakhstan introduced its new currency, the *tenge* on November 15.

With four different non-convertible currencies operating in Central Asia and neighbours refusing to accept the new currencies for trade or debt repayments, the immediate effect was hyper-inflation, a booming dollar black market, economic instability and a greater dependency on barter trade. There was no immediate agreement between the republics even to accept each other's currency. The short term impact of these new currencies was to further destabilize Central Asia and make potential economic allies into economic rivals and financial foes. Political tensions between the republics and Moscow also worsened, especially after the December elections in Russia in which the extreme nationalist Russian leader Vladimir Zhirinovsky, who views Central Asia as still being part of Russia, won more than 25 percent of the seats in the Russian parliament.

The continuing civil war in Tajikistan remained the principle security concern for Central Asian leaders. Throughout the summer of 1993 Tajik rebels launched attacks into Tajikistan from their bases in Afghanistan. Fierce clashes took place between them and Russian troops on the border, which resulted in several Russian incursions into Afghanistan itself and repeated bombardments by Russian artillery of Afghan villages along the border, which killed some two hundred Afghans. On June 21, Tajikistan's Supreme Court formally banned all the opposition parties, confiscated their assets and brought treason charges against their leaders.

In a major incident on July 14, twenty five Russian troops were killed on the border by the rebels. Russia sent in more troops, armour and aircraft to help the Tajik government. On August 24, the UN Security Council made its first but extremely strong appeal to the Tajik government to 'accept as soon as possible the need for an overall political solution and to participate in a negotiating process for the early establishment of a ceasefire and eventual national reconciliation with the widest possible participation of all political groups'. The appeal coincided with a trip by the UN Special Envoy to Tajikistan, Esmat Kittani, to Islamabad, Kabul and Dushanbe to discuss the crisis with regional leaders. The effects of the war had now spilt over into the entire region and Moscow appeared more willing to open a dialogue with the opposition and force the Tajik government to do the same. At a summit meeting of all Central Asian leaders and Russia in Moscow from August 6–9, President Yeltsin said he would back a political rather than a military solution to the civil war and he urged the Tajik government to do the same.

However, in a move that dismayed Tajik opposition leaders, the defence ministers of the CIS agreed on August 25 to set up a new coalition force to control the Tajik insurgency. The force under Russian army Colonel General Boris Pyankov would consist of contingents from Russia, Kyrgyzstan, Kazakhstan and Uzbekistan. By sending in more troops Russia appeared to be sending an entirely negative signal to the opposition, who vowed to continue their attacks until Russian forces completely withdrew from Tajikistan. Despite his pledges of peace President Yeltsin appeared to put no pressure on the Tajik government to open a dialogue with the opposition. This increased fears across Central Asia that Russia was now capable of keeping an unpopular government in power by force of arms, thereby eliminating the chances of nascent democratic and Islamic forces from winning elections.

The region will continue to be buffeted by competing international interests both economically and politically. While Russia and the West are trying to pull Central Asia away from the Islamic world, its Muslim neighbours are determined to build a greater economic and political consensus with the Central Asian states. Central Asia will also continue to be pulled in different directions by the disputes between the Arab world and Iran, between India and Pakistan, and between Iran and Turkey. It still has major problems with Russia. All this will make any Central Asian unity much more difficult to realize.

There are no easy solutions to the problems of Central Asia. In the early twentieth century this vast region had to cope with Russian colonization, tsarism, revolution, civil war, famine, collectivization and then ethnic nationhood and communism, coming one on top of another. More recently it has had to deal with independence, breaking out of diplomatic isolation, economic hardship, ethnic conflict, a civil war in Tajikistan and the revival of nationalism and Islamic fundamentalism. The republics' leaderships have so far just managed to keep their heads above water, preventing major economic and political chaos but unable to provide solutions for an increasingly demanding and demoralized public.

By and large the peoples of Central Asia have so far not risen up to demand their rights, but this somnolent attitude cannot be guaranteed for ever. The majority of the population is under thirty years of age, population growth is rapid and there is an ever-widening gulf between a new generation and a leadership still governing in the old way. Unless the increasing alienation of the young from the power structure is seriously tackled, political upheavals and uncertainty will continue.

The key to future stability will be how quickly the ruling elite will be able to change its old habits, move from centralized, controlled economic management to the market and private enterprise, give up its totalitarian methods of government and allow greater democracy and political pluralism and decentralize the huge bureaucratic apparatus so that farflung regions can decide their own economic and political paths to development. Above all the leadership will have to become more accommodating to the growing political pressures it faces, or it will be swept aside through political coups or in bloody and tumultuous movements such as have already been seen in Tajikistan. Only by adopting a more sympathetic and farsighted attitude to the Islamic revival and the appeal of nationalism, by encouraging the opposition to participate in nation-building through a more open and democratic political system, can this be avoided.

It is therefore through the revival of traditional habits, customs, methods of work, culture and ideas drawn from the historical past that national identities can be forged and become positive factors in contributing to the character of Central Asia in the future. To presuppose that narrow nationalism or fundamentalism will win the political battle in Central Asia is to underestimate the deep wells of knowledge and experience that these ancient peoples have to draw on. Central Asia will have to find its own way to real freedom, and that will have to draw upon its own magnificent past and the best modernizing influences that the outside world has to offer. This enormous landscape, these courageous people who have suffered such extraordinary calamities in the past century need time and space to rediscover their own souls.

Notes

1. *Strategic Balance, 1992.*

2. Doyle McManus (in Alma Ata), 'Kazakhstan Wants to Keep Nukes', *Dawn*, 17 September 1991.

3. Reuters, 'Kazakhs To Keep Nuclear Arms', *Dawn*, 28 January 1992.

4. *Central Asian Significants*, May 1992.

5. Jeffrey Smith (in Kiev), 'Ukraine Ready to Place Warheads Under Supervision' *Dawn*, 8 June 1993.

6. US Information Service, 24 February 1993.

7. Yuri Vishnesky, the chairman of the Russian State Committee for Safety in the Atomic Industry, said that Tajikistan was free to sell uranium ore to whomever it liked. (*Trud*, 9 January 1992). President Nabiev subsequently placed a ban on uranium sales to foreign countries.

8. Steve Coll (in Alma Ata), 'The Distant Dream on Russia's Rim', *Dawn*, 15 May 1993.

9. Interview with Isaiah Berlin in the *New York Review*, reprinted *Friday Times* (Lahore), 9 July 1992.

10. B. Rumer, 'The Gatherng Storm in Central Asia', *Orbis*, Winter 1993.

11. Anthony Bevins, 'British Plot Aimed to Destabilise Soviets', *Independent*, 26 February 1990.

12. Ahmed Rashid (in Uzbekstan), 'Revival of Sufism', *Far Eastern Economic Review*, 17 December 1992.

13. Ahmed Rashid, 'Out of Steppe', *Far Eastern Economic Review*, 17 June 1993.

Appendix:
Data and Chronologies

Uzbekistan

Data

Population: 22 million (Uzbeks 71%, Russians 10.8%, Tajiks 4% and Tatars 4.2%).
Total labour force: 8.11 million.
Area: 447,400 square kilometres.
Capital: Tashkent (population 2.1 million).
President: Islam Karimov.
Neighbouring states: Afghanistan, Kazakhstan, Turkmenistan, Tajikistan and Kyrgyzstan.
GDP:
    1990 GDP: 32,430 million roubles.
    1990 GDP per capita: 1,579 roubles.
    1991 GNP per capita: $1,350.
Exports and Imports:
    1990 total exports: 7,702 million roubles, of which:
        foreign exports: 813 million roubles,
        inter-republic exports: 6,889 million roubles.
    1990 total imports: 12,289 million roubles, of which:
        foreign imports: 1,296 million roubles
        inter-republic imports: 10,993 million roubles.
    64% of all exports were to Europe and 23% to Asia. 70% of all imports were from Europe and 17% from Asia
Grain Production:
    1990: 1.89 million tons.
    1991: 1.87 million tons.
Cotton Production:
    1991: 4.5 million tons.
    1992: 4.1 million tons.
Oil and Gas Production:
    1991: gas production: 41 billion cubic metres.
    1991: oil production: 2.8 million tons.

Armed Forces:
    Army: 15,000 men under joint CIS control.
    National Guard of one brigade of 700 men. More to be formed.

Sources: World Bank, IMF, Military Balance, Government of Uzbekistan.

Chronology

500 BC Samarkand founded by Sogdian king Afriasab.

334 BC Alexander the Great conquers Samarkand.

654 AD Arab armies first cross the Amudarya river.

874–999 Samanid empire based in Bukhara rules Uzbek region.

1220 Genghis Khan ravages Bukhara and Samarkand.

1369 Tamerlane makes Samarkand the capital of his empire.

1405 Tamerlane dies.

1417 Registan Madrasah in Samarkand built by Ulug Beg.

1500 Uzbek Shaybani Khan captures Bukhara and sets up Uzbek state.

1826–60 Amir of Bukhara, Nasrullah Khan, consolidates state power.

1861–65 American Civil War increases demand for Central Asian cotton.

1865 Russians capture Tashkent.

1868 Russians capture Samarkand.

1873 Russia forces treaties with Khiva and Bukhara. Abolition of slavery in these states.

1881 Construction of Trans Caspian Railway begins.

1894 Fortress built by Tsar at Tirmiz to guard Afghan border.

1898 Revolt in Andizan against Russian occupation.

1904 Defeat of Russia by Japan.

1916 Famine in Uzbekistan as Tsar issues conscription orders. Jadid revolt against Russian troops crushed.

1917 March: Jadids hold conference of Turkestan's Muslim leaders.
        October: Tashkent Soviet assumes authority in Central Asia.

1918 March: Treaty between Amir of Bukhara and Tashkent Soviet. Subsequently, Basmachi revolt begins in the Ferghana valley.

1920 September: General Frunze captures Bukhara. Amir flees to Afghanistan.
        ʼKhanates of Khiva and Bukhara become People's Republics.

1924 27 October: The Soviet Socialist Republic of Uzbekistan is born. 16,000 cadres are purged from the CPU on Stalin's orders.

1929 Arabic script for Uzbek language replaced by Latin script.

1932 March: Karakalpak Autonomous Soviet Socialist Republic is created.

1936 Karakalpak ASSR is transferred from Kazakhstan to Uzbekistan.

1938 President of Uzbekistan, Faizullah Khojaev, and Akmal Ikramov, secretary-general of CPU, are executed after treason trial.

1940 Latin script replaced by Cyrillic script.

1941 22 June: Tamerlane's tomb is exhumed. Hitler invades Russia.

1959 March: Sharif Rashidov becomes first secretary of CPU.

1963 19 September: 40,000 sq. kms. are transferred from Kazakhstan to Uzbekistan by order of the Supreme Soviet.

1966 25 April: Earthquake destroys much of Tashkent.

1983 October: First secretary Sharif Rashidov is removed from office and charged with corruption.

1989 26 May: Birlik party is founded.

3–4 June: Riots in Tashkent and Ferghana between Uzbeks and Meskhetian Turks. One hundred dead.

1990 February: Birlik splits into two. Erk party formed.

24 March: Islam Karimov elected as president.

20 June: Uzbekistan declares its sovereignty.

1991 20 August: Coup attempt in Moscow. Karimov supports coup.

31 August: Uzbekistan declares its independence.

14 September: CPU becomes the People's Democratic Party.

22 November: Birlik registered as a movement but not as a party.

29 December: Karimov wins election for president with 85.9% of the vote. Mohammed Salih of Erk wins 12.4% of the vote.

1992 16 January: Food riots in Tashkent; twenty-one students killed.

February: US Secretary of State James Baker visits Tashkent.

17 March: Crackdown on Islamic fundamentalists in Namangan, seventy people arrested.

April: Tamerlane declared Uzbek national hero and replaces Lenin Statue on Tamerlane Boulevard, Tashkent.

May: All Uzbek soldiers in CIS forces recalled home.

30 June: Abdulrahim Pulatov, head of Birlik, beaten up in his office.

12 October: Afghan president Burhanuddin Rabbani meets Karimov in Tashkent. Afghan–Uzbek reconciliation.

8 December: New constitution passed. Elections promised for 1993; and Parliament to be reduced from 500 to 150 members.

9 December: Birlik leaders arrested by Uzbek KGB at Beshkek human rights conference and driven back to Tashkent jail. Birlik is later banned. Independent newspaper *The Businessman* is also banned.

December: Uzbek jets and helicopter gunships help Tajik communist forces capture Dushanbe.

19 December: Uzbek helicopter gunship shot down by Tajik rebels.

1993 5 January: At Heads of State meeting five Central Asian states decide to create a Union of Central Asian people. They criticize the CIS.

21 January: Supreme Court suspends activities of Birlik for three months.

22 January: At CIS summit, Uzbekistan signs CIS treaty for closer integration.

28 January: Pulatov, leader of Birlik, freed from jail.

16 March: Foreign Minister Sadyk Safaev accuses Pakistan and Afghanistan of helping Tajik fundamentalists. Uzbek troops still deployed in Dushanbe to help Tajik government.

31 March: Malaysian Prime Minister Mahathir Mohammed visits Uzbekistan.

8 April: Turkish president Ozal visits Tashkent; agreements are signed as both leaders oppose Islamic fundamentalism.

10 April: Government arrests Mohammed Salih, chairman of Erk.

22 May: Uzbek newspapers strongly criticize President Nazarbayev.

27 May: Trial of former Vice-President Shukrulla Mirsaidov starts for nepotism and misusing state resources. He was former Mayor of Tashkent and very popular. Foreign diplomats and journalists removed from the court.

15 June: CIS abandons plans to set up joint armed forces.

22 June: US cuts short visit of Uzbek parliamentarians to Washington and threatens to freeze aid after Uzbek woman working in the US embassy in Tashkent is beaten up.

23 June: Former Vice President Shukrulla Mirsaidov confirms that he was sentenced to 3 years in jail and then pardoned.

23 July: Saidmukhtar Saidiqasimov made foreign minister. He is a former ambassador to Germany.

9 August: Karimov in Moscow for summit on Tajikistan crisis. He supports Yeltsin in calling for talks between Tajik opposition and government.

2 September: Law passed by parliament to introduce Latin script.

6 September: Russia and five republics including Kazakhstan, Tajikistan and Uzbekistan agree to common rouble zone and the Russian Central Bank as the sole centre for currency distribution.

9 September: Uzbekistan closes borders as cholera spreads in Central Asia. Daewoo setting up US$500 million car plant in Andijan to produce 80,000 cars annually.

16 September: Karimov snubs US Special Envoy Strobe Talbott on human rights and says US should not interfere in Uzbekistan.

18 October: President Rafsanjani of Iran promises in Tashkent to open road and rail links to the sea.

3 November: Uzbekistan criticises Russian rouble zone and threatens to create its own currency. Moscow delays sending new roubles. Uzbekistan and Kazakhstan need a trillion roubles (US$840 million) to maintain solvency.

14 November: New currency, the Sum, introduced. Rouble crashes against dollar. Rift with Moscow widens.

17 November: Russian Foreign Minister Andrei Kozyrev in Tashkent as Uzbeks criticise Russia's currency policy.

5 December: Lonrho signs US$250 million deal to develop a gold mine near Zarafshan. Lonrho has five companies in Uzbekistan.

Kazakhstan

Data

Population: 17 million. (Kazakhs 42%, Russian 36%, one hundred other ethnic groups also inhabit the Republic).

Total labour force: 9.2 million.

Area: 2,717,300 square kilometres.

Capital: Alma Ata (population 1.2 million). There are eighty-seven other towns
  and cities, including Karaganda (614,000), Tselinograd (277,000), Petropavlosk
  (241,000), Chimkent.
President: Nursultan Nazarbayev.
Neighbouring states: Russia, Turkmenistan, Uzbekistan, Kyrgyzia, China.
GDP:
  1990 GDP: 45,322 million roubles.
  1990 GDP per capita: 2,706 roubles.
  1991 GDP: 76,678 million roubles.
  1991 industry share of GDP: 30.4%.
  1991 agriculture share of GDP: 26.2%.
  1991 GNP per capita $2,470.
Exports and Imports:
  1990 total exports: 9,488 million roubles, of which:
    foreign exports: 1,039 million roubles,
    inter-republic exports: 8,449 million roubles.
  1990 total imports: 16,450 million roubles, of which:
    foreign imports: 1,900 million roubles,
    inter-republic imports: 14,550 million roubles.
  1992 total exports to countries outside the CIS were $1,489 million and
    total imports were $469 million.
  65% of all exports were to Europe and 18% to Asia. 72% of all imports were
    from Europe and 18% from Asia. Kazakhstan's largest trading partner
    outside the CIS is China (1992: exports to China were worth $228
    million and imports were worth $204 million).
Grain Production:
  1990: 28.5 million tons.
  1991: 11.9 million tons.
  1992: 32 million tons.
Oil Production:
  1991: 26 million tons.
  1992: 28 million tons.
  1992: 8 million tons to Russia.
Estimated oil reserves: 100 billion barrels.
Estimated gas reserves: 2.4 trillion cubic metres.
Minerals:
  Kazakhstan has 60% of the mineral resources of the former Soviet Union;
    it has ninety minerals in all.
  1991: Kazakhstan mined 130 million tonnes of coal or a quarter of the
  former Soviet Union's total. Kazakhstan produced 7% of the former Soviet
  Union's gold, and 50% of its silver. Kazakhstan also produces lead, copper,
  zinc, cadmium, iron ore, beryllium, manganese, chrome, nickel, cobalt,
  bauxite, and industrial diamonds. It has the largest uranium mines in the
  world.
Armed Forces:
  Army: 63,000 men under joint CIS control.
  Strategic nuclear force of 104 SS-18 Satan rockets with more than 1,000
    warheads. 40 bombers.

National Guard of 5,000 men to be formed.

Sources: IMF, World Bank, Caravan Business News (Alma Ata), Ernst and Young, Military Balance, Government of Kazakhstan

Chronology

600–1200 AD Some Turkic tribes united by legendary figure Alasha Khan in southern Siberia, forerunner of Kazakh people.

1200–1500 Kazakh tribes migrate southward from Siberia.

1218 Central Asia devastated by Mongol hordes under Genghis Khan.

1500–1600 Kazakh chiefs resist Uzbek confederacy. Founding of the three Ordas. Kazakhs convert to Islam.

1731–42 Kazakh ordas submit to Russian protection.

1757 Qirot tribes, who devastated Kazakhs, defeated by Chinese.

1783–1870 Kazakhs lose 1 million people in anti-Russian revolts, famine and migration.

1822–48 Kazakh territory incorporated into Russia.

1853 Russians capture Kazakh seat of resistance at Kzyl–Orda.

1854 Vierny, later Alma Ata, is founded by the Russians.

1860 Sino–Russian Treaty, which establishes the formal border with Chinese Xinjiang, furthur dividing ethnic groups such as the Kyrgyz, Kazakhs and Uighurs.

1864 Russians capture Chimkent.

1891 Some 1 million Russian migrants move into Kazakhstan.

1905 Alash Orda, the Kazakh nationalist party created.

1916 Major anti-Russian revolt by the Kazakh–Kyrgyz tribes. Several hundred thousand migrate to China.

1917 Alash Orda sets up independent government.

1920 Alash Orda joins Bolsheviks.

1920 26 August: The Kazakh Autonomous Soviet Socialist Republic is set up.

1928 First of many purges of Kazakh nationalists from CPKZ.

1930–31 Forced collectivization of Kazakh–Kyrgyz nomads. Tens of thousands killed or migrate.

1936 5 December: The Kazakh Soviet Socialist Republic is founded.

1941 Ethnic groups from Russia sent to Kazakhstan by Stalin.

1954 February: Virgin Lands Scheme begins. One millon migrants from other republics arrive.

1964–86 Dinmukhamed Kunayev is first secretary of CPKZ.

1986 17 December: Alma Ata riots begin after Kunayev is removed from office and replaced by a Russian, Gennady Klobin. Seventeen people are killed and hundreds are injured as riots spread to twelve other towns.

1989 28 February: Nevada–Semipalatinsk movement founded.

March: Nursultan Nazarbayev becomes first secretary of the CPKZ.

1990 12 January: Radbek Nisanbai becomes grand mufti of Kazakhstan as new Islamic Religious Board is set up.

February 22: Nazarbayev is re-elected as first secretary and chairman of the Supreme Soviet.

24–26 May: International anti-nuclear conference in Alma Ata organized by Nevada–Semipalatinsk movement.

26 October: Kazakhstan declares its sovereignty.

1991 20 August: Coup attempt in Moscow.

7 September: CPKZ renamed the Socialist Party.

5 October: Nevada movement turns itself into the People's Congress of Kazakhstan.

1 December: Nazarbayev elected President in the first direct presidential elections, winning 99.8% of the vote.

16 December: Kazakhstan announces its independence.

21 December: CIS formed in Alma Ata.

1992 January–February: Trade, economic agreements signed with China. Opening of railway line between Kazakhstan and China.

26 May: Russia and Kazakhstan sign military and economic agreement.

June: Semipalatinsk declared an ecological disaster zone.

29 November: Kazakhstan joins Economic Co-operation Organization (ECO).

20 December: Russia and Kazakhstan endorse call for new, tighter core for Commonwealth.

1993 3 January: START-2 signed in Moscow between Bush and Yeltsin to eliminate three quarters of their 20,000 nuclear warheads by 2003.

5 January: At heads of state meeting five Central Asian states decide to create a Union of Central Asian People.

21 January: Russia demands control of all nuclear weapons from the CIS. Ukraine, Belarus and Kazak nuclear weapons would become part of Russian strategic forces.

28 January: Kazakh Parliament passes new constitution. Kazakh language made the official state language, but Russian declared the social language beween people. State declared to be democratic, secular and unitary.

6–8 February: ECO meets in Quetta, Pakistan, and Kazakh delegation asks for roads to be opened through Pakistan via Xinjiang. Air link accord signed with Pakistan.

28 February: Yeltsin and Nazarbayev agree to military, political and economic co-operation and the creation of a single military space and single rouble zone.

6 April: After four years of talks, US oil company Chevron signs final agreement with Kazakhstan to develop the Tenghiz oilfield.

16 April: CIS summit in Minsk. Nazarbayev says seven CIS states will form a closer Union by May, including a single rouble zone.

29 April: State Committee on Statistics says economic indicators for the first quarter of 1993 worse than 1992.

13 June: Seven Western oil firms form consortium with Kazakhstan to explore 1000 kms area in Caspian Sea.

15 June: CIS abandons plans to set up joint armed forces.

27 July: IMF approves US$86 credit for Kazakhstan to help transform the economy.

6 August: Nazarbayev in Moscow for summit meeting on Tajikistan calls for greater economic and political union with Russia. Says Islamic fundamentalism a threat to Central Asia and Russia also.

3 September: Chevron agrees with Russia to build 960 km pipeline to carry Tenghiz oil to Black Sea port of Novorossiysk at a cost of US 1.2$billion.

7 September: Russia and five republics including Kazakhstan, Tajikistan and Uzbekistan agree to common rouble zone and the Russian Central Bank as the sole centre for currency distribution.

13 September: Cholera closes schools in Alma Ata.

18 September: President Mitterand in Alma Ata gives loan of US$50 dollars and 15 contracts worth US$90 million signed with French firms.

29 September: Kazakhstan, Kyrgyzstan, Pakistan and China open talks on Karakorum Highway links to Central Asia.

21 October: Nazarbayev in China to sign friendship treaty but both countries fail to resolve border dispute and deployment of Chinese troops along 1700 km border.

25 October: US Secretary of State Christopher in Alma Ata promises US 85 million for the dismantling of Kazakh nuclear weapons but Nazarbayev refuses to give a timetable. A total of US 145 million promised by US to Kazakhstan in economic aid. President Rafsanjani of Iran visits Kazakhstan.

3 November: Kazakhstan criticises Russia for demanding gold reserves in exchange for supplies of roubles.

15 November: Kazakhstan introduces new currency, the Tenge and abandons rouble zone.

25 November: President Nazarbayev blames Russia for ruining rouble zone and says the policy of protecting Russians is like expansionist moves by Hitler.

9 December: Parliament dissolves itself to hold early elections on March 7. 350 deputies resign and local councils also resign. Special powers given to Nazarbayev in interim period.

Kyrgyzstan

Data

Population: 4.4 million, (Kyrgyz 52.4%, Russian 21.5%, Uzbek 12.9%, while eighty other ethnic groups also inhabit the Republic).

Total labour force: 1.75 million.

Area: 198,500 square kilometres.

Capital: Beshkek (population 600,000).

President: Askar Akaev.

Neighbouring countries: China, Uzbekistan, Kazakhstan, Tajikistan.

GDP:

1990 GDP: 8,320 million roubles.

1990 GDP per capita: 1,893 roubles.

1991 GNP per capita: $1,550.

Exports and Imports:

    1990 total exports: 2,006 million roubles, of which:

      foreign exports: 52 million roubles,

      inter-republic exports: 1,954 million roubles.

    1990 total imports: 3,669 million roubles, of which:

      foreign exports: 759 million roubles,

      inter-republic exports: 2,910 million roubles.

    61% of total exports were to Europe and 35% to Asia. 66% of total imports were from Europe and 17% from Asia.

Wheat Production:

    1990: 1.5 million tons.

    1991: 1.36 million tons.

    1992: 1 million tons.

Armed Forces:

    Army: 8,000 men under joint CIS control.

    National forces to be formed of approximately 5,000 men.

Sources: World Bank, IMF, Military Balance, Government of Kyrgyzstan

Chronology

1500 BC Early Turkic tribes including Kyrgyz inhabit southern Siberia.

800 BC Saka kingdom in present territory of Kyrgyzstan.

500 AD Kazakh–Kyrgyz migrate south from Siberia.

1100 Osh becomes centre of Islamic scholarship.

1207 Genghis Khan defeats his Mongol rival at Tokmak. Kyrgyz later defeated by Genghis Khan.

1500 Babar takes refuge in Kyrgyzstan. Kara–Kyrgyz or Black Kyrgyz established as separate group from Kazakhs.

1856 Russians first map out Lake Issyk-Kul.

1859–60 Thousands of Kyrgyz die in freezing winter.

1860 Sino-Russian Treaty which established the border with Xinjiang divides ethnic groups such as the Kyrgyz, Kazakhs and Uighurs.

1860–70 Kyrgyz tribes accept Russian control. Land given to Russian settlers.

1916 Revolt by Kyrgyz and Kazakhs against Russia.

1918 30 April: Kyrgyzstan becomes part of the Turkestan Autonomous Soviet Socialist Republic within the Russian Federation.

1924 Kyrgyz Autonomous Region formed.

1925 Beshkek made the capital and renamed Frunze (1926).

1926 1 February: First purges of Kyrgyz communists from the CPK begin. Kyrgyz Autonomous Soviet Socialist Republic is created.

1936 5 December: Soviet Socialist Republic of Kyrgyzia created.

1961–85 Turdakun Usubaliev first secretary of the CPK.

1978 New constitution adopted.

1985 First Secretary of the CPK Usubaliev retires. Elections to the Supreme
Soviet. Absamat Masaliyev is elected as first secretary.

1989 March: Ashar becomes first political opposition group.

1990 10 April: Absamat Masaliyev re-elected as first secretary of CPK.

3 June: Rioting in Osh between Uzbeks and Kyrgyz.

28 October: Askar Akaev elected President of Supreme Soviet.

12 December: Kyrgyzstan announces full sovereignty.

1991 20 August: Coup attempt in Moscow. Akaev supports Yeltsin.

31 August: Kyrgyzstan declares independence.

1993 22 January: At CIS summit, Kyrgyzstan signs treaty for closer integration.

3 March: A battalion of Kyrgyz peacekeeping troops sent to Afghan–
Tajik border.

17 April: During debate on new constitution, Parliament agree on a new
105-member single house to replace Soviet-style system.

24 April: President Akaev visiting Tokyo, says his country may introduce
a new currency, the som, soon.

5 May: New constitution adopted by Supreme Soviet.

10 May: Government abandons rouble zone and adopts the Som as the
new currency.

14 May: World Bank approves a credit of $60 million for Kyrgyzstan.

22 May: President Akaev in Washington. US approves loan of US$100m,
Japan pledges US$60m, Switzerland US$60m.

29 May: Akaev apologises to Karimov for not informing him about
currency change.

13 June: 1500 factories lay off workers and production because of Sum.
Trading partners unwilling to offer raw materials.

21 June: President Askar Akaev visits Iran and signs 7 agreements. But
relations strained after he promises to open Kyrgyz embassy in Jerusalem.

5 July: Russian Defence Minister Pavel Grachev signs agreements on
military cooperation with Chairman of Kyrgyz Defence Committee,
Dzhanibek Umetaliev.

20 July: Monthly inflation rate has dropped since introduction of the
Sum. But many factories closed down and foreign suppliers are refusing to accept the new currency.

7 August: Akaev in Moscow for summit on Tajikistan crisis, says Islamic
fundamentalism on the decline and conflict caused by clan rivalries.
Calls for compromise and talks.

24 August: Stringent budgetary controls declared. No more funds for
state-owned industries, redundancies in many ministries and many
industries will pay 5% of sales revenue into a social protection fund.

10 December: Vice President Felix Kulov resigns after being accused of
involvement in illegal gold trading. PM Tursunbek Chingyshev denies
involvement.

Tajikistan

Data

Population: 5.4 million people (Tajiks 58.8%, Uzbeks 23%, Russians 11%. Tartar, German, Ukrainian and Kyrgyz are 1% each of the population).
Total labour force: 1.9 million.
Area: 143,100 square kilometres.
Capital: Dushanbe (population 600,000).
Presidents: Rakhmon Nabiev 23 September 1991 to 7 September 1992. Akbarsho Iskandarov 7 September 1992 to 19 November 1992. Ali Rakhmanov from 19 November .
Neighbouring countries: China, Afghanistan, Uzbekistan, Kyrgyzstan.
GDP:
    1990 GDP: 7,112 million roubles.
    1990 GDP per capita: 1,341 roubles.
    1991 GNP per capita $1,050.
Exports and Imports:
    1990 total exports: 1,999 million roubles, of which:
        foreign exports: 356 million roubles.
        inter-republic exports: 1,643 million roubles.
    1990 total imports: 3,464 million roubles, of which:
        foreign imports: 383 million roubles.
        inter-republic imports: 3,081 million roubles.
    61% of total exports were to Europe and 18% to Asia. 67% of total imports were from Europe and 17% from Asia.
Grain Production:
    1990: 3.03 million tons.
    1991: 2.83 million tons.
Cotton Production:
    1991: 600,000 tons (estimate).
    1992: 120,000 tons (estimate).
Aluminium Production:
    1990: 520,000 tonnes.
    1991: 370,000 tonnes.
    1992: 200,000 tonnes.
Oil Production:
    1989: 300,000 tonnes.
    1990: 90,000 tonnes.
Armed Forces:
    Army: 6,000 men under joint CIS command. Bolstered by another 5,000 during civil war in 1992–93.
    National forces to be created. Numerous political militias exist.

Sources: IMF, World Bank, Military Balance, Government of Tajikistan.

Chronology

329 BC Alexander invades Tajik region and creates two new cities near present-day Termiz and Khodjent.

300–140 BC Bactrian kingdom in Tajikistan.

400 AD Turkic invasions begin.

654 Arabs first cross the Oxus river.

874–999. Saminid empire. Golden era of Persian culture.

980 Ibn Sina (Avincenna) born near Bukhara. Considered to be Tajik national hero.

1220 Genghis Khan ravages Tajikistan and sacks Termiz.

1273 Marco Polo crosses the Pamirs.

1380 Tamerlane begins campaign to conquer Central Asia.

1762 Manchus annex eastern Turkestan and Tajikistan.

1868 Russia annexes northern Tajikistan.

1884 Anglo–Russian Boundary Commission is set up.

1894 Fortress built at Termiz to guard Afghan border.

1918 February: Kokand captured by Bolsheviks.
       April: Basmachi rebellion begins. Civil war begins.

1921 February: Red Army enters Dushanbe.

1922 4 August: Enver Pasha is killed by Red Army.

1923 Famine and epidemics kill thousands.

1924 October: Tajik Autonomous Soviet Socialist Republic (SSR) is created as part of the Uzbek SSR.

1925 January: Gorno-Badakhshan Autonomous Region is created.

1929 15 October: The Tajik Soviet Socialist Republic is created.

1927–31 Several purges of CPTJ.

1931 Basmachi rebel Ibrahim Beg is executed.

1937 Major purge of CPTJ.

1961 Jabar Rasulov becomes first secretary of the CPTJ.

1979 December: Soviet troops invade Afghanistan.

1982 April: First secretary of CPTJ, Jabar Rasulov, dies.

1982–85 Rakhmon Nabiev is first secretary of CPTJ.

1989 April: Soviet forces complete withdrawal from Afghanistan.

1990 February: Riots in Dushanbe over the resettlement of Armenian refugees. Dozens of people are killed.

1991 August: President Kakhar Makhamov supports Moscow coup.
       7 September: President Makhamov is forced to resign. Replaced by Kadriddin Aslonov.
       23 September: President Aslonov is replaced by Rakhmon Nabiev.
       24 November: General elections. Rakhmon Nabiev wins 58% of the vote.

1992 March: beginning of fifty-one days of demonstrations by the opposition.
       25 April: Kabul falls to the Afghan Mujheddin.
       6 May: Three people killed during demonstrations. Nabiev invokes state of emergency and curfew in Dushanbe.

7 May: Nabiev forms National Reconciliation government with opposition. Demonstrations continue.

12 May: All parties agree to implement agreement.

28 June: 100 people killed in fighting near Kurgan Tube.

31 August: Armed groups take over Parliament building.

7 September: Nabiev is forced to resign. Replaced by Acting President Akbarsho Iskandarov. Kuliab forces attack Kurgan Tube.

27 September: Kuliab forces capture four Russian tanks and seize Kurgan Tube. The next day, Russia orders 2,000 more troops to Tajikistan.

24–25 October: coup attempt in Dushanbe by Kuliab forces.

31 October: UN Security Council appeals for end to fighting.

4 November: Summit meeting in Moscow of all Central Asian leaders to discuss Tajik crisis.

19 November: President Iskandarov resigns at meeting of Parliament in Khodjent. Ali Rakhmanov elected acting President.

22 November: Abdulmalek Abdulajanov becomes Prime Minister. He appeals to Central Asian states to send troops.

23 November: 800 casualties as refugees from Kurgan Tube are attacked near Dushanbe.

25 November: Interior ministry says 50,000 killed in the fighting since June.

5 December: Sixty people killed in Dushanbe as communist militias try to capture Dushanbe but fail.

7 December: 60,000 refugees stranded on Afghan border having fled fighting in Shartuz. Many deaths reported. Russian army calls on Islamic militants to leave Dushanbe.

9 December: 200 refugees die trying to cross Amudarya river to Afghanistan. Others stranded on border. Bread rationing in Dushanbe.

11 December: Dushanbe falls to pro-communist forces. New president and Prime Minister fly in from Khodjent. Islamic forces take up positions outside the city. Fighting begins.

18 December: Islamic rebels regroup around Kofernikhon. Government forces are helped by Uzbek jets and soldiers.

19 December: 150 people are killed in fighting. Uzbek helicopter gunship is shot down by rebels.

22 December: Kofernikhon falls to the government after heavy fighting. Rebels retreat to Pamirs and to Afghan border.

30 December: Government forces capture Pyanj as thousands more refugees flee south to Afghanistan.

1993 7 January: Emergency and curfew declared in Dushanbe.

24 January: President says 3,000 more CIS troops to patrol Afghan border. Four battalions to reinforce the 3,000 troops already on border. State of emergency declared on Afghan border.

19 February: Government launches offensive against rebel stronghold in Romit Gorge, outside Dushanbe.

22 February: Government captures three rebel strongholds, including Garm. CIS forces helping government.

16 March: Government accuses Pakistan and Afghanistan of helping Tajik rebels.

30 March: Popular Front leader Sanjak Safarov is killed.

April: Government kills thirty-two rebels near Kofernikhon.

1 May: UN Secretary-General names Iraqi diplomat Ismat Kattani as his Special UN Envoy for Tajikistan.

9 May: Government accuses rebels of planning invasion from northern Afghanistan. Eighty-six rebels killed on border by CIS forces.

24 May: UNHCR repatriates some 300 refugees to Tajikistan from Afghanistan. More to follow.

31 May: Tajikistan and Russia tell Kabul to enforce order on its border after 3 Russian soldiers killed on Tajik border.

20 June: Garobsho Shahbosov, Chairman of Badakhshan parliament says Badakhshan no longer pursuing independence and it cannot survive without central government. First food convoys reach Khorog since the winter.

21 June: Supreme Court bans four opposition parties and confiscates their assets. Criminal charges against their leaders.

26 June: In first parliament session since civil war ended, Rakhmonov pledges to build democracy.

2 July: 50 IRP rebels killed by Russian troops after major incursion into Pyandzh region. Tajik complaint to Kabul government.

14 July: 25 Russian troops killed on border and Russia promises to send more troops, armour and planes. Some 200 Tajik villagers died in mortar attacks on villages 13 kms inside Tajik border.

17 July: Russia sends more troops to Tajikistan and shells Afghan villages. Russian Defence Minister Pavel Grachev visits Dushanbe.

20 July: Russian Security Minister Viktor Barannikov warns of Afghan war replay as he visits Afghan border. Russian jets bomb rebel forces near Fayzabad.

22 July: Russia says it has the moral right to launch raids into northern Afghanistan.

27 July: Tajik Foreign Minister Rashid Alimov offers 4-way talks with Russia, Uzbekistan and Afghanistan but refuses to talk to the opposition.

28 July: Some 200 Afghan and Tajik rebels killed as they try to cross Tajik border. Week long offensive against rebels around Vari continues.

30 July: Yeltsin orders more troops to Dushanbe and says he will apply to the UN to give them UN status. Grenade explodes outside office of US diplomat in Dushanbe.

1 August: IRP leader Sharif Himmatzade, deported from Pakistan to Kabul, says he is ready for talks with Moscow but not Dushanbe. Offensive starts in Tavildara region of Badakhshan after 4 soldiers are killed. Russian aircraft bomb Afghan villages. Kabul says 300 Afghan villagers killed so far.

6 August: Summit talks start in Moscow between Yeltsin and Central Asian leaders and Tajik President Imamali Rakhmonov.

9 August: Yeltsin urges Tajikistan to start talks with opposition after summit. Also calls for UN observers on Tajik-Afghan border. Tajik FM Rashid Alimov says Tajiks ready for talks.

10 August: Tajik forces recapture Khaburabad pass linking Khorog with Dushanbe after 10-day offensive against rebels. 60 reported killed in fighting.

11 August: Afghan Foreign Minister Amin Arsalla holds successful talks in Dushanbe to control cross border fighting. But 1 Kazakh and 4 Russian soldiers kidnapped and taken into Afghanistan, in a bid to sour talks.

18 August: Tajik refugees in Afghanistan suffering from cholera and malnutrition. Russia says 14 training camps in northern Afghanistan being run by Afghan Mujheddin for Tajiks.

19 August: UN Special Envoy to Tajikistan Esmat Kittani begins five days trip to Kabul and Tajikistan.

24 August: UN Security Council appeals for end to civil war and urges government to open talks with the opposition.

25 August: CIS Defence Ministers set up a coalition force to control Tajik insurgency under Russian General Boris Pyankov.

26 August: Tajik court gives death sentence to IRP presidium member Ajit Aliyev, after he is found guilty of treason.

28 August: Tajik President visits Kabul for 3 days with 40 strong delegation to discuss border crisis and the release of Russian soldiers. Tajik Airways plane crashes between Khorog-Dushanbe. 65 people killed.

30 August: Tajik President leaves Kabul with kidnapped Russian soldiers.

9 September: Russian Foreign Minister Andrei Kozyrev in Dushanbe urges Tajiks to talk to opposition.

10 September: Tajik rebels attack munitions depots outside Dushanbe and cause massive explosions.

6 October: Russian troops surround 300-400 rebels on border after fierce four day battle. Helicopters and artillery used.

9 October: Tajik rebels capture 3 Russian and 3 Kazakh troops near Khorog but free them later. Fighting between 400 rebels and troops continues for seventh day on border.

25 October: Russian border troops again shell Afghan territory around Imamsahib.

25 November: Russian troops kill 20 Tajik rebels on border.

Turkmenistan

Data

Population: 4.2 million (Turkmen 72%, Uzbek 13%, Russians 12.6%). Total labour force: 1.847 million.

Area: 488,000 square kilometres.

Capital: Ashkhabad 400,000 people. Other cities, Cardzou (162,000 people)

President: Saparmurad Niyazov.

Neighbouring states: Kazakhstan, Uzbekistan, Iran and Afghanistan.
GDP:
  1990 GDP: 7,344 million roubles.
  1990 GDP per capita: 2,002 roubles.
  1991 GNP per capita: $1,700.
Exports and Imports:
  1990 total exports: 2,641 million roubles, of which:
    foreign exports: 172 million roubles.
    inter-republic exports: 2,469 million roubles.
  1990 total imports: 3,608 million roubles, of which:
    foreign imports: 685 million roubles.
    inter-republic imports: 2,923 million roubles.
  63% of total exports were to Europe and 22% were to Asia. 71% of total imports were from Europe and 20% from Asia.
Oil and Gas Production:
  1989: 5.4 million tons of oil, 85 billion cubic metres of gas.
  1991: 5.4 million tons of oil, 80.4 billion cubic metres of gas.
  1992: 5.2 million tons of oil, 55 billion cubic metres of gas.
  8.1 trillion cubic metres of proven gas reserves.
  700 million tonnes of proven petroleum reserves.
Cotton Production:
  1991: 1.4 million tonnes.
Grain Production:
  1990: 4.44 million tonnes.
  1991: 4.47 million tonnes.
Armed Forces:
  Army: 34,000 men under joint CIS command.
  National forces to be formed.

Sources: World Bank, IMF, Military Balance, Government of Turkmenistan.

Chronology

329–327 BC Alexander the Great conquers the region.
200 BC–AD 10 Parthian civilization.
1000–1100 AD Turkmen migrate to Caspian region from the east.
1741 Turkmen first resist and then join armies of Persian king Nadir Shah.
1813 Russia defeats Persia and enters Turkman area.
1834 Russia starts building forts in Turkman territory.
1870 Turkmen begin guerrilla war against Russians.
1873 Khiva is captured by Russians.
1881 Russians capture fort of Geok Tepe and massacre 6,000 Turkmen.
1886 Turkmen territory is annexed by Russia.
1900–1905 Strikes in Ashkhabad by Russian workers.
1916 Junaid Khan captures Khiva.
1919 Bolsheviks capture Khiva.
1919–27 Guerrilla war against Russians led by Junaid Khan.

1918 Turkmenistan becomes part of Turkestan Autonomous Republic.
1925 14 February: Soviet Socialist Republic of Turkmenistan is created.
1928 Collectivization begins.
1930 Purges against CPT members begin.
1948 6 October: Earthquake destroys Ashkhabad.
1969–86 Mukhamednazar Gapurov is first secretary of CPT.
1987 November: First protest demonstrations in Ashkhabad by Afghan war veterans.
1988 May: Demonstrations in Ashkhabad over unemployment.
1989 Six hundred academics and intellectuals form the first 'informal' group, named Agzybirlik.
1990 August 22: Sovereignty of Turkmenistan is declared.
      26 October: 98 per cent of the population vote for President Saparmuradov Niyazov in first presidential elections.
1991 August: Coup attempt in Moscow is supported by Niyazov.
1992 March: New constitution is adopted.
      22 June: Niyazov is re-elected President winning 99.5 per cent of the vote.
1993 22 January: Turkmenistan refuses to sign CIS treaty for closer integration.
      18 March: President Niyazov vows to stop Islamic fundamentalism and refuses to allow political parties.
      21 April: Turkish businessmen plan to invest $800 million in Turkmenistan.
      14 May: At CIS summit in Moscow, Turkmenistan refuses to support economic union for CIS members.
      25 October: President Rafsanjani of Iran signs deals in Turkmenistan on transport and to build a pipeline for export of Turkmen gas to the West via Iran; 160 km. railway link between Iran and Turkmenistan being completed.
      29 October: New currency Manat replaces rouble. US$300 million of reserves set aside to back it. Huge price rises as subsidies lifted.

Bibliography

Books

Akiner, S. (1983) *Islamic Peoples of the Soviet Union*. Kegan Paul International, London.

Ali Kettani, M. (1986) *Muslim Minorities in the World Today*. Mansell Publishing, London.

Al-din Attar, F. (1990) *Muslim Saints and Mystics: episodes from the Memorial of the Saints*. Arkana Penguin, London.

Allworth, E. (1990) *The Modern Uzbeks: from the fourteenth century to the present, a cultural history*. Hoover Institution Press, USA.

Arrian. (1971) *The Campaigns of Alexander*. Penguin, UK.

Asimov, M. (1987) *Tajikistan*. Novosti Press, Moscow.

Avineri, S. (ed.) (1969) *Karl Marx on Colonialisation and Modernization*. Doubleday, USA.

Babur. (1921) *Babarnama*. Transalated by Annette Beveridge. Reprinted by Sang-e-Meel, Lahore.

Battuta, I. (1984) *Travels in Asia and Africa 1325–1354*. Routledge and Kegan Paul, London.

Bailey, F. M. (1992) *Mission to Tashkent*. Oxford University Press, England.

Bennigsen, A. and Wimbush, E. (1979) *Muslim National Communism in the Soviet Union: a revolutionary strategy for the colonial world*. University of Chicago Press, USA.

Bowles, G. (1977) *The People of Asia*. Charles Scribners, USA.

Bukharin, N. and Preobrazhensky, E. (1969) *The ABC of Communism*. Penguin, UK.

Cameron, I. (1984) *Mountains of the Gods*. Facts on File, USA.

Carr, E. H. (1952) *The Bolshevik Revolution, 1917–23*. 3 volumes. Macmillan, London.

— (1958) *Socialism in One Country, 1924–26*. 3 volumes. Macmillan, London.

Carrere d'Encausse, H. (1979) *Decline of an Empire: the Soviet Socialist Republics in revolt*. Newsweek Books, USA.

— (1988) *Islam and the Russian Empire: reform and revolution in Central Asia*. I.B. Taurus, London.

Chaudri, K. N. (1990) *Asia before Europe: economy and civilization of the Indian Ocean from the rise of Islam to 1750*. Cambridge University Press, UK.

Cockburn, P. (1989) *Getting Russia Wrong: the end of Kremlinology.* Verso Books, London.

Conquest, R. (1988) *Harvest of Sorrow.* Arrow Books, London.

— (1990) *The Great Terror: a reassesment.* Plimlico Press, London.

Crawshaw, S. (1992) *Goodbye to the USSR: the collapse of Soviet power.* Bloomsbury, London.

Critchlow, J. (1991) *Nationalism in Uzbekistan: a Soviet Republic's road to sovereignty.* Westview Press, USA.

Davis, H. B. (1978) *Towards a Marxist Theory of Nationalism.* Monthly Review Press, USA.

Denikin, A. I. (1992) *The White Army.* Ian Faulkner Publishing, Cambridge.

Doder, D. and Branson, L. (1990) *Gorbachev: heretic in the Kremlin.* Futura Books, London.

Emperor Taimur. (1975) *Mulfuzat Taimury.* Sang-e-Meel Publications, Lahore.

Erskine, W. (1974) *A History of India under Babur.* Oxford University Press, UK.

Hauner, M. (1990) *What is Asia to Us: Russia's Asian heartland yesterday and today.* Unwin Hyman, London.

Hitti, P. (1946) *History of the Arabs.* Macmillan, London.

Hopkirk, P. (1984) *Setting the East Ablaze.* John Murray, London.

— (1990) *The Great Game.* John Murray, London.

Hosking, G. (1990) *A History of the Soviet Union.* Revised edition. Fontana, London.

Isphani, M. (1989) *Roads and Rivals: the politics of access in the borderlands of Asia.* I. B. Taurus, London.

Kalter, J. (1984) *The Arts and Crafts of Turkestan.* Thames and Hudson, London.

Kekilbayev, A. (1987) *Kazakhstan.* Novosti Press, Moscow.

King, P. (1986) *Curzon's Persia.* Sidgwick and Jackson, London.

Krist, G. (1992). *Alone Through the Forbidden Land: journeys in disguise through Soviet Central Asia.* Ian Faulkner, Cambridge.

Kublitsky, G. (1990) *Peoples of the Soviet Union: traditions and customs.* Novosti Press, Moscow.

Lamb, H. (1989) *Tamerlane the Earth Shaker.* Deep Publications, Delhi.

Lawton, J. (1991) *Samarkand and Bukhara.* Tauris Books, London.

Lenin, V. I. (1968) *Selected Works.* 3 volumes. Progress Publishers, Moscow.

— (1978) *Lenin and National Liberation in the East.* Progress Publishers, Moscow.

Lewin, M. (1975) *Lenin's Last Struggle.* Pluto Press, London.

Lewis, R. (1992) *Geographic Perspectives on Soviet Central Asia.* Routledge, London.

Maalouf, A. (1992) *Samarkand.* Quartet Books.

Maclean, F. (1951) *Eastern Approaches.* Jonathan Cape, London.

Magowan, R. (1989) *Fabled Cities of Central Asia: Samarkand, Bukhara, Khiva.* Abbeville Press, New York.

Maillart, E. (1985) *Turkestan Solo.* Century Publishing, London.

Manz, B. F. (1989) *The Rise and Rule of Tamerlane.* Cambridge University Press, UK.

Marlowe, C. (1969) *The Complete Plays.* Penguin, UK.

Marwat, F. R. (1985) *The Basmachi Movement in Soviet Central Asia.* Emjay Books, Karachi.

Mcrindle, J. W. (1896) *The Invasion of India by Alexander the Great.* Reprinted by Indus Publications, Karachi.

Mnatsakanian, R. (1992) *Environmental Legacy of the Former Soviet Union,* Centre of Human Ecology, University of Edinburgh.

Nahaylo, B. and Swohboda, V. (1990) *Soviet Disunion: a history of the nationalities problem in the USSR.* Hamish Hamilton, London.

Omurkulov, K. (1987) *Kirigzia.* Novosti Press, Moscow.

Phillips, E. D. (1965) *The Royal Hordes: Nomad peoples of the steppes.* Thames and Hudson, London.

Polo, M. (1961) *The Travels of Marco Polo.* Introduction by F. W. Mote. Dell Publishing, USA.

Rawlinson, H. (1875) *England and Russia in the East: the political and geographical condition of Central Asia.* London, reprinted by Indus Publications, Karachi.

Rice, T. T. (1965) *Ancient Arts of Central Asia.* Praeger, New York.

Roi, Y. (ed.) (1984) *The USSR and the Muslim World.* George Allen and Unwin, London.

Rumer, B. (1989) *Soviet Central Asia: a tragic experiment.* Unwin Hyman Press, London.

Shah, I. (1990) *The Way of the Sufi.* Arkana Penguin, London.

— (1991) *Thinkers of the East.* Arkana Penguin, London.

Sheridan, C. (1992) *Russian Portraits.* Ian Faulkner Publishing, Cambridge.

Sikorski, R. (1989) *Dust of the Saints: a journey to Herat in time of war.* Chatto and Windus, London.

Smith, A. D. (1981) *The Ethnic Revivial in the Modern World.* Cambridge University Press, UK.

Smith, H. (1990) *The New Russians.* Vintage Books, USA.

Solzhenitsyn, A. (1991) *Rebuilding Russia.* Harvill, London.

Spector, I. (1959) *The Soviet Union and the Muslim World, 1917–1958.* University of Washington Press, USA.

Stalin, J. (1975) *Marxism and the National Question.* Proletarian Publishers, San Francisco.

Stone, P. (ed.) (1992) *The State of the World's Mountains: a global report.* Zed Books, London.

Swift, G. (1990) *The Nationalities Question in the Soviet Union.* Longman, London.

Taheri, A. (1989) *Crescent in a Red Sky: the future of Islam in the Soviet Union.* Hutchinson, London.

Trotsky, L. (1967) *The History of the Russian Revolution.* Sphere Books, USA.

Ulyanovsky, R. A. (1979) *The Comintern and the East.* Progress Publishers, Moscow.

Vambery, A. (1873) *History of Bukhara.* Reprinted by Indus Publications, Karachi.

Verrier, A. (1991) *Francis Younghusband and the Great Game.* Jonathan Cape, London.

Weekes, R. (1978) *Muslim Peoples: a world ethnographic survey.* Greenwood Press, USA.

Wohl, L. (1961) *Attilla.* Bestsellers Library, USA.

Yazkuliev, B. (1987) *Turkmenia.* Novosti Press, Moscow.

Journals

Bennigsen, A. 'Panturkism and Panislamism in History and Today'. *Central Asian Survey*. Vol. 3, No. 3.

Brill Olcott, M. 'Central Asia's Post-empire Politics', *Orbis*, Spring 1992.

— 'Central Asia's Catapult to Independence'. *Foreign Affairs*, Summer 1992.

— 'Central Asia on its Own'. *Journal of Democracy*, Winter 1993.

Brown, B. 'The Public Role in Perestroika in Central Asia', *Central Asian Survey*, Vol. 9, No. 1.

Buttino, M. 'A Study of the Economic Crisis and Depopulation in Turkestan, 1917-20', *Central Asian Survey*, Vol. 9, No. 4.

Carley, P. 'The Price of the Plan', *Central Asian Survey*, Vol. 8, No. 4.

Central Asia Significants. Centre on Central Asia, Government of Pakistan, Islamabad.

Critchlow, J. 'Did Faizulla Kohjaev really oppose Uzbekistan's land reforms?' *Central Asian Survey*, Vol. 9, No. 3.

Fierman, W. 'Glasnost in Practice: the Uzbek experience', *Central Asian Survey*, Vol. 8, No. 2.

Oraltay, H. 'The Alash Movement in Turkestan'. *Central Asian Survey*, Vol. 4, No. 2.

Oxford Analytica Papers.

Rumer, B. 'The Gathering Storm in Central Asia', *Orbis*, Winter 1993.

Saray, M. 'Russo-Turkmen Relations up to 1874', *Central Asian Survey*, Vol. 3, No. 4.

Togan, Z. 'The Current Situation of the Muslims in Russia', *Central Asian Survey*, Vol. 9, No. 1.

Watters, K. 'The Current Family Planning Debate in Soviet Central Asia', *Central Asian Survey*, Vol. 9, No. 1.

Wright, R. 'Islam, Democracy and the West'. *Foreign Affairs*, Summer 1992.

News Agency Reports, Newspapers and Magazines

Pakistan: *Dawn*; *Herald*; *Frontier Post*; *Nation*; *News*.

USA: *Atlantic*; *International Herald Tribune*; *New York Times*; *Washington Post*.

Europe: Agence France Press; Interfax; Moscow News; Reuters; Tass; *Economist*; *Far Eastern Economic Review*; *Guardian*; *Independent*; *Sunday Times*; *The Times*.

Index